THE LITERATURE OF CO

(34011/33)

Dr Alan M. Kent was born in St Austell and grew up in the china clay mining region of mid-Cornwall. In addition to being a poet, novelist and dramatist, he has several academic publications to his name. Recent books include *Wives, Mothers and Sisters: Feminism, Literature and Women Writers of Cornwall* (1998), *Voices from West Barbary: An Anthology of Anglo-Cornish Poetry 1549–1928* (2000) and *Looking at the Mermaid: A Reader in Cornish Literature 900–1900* (2000) which he co-edited with Tim Saunders. He is presently researching Anglo-Cornish poetry from 1928 to the present and the history of Cornish theatre. He is also currently completing a new verse adaptation of the Cornish mystery play trilogy known as *Ordinalia*.

Cover picture: From Under the Sea, *James Clarke Hook*, *courtesy of Manchester City Galleries*.

The Literature of Cornwall
Continuity • Identity • Difference

1000–2000

Alan M. Kent

 *redcliffe*

First published in 2000 by Redcliffe Press Ltd.,
81g, Pembroke Road, Bristol BS8 3EA

© Alan M. Kent

ISBN 1 900178 28 1

British Cataloguing-in-Publication Data

A catalogue record for this book is available
from the British Library.

The publishers gratefully acknowledge the financial support
of the Patten Press (Publishers), The Old Post Office, Newmill,
Penzance, Cornwall TR20 8XN.

Typeset in 11/12 Monotype Baskerville
by Mayhew Typesetting, Rhayader, Powys
Printed in Great Britain by Hackman Print, Tonypandy, Rhondda

CONTENTS

To Amy, whose accent is comin' on proper. . .

ACKNOWLEDGEMENTS

In my researches for this book, I owe a debt of gratitude to numerous colleagues. I remain especially grateful to all the scholars of the Cornish academic community. In particular I greatly benefited from discussions with Charles Thomas, former Director of the Institute of Cornish Studies, Brian Murdoch of the University of Stirling, Bernard Deacon of the Open University, Allen Ivey of the University of Massachusetts, Ella Westland, John Hurst and Richard Gendall of the University of Exeter, Ken George of the University of Plymouth, A. Robert Lee of the University of Kent, Alison Light of Royal Holloway and Bedford New College, Nickianne Moody of Liverpool John Moores University, Roger Ellis and Norman Schwenk of the University of Wales, College Cardiff and the late and very missed Kenneth Phillipps of the University of Leicester.

Several friends and colleagues have provided a continuing conversation about the issues raised in this book. In particular my sincere thanks goes to Tim Saunders, with whom I complete a continuing daily dialogue about Cornish literary matters. I am also deeply grateful to the many other individuals who have helped, inspired and commented: Richard Jenkin, Donald R. Rawe, Paul Newman, Neil Kennedy, Andrew C. Symons, Oliver Padel, Myrna Combellack, Paul Thornton, Julyan Holmes, Kenneth MacKinnon, Garry Tregidga, Audrey Pool, Mark Stoyle, Benjamin Luxon, Anton Minard, Ronald Perry, Ray Edwards, N.R. Phillips, Graham Sandercock, Jim Pengelly, Howard Crowe, Les and Gill Goldman and Clive Boutle. The discussions I had with them and their correspondences and commentaries on the material presented here were invaluable.

Special thanks, too, should go to Angela Broome, Les Douch and Roger Penhallurick at the Royal Institution of Cornwall, the ever-helpful Kim Cooper and Kay Phillips of the Cornish Studies Library and to Terry Knight's unending patience, and to the staff of the University of Exeter Library, University of Wales, Cardiff and Aberystwyth Libraries, Cambridge University Library and the Bodleian Library, Oxford. Additional authors such as Peter Berresford Ellis, Denys Val Baker, Peter Stanier, John Rowe, Craig Weatherhill, David Fowler, James Whetter, Nicholas Orme and the late A.L. Rowse have in their important contributions to Cornish Studies provided much of the secondary source material upon which I have been able and fortunate enough to draw. I am equally indebted to the Sir Arthur Quiller Couch Memorial Fund and the Cornwall Educational Research Trust for providing financial assistance. In particular Courtney V. Smale deserves my thanks. I am also grateful for the support given to this publication by Melissa Hardie, the Patten Press and the Hypatia Trust: literary culture in Cornwall has been greatly enhanced by the Trust's work over recent years.

Above all I should like to thank my two supervisors at the University of Exeter. Firstly, Peter Faulkner of the School of English and American Studies. Secondly, Philip Payton, Director of the Institute of Cornish Studies. Both of them oversaw all the stages of this book with good humour and the eyes of friendly critics. Special thanks here also goes to my wife and partner in Cornish Studies, Amy Hale, for her comments on all stages of the work. Finally my thanks to John Sansom of Redcliffe whose belief and support in this publication has been enormously helpful. To him and all at Redcliffe I am very grateful.

Dr Alan M. Kent,
Lanbrebois/Probus,
Kernow/Cornwall.

FOREWORD

Iceland is a country whose inhabitants are fantastically well-read and practise just about every variety of the Christian religion. It used to be said that, because of the long nights half the year and until recently prohibition (of liquor), they hadn't much else to do; the day's work ended, you read the Sagas in the original or battled out to the nearest chapel. The same was actually claimed of pre-nineteenth-century Cornwall – no towns of any size, hardly any newspapers, plenty of beer and hundreds of Methodist chapels, but you had to make your own amusements. One of these was writing, and those too poor to get hold of a pencil and paper were not discouraged; they were prepared to use a nail and a bit of slate, or in the poet John Harris' case blackberry juice instead of ink. Did this happen elsewhere in Britain? Probably, but in Alan M. Kent's sub-title, while I think readers may take 'Identity' and 'Difference' for granted (and self-explanatory), to me the key word is 'Continuity'.

What is 'the literature of Cornwall'? The term has to be very wide indeed, and rightly so. It covers just about everything written by Cornish people, whether or not penned within Cornwall – much of it, perforce, was not – and also, to be fair, everything written about Cornwall. In the mid-tenth century Cornwall probably had about 40,000 inhabitants; in the mid-twentieth, this began to reach 400,000. The latter is still less than the population of most large towns or cities in England. Yet today, especially, with the happy advent of new printing technologies and printing-shops everywhere, Cornwall not only seems to possess more private imprints than one would have thought possible; there are also more people free to compose and to publish, in prose, fiction and verse, in both languages. This is not really a complete innovation. It is a steep upward curve, in a creativity-graph, rooted way back in the eighteenth century. And Cornish writing itself, of course, is older still. The earliest, signed and dated, scrap known to me – and it is nearly a thousand years old – is the short message carved on Penzance Market Cross. It says *Procumbunt in foris – Quicumque pace venit hinc oret*, 'They lie here in the open – Whoever in peace comes here, let him pray'. This is a kind of Latin verse, and in curious ways it contains both the author's name (Wiweht, a priest) and the date MVII, AD 1007. Nineteenth-century composers of epitaphs in Cornish churches were simply exhibiting continuity from this!

We have never had anything like a full survey of the literature of Cornwall. There have been (selective) anthologies of verse, many collections of multi-authored essays on Cornish themes and, usually as articles, partial investigations of writing on specific topics like Methodism, or the railways, or holiday experiences. The task of compiling anything like an all-embracing discussion gets more and more formidable, as the material itself increases. But it is high time that the attempt was made, the more so because in the last few years the wheel has gone full circle; original poetry in the Cornish language (not translations of existing verse), and of a notable quality and buoyancy, is being offered by a fresh generation of Cornish poets. With this comes a new sense, new and personal perceptions, of identity and therefore of difference. Cornwall through its writers, known or unknown, has much to give the world of European letters; right back to Tristan and Isolde, *Drustan* and *Esselt*, which somehow took shape in pre-Norman Cornwall and was then enthusiastically embellished across much of Europe.

Alan M. Kent's own training and inclinations, experience in teaching and writing, together make him the ideal author. Most of us would be daunted by the scope. What he has to say will strike a chord in Cornish hearts, and by that territorial adjective I mean anybody, whether he or she is surnamed Penhaligon or Postlethwaite, personally concerned with the distinctive culture of our peninsula. It is necessary to re-state certain things; for instance, that 'Q', Sir Arthur Quiller Couch, despite his denigration by the Leavises, was for his time a more than competent poet but above all a master novelist and short story writer. It is desirable to bring to light some of the medieval Cornish writers, who may be known to specialist scholars but whose names are hardly household words. All this is here, spanning a millennium and enlivened throughout by informed and sympathetic comment. *The Literature of Cornwall* is a work that has been overdue for quite a time. Alan M. Kent truly merits our thanks.

Charles Thomas
Professor Emeritus in Cornish Studies

Introduction

'Nor do I know anything of the existence of islands
called the Tin Islands, whence we get our tin.'

Herodotus, The Histories (c.425BC)[1]

'I should like to take this opportunity to make a bit of
history by saying:
  "Me am beth hanow
  Heb dewath ha bry
  Bisgwethack rag nevra"
  [I shall have a name perpetual and a fame per-
manent and immortal]
  Those words are Cornish. They were spoken by a
blacksmith from St Keverne, in my constituency,
where I come from.'

Andrew George MP (May 22nd 1997)[2]

As the Member of Parliament for St Ives – Andrew George – explores
in his maiden speech, Cornwall occupies a fascinating if difficult
position within the Atlantic archipelago. It *is* and *is not* an English
county. It *is* and *is not* mentioned in the same breath as Wales,
Scotland and Éire. It is one of the poorest regions in western Europe.
It is a Duchy, a bi-lingual territory, and claims its own nationhood.
Debate on these issues alone in present-day Cornwall could fill
countless volumes; and yet, as the much older words of the great
Greek historian, Herodotus prove, Cornwall has been constructed in
the minds of successive Europeans for a much longer time. It has
mined tin for some two millennia, and yet despite its sometime
oppression in history, despite early accommodation into the English
nation-state, despite the near-loss of the Cornish language, mass
immigration outwards (to the rest of the world) and inwards (from the
rest of these islands), despite economic collapse and the effects of
globalization, its people continue to argue their distinctiveness – their
Cornishness – at the beginning of the third millennium. Perhaps
paradoxically, it is this very reaction against historical adversity which

11

explains why Cornish identity has persisted so strongly and continues to be celebrated. As both the words of Herodotus and Andrew George demonstrate, Cornwall is one of the most intriguing territories of these islands.

For its relatively small size, Cornwall has been imagined and written about perhaps more than any other equivalent territory within western Europe.[3] Despite its seemingly tiny bounds, Cornwall generates an enormous number of publications about it every year. Cornwall continues to ignite an incredible passion, while its narratives and legends continue to fascinate a world-wide audience.[4] In short, Cornwall's history is full of paradoxes, but they are paradoxes which continue, even today, to fire the imagination of thousands of poets, novelists, dramatists and writers of all kinds.

To achieve an understanding of how Cornwall has been imagined in literature, we need to ask many questions about its past, present and future. How is Cornwall written about? More importantly, what has this literature to say about Cornwall and the Cornish? Why, in the perceived face of extinction and dissolution into a greater English literature, has there remained a cultural and literary sense of 'Cornishness' and 'difference'? When, and what, are the moments and texts which demonstrate cultural continuity in the Cornish context? How, in the face of tourism on a seemingly cataclysmic scale, is there now a distinctively Cornish nationalist literature?

In answer to these questions, the core aims of this book are to examine both the linkages and breaks in the continuity of the literature of Cornwall; at the same time aligning these to the social, political and economic influences which affected both British and Cornish history. As a result of this explanation of continuity, we should arrive at a more comprehensive picture of how Cornishness and Cornish identity have been explored and asserted in writing. In better understanding the continuity and discontinuity of Cornish literature and how Cornish identity has been 'written' throughout history, such a paradigm will also allow us to understand why Cornwall's difference emerged, how it altered, faltered and continued, and finally how it is presently seen at the start of the third millennium.

The reader might consider that such a project would be built on 'shifting sands' and wonder why there should be a need for a specific study of literary constructions of Cornwall. Other parts of these islands – Devon for instance – have claims to an impressive range of literary texts and their own literary histories, so what makes Cornwall special? The fact is that Cornwall's difference has been asserted by conclusive research in a number of academic modes of enquiry ranging from archaeology, anthropology and history, to politics, linguistics and geography.[5] Such a multitude of fields have all asserted that despite apparent assimilation into England, Cornwall has retained and continues to exhibit 'difference'. In this sense, literary texts generated in Cornwall are likely to be important expressions of that difference over time, as well as being a 'suitable case' for academic treatment.

Similarly, this study is written as a response to moves in the field of literary and cultural studies away from the apparent homogeneity and hegemony of dominant literatures, to reassertions and readings of those groups who have either been mistakenly included in those groupings, or lost in the literary void, or are genuinely new voices. Throughout time, conceptualisations of literary histories and their relationships with particular territories have altered and changed. During the mid-twentieth century, literatures of both western countries and the United Kingdom were written of by scholars as unified and homogenous as part of singular and established literary 'traditions'.[6] However, new methods of enquiry and responses to political change in the latter half of the twentieth century began to show that this apparent unity and homogeneity did not exist. This view of literature was also dependent on the apparent distinctiveness of existing and dominant nation-states, so that literary history upheld and reflected the powers and structures of those states. Inevitably, this particular ideological conception of literary history began to be seen as flawed and problematical. As the power of existing centralized nation-states has been progressively thrown into question by devolution, the European focus on regionalism, challenges to unacknowledged cultural imperialism, and successive recasting of territories, such changes have been matched by academic enquiry into new, or perhaps previously hidden literatures.

In part, this myth of literature had been progressively eroded towards the latter part of the twentieth century by (to use Bill Ashcroft, Gareth Griffiths and Helen Tiffin's phrase) 'the empire writing back', opening up assumptions underlying Eurocentric and Anglocentric notions of literature and language,[7] as well as a wide range of other scholars who have debated questions of ethnicity, race and cultural difference in the post-colonial era.[8] In addition, as Keating (among others) has argued, the myth of the enduring nation-state and the unproblematic unity of the United Kingdom was undermined by an unexpected upsurge in nationalism in the late twentieth century.[9] As well as questioning the territorial identity of such nation-states, notions of literary and linguistic integrity and unity were also challenged.[10]

In general, literary scholarship in the United Kingdom has embraced the concept of multi-nationalism within these islands, allowing for new studies of the literatures of Éire, Northern Ireland, Scotland and

Wales.[11] In addition, some analysis has also attempted to elucidate and explain other issues of diversity and peripheral literatures in the United Kingdom.[12] The work of Bell *et al* has redefined literary visions of the periphery by reassessing the ways in which writers promote distinctive local and national identities, and how writers have resisted stereotypical portrayals of their territories in centrally generated accounts.[13] As well as Celtic literatures from Wales, Scotland, Éire, Northern Ireland and Cornwall, Bell also considers the north-east of England and London itself. The reassessment has also been advanced by A. Robert Lee in his work on multi-cultural fiction in Britain, who argues that now 'Britain speaks from infinitely beyond Middle-England' and by Ludwig and Fietz who assert a discussion of poetry in the British Isles from a 'non-metropolitan perspective . . . and its role in the self-definition of communities'.[14]

Yet despite the overwhelming evidence of this diversity within the United Kingdom, which emphasises the existence and importance of this diversity in terms of nations and communities and their separate literatures, some territories have received little attention.[15] The larger territories of Wales, Scotland, Éire and Northern Ireland have seen most enquiry,[16] perhaps to the detriment of the smaller off-shore territories such as the Channel Islands and the Isle of Man, yet also the distinctive English regions of Cumbria and Northumberland. It is perhaps within this category of smaller territories that Cornwall sits, usually receiving only brief attention in any discussion of the United Kingdom's literary history, or else dominated by specifically English literature.

Alongside this, a particular ideological conception of Cornwall has developed. It tends to be seen as an important, if peripheral, part of England, but comes with a particular set of other characteristics which have guaranteed its distinctiveness over time. One important construction of Cornwall is its particular association with 'romance' and 'legend', attesting partly to the reason why it is seen as a special and unique territory within the United Kingdom. Additionally, as successive commentators have indicated, since the beginning of the twentieth century Cornwall has also increasingly been recognized as a 'Celtic' territory within Britain, comparing it with other Celtic territories along the Atlantic shores of Europe.[17] However, it has only been very recently that the kind of academic enquiry afforded to such territories has been applied to Cornwall.

Indeed, for the most part, the very discipline of 'Celtic Studies' has given Cornwall short shrift in the past; either ignoring Cornish literature and culture completely, or else being 'critical' of Cornwall, for somehow not offering the kind of mythological or epic literature found in territories such as Wales and Éire.[18] Put simply, Cornwall has been viewed as not being 'Celtic', or not 'Celtic enough', when certain scholars were basing their conceptualisation of what was or what was not Celtic on only narrow and restrictive models. Put another way, if performances of Cornish Celticity did not fit into the wider pan-Celtic model, they were deemed inferior or insubstantial. In 1902, as Celtic Studies was beginning to emerge as an academic discipline, Magnus Maclean – a Professor at Glasgow Technical College – commented that '[Cornwall] never produced much of a Celtic literature' and that 'Cornish dialect [sic] has no literature to show, and therefore is not concerned in the special Celtic revivals characteristic of the literature in other dialects'.[19] Given the lack of an institute of higher education in Cornwall during this period, such a critique had a powerful effect in the world of Celtic Studies and once asserted, such arguments have been difficult monoliths to counter and destroy throughout the twentieth century. Murdoch has drawn much attention to the problems of this kind of approach to Cornish literature, criticising observers for accepting 'glib comments'.[20] Such past scholarship was inherently flawed: it asked Cornwall to fit into a literary model which was alien to it. Whilst Cornish literature (based on surviving dramatic texts from the medieval period) would seem to be produced and 'marketed' for a popular audience in the context of festival and celebration, other territories developed their own traditions of texts, which were not always circulated to the wider non-literate community.[21] Thus more productive readings of Cornish literature are to be gained by asking how does the particular literature of Cornwall demonstrate its version of Celticity?

This new critique of the discipline of 'Celtic Studies' – for its lack of contextualisation, its focus on linguistics and, to use Chapman's term, its 'construction of the myth' of the Celts has paradoxically been central in helping scholars to re-evaluate approaches to 'Celtic' territories like Cornwall.[22] Though criticised for being dismissive about the position of ethnic Celts within the Atlantic archipelago, the work of Chapman and James have, in part, been helpful in re-conceiving the very notion of Celtic Studies.[23] Despite, for the most part, fitting into the trend of Celtic scholarship itself by ignoring Cornwall, James reasserts the idea of how insular Celtic identity is actually a product of the rise of nationalism in the eighteenth century, and that the 'Celticness' of the Atlantic archipelago may be 'a romantic fantasy', even 'a politically dangerous fabrication of history which has implications in the current debate on devolution and self-government for the Celtic regions'.[24] In the field of literary studies, it is also helping to reform the ways in which Celticists in particular approach their discipline, and is promoting the use of other tools and methodologies within Celtic Studies. Both Helen Fulton and myself have drawn attention to the ways in which the established study of Celtic literatures can benefit from cultural materialist, new historicist and feminist perspectives, drawing on applicable developments in studies of other literatures.[25]

Thus, despite the sometimes widely perceived difficulties of Chapman and James' position, this new enquiry has helped to confront the notion of Cornwall as an interesting but difficult foot-note in history, and reasserted its specific cultural history. Following the research of the Cornish Social and Economic Research Group, Deacon, George and Perry noted that Cornwall had reached a 'crossroads' in its development and questioned whether it was a 'living community' or a 'leisure zone'.[26] A reassessment of Cornwall's history at home and abroad has been completed by Payton,[27] and a number of scholars have begun to reconsider issues of Cornish identity, language and literature.[28] More recently, Westland et al have opened up discussion on the different ways in which Cornwall has been imagined by writers, prompting further enquiry into the 'cultural construction of place'.[29]

The most comprehensive works to date covering the history of Cornish literature have been those by Peter Berresford Ellis and Brian Murdoch. Given the field, it is impossible to ignore their tremendous contribution. Likewise, in the field of Anglo-Cornish writing the criticism of John Hurst and the research of Peter Stanier have been enormously helpful in allowing us to understand post-war literature in Cornwall. Obviously, the present study is greatly indebted to their research and their understanding of textual chronology. However, in light of new developments in literary theory and a better historical reconsideration of Cornwall itself, a fresh look at Cornish literature is now needed, not only tracing texts in Cornish, or traces of Cornish literature, but understanding their interaction with the development of writing in English in Cornwall, aiming to explain how performances of identity and difference have been sustained.

To take this enquiry further, any study of literature about Cornwall and the Cornish requires knowledge of contexts as well as texts. What forces acted upon writers as they wrote? What was the historical, the political, the philosophical, the religious, the economic, the cultural background of writers in a Cornish context? Was the writer accepting or rejecting the literary conventions of the time, or developing them, or creating entirely new kinds of literary expression? Are there interactions between literature and the art or architecture of Cornwall? Was the writer affected by contemporaries or isolated? Such questions stress the need for scholars of Cornish literature to go beyond the reading of texts, to extend their knowledge by developing a sense of chronology, of action and reaction, and of the varying relationships between Cornish writers and Cornish society.

Histories of any literature can encourage readers to make comparisons, can aid in understanding the purposes of individual authors and in assessing the totality of their achievements. The same process holds true for Cornwall. Cornish writers' development can be better understood and appreciated with some knowledge of the background of their time and culture. Such histories also demonstrate the great wealth of Cornish writing that there is to be enjoyed. We need to be wary of reducing the stories of past and recent Cornwall into a simple narrative. For just as 'Cornish' itself subdivides into a multitude of classes, genders, religions, regions and languages, so combinations like 'New-Cornish', 'Scillonian', 'Chinese-Cornish', 'Australian-Cornish', 'American-Cornish' come with their own internal dynamics.[30] Yet even within those combinations there exist tensions; all that aside from other occasions when these different performances of 'Cornish' come into contact.

At this point, some other nomenclature – and the destruction of a few myths – may be helpful to the reader in understanding the literary culture of Cornwall. Many scholars have presented the overall picture of 'the literature of Cornwall' from 1000 to 1900, as a kind of 'decline' – from a somehow once 'healthy', fully operational Cornish-Celtic culture, to a corrupted English-speaking territory where the ethos of the 'cult of loss' is central.[31] That model fails, because its mythic version of events in Cornish literary culture is too simple. Conceived this way, if it were to be true, then the so-called 'revival' of Cornish culture in the twentieth century would not have happened. Instead, Cornwall would be descending into English-speaking-and-writing oblivion. A more realistic and accurate model of Cornwall's literary continuum – and the one posited here – is to see the process within a paradigm of language shift and change over time, which has brought about a multitude of linguistic and literary features and events throughout the past thousand years. These shifts and changes have resulted in the continuum altering – sometimes gradually, sometimes more dramatically, with a set of inherent declines, revivals and events paralleling these moves. Constructions of Cornish difference have matched these alterations in the literary culture of Cornwall as well as wider movements in Cornish and world history.

Labels are easy to apply, but are still often inconvenient. For the purposes of this study, I use the following terms to label particular pieces of writing about Cornwall, to show the present three major linguistic and therefore literary groups operating. Firstly, Cornish Literature. By

this, I mean texts written in Cornish. Secondly, Anglo-Cornish Literature. Here, I refer to texts written about Cornwall in English. Thirdly, I
use the term Cornu-English to show those texts which form the canon of
Celtic-English writing in Cornwall; that is those texts written in what
some observers might label the Cornish dialect of English.[32] To be sure,
these terms are not perfect and for the most part, they overlap and
interconnect all the time, and yet they will help us to understand the
continuum of writing under consideration.

Chapter One, examining the period 1000–1660, offers initially a
historical survey of early and medieval Cornish literature, and
demonstrates how scholars have failed to recognise the place of this
literature in a wider European context. Far from being a periphery of
Europe, evidence suggests that during this phase, Cornwall was a
thriving cultural centre influencing the traffic of literature and narratives – Arthurian, Saintly and otherwise – between central Europe
and these islands. It then considers a subsequent period of alignment
with English culture in medieval and early modern Cornwall, followed
by a consideration of the often neglected literary politics and paralysis
of the Renaissance and seventeenth-century Cornwall. In doing so, I
hope to explore the literary imaginings of the shift from pre-modern to
modern and the continuum of writing in Cornish during this phase.

Chapter Two begins with an exploration of the period 1660–1820,
when new constructions of modern Cornish identity were being forged
by both native and visiting writers, paralleling the fragmentation of
continuity within writing in Cornish, as it moved towards secular
themes. An analysis is then offered in Chapter Three of nineteenth-
century Cornwall between 1820 and 1890, studying how the effects of
industrial change were crucial in redefining Cornwall's difference. The
impact of travel and tourism, and their meeting with Celtic Revivalism
of the early twentieth century is next explored in Chapter Four,
arriving at a further refinement of Cornish difference between 1890
and 1940.

Chapter Five considers the structural and thematic concerns of
writers between 1940 and 1980, examining post-modern and post-
industrial Cornwall, as well as how Cornish identity came to be
asserted in new ways. Finally in Chapter Six, we examine the period
1980–2000. Here, the book comes full circle, exploring the impact of
'devolved' small nations within the European context, with Cornwall
asserting both its importance as a romantic periphery, and its confident
contemporary literature. The achievements of Cornish, Anglo-Cornish
and Cornu-English literature are summarised in the Conclusion,
alongside a discussion of Cornwall's literary future. Inevitably, as we
move through the continuum and the means of literary production

have grown, we shall find ourselves covering more texts in smaller time periods.

All the chapters exploring the continuum fit around difficult questions and more difficult answers about Cornwall's place in both past and contemporary Britain and Europe. As a response to cultural imperialism and devolution, Cornwall has an important story to tell within European writing and culture. I cannot say that this book will answer all the questions the reader may have about the eclectic and changing literature of Cornwall, but part of my hope here is that it will begin to ask the right kind of questions. The following study therefore, both considers and celebrates the achievement of the literature of Kernow and Cornwall.

NOTES

1. See Aubrey de Sélincourt (tr.) and A.R. Burn (ed.), *Herodotus: The Histories* (Harmondsworth 1954), p. 250.
2. *Parliamentary Debates: Hansard*, 294, 11 (1997), pp 880–3.
3. See Denys Val Baker, *The Timeless Land: The Creative Spirit in Cornwall* (Bath 1973), *A View from Land's End: Writers Against a Cornish Background* (London 1982).
4. For two examples, see Craig Weatherhill and Paul Devereux, *Myths and Legends of Cornwall* (Wilmslow 1994); Peter Berresford Ellis, *The Chronicles of the Celts: New Tellings of their Myths and Legends* (London 1999), pp 349–430.
5. See Charles Thomas (ed.), *Cornish Studies/Studhyansow Kernewek 1–15* (Redruth 1973–1987).
6. For a critique of this process, see John Dixon, *A Schooling in 'English': Critical Episodes in the Struggle to Shape Literary and Cultural Studies* (Milton Keynes 1991). For the way this ideology informed critical practice, see F.R. Leavis, *The Great Tradition* (London 1948). For a 'Celtic' perspective, see Matthew Arnold, *The Study of Celtic Literature* (London 1867).
7. See Bill Ashcroft, Gareth Griffiths and Helen Tiffin, *The Empire Writes Back: Theory and Practice in Post-Colonial Literatures* (London 1989).
8. For differing views of this debate, see Gopal Balakrishnan (ed.), *Mapping the Nation* (London 1996); Stuart Murray (ed.), *Not on Any Map: Essays on Postcoloniality and Cultural Nationalism* (Exeter 1997); David Bennett (ed.), *Multicultual States: Rethinking Difference and Identity* (London 1998).
9. Michael Keating, *State and Regional Nationalism: Territorial Politics and the European State* (London 1988), p. 1. See also Michael Hechter, *Internal Colonialism: The Celtic Fringe in British National Development, 1536–1966* (London 1975); Sharon Macdonald (ed.), *Inside European Identities: Ethnography in Western Europe* (Oxford and Providence, RI 1993); Peter Lynch, *Minority Nationalism and European Integration* (Cardiff 1996).

10. For such arguments, see Ned Thomas, *The Welsh Extremist: Modern Welsh Politics, Literature and Society* (Talybont 1991 [1973]); Peter Berresford Ellis, *Celtic Dawn: A History of Pan-Celticism* (London 1993); Murray G.H. Piltock, *Celtic Identity and the British Image* (Manchester 1999).

11. For example, see Robert Welch, *Changing States: Transformations in Modern Irish Writing* (London 1993); Gavin Wallace and Randall Stevenson (eds.), *The Scottish Novel since the Seventies* (Edinburgh 1993); Tony Brown (ed.) (1995) *Welsh Writing in English: A Yearbook of Critical Essays* (Bangor 1995).

12. See Alan Sinfield (ed.), *Society and Literature 1945–1970* (London 1983); Mike Storry and Peter Childs (eds.), *British Cultural Identities* (London 1997); Geoffrey Cubitt (ed.), *Imagining Nations* (Manchester 1998).

13. Ian A. Bell (ed.), *Peripheral Visions: Images of Nationhood in Contemporary British Fiction* (Cardiff 1995).

14. A. Robert Lee (ed.), *Other Britain, Other British* (London 1995), p. 3; Hans-Werner Ludwig and Lothar Fietz (eds.), *Poetry in the British Isles: Non-Metropolitan Perspectives* (Cardiff 1995), p. 321.

15. Cornwall, Brittany and the Isle of Man receive scant attention in Paul Russell, *An Introduction to the Celtic languages* (London 1995).

16. See Victor Edward Durkacz, *The Decline of the Celtic Languages* (Edinburgh 1983).

17. See Len Truran, *For Cornwall – A Future!* (Redruth 1976); James Whetter, *Cornish Essays / Scryvow Kernewek 1971–76* (Gorran 1977); Peter Berresford Ellis, op.cit., *The Celtic Revolution: A Study in Anti-Imperialism* (Talybont 1988 [1985]); R.A. Pascoe (ed.), *Cornwall: One of the Four Nations of Britain* (Redruth, 1996). For a more militant Cornish position, see John Angarrack, *Breaking the Chains: Propaganda, Censorship, Deception and the Manipulation of Public Opinion in Cornwall* (Camborne 1999).

18. A position reflected in Charles Squire, *The Mythology of the British Islands* (London 1905); Alwyn Rees and Brinley Rees (eds.), *Celtic Heritage: Ancient Tradition in Ireland and Wales* (London 1961); J.E. Caerwyn Williams (ed.), *Literature in Celtic Countries* (Cardiff 1971) and more recently in John T. Koch and John Carey (eds.), *The Celtic Heroic Age: Literary Sources for Ancient Celtic Europe and Early Ireland and Wales* (Malden, Massachusetts 1994).

19. Magnus Maclean, *The Literature of the Celts* (London 1902), pp 248–9. Maclean was heavily criticised by the Cornish cultural activist L.C. Duncombe-Jewell for these comments. See 'Dr. Magnus Maclean and Cornish literature' in *Celtia*, November (1902), p. 173.

20. Brian Murdoch, *Cornish Literature* (Cambridge 1993), p. 6. This is the best analysis of the continuum of writing in Cornish.

21. See Rosalind Conklin Hayes and C.E. McGee (Dorset) and Sally L. Joyce and Evelyn S. Newlyn (Cornwall) (eds.), *Records of Early English Drama: Dorset / Cornwall* (Toronto 1999), pp 397–505. Compare with Kenneth Hurlstone Jackson (ed. and tr.), *A Celtic Miscellany* (Harmondsworth 1971) and Dafydd Johnston, *The Literature of Wales* (Cardiff 1994).

22. See Malcolm Chapman, *The Celts: The Construction of a Myth* (Basingstoke 1992); Simon James, *The Atlantic Celts: Ancient People or Modern Invention?*

(London 1999). Compare with Henry Jenner, *Who are the Celts and what has Cornwall to do with them?* (Cornwall 1928).

23. For new approaches to Celtic studies, see contributors to Terence Brown (ed.), *Celticism* (Atlanta 1996), Graham Harvey and Charlotte Hardman (eds.), *Paganism Today* (London 1996); Amy Hale and Philip Payton (eds.), *New Directions in Celtic Studies* (Exeter 2000).

24. James, op.cit., pp. 136–44.

25. See Helen Fulton, 'Individual and Society in the Welsh and French Romances of Owein/Yvain' – paper given at the Celtic Studies Association of North America, Annual Meeting 1999; Alan M. Kent, 'Cornish Politics, Society and Literature: A Plea for Correlation' in *An Baner Kernewek/The Cornish Banner*, 72 (1993), 'One and all: Unity and Difference in Cornish literature' in Eurwen Price (ed.), *Celtic Literature and Culture in the Twentieth Century* (Bangor 1997), *Wives, Mothers and Sisters: Feminism, Literature and Women Writers of Cornwall* (Penzance 1998).

26. Bernard Deacon, Andrew George and Ronald Perry, *Cornwall at the Crossroads: Living Communities or Leisure Zone?* (Redruth 1988).

27. Philip Payton, *The Making of Modern Cornwall: Historical Experience and the Persistence of "Difference"* (Redruth 1992); *Cornwall* (Fowey 1996); *The Cornish Overseas* (Fowey 1999).

28. See for example, Bernard Deacon and Philip Payton, 'Re-inventing Cornwall: Cultural Change on the European Periphery' in Philip Payton (ed.), *Cornish Studies: One* (Exeter 1993), pp 62–79; Bernard Deacon, 'Language Revival and Language Debate: Modernity and Postmodernity' in Philip Payton (ed.), *Cornish Studies: Four* (Exeter 1996), pp 88–106; John Hurst, 'Literature in Cornwall' in Philip Payton (ed.), *Cornwall Since the War: The Contemporary History of a European Region* (Redruth 1993), pp 291–308.

29. Ella Westland (ed.), *Cornwall: The Cultural Construction of Place* (Penzance 1997).

30. See Australian and North American examples in Payton, op.cit. (1999), pp 393–99.

31. For the best of numerous examples, see Peter Berresford Ellis, *The Cornish Language and its Literature* (London and Boston 1974); Crysten Fudge, *The Life of Cornish* (Redruth 1982); P.A.S. Pool, *The Death of Cornish* (Redruth 1982).

32. For 'Celtic-English' see L.C. Hildegard Tristram (ed.), *The Celtic Englishes* (Heidelberg 1997). For Cornu-English, see Uncle Jan Trenoodle (ed.), *Specimens of Cornish Provincial Dialect* (London 1846); Alan Pearson (ed.), *Cornish Dialect: Prose and Verse* (Cornwall 1982); K.C. Phillipps, *A Glossary of Cornish Dialect* (Padstow 1993).

From King Arthur to An Gof: The Literary Politics of Medieval and Renaissance Cornwall, 1000–1660

'Those who retreated to the southern corner of the island could not continue their resistance, for their territory has no natural protection. It is called Cornwall, after their leader Corineus.'

Gerald of Wales, *The Description of Wales* (c.1188)[1]

'C'era una volta un castello in Cornovaglia. . . [There was once a castle in Cornwall. . .]

Anon, *Traditional Preface to Italian folktales* (n.d.).[2]

Much of the emphasis of studies of medieval Cornwall has concluded that the territory was something of a backwater, having little literature and culture to offer its people; let alone having any effect on wider British or European writing. A.L. Rowse was to conclude that 'Cornwall in the Middle Ages was a little land very much on its own, living its own inner life, wrapped up in its Celtic tongue, in its dream of the Celtic past, rather a backwater, a dead end'.[3] However, a closer reading of literary history shows that medieval Cornwall was a complex, multi-lingual European territory, which since post-Roman Britain has produced a series of texts which not only reflected the identity and continuity of writing from Cornwall, but which were also highly influential in the wider development of European literature.

Far from being a literary backwater, Cornwall, Cornish subject-matter and applied liturgical themes with a resolutely Cornish face, were shaping the literary politics of much of these islands and some of the central themes of continental literature. Thus, Cornwall, rather than being on the periphery may be seen as an important destination on the Atlantic shores of Europe, lying as it does between Ireland and Wales in the north, and Brittany, France and the Iberian peninsula to the south. With travel, came the movement and retelling of narratives and myths, poems and dramas, romances and saints' lives. This complexity of culture may be seen in the light of L.E. Elliot-Binns' observation that 'it may be certain that in medieval Cornwall four different tongues were in use – Latin, French, English and Cornish'.[4] Later, during the Renaissance, the multi-lingual society of Cornwall was to undergo a complete re-shaping, so that in retrospect the dynamic literary politics of the earlier period were to undergo a kind of paralysis which would last until the construction of modern Cornwall. The literary continuum fully established in Cornwall in the Renaissance (but also emergent even in medieval Cornwall) is one whereby conscious revival of explicitly 'Cornish' culture is held in opposition to an apparently on-going Anglicisation project, which seeks to rid Cornwall of Cornish and synthesize it ever more fully into England. However, as this chapter will show (and the rest of this book will demonstrate), that is all too simplistic a model of the literary continuum of Cornwall, and throughout history, performances of Celticity, of Cornish identity and difference, have been constructed in an enormous variety of texts, which have demonstrated the changing nature of that identity and difference over the literary continuum.

In order to more fully understand constructions of Cornwall and Cornish identity during the medieval period, it is perhaps necessary to go a little further back in history to the development of parent Brythonic writing in post-Roman Britain. The Celtic languages of Britain may be divided into two main sub-groups – the Goidelic (comprising Irish, Scottish Gaelic and Manx) and the Brythonic. The parent Brythonic language was that tongue spoken by British peoples in the post-Roman period which later subdivided into Cornish, Breton and Welsh. Much of what is considered today to be 'early Welsh' writing was in fact, not Welsh at all in the contemporary sense. It is possible that texts from other Brythonic-speaking regions of Britain have been perhaps anachronistically labelled as Welsh. For instance, the sixth century AD 'Welsh' poem known as *The Gododdin* was actually composed in the British-speaking region of what is now known as southern Scotland. In this light, Cornish writing potentially has a much longer pedigree.[5] It is with this Brythonic continuum that we must begin our study, but soon the parent Brythonic in the south-western part of the island of Britain starts to delineate into Cornish, and a separate Cornish language and literature begins to develop.

Also demonstrative of this early phase is the Saintly culture of these islands from the early fifth century onwards. After the Briton St Patrick's conversion of Ireland, countless missionaries travelled to Wales and Cornwall and founded monasteries in both territories. Other saints passed back and forth between Wales, Cornwall and

Brittany, so demonstrating an advanced seafaring culture.[6] These early Christian travellers are now commemorated around Cornwall in various sites – ranging from churches, erection and later rededication of granite crosses, cells and holy wells.[7] Numerous stories about the lives of these saints remain: for example, St Ia's journey to Cornwall upon a leaf, St Austell's battle with the devil high on Hensbarrow Downs, St Neot's protection of the animals, St Petroc's journey to Rome and Jerusalem; not to mention the lives of St Piran and St Meriasek.[8] Their often magical and embellished narratives have been recorded by various authors throughout the centuries, used as 'touchstones' for imagining Cornish experience. The useful work of Gilbert H. Doble has given us much insight into the individual saints' lives in Cornwall, and in his research he has drawn upon a wealth of documentation, depicting these important early narratives, which have remained in the Cornish literary continuum as reference points until the present day.[9]

Some evidence of the slowly emergent writing and culture in post-Roman Britain can also be gleaned from research into the corpus of fifth to eighth century inscribed stones. Though not literary texts in the narrowest sense, such inscriptions and memorials do provide us with a picture of the narrative culture which existed during this early phase. Among the most recognizable and distinctive are the Mên Scryfa, near Morvah which is adorned with the Latin text *Rialobrani-Cvnovali-Fili* [Rialobran, son of Cunoval].[10] These names translate to 'Royal Raven' and 'Famous Chieftain' respectively and the type of lettering used indicates that the inscription is from the sixth century. Such a memorial stone indicates a fascinating, yet lost narrative. A more visible story is to be gleaned from the inscription on King Doniert's Stone, near St Cleer, which reads *Doniert Rogvavitt Pro Anima* [Doniert ordered this memorial for the sake of his soul]. As Weatherhill has argued, Doniert could be the Cornish king Donjarth who drowned in the River Fowey c.AD875 – an event recorded in the *Annales Cambriae*.[11] However, perhaps the most famous source of this type is the so-called Tristan stone, near Fowey. The sixth-century inscription here may be linked to the narrative of Tristan, since it reads *Drvstanvs Hic Iacit Cvnomori Filivs* [Drustanus (Tristan?) lies here, son of Cunomorus].[12]

Meanwhile, the ground-breaking work of the Cornish scholar Charles Thomas has shown how such stones and memorials may be used as 'literary sources' demonstrating how, far from being a land of saints, Cornwall in fact remained largely pagan until the sixth century.[13] In the volume *Christian Celts: Messages and Images*, Thomas advances his inspired theory further by showing that by the year 500,

1. The Mên Scryfa: *Rialobrani-Cvnovali-Fili.*

2 + 3. The final battle between King Arthur and Sir Mordred, as depicted in William Hatherell's painting of 1928 at King Arthur's Great Halls, Tintagel and, *below*, one of 72 stained glass windows shows Arthur pulling the sword from the anvil in the stone.

memorial stones offered ingenious and cryptic codes, which we are able to interpret as a form of structured meaning.[14] Another inscribed piece of stone, found in 1998, advanced further the possible association of King Arthur with Cornwall, and Tintagel in particular. The stone was a piece of slate bearing the Latin inscription *Pater Colliavficitt Artogno* [Artognou (Arthur?), father of a descendant of Coll, has had this built], and has now been labelled 'the Arthur Stone' – perhaps providing some interesting if tenuous evidence of the link between Arthurian narrative and western Britain.[15]

However, we have already been able to speculate on a Cornish origin for the beginnings of Arthurian legend for some time. The legend articulates a mythology and ideology so vast that tales of Arthur were not only transmitted across the rest of the Atlantic archipelago but also to continental Europe.[16] Though now much embellished with medieval tales of chivalry and knighthood,[17] Arthur was most probably a Celtic ruler, or possibly a Romano-British military leader, born in the late fifth century AD who led one of the last major campaigns against the Anglo-Saxon invasion of Britain.[18] The main source for a Cornish provenance of Arthurian material is in Geoffrey of Monmouth's *Historia Regum Britanniae / History of the Kings of Britain*. Geoffrey refers only to one major source for his narrative:

> Walter, Archdeacon of Oxford, a man skilled in the art of public speaking and well informed about the history of foreign countries, presented me with a certain very ancient book written in the British language.[19]

A number of scholars have argued that this book written in the 'British language', which has given rise to all the European constructions of Arthur over the centuries, and specifically locates Tintagel as a starting point, might well have been written in Cornwall.[20] Thorpe has argued that 'Geoffrey's inspiration was a patriotic one' and that 'his inspiration was a pageant of striking personalities'.[21] Put another way, the *History* was a massive compendium of historical and mythological material blended into a continuous narrative that displays the glory of the Britons. Here Geoffrey describes their first arrival as refugees from Troy, and Corineus' acquisition of Cornwall:

> Corineus, however, following in this the example of his leader, called the region of the kingdom which had fallen to his share Cornwall, after the manner of his own name, and the people who lived there he called Cornishmen. Although he might have chosen his own estates before all the others who had come there, he preferred the region which is now called Cornwall, either for

its being the *cornu* or horn of Britain, or through a corruption of his own name.[22]

As well as Corineus' wrestling match with the giant Gogmagog on Plymouth Hoe (conveniently providing a mythical origin for the Cornish sport), Geoffrey's *History* also has a section titled 'The Prophecies of Merlin', which argues, among other things, that the 'Boar of Cornwall shall bring relief from these invaders, for it will trample their necks beneath its feet', that 'the Cornish oaks shall flourish' and that a 'soldier in a chariot will resist the Wolf and transform the Cornish people into a Boar. As a result the boar will devastate the provinces, but it will hide its head in depths of the Severn'.[23] Many of these references and allusions are now unfortunately lost, yet clearly this text has a link to another of the same period.

The earliest work purporting to have been written in Cornish is *Prophetia Merlini/The Prophecy of Merlin* which John of Cornwall re-rendered in Latin hexameters.[24] The text again belongs to the widespread medieval tradition of expressing political and religious propaganda in the guise of ancient prophecy:

> Disce modum tandem, Cornubia, disce laborem!
> Nostraque Saxonicum referunt cunabula luctum;
> quae nostra large manus? quis postmodo liber habendus?
> Qua spectat plaustrum, qua Tamarus exit in Austrum,
> per iuga Brentigie Galli dominantur ubique.
> Viuere si pergis, regina, seres et arabis,
> ex quo murilegi praecio comulantur et hirci.

> [Learn the way at last, Cornwall, learn the work!
> And our cradles shall bring back the Saxon mourning.
> Why is our hand so generous? Who afterwards will be considered free?
> Where the Great Bear looks, where the Tamar goes out into the South,
> by the yoke of Brentigia the French lord it everywhere,
> if you would continue to live, o queen, you will so unplough,
> out of which rodent-catchers and buck goats are multiplied in value.][25]

What distinguishes John of Cornwall's *Prophecy of Merlin* is that his notes reveal his sources included documents in Old Cornish, so demonstrating that the Cornish literary continuum was healthy during this phase, despite the loss of noble patronage. Here, among the points John of Cornwall refers to, are Cornish methods of counting, the ancestral lineage of Cornish characters, the achievements of Viscount Frewin and other Cornish who killed their enemies at a town called Treruf, reference to Bodmin Moor (then known as Brentigia), as well

as the siege of the castle at 'Periron' called Tintagel.[26] As it is dedicated to Bishop Warelwust it clearly belongs to the mid-twelfth
century, though the only manuscript, now in the Vatican Library,
comes from the fourteenth.

Centrally, therefore, Cornish writers and scholars were having an
impact in the literary constructions of King Arthur and other mani-
festations of Arthuriana – a process which was to be present
throughout the Cornish literary continuum.[27] Evidence of a Cornish
origin for the stories of Tristan and Isolde also exists. The tale of
Tristan has developed into one of the greatest love stories ever written,
and during the twelfth and thirteenth centuries, various poets and
scholars embellished the legend with their own re-tellings, assimilating
material relevant to their audience. The first scholar to assert that all
the narratives could be traced back to a single original poetic source
was Joseph Bédier.[28] From this source other versions developed, and
the tale began to diversify, yet it maintained its Cornish base. Thomas,
a French-writing poet of the twelfth century, prepared the oldest
extant text, yet he is thought to have come from Britain or Brittany –
which may indicate a familiarity with Cornwall. Gottfried von
Strassburg composed his German version based upon Thomas.[29] This
text then became the dominant 'European' version of the story,
inspiring many others – among them Wagner. An additional poet
from the twelfth century, Béroul, about whom we know very little,
completed a version of the Tristan Romance (also in French) which
inspired other later poets.[30] Henry Jenner (basing at least some of his
observations on the work of Joseph Loth[31]) makes three significant
points about the narrative:

1. That the author of the original story from which Thomas
   and Béroul derived their poems, and of the ground-breaking
   work on which the whole Tristan literature, whether in
   prose, verse or music, and whether in French, English,
   German, or any other tongue, is built, was, if not actually a
   Cornish-man, a man well acquainted with Cornwall.
2. That he laid the scene of his story along the south coast of
   Cornwall from the Fowey estuary to St. Michael's Mount,
   taking real and identifiable places for it, and not only real,
   but likely places.
3. That he wrote when French had been added to the Celtic
   and English which had for some time been concurrently
   spoken in Cornwall.[32]

Successive re-tellings and scholarship have placed constructions of
Cornwall and Cornish identity at the centre of the text, and, alongside
other Arthurian evidence, prove the centrality of Cornish texts in

the European continuum.[33] More recent commentators have also advanced evidence for a Cornish provenance of the narrative. Roberts has argued that Béroul

> . . . may have deliberately relocated a traditional Cornish legend into the Fowey area from a more western location, simply to heighten the drama for his patrons. He was probably writing to entertain members of the powerful Cardinham family. Their estates lay beside the Fowey river, where Robert de Cardinham built the first castle at Restormel.[34]

However, a brief sample of the geography of Béroul's text shows us there is little doubt as to the Cornish location, as we travel from north Cornwall through mid-Cornwall and the Manor of Dimelioc towards the present-day Fal Estuary. With reference to the latter location, the poet first presents a picture of the forest of Moresk, near Truro; and secondly, the Lande Blanche near to Malpas:

1275   En la forest de Morrois sont;
       La nuit jurent desor un mont.
       Or est Tristan si a seür
       Con s'il fust en chastel o mur.

3298   'Di li qu'il set bien le marchès,
       Au chief des plannches, au Mal Pas:
       G'i sollai ja un poi mes dras.
       Sor la morte, el chief de la planche,
       .I. poi de ça la Lande Blanche,
       Soit, revestuz de draz de ladre;
       .I. hanap porte o soi de madre,
       Une botele air dedesoz
       O coroie atachie a noz;
       A l'autre main tienge .I. puiot.
       Si aprenge de tel tripot.'

1275   [They were in the forest of Moresk;
       That night they lay on the hill.
       Now Tristan is as safe
       as if he were in a castle with a wall.]

3298   ['Tell him that he knows the marsh well,
       at the end of the plank-bridge at Malpas:
       There, I soiled my clothes a little.
       On the mound, at the end of the plank-bridge,
       and a little this side of the Lande Blanche,
       let him be dressed in the clothes of a leper;
       let him carry a wooden cup,
       let him have a bottle beneath

4. King Mark stabbing Tristan in the presence of Isolde, engraving after a miniature in a fifteenth-century manuscript.

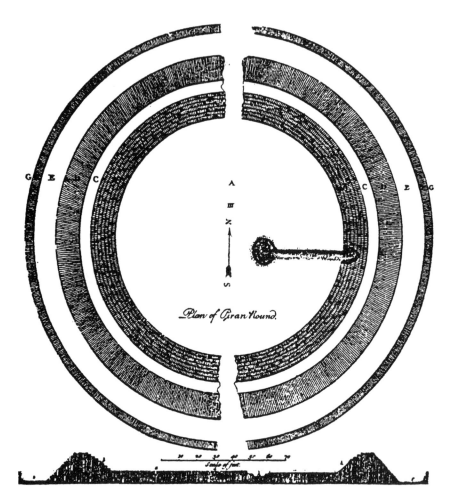

G E C   A   C E G
                       H
                       N
                       S

Plan of Giran Hound.

Scale of feet.

5.   The medieval *plen an gwary* – playing place – near Perranporth, from William
Borlase's *The Natural History of Cornwall*, 1758.

tied on with a strap;
in the other hand, let him carry a stick.
This is the strategem he must keep in mind.']35

In such ways, whilst the beginnings of a Cornish literary continuum were gradually beginning to assemble, change was on its way. After Athelstan's subjugation of the western Celts in AD936, with what some observers have termed the 'ethnic cleansing' of the city of Exeter and what is now west Devon, and then the fixing of the River Tamar as the boundary between his Saxon kingdom and the 'west wealhas', the territory of the west Britons had been surrendered.36 Whilst Athelstan's actions are deplored and although it had ceased to be an independent state, the fact remains that Cornwall did retain some independence.37 Later when the Saxon kingdoms joined together, under English rule, the individuality and difference of Cornwall was at least recognized.38

Whether the Cornish 'Celts' and others fully self-ascribed during this period is unclear. James argues they never did.39 His argument holds some water, and yet there is literary evidence showing that at least a wider understanding of British identity did exist in the face of territorial loss. During the conquest of Cornwall, a Welsh poet wrote 'Armes Prydein [The Prophecy of Britain]'. The poem was written in AD930, six years before Athelstan's cleansing of Exeter and subjugation of the Cornish. It calls upon the Celts of Wales, Cornwall, Scotland, Ireland and the Isle of Man, to unite and throw the 'English' out of Britain:

> And concord of Welshmen and Dublin's men,
> Gaelic men of Ireland, Man and Scotland,
> Cornishmen and Clydesmen at one with us.40

The poem's aim – for the Celts to rid Britain of its conquerors – was an ambitious one. However, in essence, from this period onwards to the Renaissance, Cornwall was to become the first Celtic territory to be incorporated into the English nation-state, and this is one of the reasons why Cornwall's literary construction of itself is different from other 'Celtic' territories. However, all through the medieval period, the phrase 'in Anglia et Cornubia' was commonly used, and 'west Wales' was used to refer to Cornwall until the early modern period.41 Cornwall's difference thus continued (and was officially recognised), as did a flourishing literary culture.

It is unfortunate that much Cornish literature from both this period and the medieval one following has been lost, yet though there are only a few surviving texts, they give us enough evidence of what kind of literary culture existed in Cornwall as post-Roman Britain moved towards the medieval period. The earliest evidence of Old Cornish consists of several glosses from the tenth century. The earliest were written on a text named *Smaragdus's Commentary on Donatus*.[42] Originally, these glosses were thought to be Old Breton, but in 1907, Loth proved that they were Old Cornish. This confusion demonstrates the close relationship between Cornish and Breton, which was to continue within literary culture in Cornwall until the Reformation. Three more glosses are to be found in a Latin text of the *Book of Tobit* contained in a manuscript called *Oxoniensis Posterior*.[43] More substantial glosses (or rather names) are to be found in the *Bodmin Manumissions*. They are copies of New Testament stories, written in Latin at the start of the tenth century. As well as its Cornish names, the Latin text also records the freeing of 122 slaves (of which 98 were Cornish).[44] As in a number of countries, it was the custom to record legal transactions on the blank spaces of sacred texts, and the feudal overlords probably freed the serfs as acts of piety. Generally, most of the landlords have Saxon names while most of the serfs have Cornish ones. However, certain Cornishmen, like Cenmennoc, had learned to work the system for his own ends:

> Hoc est nomen illius hominis quem liberavit Cenmenoc pro anima sua super altare Sancti Petroci, Benedic, coram istis testibus videntibus, Osian presbiter, Morhaitho diaconus.

> [This is the name of that man whom Cenmenoc freed for his soul on the altar of Saint Petrock, Benedic, in the presence of these beholding witnesses, Osian the priest, and Morhaitho the deacon.][45]

Whilst these early Latin narratives are interesting and tell us much about the ethnic politics of early medieval Cornwall, by far the longest piece of Old Cornish literature is the *Vocabularium Cornicum* (*The Old Cornish Vocabulary*) which dates from around AD1000. It provides a long list of Latin words with their Cornish equivalents.[46] Previously only viewed as a source for scholars of the Cornish language, the text actually tells us much about the vitality of literary language a millennium ago. As a thesaurus of the age it classifies everything in the known cosmos ranging from the Biblical creator to inanimate objects, as well as creatures from distant lands such as camels and lions, proving the cosmopolitan writing of Cornish during this phase.[47]

When it came, the Norman Conquest of 1066 actually made very little impact on the Cornish cultural continuum. Most Cornish speakers and writers were a culture and territory away from their overlords, and so the continuum of writing was allowed to progress. A single fragment of Cornish is found in a story which recounts the founding of the church of St Thomas at Glasney in 1265. St Thomas appeared in a dream to the Bishop of Exeter and told him to go to Polsethow in Penryn and consecrate an altar there. The storyteller was fulfilled with the prophecy – 'In Polsethow ywhylyr anethow' [In Polsethow shall be seen dwellings (or marvels)].[48] The line is significant, since as Whetter has demonstrated, Glasney College, founded in Penryn, was to be an important centre of literary production in medieval Cornwall; in very many ways a kind of 'proto-university' and certainly the locus of much scholarship, writing and drama.[49]

The earliest 'true' piece of written Cornish literature extant from the middle Cornish period was discovered by Henry Jenner in the British Museum in 1877. Jenner was looking at some charters relating to the mid-Cornish parish of St Stephen-in-Brannel, when he glimpsed on the back of one of them some faint writing which turned out to be forty-one lines of Cornish. The charter is dated 1340 but Jenner dates the Cornish to around 1400. The content of the endorsement is different from that of any other Middle Cornish literature, since its subject-matter is secular:

> an bar ma ze pons tamar
> my ad pes worty byz fa
> ag ol se voz hy a wra
>
> [On this side to the Tamar bridge
> I pray thee be good to her
> And all thy pleasure she will do][50]

The text's theme is marriage and it offers a young man advice on the treatment of his bride, and a girl advice concerning the way to achieve mastery over her husband. Scholarship has ranged from viewing the writing to be a fragment of a play to a best man's speech.[51] Toorians, who has completed the most comprehensive study of the endorsement, has opined that it is most probably 'an independent poem',[52] whilst of late, I have tried to show how a feminist analysis of the endorsement affords us much productive insight into the relationships between Cornish men and women of this time.[53]

As mentioned at the beginning of this chapter, too much energy has been spent showing how 'backwards' Cornwall was during the medieval period. However, the most significant literary trend during this phase was the development of popular, community-based liturgical and biblical drama, though with a resolutely Cornish treatment. Much scholarship has been devoted to the language, theme and context of such plays and it is not my aim here to tread that path again.[54] Rather, it is to explore the place of that drama within the continuum. The sole surviving example is the *Ordinalia*, a long mystery cycle of three separate plays which recounts the story of humanity's fall and redemption.[55] The cycle, whilst bearing some similarities to the English mystery plays, is a highly sophisticated text and has a unified structure, since as both Halliday and Murdoch suggest, it is a compelling dramatic study of the legend of the Holy Rood.[56] The place-names of the text point to Glasney College being where the play was written. The *Ordinalia* probably took three days to perform. On the first day, *Origo Mundi* (*The Beginning of the World*) the audience is told of the sin of Adam and Eve and of its consequences, man's search for and God's promise of forgiveness. On the second day, *Passio Christi* (*The Passion*) shows how Christ's death brings that forgiveness to earth, and on the third day, *Resurrexio Domini* (*The Resurrection*) shows the results of that forgiveness, as Christ rises from the dead and enters Heaven. A sub-plot to the third play is *The Death of Pilate*. The trilogy worked for Cornish audiences by offering a biblical landscape placed onto the local environment, synthesizing two worlds and thus making the play's message all the more real for the audience. When Adam names the animals of the world in *Origo Mundi*, the creatures of the ocean reflect the maritime culture of medieval Cornwall, which the players and audience fished for and saw off the Cornish cliffs:

135   y rof hynwyn the'n puskes
       corpus sowmens syllyes
          ol thy'm gustyth y e vyth
       lenesow ha barfusy
       pysk ragof ny wra skvsy
140   mar corthyaf dev yn perfyth

135   [I give names to the fishes,
       Porpoises, salmons, congers,
          All to me obedient they shall be;
       Ling and cod,
       A fish from me shall not escape,
140   If I honour God perfectly.][57]

As well as the cultural geography of immediate Cornwall, the dramatists were able to weave in other contemporary elements. Whilst David is having an affair with Bathsheba, we meet her husband Uriah, who is presented as the very embodiment of courtly love, almost Arthurian in his quest to serve his king:

2150   ha del oma marrek len
       venythe ny thof a'n plen
          er na'n prenne an guas-na.

2150   [And as I am a trusty knight,
        Never will I come from the place
            Until I take that fellow.][58]

Whilst Uriah reflects perhaps the imaginary construct of knightly chivalry for the audience, elsewhere in the plays, the very geography of Cornwall itself becomes more immediate. In the sequence when labourers and workmen are constructing King Solomon's temple, as rewards for their efforts, he offers them tracts of Cornish land, which increase in size as the drama continues, and the temple nears completion:

2398   ha rag why thu'm kerune
        my a re thyugh bosuene
            lostuthyel ha lanerchy

2398   [And to you, by my crown,
        I will give you Bosvene
            Lostwithiel and Lanerchy.][59]

Then later:

2462   ha rag bos agas whey tek
        my a re thyugh plu vuthek
            ha'n garrack ruan gans hy thyr

2462   [And because your work is fair,
        I will give you the parish of Vuthek,
            And the Carrack Ruan, with its land.][60]

Another interesting example is the shift in geography which accompanies the play of the Passion. Up until this point, the geography is centred around Penryn and the present-day estuary of Carrick Roads, but when the torturers require nails, they head westwards towards Market Jew Street in Penzance. We have no way of knowing whether this was because the audience considered those in the west more barbarous than themselves, or it may well be some now long forgotten piece of topical humour:

2663   ye a . . . cowyth da ye
        leuereugh thy'mmo wharre
            mar cothough ple ma kentrow
        yn pen crous rak y fastie
        eugh the wovyn hep lettye
            worth an gof yn marghes yow

2663   [Ye . . . good companions, ye
        Tell me directly
            If you know where there are nails,

> To fasten him on the wood of the cross,
> Go to ask, without delay,
> Of the smith in Market Jew.][61]

There were also a stock set of images which the dramatists drew upon, and which are reflected in design and architecture from this period. One of the central images of the motif of the legend of the Rood in *Origo Mundi*, is Seth's planting of the apple seeds into the dead Adam's mouth; an image – amongst many others from the *Ordinalia* – which is to be found in the windows of St Neot church in East Cornwall:

> 870   an try spus un y anow
>   my a's gor hep falladow
>   kepar del ve thy'm yrghys

> 870   [The three grains into his mouth
>   I will put them without fail,
>   Like as it was enjoined to me.][62]

The Cornish interpretation of biblical themes is also given localised metaphor. Considering how Christ can be both God and man in *Passio Christi*, the First Doctor connects this with the mermaid of Cornish folklore:

> 1739   y gorthyby me a wra
>   ef a alse bos yn ta
>   hanter den ha hanter dev
>   den yv hanter morvoron
>   benen a'n pen the'n colon
>   yn della yw an ihesu

> 1739   [I will answer him;
>   He might be well
>   Half man and half God.
>   Human is half the mermaid
>   Woman from the head to the heart;
>   So is the Jesus][63]

In this way, though the authors of the central texts of medieval Cornwall did not always base their texts on what many twentieth-century scholars have viewed as 'Celtic' (mythological adventures and acts of heroism), the Cornish variant offered its own particular and highly distinctive performance of biblical myth synthesized onto local and very real landscape.[64] Scholars have perhaps also underestimated two other significant factors – firstly, the direct traffic of liturgical performance and biblical narrative back and forth between Cornwall

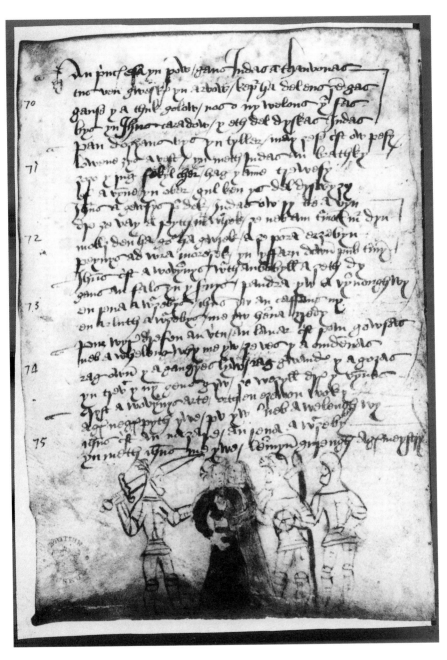

6. A Middle Cornish language text: Passyon Agan Arluth.

7 + 8. Passion poem illustrations.

and mainland Europe,[65] as well as the legends concerning Joseph of Arimathea's visit with the child Jesus to Cornwall, which may well have been a central imaginative construct for most Cornish people of this period, embodied even today in the name of the Jesus Well in north Cornwall.[66] The extant text of the *Ordinalia* stops short of Judgement Day – which is featured in most of the other cycles of these islands. There is perhaps an argument here that the cycle was part of an even longer work. Recent observers have commented on how there might have been a nativity play between *Origo Mundi* and *Passio Christi*.[67]

Cycle dramas like the *Ordinalia* were probably performed in the open air, in a large amphitheatre called a plen-an-gwarry, or a 'playing place'. There is some debate as to how these cycle dramas were performed. Traditional scholarship has considered that the cast, usually local people, were positioned around the edge of the 'plain' and at the appropriate moment, they would parade in front of their station and deliver their lines, with the audience seated upon the bank.[68] The meticulous work of Sydney Higgins has suggested that the performance was perhaps more likely to be a promenade style with a mobile audience, marshalled to where the action was occurring, or just naturally following the flow of the drama.[69] To some extent, performance must have been restricted by the local environment, and in all probability a combination of these two methodologies seems likely.[70]

Bakere has suggested that although only two 'playing places' now survive at St Just and Perranzabuloe, in fact, it can be deduced from church records, archaeological and place-name evidence that many more amphitheatres existed across Cornwall, suggesting a highly developed theatrical continuum.[71] Recent work by Padel has suggested these might number above thirty.[72] Meanwhile, as Joyce and Newlyn's historical survey of sources of early drama in Cornwall suggests, within Cornwall there was 'an extended pattern of popular entertainment and dramatic performance' and 'a richness of entertainment occurred in Cornwall in the period right down to 1642', with records showing an 'Enterlude' [sic] at Launceston, a Susanna play performed at St Breock, a 'mirable' [sic] play at Sancreed, a Corpus Christi play at Bodmin and a full cycle drama at St Ives.[73] The high concentration of dramatic activity in the comparatively small territory of Cornwall may have made for again an exchange of ideas, not only within the rest of Britain, but also on the continent. Other plays existed in other parts of Cornwall, again taking for their themes a retelling of the bible or the life of the particular community's saint, for a largely illiterate audience. Accounts of income show how central the dramas were in their contribution towards local economies and tell us that in contemporary parlance, the plen-an-gwarry was probably devised with 'multiple leisure usage' in mind.[74]

Elsewhere, there is substantial evidence of travelling theatre companies operating in Cornwall, demonstrative, in part, of a complex musical, minstrel and dance culture, operating in parallel with dramatic performances. Even now, this continuum of festival combined with drama is embodied in the Obby Oss survivals of Padstow, and Helston's Flora Day, Furry Dance and the Hal-an-Tow song.[75] Also extremely popular throughout Britain in the fourteenth and fifteenth centuries were dramas based on Robin Hood, and there is substantial evidence that the legend was given Cornish 'spin' in local communities.[76] Though the cycle plays and these dramas appear to have appealed to all classes of people, being a truly socially unifying spectacle, sources also suggest that by the fifteenth century, private household performances of dramas were held in the rich family houses of Cornwall – in the homes of the Carmynows, the Arundells, the Carews, St Aubyns and the Trevanions – ultimately, as we shall see later with Richard Carew, a process that would assist in the decline of the larger-scale productions.[77]

Emerging at broadly the same time in the late fourteenth century was the liturgical poem *Passyon Agan Arluth* (*The Poem of Mount Calvary*).[78] This is an account in verse based on the canonical gospels with various apocryphal additions. Several manuscripts are known, of which the oldest, mistakenly regarded by some scholars as the original, was found at Sancreed. The poem is a stunning and elaborate work; the poetic mirror-image of the dramas being performed. It has many similarities to the Passion play of the *Ordinalia*, though it bears no explicit Cornish references. Here, the poem's quatrains are used to great effect at the moment of the crucifixion:

> Newngo devethys an prys may tho agas theweth
> Yn erna y fe dorgis ha dris ol an bys ef eth
> Tewolgow bras a ve guris an houll a gollas y feth
> Hay moy mer thus me agris ys a rena ve yn wethe

> [Twas not come the time, but twas near his end,
> In that hour there was an earthquake, over all ye world it was
> Darkness great was made ye sunn left his face
> And more wonders I believe then there were also.][79]

Other poems and dramas obviously existed. For instance, the Renaissance hagiographer Nicholas Roscarrock saw a copy of the Life of St Columb, but this has not survived:

This I haue taken out of an olde Cornish Rymthe containing her Legend, translated by one Mr Williams, a Phis[it]ion there, but howe Autentick it is I dare not saye, being loath to comptrowle that which I cannot correct.[80]

Thus, as we have now clearly seen, unlike many of the other Celtic territories during the medieval period, Cornwall's literary energies did not, for the most part, appear to focus on a mythic or heroic Cornish age – as it did in territories such as Wales and Ireland, but rather, the focus was on a merging of European-wide biblical narrative onto Cornish experience. As we might expect, considering its close cultural development with Cornwall, Brittany was the only other territory to hold such a fully developed continuum.[81] Presumably some of the narratives eventually to be found in the nineteenth-century folktale collections of Robert Hunt and William Bottrell, were originally conceived in Cornish, later to be re-told in English, but we shall see more of this in later chapters.[82] The heroic age of Arthur, and Tristan and Isolde which preceded this epic, popular drama, perhaps continued in oral form as well, helping to shape and inform Cornish identity.

One of the most interesting figures of the middle Cornish period was the Cornish scholar John Trevisa (c.1342–1402). In a number of significant ways, Trevisa stands as symbolic of many Cornish scholars and writers who came after him. Trevisa's fame as a writer is usually derived from how he helped to save the English language. As Weatherhill details, the Norman Conquest saw the status of English relegated to the role of the subjugated.[83] With Norman-French the language of the new rulers, English was rapidly becoming extinct. Campaigns to revive English seemed doomed to fail, until the work of Trevisa. First, Trevisa wrote how John Cornwall, a master of grammar, replaced French with English in grammar schools, and how he had taught Richard Pencrych – a Cornishman – English. Pencrych in turn, taught others and English was revived. Trevisa himself contributed to the process by translating Ranulf Hidgen's *Polychronicon*, providing the English with the largest history and encyclopaedia of the time in their own tongue.[84] David C. Fowler has also advanced that Trevisa was one of the scholars responsible for the first complete translation into English of the Wycliffite Bible, as well as providing problematical evidence contending that he was also responsible for the revisions of *Piers the Plowman*, now known as the B and C texts.[85] In this way, Trevisa typifies the Cornish medieval scholar, who though very obviously connected with the territory of Cornwall, was also operating on a Britain-wide level. Elliott-Binns also records a number of other medieval Cornish writers and scholars – among them Robert Luc de Cornubia, Michael Trewinnard, Thomas Trevett, Godfrey of Cornwall and Michael of Tregury but none of their work has survived.[86]

Whilst literary activity in medieval Cornwall continued to grow, as I have argued elsewhere, in this period and after, the colonizing English state moved beyond its earlier accommodation of Cornwall to attempt full integration. Using the words of Pistol from William Shakepeare's *Henry V* ('Le Roy! a Cornish name: art thou of Cornish crew?'), I have demonstrated how Shakespeare – writing from the perspective of 1599, but projecting a vision of Agincourt in 1415 – saw that in contrast with the more easily explained and predictable portrayal of the Irish, Welsh and Scots in the play, the Cornish are afforded special treatment – an indication that for England in the medieval and early modern period, Cornwall had become a sort of 'manageable junior partner'.[87] The 'Cornish crew's' place in Henry V's army is seen as one of proud inclusion; Cornish archers were central in Henry's army against the French. However, this relationship between the colonizer and colonized is filled with considerable tension. For the Cornish, what cannot be explicitly acknowledged is their possession of an alternative language, literature and culture, for to do so would be to stage the presence of the very contradictions which the play denies in its attempt to stage the ideal of a unified English nation state.[88]

The play therefore tells us that after the medieval period, the Cornish had either been so well anglicized at this early phase that they were reduced to this status, or more probably, due to a combination of geographical, social and military reasons, were accepted as a dynamic force and territory. However, events in the early modern period were to have a cataclysmic effect on Cornish. Much of the decline of Cornish language and literature was due to Tudor central-ism.[89] New laws and taxation gave rise to a reaction among Cornish people. William Antron, a Member of Parliament for Helston, denounced this imperialism, as well as the imposition of taxes to fund an invasion of Scotland. Nevertheless despite attempts to further draw Cornwall into England, the Cornish continued to resist, sometimes with great passion and vigour.[90] The now infamous '1497 Rebellion' was one example of this, when an army of 15,000 was raised to march to London from St Keverne on the Lizard to oppose taxation levied on the Cornish to fight the Crown's war with Scotland.[91] A blacksmith from St Keverne called Michael Joseph 'An Gof' (Cornish language for 'the smith') was joined by a Bodmin lawyer, Thomas Flamank who together led the army. After a royal army was beaten back by the Cornish at Guildford, Henry VII met the Cornish 'crew' with his own army of 25,000 at Blackheath, where the Cornish surrendered. An Gof and Flamank were hung, drawn and quartered at Tyburn.[92] Their mission and martyrdom is one of the most significant events in Cornish history, and is still commemorated annually. The English monarchy's view of the Cornish as a fond 'crew' had changed considerably.

This change in England's perception of Cornwall, and in Cornwall's perception of England, is central to Cornish literature in the aftermath of the rebellion. *Beunans Meriasek* (1504), a pre-Reformation saint's play which is set in the district of Camborne, celebrates the life and work of St Meriasek, a saint found in both Cornwall and Brittany.[93] As well as references to Camborne itself, Carn Brea and 'a hobby horse', the play is a wonderful depiction of the cross-channel culture which existed between these two territories. Some of the finest sequences involve the maritime journeys back and forth between Brittany and Cornwall. Here, Meriasek is welcomed aboard a vessel travelling to Cornwall:

> 593   Wocum oys genen dremas
> ny ath wor the pen an gluas
>   dre voth du kyn pen sythen
> dus abeveth oma scon
> hav marners tennogh dyson
>   an goyl thym in ban lemen

> 593   [Welcome art thou with us, honest man.
> We put thee to Land's End
>   Through God's will, before a week's end.
> Come thou in here at once:
> And, my mariners, quickly haul
>   The sail up for me now.][94]

Later, he returns to Brittany, where, as observed by the sailor's servant, he appears to control the very rocks before them:

> 1088   Tremenys yv dyogel
> lemen genen an chanel
>   may fe holmyv spede dek
> devethys on bys in tyr
> lemen quik thagis desyr
>   grueghwy londia meryasek
> an men re ruk inclynya
> in tyr rag the receva
>   gras the ihesu galosek

> 1088   [Passed is safely
> Now by us the Channel
>   My faith, this is fair speed.

Come we are to shore
Now quick to your desire
   Do you land, Meriasek.
The stone has bent down
On the shore to receive thee.
   Thanks to mighty Jesu!][95]

In such sequences we can see that the play's construction fits the wider European dramatic model for presenting medieval Christendom and is based upon four important themes, which are closely linked. According to Murdoch, these are,

> the relations between Church and State, the combating of evil and the conversion of unbelievers, healing in the physical and soteriological sense, and the role of saints (and the clergy) as intercessors with special emphasis on the Virgin.[96]

Although Murdoch recognizes that the Duke of Cornwall's eventual victory must be viewed in the light of the play's wider themes, recent scholarship has asserted a more explicit link between *Beunans Meriasek* and the aftermath of 1497. Payton, for instance, argues that the text is actually a subversive document, rather than just a saint's play:

> At the very least, the theme of tyranny and the choice of Teudar (Henry VII was known popularly as Henry Tudor) would have struck a Cornish audience as being particularly apposite, while the specific desire to stage the play in 1504 may have been a good indication of the strength of Cornish feeling at that time.[97]

The play had therefore become 'a subversive document, a vehicle for Cornish identity as well as a statement of global Papal pretensions'.[98] Likewise, Wooding has observed,

> that Teudar's defeat by the Duke of Cornwall may well have been a statement of the locals' disillusionment with the distant king. The fact that the play itself was in the local language, probably not understood by English onlookers might serve to reinforce the 'underworld', or slightly subversive quality of it.[99]

Payton points to examples of where the Duke of Cornwall might be seen as fighting for Cornwall, as well as the universal church:

2205   Me yv duk in oll Kernow
           indella ytho ov thays
      hag vhel arluth in pov
           a tamer the pen an vlays
      tregys off lemen heb wov
           berth in castel an dynas
               sur in peddre

ha war an tyreth vhel
thym yma castel arel
a veth gelwys tyndagyel
    henna vy o[v] fenn tregse

2205   [I am Duke in all Cornwall:
    So was my father,
And a high lord in the country
    From Tamar to Land's End.
I am dwelling now, without a lie,
    Within the castle of Dynas
        Surely in Pidar,
And in the high land
I have another castle,
Which is called Tintagel:
    That is my chief dwelling-seat.][100]

Textual evidence also shows how the words of King Teudar would have put fear into the Cornish audience; Payton concluding that Murdoch's assertion that Teudar is 'seen as an interloper in Cornwall' was correct.[101] He was 'an outsider imposing his power':[102]

759   Tevdar me a veth gelwys
    arluth regnijs in kernov
may for mahum enorys
    ov charge yv heb feladov
        oges ha pel
penag a worthya ken du
y astev peynys glu
    hag inweth mernans cruel

759   [Teudar I am called,
    Lord reigning in Cornwall.
That Mohammed be honoured
    Is my charge without fail,
        Near and far.
Whosoever worship another god,
They shall have keen pains,
    And likewise a cruel death.][103]

And later, without reference to Teudar's non-Christian faith:

2397   Duk Kernow hag oll y dus
indan ov threys me as glus
    poren kepar ha treysy

2397   [Duke of Cornwall and all his folk,
Under my feet I will crush them
    Just like grains of sand.][104]

Interestingly, despite its radical subject-matter, the play still fits into the continuum of Cornish drama. It attempted to progress the form forward by the incorporation of political commentary, calling for a renegotiation of Cornwall's relationship with the powers at the centre. It is known that the manuscript of *Beunans Meriasek* was completed by Radolphus Ton who is believed to have been a canon at Glasney College.[105] It seems clear that this period saw the final efflorescence of Cornish literary culture at the College, when Cornish influence, by way of personnel, was also at its greatest. There were no doubt other plays commemorating individual saints which have not survived.

The First Act of Uniformity came in January 1549. This introduced the English language (and therefore its literature) into church services, replacing Latin and Cornish. In response to this, the Cornish rioted in defence of their traditional service patterns.[106] When the law was instated six months later, a full insurrection began. This was led by Humphrey Arundell of Helland and Nicholas Boyer of Bodmin. Their concerns are reflected in the articles of what became the '1549 Prayer Book Rebellion':

> Item we wil not receyue the new seruyce because it is but lyke a Christmas game, but we wull haue oure olde seruice of Mattens, masse, Euensong and procession in Latten, as it was before. And so we the Cornysche men (whereof certen of vs vunderstande no Englysh) vtterly refuse thys newe Englysh.[107]

After some preliminary successes, the Cornish rebels were eventually defeated by Lord Bedford's army.[108] As Ellis has convincingly argued, 'hangings, burnings, and ruthless suppression followed as harsh as anything under Cromwell in Ireland, or Cumberland in Scotland'.[109] The Cornish may have declared in 1549 that they refused English, but in reality, in the aftermath of rebellion, they were to choose collusion rather than collision in defining their relationship with the English state. Collision having already failed twice, collusion was Cornwall's only option. By the time *Henry V* was written, this collusion was accepted; the rebellion against the nation-state, if not forgotten, at least forgiven. Put another way, the colonizer had gone a significant way in persuading the colonized to accept their subordinate status. The memory of the 1497 Cornish rebellion meanwhile had moved into the conscience of wider European literature. Some twenty years later, in his speculative essay *Utopia*, Thomas More notes how the English are like 'incompetent schoolmasters' in their dealings with troublesome territories like Cornwall, but likewise praises the 'disabled soldiers, who lost a limb in that battle with the Cornish rebels'.[110]

Despite More's negative view of the Cornish during the early modern period, other writers, now writing more confidently in English, were prepared to champion Cornish identity and difference. One of those writers was Andrew Boorde. Boorde was born at the start of the sixteenth century and only a few fragments of his writing are extant.[111] Boorde's lasting contribution to Cornu-English literature was to write a fascinating tourist handbook of Britain, the *Fyrst Boke of the Introduction of Knowledge*, written in 1542 and published in 1547. Boorde writes that 'In Cornwall is two speches, the one is naughty Englysshe and the other is Cornysshe speech. And there be many men and women the which cannot speake one word of Englysshe but all Cornysshe'.[112] Additionally Boorde wrote twenty-six lines of English, which Wakelin has argued is of an east Cornish variety[113]:

Iche cham Cornysche man, al[e] che can brew;
It wyll make one to kacke, also to spew;
It is dycke and smoky, and also it is dyn;
It is lyke wash, as pygges had wrestled dryn.
Iche cannot brew, nor dresses Fleshe, nor vyshe;
Many folke do segge, I mar many a good dysche.
Dup the dore, gos! iche had some dyng to seg,
"Whan olde knaues be dead, yonge knaues be fleg."
Iche chaym yll afyngred, iche swere by my fay
Iche nys not eate no soole sens yester daye;
Iche wolde fayne taale ons myd the cup;
Nym me a quart of ale, that iche may it of sup.
A, good gosse, to me iche hab a toome, vysche, and also tyn;
Drynke, gosse, to me, or els iche chyl begyn.
God! watysh great colde, and fynger iche do abyd!
Wyl your bedauer, gosse, come home at the next tyde.
Iche pray God to coun him wel to vare,
That, whan he comit home, myd me he do not starre
For putting a straw dorow his great net.
Another pot of ale, good gosse, now me fet;
For my bedauer wyl to London, to try the law,
To sew Tre poll pen, for waggyng of a straw.
Now gosse farewell! yche can lon lenger abyde;
Iche must ouer to the ale howse at the yender syde;
And now come myd me, gosse, I thee pray,
And let vs make merry, as long as we may.[114]

Though brief, Boorde's inclusion in the literary continuum of early modern Cornwall is significant. First, it is perhaps the earliest example of a Cornu-English dialect literature, and the fact that it is written in couplets, suggests a more satirical and wittier edge. The categorical assertion of identity ('Iche cham a Cornysche man') is important since it suggests a certain Cornish independence. Wakelin notes that it has characteristics of 'Mummerset stage dialect as conceived in the sixteenth century',[115] but this misses some of the meaning of the piece, which was partly political, for it demonstrates the complexity of literary politics in early modern Cornwall. The text was written in 1542 in a period where the dissolution of the smaller monasteries of Cornwall had just been ordered by Henry VIII. His government knew that they would have to keep a careful eye on the Cornish. The delay of some five years from its composition to publication tells us something of how turbulent this period of history was for Cornwall. Thus Boorde's 'some dyng to seg' is an angrier voice and the text might well be a projected account, to the English at least, of the 'by-now-typical' Cornishman travelling once again to London in order to rebel and to try confronting the law.

Boorde's significance does not end here however. A much ignored piece of early Cornish literature is also offered by him, which comes in the form of a conversation between a traveller to Cornwall and a serving maid. With its reading much like a phrasebook of its time, Robert Morton Nance has criticised the passage for offering corrupted Cornish, and yet to other observers it reads as a genuine passage from the late sixteenth century. What is perhaps of most interest, is the fact that it is a secular conversation, and demonstrates that at this point travellers to Cornwall could still expect to hear Cornish in use:

> *Mayde, brynge me egges and butter.*
> Mathtath, drewgh me eyo hag a manyn de vi.
> *Syr, much good do it you.*
> Syrra, betha why lowe weny cke.
> *Hostes, what shall I pay?*
> Hostes, pendra we pay?
> *Syr, your reckenyng is .v. pens.*
> Syrra, iges rechen eu pymp in ar.
> *How many myles is it to London?*
> Pes myll eus a lemma de Londres?
> *Syr, it is thre houndred myle.*
> Syrra, tray kans myle dere.
> *God be with you, good hostes.*
> Bena tewgana a why, hostes da.
> *God gyve you a good night.*
> Dew rebera vos da de why.[116]

As Boorde's phrasebook for visitors indicates, change was occurring swiftly and unrelentingly. Industry in Cornwall had been around since the days of Herodotus, but moves towards modernisation and the development of that industry were already causing problems. When John Leland took his tour of Cornwall around 1540, we see the pollution surrounding the Hayle estuary:

> From Mr. Godolcan to Pembro, wher the paroch chirch is [i.e. appertains] to Mr. Godolcan. The personage impropriate to Heyles in Gloucestreshir. The south se is about a mile from Pembro. From Mr. Godolcan to Lannate a 4 miles. Passages at ebbe over a great strond, and then over Heyle river. No greater tynne workes yn al Cornwall than be on Sir Wylliam Godolcan's ground. Heyle Haven shoken [choked] with land of tynne works.[117]

The realism of Boorde and Leland only slightly revealed the cultural, material and linguistic devastation that Cornwall was facing during the Reformation. The English writer Nicholas Udall argued that the Bible, Service and Prayer book should be available in Cornish. In 1560 the Church resolved 'that it may be lawful for such Welsh or Cornish children as can speak no English to learn the Premises of the Welsh tongue or Cornish language'.[118] Although this resolution was not followed, the fact that many Cornish remained Catholic following the Reformation contributed much to what we know of the language and its literature in the sixteenth century. For example, the extensive prose work of John Tregear consists of homilies translated into Cornish around 1558. Tregear is one of the few Cornish priests known to have made translations of Christian works for his Cornish-speaking congregation.[119] *The Tregear Homilies* consist of thirteen translations into Cornish of homilies, twelve originating from Edward Bonner, the bishop of London. In 1555, through a series of sermons, Bonner celebrated Mary Tudor's accession, and the temporary end of the Reformation. The Creation Homily refers to Cornish itself – that people should know God is their Lord in their language:

> Ima an profet Dauit in peswar vgans ha nownsag psalme ow exortya old an bobyll the ry prayse hag honor the du ha thy servya in lowendar ha gans perfect colononow the reiosya in sight agan creator ha redemar. yma an profet dauid ow allegia helma kepar ha dell ewa sufficiant cawse again redempcion. *Scitote Quoniam Ipse Est Dominus. Ipse Fecit Nos, Et Non Ipsi Nos*, henna ew tha leverall in agan eyth ny.

> [The prophet David in the ninety-ninth psalm, exhorts all the people to give praise and honour to God and to serve him in joy and with perfect hearts to rejoice in the sight of our Creator and

Redeemer. The prophet David alleges this as being a sufficient cause of our redemption. *Know ye that he is the Lord. He made us and not we ourselves*, that is to say in our language, know God is our Lord, and He our maker, for we did not make ourselves.][120]

Very little is actually known about Tregear himself, but within the manuscript we can see him exercising his own poetic talents regarding the sacrament of the altar. The following sequence shows how the eventual couplet is formed from the source material available to him; a process that no doubt formed a regular part of Cornish writers' work during this phase. By the third line, he has created the desired couplet effect:

[An bara ha]n gwyn dir goir Dew ew trylis the corf ha gois chris[t]
Bara han gwyn dir geir Dew ew gwris corf ha [gois Christ]
Bara ha gwyn dir gyrryow Dew, Corf ha gois Christ gwrie a thew.

[The bread and the wine, through the word of God, are changed into the body and blood of Christ.
The bread and the wine, through the word of God, is made the body and blood of Christ.
The bread and the wine, through the words of God, the body and blood of Christ are made.][121]

However, despite the efforts of writers like Tregear, when Elizabeth succeeded her sister in 1558, the Reformation continued once again. This was the turning point, not only for the continuum of literature in Cornish, but also the complex multi-cultural society that Cornwall had been in the medieval period. Ellis cites Jenner as stating:

> After the Reformation, English came in like a flood: and the fact that neither the Book of Common Prayer nor the Bible was translated into Cornish shows that, even if Cornish was still in use, the people also had a knowledge of English. The chief reason for the decay was undoubtedly the failure of Cornwall to produce a literature for it is through literature that language achieves permanent form and can struggle successfully with competing tongues.[122]

Jenner was correct to some degree, but actually a literature had been produced. That it has been lost is a point he fails to make. The reality of the Reformation, however, was that during the seventeenth century the language and therefore literature's decline was fast and abrupt, in spite of the fact that a small number of Cornish gentlemen became interested in developing its literature. Neither the oral nor the written continuum of Cornish would long survive.

It is, however, worth drawing our attention to some texts which were constructed despite the effects of the Reformation process. Oliver Oldwanton's bawdy play *The Image of Idleness* (c.1565–70) is a reworking of the story of Pygmalion, given a Cornish context and performed on the London stage. The story was 'translated out of the Troyance or Cornysche tounge' and contains the Cornish line 'Marsoye thees duan Guisca ancorne Rog hatre arta [If there is to thee grief to wear the horn, give it home again]'.[123] The central character is a Cornish priest – John Polmarghe – who is from the college of Penborgh (perhaps a stage 'Glasney'), and two other Cornish characters add to the comedy: Maistur Jewgur and Syr Ogier Penkeyles. The play needs further study, but it seems likely that by this phase, Cornwall had already gained a reputation for being barbarous, and bringing Cornish characters to the London stage was difficult for the playwright to resist. Back in Cornwall, dramas equivalent to those happening on the London stage – and telling us much about the linguistic and literary culture of the period – were occurring in individual parishes. The 1572 Bishops' Consistory Court Depositions at Exeter tell us how a William Hawysche heard the following

> . . . upon Dew Whallan Gwa Metten in Eglos Da Lalant, viz. upon all hallow day late paste about the mydds of the service in the parish church of Lalant Moryshe David's wife and Cicely James came into the church of Lalant together and in chiding with words together Cycely called Agnes Davey whore and whore bitch in English and not in Cornowok.[124]

The bi-lingual west Cornish society of this time is ably described here, with both Agnes and Cycely seemingly able to move between tongues quite easily; but we receive a picture of the clerk of the court as well, who was clearly proficient in Cornish. An observer of the period – John Norden – wrote his *Topographical and Historical Description of Cornwall* in the year 1584, and makes some interesting observations on language shift and change within Cornwall:

> [Of] late the Cornishe men haue much conformed themselues to the vse of the Englishe tounge, and their Englishe is equall to the beste, espetially in the easterne parts; euen from Truro eastwarde it is in manner wholy Englishe. In the weste parte of the Countrye, as in the hundreds of Penwith and Kerrier, the Cornishe tounge is moste in vse amongste the inhabitantes and yet (which is to be maruelyed) thowgh the husband and wife, parentes and children, Master and Seruantes, doe mutually comunicate in their natiue language, yet ther is none of them in manner but is able to conuers with a Straunger in the English tounge, vnlesse it be some obscure

53

people, that seldome conferr with the better sorte: But it seem that in few yeares the Cornishe Language wilbe by litle and litle abandoned.[125]

As well as linguistic symbols of identity and difference, Norden alludes to the difficult politics (both historical and contemporary) of Cornwall's relationship with England; perceptively noting the frustration of the Cornish in the face of their more powerful neighbour:

> [A]nd as they are amonge themselve litigious so seeme they yet to retayne a kinde of conceyled enuye agaynste the Englishe, whome they yet affecte with a desire of reuenge for their fathers sakes, by whome their fathers recuyued the repulse.[126]

From this it appears that though the English, at least, had forgiven the Cornish for their insurrections of 1497 and 1549, what we may term the 'folk memory' of those events continued for some time into the early modern period. The other important text regarding Cornish literature at this time is the 'Relation of the visit of the Catholic Kings' by Don Antonio Ortes, which details a sermon spoken in Cornish to Philip III and his wife Queen Margaret in 1600 at Valladolid in Spain:

> *La lengua Cornaica*: The Cornish Language
> 'His honour is great in thy salvation: glory and great worship shalt thou lay upon him.' Verse 5.
> There spoke in this language a student, a native of that Province of England, whose language is distinct from English, as is in Spain the Biscayan from the Castilian; and it has some ways and manner of speaking, with that rapidity of the Basques: and it is that part of England which look directly towards Biscay and in his manner he spoke it excellently.
>
> *Interprete*: Translation
> Said the Cornishman: that all men aim at honour and glory, but few find it, because they do not seek it where it is; they seek it in vanity and deceitful splendour of the world and they find themselves deceived and vain: because it is only found in virtue in which the Catholic Kings seek it, and therefore the true honour follows them as the shadows follow the body.[127]

They were part of a state visit to an English college which trained Catholic priests, and though Ortes fails to record the name of the Cornishman, various scholars have offered a name: Richard Pentrey.[128] Pentrey therefore embodies the notion that in Cornwall, Catholicism lasted a long time after the Reformation. The other significant change to occur was that the close relationship between Cornwall and Brittany was to cease after the Reformation. Previously, the *Lay Subsidy Rolls* (especially for the years 1540–1560) and the old parish registers, showed that there were many Bretons living in Cornwall. Then suddenly these names cease. As Smith has argued, 'the probability is that the ill-treatment these people received under Queen Elizabeth made them return to Brittany' and that 'the loss of this centuries-old friendly intercourse between these two Celtic-speaking countries must have had an adverse effect on Cornish'.[129]

The writing was on the wall for Cornish by the end of the sixteenth century, and by the mid-seventeenth century, as this Cornwall began to coalesce under the pressure of English, the old Cornish literature and culture crumbled, eventually to be replaced in the next century by the dynamic cultural forces of counter-Reformation Methodism and industrialization. The age of King Arthur had long since passed, and now after the age of An Gof, a number of post-Reformation, Renaissance writers begin to emerge, who will come to exemplify the literary politics and paralysis in the period after. These literary politics pattern the wider economic, religious and social conditions of Renaissance Cornwall, yet they also interrelate in such a way as to be become a productive reading of all future literary production in Cornwall from 1600 onwards. Thus, two continuums emerge simultaneously, and it is these two continuums and their collisions and collaborations which will define the next phase of Cornish literary development. Two major writers of Renaissance Cornwall problematicize the successive literary politics for generations afterwards. They are Nicholas Roscarrock (c.1550–1634) and Richard Carew (1555–1620): the first exemplifying the older conceptualization of Catholic Cornwall – rooted in saints' lives, superstition and folklore (in a way 'proto-revivalist'); the second promoting Protestantism, new Renaissance humanism and an alignment with 'English' culture and literature. In their own ways, each also offered new developments of old themes – thus enhancing the overall continuum of literature emerging from Cornwall. In addition, the writer Sidney Godolphin looked as if he might well progress a gentrified Anglo-Cornish poetic of Cornwall, but this never fully materialized. The reason for this paralysis will be explored later in this chapter.

As Orme has shown, one major writer facing difficulties in an era of Catholic persecution was Nicholas Roscarrock.[130] Roscarrock's *Lives of the Saints* occupies a unique place in Cornish Renaissance literature. He was, like Trevisa, a scholar who left Cornwall to write. However, he was writing what was by now typical Cornish subject-matter, the lives of the saints. Saints' lives had formed the basis of some of the drama in the medieval period, and the material was to provide the thematic base for later literature. Though written in English, the subject-matter of his work was resolutely of medieval Cornwall. As well as symbolizing the end of this period, Roscarrock was effectively an early folklorist – or even proto-revivalist, who was collecting the fragments of post-Roman and medieval Britain; the volume an affirmation of these islands as a nursery of saints. In this respect, Roscarrock was of the era of An Gof, yet his scholarship pointed to the work of an emergent Renaissance Cornwall. Roscarrock catalogues and narrates the lives of all the major saints of Cornwall, but also demonstrates his knowledge of feast days and popular religious celebrations. Connecting to the earlier dramas themselves, the lives of the saints were important liturgically, and were often as influential at times of public and community activity. Typical of the narratives is the life of St Piran:

> Being in Ireland, boares, wolves and other brute beastes did obey him; he converted many and miracles were wrought betwixt him and Sct Brendan who turned water into milke by blessing it, showing therby he has no vse for a cow, when Sct Piran by blessing the same milke turned it againe to water, perswading him therby not to refuse ordinary meat . . .[131]

Roscarrock stands as a writer at the very end of pre-Reformation Cornwall, a Cornwall which was trying to hold onto a mythic and 'spiritually correct' past. The literature and politics of pre-Reformation Cornwall, being somehow 'more' Cornish than that which was to follow, first begins to emerge here, with Roscarrock as the recorder of past glories, a Catholic religion and heritage, and though an English speaker, primarily a writer concerned with a 'past greatness'. Richard Carew was to offer something radically different to this and it is between these two Renaissance writers that the debate over the direction and purpose of what we may term a truly modern Anglo-Cornish literature first surfaces.

Several observers have noted what we may term Carew's 'Renaissance individuality',[132] but have failed to note his importance to this period of Anglo-Cornish literature. Carew's understanding of the changing nature of the new, emerging Cornwall is what we perceive within his work.[133] In direct contrast to Roscarrock's belief in the ideology of an earlier Cornwall, Carew, whilst recognizing and sometimes lamenting the loss of the old, actually reinforces the development of Cornwall into the modern era. This process becomes clear from Carew's subject-matter, methodology and metaphor.

As Halliday asserts, Cornish difference was merged, but never submerged, into a greater English nationalism, which meant enmity with Spain and abhorrence of its religion.[134] Cornwall was no longer the virtually independent land it had been before; in the war with Spain it found itself at the English frontier and as a springboard in the race for the New World. Centrally, what we find in Carew is a tension between a traditional order and the disruption of that order. It is this tension which is at the heart of works like his Arthurian poetic satire, *A Herring's Tail*, which mocks a previous generation's interest in chivalry, knightly honour and the very foundations of 'old' Cornwall, by having a snail named Sir Lymazon questing to climb a weathercock on Tintagel castle:

> I sing the strange adventures of the hardy snail,
> Who durst (unlikely match) the weathercock assail:
> A bold attempt, at first by fortune flattered
> With boot, but at the last to bale abandoned.
> Help, sportful Muse, to tune my gander-keaking quill,
> And with ink bottles of sad merriments it fill. . .
> Fame says, when Uther to the fair Igerna's bed
> Made way on carcass of her husband slaughtered,
> She, causer of the fact not partner of the guilt,
> Washt with her tears the blood by other's hand yspilt,
> And sought with the price of borrow'd merits to enrich
> Her either mate, who did, and suffered too much.
> Tintagel was the place where she exchanged loves,
> Tintagel was the place where to both their behoves.[135]

In his use of rhyming couplets and puns, Carew was able to construct a striking satire on imagined past Cornwall. In this way and through his embracing of the 'English language' in his essay *The Excellency of the English Tongue* and his rejection of Cornish (though he does record a few phrases and concepts in the language),[136] Carew shapes a new literary consciousness, far removed from writers like Roscarrock. His 'rather fancy sporting than gain-seeking voyage' equally illustrates the identity of a Cornwall undergoing much transition:

> Besides, the state of our country, hath undergone so many alterations since I first began these scribblings, that in the reviewing I was driven likewise to vary my report or else to speak against my knowledge.[137]

Additionally, throughout *The Survey of Cornwall* Carew self-consciously uses literary devices to demonstrate his wit, learning and skill with the English language, something which only Boorde, in his clumsy manner, had attempted before. Carew turns his back on the continuum of Cornish writing, and instead, like all gentry of his time, attempts to develop the literature of the English continuum. The work

9.   Richard Carew, engraving from frontispiece of the 1811 edition of his *The Survey of Cornwall* first published in 1602. From original painting at Antony House dated 1586.

of Greenblatt has demonstrated the process of 'self-fashioning' which
Carew and other gentry underwent during the period.[138] Thus in *A
Herring's Tail*, Carew turns Arthurian legend into farce, when the very
fabric of Cornwall's heroic past, was increasingly, in the light of a
Spanish invasion, difficult to maintain.[139] The *Survey* itself, meanwhile,
was a remarkable account of a Cornwall in transition. Among the
material considered are the problems of mining, adventuring and the
growth of the economy, as well as the farce of a late performance of
one of the mystery plays:

> The players con not their parts without book, but are prompted
> by one called the ordinary, who followeth at their back with the
> book in his hand, and telleth them softly what they must
> pronounce aloud. Which manner once gave occasion to a
> pleasant conceited gentleman of practising a merry prank; for he
> undertaking (perhaps of set purpose) an actor's room, was
> accordingly lessoned (beforehand) by the ordinary, that he must
> say after him. His turn came: quoth the ordinary, 'Go forth man,
> and show thyself.' The gentleman steps out upon the stage, and
> like a bad clerk in scripture matters, cleaving more to the letter
> than the sense, pronounced these words aloud. 'Oh (says the
> fellow softly in his ear) you mar all the play.' And with this his
> passion the actor makes the audience in like sort acquainted.[140]

Prompt books, amateur acting and slapstick were not in vogue for
an age which in Cornwall and elsewhere demanded learnt lines and
sophisticated drama. Carew's success with the English language and
his notion of English as the future language of Britain was timely. The
Celtic languages were seemingly doomed to failure in the growing
mechanical and military revolution in which Cornwall found itself
placed. However, the emergent gentrified class in Cornwall, writing in
English, exemplified by writers like Carew and, to a lesser extent, the
work of William Carnsew,[141] could not quite hold its own, being so far
away from theatrical and publishing centres, and there was now little
time for popular audiences with the abeyance of the mystery plays.
The literary future of Cornwall was suddenly dependent on the oral
tradition and a tiny, but developing, Cornu-English and Anglo-
Cornish literature.

One text of note here is the Anglo-Cornish narrative known as *The
Black Letter Pamphlet* (1618), originally a chapbook titled *Newes from
Pe[n]rin in Cornwall*. The story is a moral tale – drawing again on some
of the central narratives of European literature, such as wicked
stepmothers, over-ambition and what was later to develop into the
genres of the German *Bildungsroman* and British chapbooks. Also
present are the themes of greed and disguise, yet again the story is

characterized by a Renaissance Cornishman, who consciously decides to alter his fate, rather than be a victim of it. Again, growing economic activity and trade are central to the story's themes:

> A Most Bloody and Un-exampled Murder Very lately committed by a Father on his owne Sonne (who was lately returned from the Indyes) at the Instigation of a Mercilesse Step-mother Together with their severall most wretched endes, being all performed in the Months of September last Anno 1618.[142]

Elsewhere in Britain, interest in 'modern' Cornwall was growing, alongside a celebration of its 'heroic' past, as in the work of the somewhat neglected Warwickshire-born poet Michael Drayton (1563–1631). As part of the on-going creation of the English nation-state, Drayton embarked on writing an epic poem, written in twenty cantos or songs, titled *The Poly-Olbion*,[143] in which he endeavoured to demonstrate to his reader the glories and beauty of this apparently swiftly unifying country. Paradoxically, in order to show this, Drayton elected to show the regional features and particularities of the territory and so catalogues topics ranging from topography and history to mythology and legend. The overall aim was to create a grand depiction of English culture, yet as the opening section on Cornwall suggests, in actual fact the poem asserts the strength of regional culture. The cantos begins with a summary of the argument:

> The sprightly Muse her wing displays,
> And the French islands first surveys:
> Bears up with Neptune, and in glory
> Transcends proud Cornwall's promontory:
> There crowns Mount-Michael, and descries
> How all those riverets fall and rise,
> Then takes in Tamer [sic], as she bounds
> The Cornish and Devonian grounds.[144]

The image of Neptune in the seas is followed through, after this almost cinematic opening, though here Drayton writes with more awareness of the difference of Cornish history, recalling Brutus and Corineus, and then also referring to the drowning of Lyonesse and to an English translation of the Cornish for St. Michael's Mount:

> Strange things that his days time's course had brought to pass,
> That forty miles now sea, sometimes firm fore-land was,
> And that a forest then, which now with him is flood,
> Whereof he first was call'd the Hoar-rock in the wood.[145]

And yet for all its tone of celebration, the poem concludes with a more cautious note that the Cornish 'after long expulst the inner land, when they the Saxon power no longer could withstand'.[146] Drayton clearly realises that despite his wish for unity, and despite this period's attempt at full integration, Cornish identity was going to try to persist.

Best exemplifying this new 'modern' phase, however, was the poet Sidney Godolphin (1610–43). Godolphin took up Carew's faith in English and wrote a series of poems and lyrics distinguished by short lines, precise but idiomatic diction, and an urbane and graceful wit. Like other 'Cavalier' poets, Godolphin was influenced by Ben Jonson and paid little attention to the sonnet, as exemplified in 'Song':

> Let some nobler torture find
> > Than of a doubting wavering mind:
> Take all my peace; but you betray
> > Mine honour too this cruel way.[147]

Godolphin was among the leading Royalists in Cornwall. When the Civil War began on August 22nd 1642, in Cornwall, there was a preliminary period of manoeuvring for the allegiance of towns and control of the militia, and it was another month before Bodmin and Truro had been secured for the King. Here, the war became a battle between Royalist Cornwall (seeking to retain some degree of independence) and Parliamentary Devon, and in February 1643, the Royalists were driven back to Tavistock. As Stoyle has shown it was on a raid during this operation that Godolphin was killed by a stray shot in the dark, 'from an undiscerned and undiscerning hand'.[148] Godolphin's bravery and awareness of the political situation is found at the end of 'Meditation upon the Nativity' where we observe his depiction of the Cornish in the Civil War in the winter of 1642–43:

> When then our sorrows we apply
> To our own wants and poverty,
> When we look up in all distress
> And our own misery confess,
> Sending both thanks and prayers above:
> Then, though we do not know, we love.[149]

When one reads such political poetry, it seems unfortunate that Godolphin was killed so young. He was a sad loss to the Cornish Royalists and Anglo-Cornish literature. A number of critics dismiss Godolphin for not being 'Cornish enough',[150] but as the evidence of this chapter suggests, given the conditions of production in this period of literature, this was not about to happen. Besides, just because Cornwall is not always explicit in Godolphin's poetry, does not take away its Cornish nature and value – in particular in writing Cornish identity during the Civil War. In Godolphin, we see the manifestation of Carew's hope – and certainly the language of Carew and Godolphin were to remain dominant for the next three centuries – yet the literature of the later seventeenth and eighteenth centuries was to be short-lived and undeveloped. As it was, Godolphin's work pioneered a new literature of the Cornish gentry, but given their defeat in the Civil War, it was not a confident Cornish society which emerged in the latter years of the seventeenth century. There may have been the potential for a sophisticated new literature, but its actual production, given the political and cultural circumstances, would be near-impossible. Coupled with the by now virtual shut down of literature in Cornish and the old order – exemplified in the work of Roscarrock and any continuation of the cycle dramas – the literary future of Cornwall looked grim.

Far from Cornwall being the complex multi-lingual territory that it was in the post-Roman and medieval periods – asserting not only its own confident telling of its romances and dramas to its people, as well as circulating its narratives and poetry across Europe – at the end of the seventeenth century, a devastating paralysis had been reached.[151] Cornish was near to being lost, Cornwall had apparently been even further assimilated into England, and it had been on the losing side at the end of the Civil War. Cornish self-confidence and identity were at an all-time low; difference seemed to be negated and the continuum of writing had come to a halt. It was only in the eighteenth and nineteenth centuries, given a healthy economy, that Cornwall would be able to re-invent itself into one of the first industrial societies on earth, reviving its confidence and literary culture. It is to this construction of modern Cornwall that I now turn.

NOTES

1. Lewis Thorpe (ed. and tr.), *Gerald of Wales: The Journey through Wales and the Description of Wales* (Harmondsworth 1978), p. 220.
2. Cited in Craig Weatherhill and Paul Devereux, *Myths and Legends of Cornwall* (Wilmslow 1994), p. iii.
3. A.L. Rowse, *The West in English History* (London 1949), p. 67.
4. L.E. Elliot-Binns, *Medieval Cornwall* (London 1955), p. 398. Breton might also have been spoken. On medieval Cornwall, see James Whetter, *The Bodrugans: A Study of a Cornish Medieval Knightly Family* (Gorran 1995), *Cornwall in the 13th Century: A Study in Social and Economic History* (Gorran 1998).
5. See Ifor Williams (ed.) *Canu Taliesin* (Cardiff 1960), (ed.) *Canu Aneirin* (Cardiff 1970). There are many references to the Cornish and Cornwall

in other early Welsh texts. For example, see Patrick K. Ford (ed. and tr.) *The Mabinogi and Other Medieval Welsh Texts* (Berkeley 1977).

6. See William Copeland Borlase, *The Age of Saints: A Monograph of Early Christianity in Cornwall with the Legends of the Cornish Saints* (Truro 1893); E.G. Bowen, *Britain and the Western Seaways* (London 1972), pp 70–91.

7. For a detailed analysis of this process, see Nicholas Orme, 'From the Beginnings to 1050' in Nicholas Orme (ed.), *Unity and Variety: A History of the Church in Devon and Cornwall* (Exeter 1991), pp 1–22. For granite crosses, see Arthur G. Langdon, *Old Cornish Crosses* (Exeter 1988 [1896]). For Holy Wells in Cornwall, see M. and L. Quiller Couch, *Ancient and Holy Wells of Cornwall* (London 1894), Paul Broadhurst, *Secret Shrines: In Search of the Holy Wells of Cornwall* (Launceston 1991).

8. Catherine Rachel John, *The Saints of Cornwall* (Padstow and Redruth 1981); Weatherhill and Devereux, op.cit., pp 29–40.

9. Gilbert H. Doble, *The Saints of Cornwall: Parts One to Six* (Felinfach 1997 [1923–1944]). For an innovative analysis of saints in Cornwall, see Nicholas Orme, *The Saints of Cornwall* (Oxford 2000).

10. Henry Jenner, 'The Men Scrifa' in *Journal of the Royal Institution of Cornwall*, 69 (1922), pp 56–62.

11. Craig Weatherhill, *Cornovia: Ancient Sites of Cornwall and Scilly* (Penzance 1985), p. 35.

12. See Charles Thomas, *Tintagel: Arthur and Archaeology* (London, 1993), p. 126.

13. Charles Thomas, *And Shall These Mute Stones Speak? Post-Roman Inscriptions in Western Britain* (Cardiff 1994).

14. Charles Thomas, *Christian Celts: Messages and Images* (Stroud 1998).

15. *The Western Morning News*, August 7th 1998.

16. See James J. Wilhelm (ed.), *The Romance of Arthur: An Anthology of Medieval Texts in Translation* (New York and London 1994).

17. See, for example P.M. Matarasso (ed. and tr.), *The Quest of the Holy Grail* (Harmondsworth 1969), James Cable (ed. and tr.), *The Death of Arthur* (Harmondsworth 1971), William W. Kibler and Carleton W. Carroll (ed. and tr.) *Chrétien de Troyes: Arthurian Romances* (Harmondsworth 1991). For an interesting overview, see Alfred Nutt, *The Influence of Celtic upon Medieval Romance* (London 1904).

18. Detailed discussions of this resistance are given in Charles Thomas, *Celtic Britain* (London 1986), Peter Berresford Ellis, *Celt and Saxon: The Struggle for Britain AD 410–937* (London 1993). For a Cornish perspective, see Henry Jenner, 'Some Possible Arthurian Place-Names in West Penwith' in *Journal of the Royal Institution of Cornwall*, 19 (1912), pp 46–89. For an introduction to numerous aspects of Arthuriana, see Fran and Geoff Doel, and Terry Lloyd, *Worlds of Arthur: King Arthur in History, Legend and Culture* (Stroud 1998).

19. Lewis Thorpe (ed. and tr.), *Geoffrey of Monmouth: The History of the Kings of Britain* (Harmondsworth 1966), p. 51.

20. See Peter Berresford Ellis, *The Cornish Language and its Literature* (London

1974), pp 22–3, Charles Thomas, 'Hardy and Lyonesse: Parallel Mythologies' in Melisssa Hardie (ed.), *A Mere Interlude: Some Literary Visitors in Lyonnesse* (Penzance 1992); Paul Broadhurst, *Tintagel and the Arthurian Mythos* (Launceston 1992).

21. Thorpe, op.cit., p. 9.
22. Ibid., p. 72.
23. Ibid., p. 171, p. 175 and p. 184.
24. See John of Cornwall, *Prophetia Merlini*. Cod. Ottobonianus Lat. 1474, Vatican. For an excellent exploration of literary imaginings of Merlin, see Peter Goodrich (ed.), *The Romance of Merlin: An Anthology* (New York and London 1990).
25. Michael J. Curley (ed.) 'A New Edition of John of Cornwall's Prophetia Merlini' in *Speculum* 57 (1982), pp 217–49. For a Cornish edition, see Julyan Holmes (ed. and tr.), *An dhargan a Verdhin gans Yowann Kernow* (Cornwall 1998).
26. For the Cornish notes, see Curley, ibid., pp 240–49.
27. For evidence of this, see Alan Lupack (ed.), *Modern Arthurian Literature: An Anthology of English and American Arthuriana from the Renaissance to the Present* (New York 1992).
28. Joseph Bédier, *Le Roman de Tristan* (Paris 1902–05).
29. See A.T. Hatto (ed. and tr.), *Gottfried von Strassburg: Tristan with the 'Tristan' of Thomas* (Harmondsworth 1960).
30. See Ernest Muret (ed.), *Le Roman de Tristan par Béroul* (Paris 1903). See also Alan S. Fredrick (ed. and tr.), *Béroul: The Romance of Tristan* (Harmondsworth 1970).
31. See Joseph Loth *De Nouvelles Théories sur l'origine du Roman Arthurian* (Paris 1892).
32. Henry Jenner, 'The Tristan Romance and its Cornish Provenance' in *Journal of the Royal Institution of Cornwall*, 14 (1914), pp 464–88.
33. E.M.R. Ditmas, *Tristan and Iseult in Cornwall* (Brockworth 1970); Joan Tasker Grimbert (ed.), *Tristan and Isolde: A Casebook* (New York 1995).
34. Forrester Roberts, *The Legends of Tristan and Iseult: The Tale and the Trail in Ireland, Cornwall and Brittany* (Gloucester 1998), p. 6.
35. Muret, op.cit., p. 40 and p. 102.
36. Ellis, op.cit. (1993), pp 202–23.
37. Philip Payton, *The Making of Modern Cornwall* (Redruth 1992), pp 46–7.
38. See Peter Berresford Ellis, *The Celtic Revolution: A Study in Anti-Imperialism* (Talybont 1985), pp 134–5.
39. Simon James, *The Atlantic Celts* (London 1999).
40. J. Gwenogvryn Evans (ed.), *The Book of Taliesin* (Llanbedrog 1910), p. 10. See also Ellis, op.cit. (1974), p. 26.
41. See Philip Payton, *Cornwall* (Fowey 1996), pp 86–7.
42. See Crystan Fudge, *The Life of Cornish* (Redruth 1982), p. 5.
43. Ibid.
44. Henry Jenner, 'The Bodmin Gospels' in *Journal of the Royal Institution of Cornwall*, 70 (1922), pp 113–45. Compare with the detail of society in the

Doomsday Book. See Caroline and Frank Thorn (ed.), *Doomsday Book: Cornwall* (Chichester 1979).

45. Henry Jenner, 'The Bodmin Manumissions' in *Journal of the Royal Institution of Cornwall*, 71 (1924), p. 242.

46. Richard Gendall, *1000 years of Cornish* (Menheniot 1994), p. 1.

47. On this, see Eugene van Tassel Graves, *The Old Cornish Vocabulary* (Diss. Ph.D, Columbia 1962). For the vocabulary itself, see Edwin Norris, *The Ancient Cornish Drama* (London and New York 1968 [1859]), pp 311–435.

48. Quoted in Fudge, op.cit., p. 9. For the use of prophecy in Cornish culture, see R. Morton Nance, 'Cornish Prophecies' in *Old Cornwall* (1931), pp 443–53.

49. James Whetter, *A History of Glasney College* (Padstow 1988).

50. Ray Edwards (ed.), *The Charter Fragment* (Sutton Coldfield 1991), p. 5.

51. For various standpoints, see Henry Jenner, 'The Fourteenth-Century Charter Endorsement' in *Journal of the Royal Institution of Cornwall*, 20 (1915–1916), pp 46–7; Robert Morton Nance, 'The Charter Endorsement in Cornish' in *Old Cornwall* (1947), pp 34–36; Brian Murdoch, *Cornish Literature* (Cambridge 1993), pp 3–13.

52. Lauran Toorians (ed.), *The Middle Cornish Charter Endorsement: The Making of a Marriage in Medieval Cornwall* (Innsbruck 1991), p. 14.

53. See Alan M. Kent, *Wives, Mothers and Sisters: Feminism, Literature and Women Writers of Cornwall* (Penzance 1998) pp 8–9.

54. Some of the core research here is Robert Longsworth, *The Cornish Ordinalia: Religion and Dramaturgy* (Cambridge Massachusetts, 1967); Jane A. Bakere, *The Cornish Ordinalia: A Critical Study* (Cardiff 1980); Brian Murdoch, op.cit., 'The Cornish Medieval Drama' in Richard Beadle (ed.), *The Cambridge Companion to Medieval English Theatre* (Cambridge 1994), pp 211–39. There are countless other articles and papers. See Evelyn S. Newlyn (ed.), *Cornish Drama of the Middle Ages: A Bibliography* (Redruth 1987).

55. See *Ordinalia*. MS Bodl. 791, Oxford; Norris, op.cit.; Markham Harris (ed. and tr.), *The Cornish Ordinalia: A Medieval Dramatic trilogy* (Washington 1969). See also R. Morton Nance, A.S.D. Smith and Graham Sandercock (eds. and trs.), *The Cornish Ordinalia, Second Play: Christ's Passion* (Cornwall 1982), *The Cornish Ordinalia, Third Play: Resurrection* (Cornwall 1984); Keith Syed and Ray Edwards (eds.), *Origo Mundi* (Cornwall 1998). See also the adaptation by this author.

56. See F.E. Halliday (ed. and tr.), *The Legend of the Rood* (London 1955); Brian Murdoch, op.cit. (1993), pp 41–74, 'Legends of the Holy Rood in Cornish Drama' in *Studia Celtica Japonica*, 9 (1997), pp 19–34. For an alternative approach, see Jim Hall, 'Maximilla, the Cornish Montanist: The Final Scenes of Origo Mundi' in Philip Payton (ed.) *Cornish Studies: Seven* (Exeter, 1999), pp 165–92.

57. Norris, op.cit., pp 10–11.

58. Ibid., pp 162–3.

59. Ibid., pp 182–3.
60. Ibid., pp 186–7.
61. Ibid., pp 432–3. Line 2668 has been amended here.
62. Ibid., p. 67. See also Patricia Burke, 'The Stained Glass Windows of the Church of St. Neot; Cornwall' in *Devon and Cornwall Notes and Queries*, 33 (1974–78), pp 65–68.
63. Ibid., pp 360–1.
64. See Bakere, op.cit., pp 14–49.
65. The exception is Murdoch. See Murdoch, op.cit., pp 44–74.
66. See Tony Deane and Tony Shaw, *The Folklore of Cornwall* (Totowa, New Jersey 1975), p. 22; Quiller Couch, op.cit., pp 89–92. See also Keith Pearce and Helen Fry (eds.), *The Lost Jews of Cornwall* (Bristol 1999).
67. See Rosalind Conklin Hays and C.E. McGee (Dorset) and Sally L. Joyce and Evelyn S. Newlyn (Cornwall) (eds.), *Records of Early English drama: Dorset/Cornwall* (Toronto 1999), p. 542. The editors of this comment that the word 'flogholeth' [childhood] is written above the word 'passyon' [passion], so suggesting a nativity. Most other European cycles have a Doomsday play.
68. For this view, see Halliday, op.cit., p. 33. The 1969 revival of the Ordinalia at Piran Round near Perranporth utilised this method of performance.
69. See Sydney Higgins, *Medieval Theatre in the Round: The Multiple Staging of Religious Drama in England* (Camerino, Italy 1995).
70. Hays and McGee, Joyce and Newlyn, op.cit., pp 549–56.
71. Bakere, op.cit., p. 29.
72. See Oliver Padel, 'Ancient Parishes with Possible Examples of the Plain-an-gwary' in Hays and McGee, Joyce and Newlyn, op.cit., pp 559–63.
73. Ibid., pp 397–399.
74. Ibid., pp 417–538.
75. See Donald R. Rawe, *Padstow's Obby Oss and May Day Festivities: A Study in Folklore and Tradition* (Padstow 1990 [1971]; Deane and Shaw, op.cit., pp 173–75. The Cornish Hal-an-tow may mean 'in the country and in the town', though there are numerous other possibilities.
76. See Jane Bakere, op.cit., p. 18; Hays and McGee, Joyce and Newlyn, op.cit., p. 400.
77. Ibid., pp 395–96.
78. See Davies Gilbert (ed.), *Mount Calvary* (London 1826). See also Ray Edwards (ed.), *The Poem of Mount Calvary* (Sutton Coldfield 1993). For criticism, commentary and bibliography, see Brian Murdoch (ed.), *The Medieval Cornish Poem of the Passion: A Bibliography* (Redruth 1979), op.cit., pp 19–40.
79. Gilbert, op.cit., pp 70–1.
80. Nicholas Orme (ed.), *Nicholas Roscarrock's Lives of the Saints of Cornwall and Devon* (Exeter 1992), p. 68.
81. See Jean-Pierre Le Mat, *The Sons of Ermine: A History of Brittany* (Belfast 1996), p. 52.

82. Robert Hunt (ed.), *The Drolls, Traditions, and Superstitions of Old Cornwall: Popular Romances of the West of England (First and Second Series)* (London 1865); William Bottrell (ed.), *Traditions and Hearthside Stories of West Cornwall: First, Second and Third Series* (Penzance 1870–1880).

83. Craig Weatherhill, *Cornish Place Names and Language* (Wilmslow 1995), p. 82.

84. David C. Fowler, *John Trevisa* (Aldershot 1993), pp 3–13.

85. David C. Fowler, *The Life and Times of John Trevisa, Medieval Scholar* (Seattle 1995), pp 241–7. A curious reference to a 'Book of the Acts of King Arthur' by John Trevisa is found in William Hals, *The Compleat History of Cornwall* (Truro c.1736), p. 103.

86. Elliot-Binns, op.cit., pp 406–9.

87. Alan M. Kent, '"Art thou of Cornish crew?": Shakespeare, Henry V and Cornish Identity' in Philip Payton (ed.), *Cornish Studies: Four* (Exeter 1996), pp 7–25.

88. For a good exploration of state formation during this period, see Brendan Bradshaw and John Morrill (eds.), *The British Problem, c. 1534–1707: State Formation in the Atlantic Archipelago* (Basingstoke 1996).

89. See the observations of Ellis, op.cit. (1974), pp 52–69; A.S.D. Smith, *The Story of the Cornish Language: Its Extinction and Revival* (Camborne 1947).

90. A.L. Rowse, *Tudor Cornwall* (Redruth 1990 [1941]), pp 114–41.

91. The story of the 1497 rebellion is well-documented in Simon Parker (ed.), *Cornwall Marches On!/Keskerdh Kernow* (Truro, 1998), pp 5–35.

92. See Ian Arthurson, *The Perkin Warbeck Conspiracy 1491–1499* (Stroud 1997), pp 162–68.

93. See *Beunans Meriasek* MS Peniarth 105, NLW Aberwystwyth, and Whitley Stokes (ed. and tr.), *The Life of Saint Meriasek, Bishop and Confessor: A Cornish Drama* (London 1872). A useful verse translation is Myrna Combellack (ed. and tr.), *The Camborne Play: A Verse Translation of Beunans Meriasek* (Redruth 1988).

94. Stokes, op.cit., pp 34–5.

95. Ibid., pp 62–3.

96. Murdoch, op.cit. (1993), p. 102.

97. Philip Payton (1993) '"a. . . concealed envy against the English": A Note on the Aftermath of the 1497 Rebellions in Cornwall' in Philip Payton (ed.), *Cornish Studies: One* (Exeter 1993), pp 4–13.

98. Ibid., p. 10.

99. Jonathan Wooding, *St Meriasek and King Tudor in Cornwall* (Sydney 1992).

100. Stokes, op.cit., pp 126–7. In Payton's article, he uses Combellack's translation. For consistency and to show the Cornish text, I use Stokes' edition here.

101. Murdoch, op.cit., p. 114.

102. Payton, op.cit., p. 11.

103. Stokes, op.cit., pp 44–5.

104. Ibid., pp 136–7.

105. Whetter, op.cit., p. 104.
106. Payton, op.cit. (1996), p. 138.
107. Francis Rose-Troup, *The Western Rebellions of 1549* (London 1913), p. 221.
108. For a useful account of the Prayer Book Rebellion, see John Sturt, *Revolt in the West: The Western Rebellion of 1549* (Exeter 1987).
109. Peter Berresford Ellis, *The Celtic Revolution* (Talybont 1985), p. 137. Numerous Cornish texts must have been lost during this phase.
110. Paul Turner (ed. and tr.), *Thomas More: Utopia (1516)* (Harmondsworth 1965), pp 43–4.
111. For background on Boorde, see Brian Murdoch (ed.), *The Dedalus book of Medieval Literature: The Grin of the Gargoyle* (Sawtry 1995), p. 201.
112. R. Morton Nance, 'Andrew Boorde on Cornwall, circa 1540' in *Journal of the Royal Institution of Cornwall*, 75 (1928), pp 366–81. On this subject see F.J. Furnivall (ed.), 'Andrew Boorde: The Fyrst Boke of the Introduction of Knowledge' in *Publications of the Early English Text Series*, 10 (1870 [1547]), pp 122–3.
113. Martyn F. Wakelin, *Language and History in Cornwall* (Leicester 1975), p. 25.
114. Nance, op.cit., pp 367–68.
115. Wakelin, op.cit., p. 210.
116. Nance, op.cit., pp 369–70.
117. John Leland, 'The Itinerary: So far as it relates to Cornwall' in Davies Gilbert (ed.), *The Parochial History of Cornwall*, 4 (London 1838), p. 267.
118. Cited in Ellis, op.cit. (1974), p. 63.
119. See *Tregear Homilies* BL MS Add, 46397, London; Ray Edwards (ed.), *The Tregear Homilies* (Sutton Coldfield 1994).
120. Ibid., p. 5.
121. Ibid., pp 45–6.
122. Ellis, op.cit., p. 66.
123. Henry Jenner, 'Some Miscellaneous Scraps of Cornish' in *Royal Cornwall Polytechnic Society* (1929), pp 238–55.
124. See 'The Consistory Court Depositions, 1569–1572' in *Old Cornwall* (1936), p. 11.
125. John Norden, *Speculum Magnae Britanniae pars Cornwall – A Topographical and Historical Description of Cornwall* (Newcastle upon Tyne 1966 [1584]). p. 21.
126. Ibid., p. 22.
127. Henry Jenner, 'A Cornish Oration in Spain in the Year 1600' in *Royal Cornwall Polytechnic Society* (1923), pp 61–69.
128. Ibid.; Murdoch, op.cit. (1993), p. 9.
129. Smith, op.cit., p. 8.
130. See Nicholas Roscarrock. *Lives of the Saints* MS Add, 3041, Cambridge. See Orme, op.cit. (1992), pp 1–52.
131. Ibid., p. 105.

132. See A.L. Rowse, op.cit., pp 421–30; F.E. Halliday, *A History of Cornwall* (London 1959), p. 206.
133. F.E. Halliday (ed.), *Richard Carew: The Survey of Cornwall* (London 1953).
134. Ibid., p. 30.
135. Ibid., pp 281–2.
136. Ibid., pp 303–8. For Carew on Cornish language, see pp. 126–8.
137. Ibid., p. 79.
138. Stephen Greenblatt, *Renaissance Self-Fashioning: From More to Shakespeare* (Chicago 1980), p. 256.
139. Halliday, op.cit., p. 281.
140. Ibid., p. 145.
141. See N.J.G. Pounds (ed.), 'William Carnsew of Bokelly and his Diary, 1576–7' in *Journal of the Royal Institution of Cornwall*, 8 (1978).
142. *The Black Letter Pamphlet: News from Perin in Cornwall of a most Bloody and un-exampled Murder Quarto*, Bodley, 4 M G29(2), Oxford.
143. *Poly-Olbion* (from the Greek) means 'having many blessings'.
144. Michael Drayton, 'The Poly-Olbion' in Gilbert, op.cit. (1838), p. 294.
145. Ibid., p. 297. 'Hoar-rock in the wood' is a translation of Cara Clowse in Cowse. Variations of this are found in many antiquarian Cornish texts.
146. Ibid., p. 310.
147. Cited in Alistair Fowler (ed.), *The New Oxford Book of Seventeenth Century Verse* (Oxford 1992), p. 484.
148. Mark Stoyle, *Loyalty and Locality: Popular Allegiance in Devon during the English Civil War* (Exeter 1994), p. 67.
149. Fowler, op.cit., p. 484.
150. See D.M. Thomas (ed.), *The Granite Kingdom: Poems of Cornwall* (Truro 1970), p. 9; Muriel Hawkey (ed.), *A Cornish Chorus: An Anthology of Prose and Verse* (London 1944). Godolphin is not included in this collection.
151. Payton, op.cit. (1996), pp 167–76.

The Tongueless and the Travellers: The Fragmentation of Continuity and New Constructions of Cornish Identity, 1660–1820

An Lavor gôth ewe lavar gwîr,
Na vedn nevra doas vâs a tavaz re hîr;
Bes dên heb tavaz a gollas e dîr.

[The old saying is a true saying,
Never will come good from a tongue too long;
But a man without a tongue shall lose his land].

Cited in William Pryce,
Archeologia Cornu-Britannica (1790)[1]

On my offer of English money for Cornish words to the men at Land's End they referred me to an old man living about three miles off towards the south at St Levan (I think) a second chapelry with St Sennen in the parish of St Buryan, and intimated that I might have as many words as I would wish to purchase.

John Whitaker, *Supplement to the First and Second Books of Polwhele's History of Cornwall* (1804)[2]

As Chapter One has demonstrated, the question of Cornwall's literary development has thus far been answered by three significant historical moments. During the medieval period, separated and isolated from the rest of Britain yet still influencing European literature, Cornish literary culture was dependent upon the Cornish language and the impact of Catholicism upon its culture and ideology. Cornwall was first pushed into reform in the fifteenth and sixteenth centuries, reluctant and making protest in the rebellions of 1497 and 1549 respectively. Secondly, during this early modern period, England had

70

attempted to integrate Cornwall as a colony into its vision of a nation-state. In the next century, Cornwall's devotion to the Royalist cause made the Cornish army the King's best fighting instrument in the West, until it was defeated in the siege of Bristol.[3] This third phase, coupled with a further loss of the Cornish language, resulted in a temporary cessation in literary production. In one language at least, as the traditional poem above alludes to, Cornwall was losing a 'tongue'.

Cornwall's next most important period of development came with the Industrial Revolution.[4] With tin and copper mining and a series of developments in steam and engineering technology, Cornwall was re-invented, giving the world this technology and its people a renewed sense of self-confidence which had been lacking for well over a century. This not only produced an explosion of talent in engineering and science, but in literature as well. It is to the beginnings of this Anglo-Cornish literature – its production, problems and development – that I shall turn later in this chapter.

Initially however – and paradoxically as part of the development of this new Anglo-Cornish and Cornu-English literature – it is necessary to briefly examine Cornwall's limited literary production in Cornish in the aftermath of the Civil War. With Cornwall denied a Prayer Book and Bible, regarded as unrefined by the gentry and ruling classes, and subject to the advance of English, two major literary trends may be discerned in this period of its literary history. These mirror exactly the historical process and begin to answer our question as to how Cornwall imagined itself as the seventeenth century unfolded. The two trends were at once close, yet far removed from each other. The first, as Weatherhill argues, was a 'late Renaissance' in writing in Cornish,[5] arising from the realization of Cornish middle-class intellectuals of the age that the language might be permanently lost if corrective actions were not taken. The second, as noted by Mattingly and Palmer, was the growing trend of English travellers and diarists who were coming to an increasingly accessible Cornwall and recording what they observed in what we may term as a first phase of proto-tourism from England.[6]

In a sense, neither of these is surprising given the circumstances. Human activities and especially 'dying' languages often burn brightest at their end – as in the case of Cornish – and ironically, as Cornwall became less isolated and linguistically 'modern' with its adoption of English, the observers and recorders started to arrive and began to discover, for English readers, what Cornwall was like, and to find that, despite those three significant phases of history, Cornwall was still displaying difference. Despite an old medieval identity being stamped out, a new modern one was beginning to emerge, and they took delight in recording this process.

Paralleling this were two other significant issues: the first was an 'ennobling' of the Cornish themselves as they experienced both linguistic, industrial and economic shifts. This 'ennobling' process was read and perceived on many levels – racial, literary, linguistic and societal. The second trend was amongst the observers and antiquarians themselves, who seemingly flocked to Cornwall during this period desperate to record and observe the last of this ennobled 'race' apparently reaching near extinction. Yet as Mitchell has shown, such antiquarians as Daines Barrington often had their own agendas and did not always bring objectivity with them;[7] thus on occasions pre-empting the death of the language, when in actuality it continued a lot longer.[8] As the words of the historian and traveller John Whitaker show above, this piece of social engineering on the part of the antiquarians also assisted the process of ennobling the Cornish, whilst as the same time using the ancient culture of Cornwall as an important contribution to the forging of a wider British identity.

The other important and interesting issue in this phase is the distinctive initial lack of an Anglo-Cornish literature, though upon closer examination, the reasons for its non-appearance are quite clear. As we have already seen, the turmoil of the Civil War had taken a great toll of the potential writing class of the age – the Cornish gentry – and still isolated from the centres of English literary culture, like Bristol and London, their efforts were passed by. It is likely that many texts were written, but never published. This was coupled with the fact that for almost two centuries, Cornwall had no centre of learning or scholarship. Creative energies were being directed elsewhere; into religious reform or into industrial development. Only when the culture had been fully reformed and re-invented could the true 'songs of the Western men (and women)' be written. This was to occur initially in the later years of the eighteenth century and then more fully in the nineteenth century.

Earlier, a Cornish literature had struggled on in the opening years of the seventeenth century. *The Creacion of the World, with Noye's Flude*, transcribed by William Jordan of Helston in 1611 from an older source, is the sole surviving literary text in Cornish written in the first half of the seventeenth century.[9] Based on *Origo Mundi*, from the *Ordinalia*, its character is noticeably medieval, although Jordan himself was responsible for modernizing its language. There are some significant differences between the two texts however. As Murdoch has argued, first of all, *The Creacion of the World* is twice as long as the corresponding part of *Origo Mundi*, and secondly there are some additional sequences: an expanded flood and a developed depiction of the fall of the angels.[10] Thirdly, there is the depiction of the character

Lamech, who must have entertained the Cornish spectators with his womanising ways:

> 1449   Moy es un wrek dhym yma
> dhe'm plesour rag gul gans'y,
> ha sur my yu an kensa
> bythqueth whath a'n jeve dyw wrek
> Ha'n mowysy lowr plenty
> yma dhym – nyns yns denty –
> my a's kyf pan vynnaf-vy.
> Ny sparyaf anedha-y
> malbew onen a vo tek.

> 1449   [More than one wife have I
> to deal with at my pleasure,
> and, surely, I am the first
> that ever yet had two wives.
> And girls in sufficient plenty
> I have – they are not particular –
> I get them when I will.
> I do not spare a single one
> of them that is pretty].[11]

The language of this would indicate a slightly more secular feel to the drama, suggesting that such plays needed to reform their action to sustain interest. It is difficult to know the exact dates of performance of Jordan's text, or even where it was performed. If it was still performed in Helston during the early part of the seventeenth century, then we have a picture of Cornish culture which was still remarkably un-Anglicised. Indeed, it may well have been the kind of drama which Carew had observed around the same time.

In terms of Jordan's recording of the flood itself, we perhaps need to consider other issues surrounding Cornish identity and ideology during this phase. Though dramatizations of the flood were popular elsewhere in these islands during the medieval period, Cornish audiences would have viewed the flood as a very real and material event in the history of the world, providing a God-given re-casting of the earth's resources – especially tin – for their material benefit.[12] The retelling of the flood was in effect a retelling of some of the central strands of Cornish history (Lyonesse and otherwise), hence its special emphasis in the title and its obvious popularity. Material mineral benefits were to be thanked with a dramatization of Cornish religiosity:

> 2391   Rag dre er oll a vu gwrys,
> nef ha'n nor, myns us omma,
> ha der er arta, dhym crys,

Ef a yl, mara mynna,
y dhystrewy der an dowr.

2391   [For by a word all was made,
heaven and earth, all that is here,
and by a word again, believe me,
He can if He should wish
destroy it by the water.][13]

Elsewhere, Cornwall was finding expression in other ways, via a bizarre single sentence of garbled Cornish found in Richard Brome's first extant play *The Northern Lasse* (1632). The character Salmon Nonsense is both a suitor of Constance, the 'northern lasse' of the play's title, as well as the son of Sir Hercules Nonsense of Cornwall. Matching the notion of Cornwall as England's Atlantic seaboard territory, the characters discuss Sir Percy Squelch, who enters disguised as a Spaniard:

> Bullfinch: Alasse what shall wee doe then? Gentlemen, have any of you any Spanish to help me to understand this strange stranger.
> [They all disclaim knowledge.]
> Bullfinch: What shiere of our Nation is next to Spain? Perhaps he may understand that shiere English.
> Tridewell: Devonshire or Cornwall, sire.
> Nonsense: Never credit me but I will spurt some Cornish at him.
> *Peden bras, vidnae whee bis cregas.*[14]

The work of Jordan and Brome offer us some understanding of the way Cornish literature was progressing at the beginning of the seventeenth century. It was, however, as shown in Ellis, and Payton, a vice-warden of the Stannaries, William Scawen, who kick-started the renaissance of writing in Cornish. In a comprehensive argument titled *Antiquities Cornuontanic: The causes of the Cornish Speech's Decay* (1680),[15] Scawen reviewed the problems associated with the decline of Cornish, hoping that others might start to reverse the process. Scawen was a perceptive scholar. Among the sixteen reasons he considered contributing to the decline of Cornish were: the lack of a distinctive alphabet, the persecution of the druids, the decline of the Celtic church, the loss of contact with Brittany, the lack of performances of the "Guirremears" (the mystery plays), the loss of ancient records of the Duchy and Earldom at Restormel Castle, the lack of general usage of the language, the lack of support by the gentry, the 'coming-in of strangers of all sorts', and a 'general stupidity in the whole county'. This was coupled with his anger over the failure to teach the Lord's Prayer in Cornish and the lack of surviving literature.

Scawen was the central motivator of a crucial group of writers and scholars who became hugely important in shaping this next phase of Cornish. He encouraged these writers to begin composing in Cornish and to resume the continuum in ways they felt appropriate. In so doing, Cornish moved from being a community, popular literature to more of an exclusive entity, read and written by gentlemen. Although writers from other parts of Cornwall contributed to this new movement, the school was primarily focused around Penzance, Newlyn and Mousehole – an area of Cornwall which at this time still spoke Cornish.

The lead writer and scholar of this group was John Keigwin (1641– c.1720). Keigwin lived in Mousehole and was probably a native speaker. He helped to translate a number of texts including the *Ordinalia*, and also assisted outside scholars (such as Edward Lhuyd) in their work. Keigwin knew the difficulty of the task. In 1702, he tellingly wrote:

> Go forth, ye sacred Cornish tragedies. Remember that the Cornish language is nearly the same as that of Wales and Brittany. From these three languages it is possible to see what the British language was. Anxious lest our language should fall into disuse and utterly perish, of my own accord I have rendered these tragedies into English in face of the oncoming tide of the English language, so that at least some lasting trace of this ancient language of ours (for it claims that [it] has taken nothing from Latin, French, Greek, or English) should be remembered by posterity; of his country and race the dearest lover.[16]

Fortunately, Keigwin was assisted in his task by the work of the Newlyn-based Boson family, consisting of the merchant Nicholas Boson, his son John (1665–1720) and his cousin Thomas. The barrister William Gwavas (1676–1741) was based in Paul and he recorded many of the smaller proverbs and poems. Working alongside this group were the Reverend Henry Usticke and John Tonkin, both of St Just, William Rowe (c.1630–1690), a farmer living at Sancreed, and James Jenkins of Alverton, Penzance. Meanwhile, eastwards at Trevaunance, St Agnes, the Cornish historian Thomas Tonkin completed additional study of the language, corresponding with Lhuyd. These writers were ambitious and seeing the benefits of preserving and developing Cornish collectively took up the challenge that had been laid down by Scawen.[17] This group planned to complete a translation of the bible, an activity which was known elsewhere in Britain, as the Exeter-based playwright and printer Andrew Brice recorded in 1727.[18] However, though central sections of the bible were finished, the full translation was never completed.

There is not the space here to enter into a full analysis of all the literature in Cornish produced during this period; besides important enquiry has already been completed by Ellis, Pool, and Murdoch,[19] but, for the purposes of comparison and the historical development of writing from Cornwall, a few issues and texts are worthy of our attention. Unlike the religious verse of middle Cornish, the literature of this period contains a greater variety of forms, structures and subject-matter. To an extent this is demonstrated by some of the small fragments of poetry and proverbs which were recorded. Often folk-loric or moralistic in their themes, they demonstrate some of the poetic skills of those remembering the 'oral continuum', as well as those members of the 'late Renaissance' who were actively recording these texts. This is seen in the poems 'On a Lazy Weaver' and 'Verses on the Marazion Bowling-Green, and Club':

> Why lader gweader,
> Lavarro guz pader,
> > Ha ro man do higa an cath:
> Gra owna guz furu,
> Hithow, po avorou,
> > Ha whyew boz dean dah whath.

> Ny ol devethes war tyr glaz,
> Dho gware peliow, rag gun ehaz;
> Dibre tabm dah, hag eva badna,
> Mal nag wonnen, moaz gwadn trea,
> Mez ol krêv, an kerensa vâz,
> Dho ara tyr, gunnes hâz.

> [You thievish weaver,
> Say your prayer,
> > And give up to play with the cat:
> Do mend your ways,
> To-day or to-morrow,
> > And you may be a good man yet.]

> [We all come upon green land,
> To play at bowls, for our health;
> To eat a good bit, and drink a drop,
> That not one goes weak home,
> But all strong, in good friendship,
> To plough the land, and sow the seed.][20]

Other writers turned to the explicit material concerns of the seventeenth century, by describing the working patterns of daily life in west Cornwall. Around 1700, John Boson wrote a poem on the theme of

76

pilchard curing. As well as the technicalities of the curing process – the couplets reinforcing the task in hand – the poet gives useful insight into how Cornish people imagined themselves and constructed others in different territories:

> Blethan wor blethan Gra Gorollion toas
> Ha gen Hern lean moas ort Dour Gwavas
> Wor duath Gra Gwenz Noor East wetha pell
> Rag an Poble pow tooben debra ol
> Ma Peath Hern pokar ol an Beaz
> Moy Poble Bohodzack vel poble Broaz.

> [Year after year ships will come
> And full of pilchards they will leave Gwavas Lake
> At last, the wind of the North East will blow far
> For the people of hot countries will eat them all.
> The wealth of pilchards is like all the world
> More poor people than rich people.][21]

In such ways, Cornish literature was modernizing itself – effectively creating a new route for the continuum to follow. Elsewhere, more philosophical questions were being discussed in the literature – including debate over the role and place of men and women in Cornish society, and how best to bring up children. Such writing is sophisticated, and demonstrates that this later phase of Cornish literature was far from 'impure' or 'marginal' compared to the canon of earlier work, but displays engagement with issues surrounding all European cultures of the same period. Put another way, conditions were allowing Cornish literature to progress in ways perhaps unimagined by writers such as Carew, as in this 'Poem of Advice' by James Jenkins (c.1700):

> Ma leezz Greage. Lacka vel Zeage.
> Gwel gerres. Vell commerez.
> Ha ma leeaz Bennen. Pocare an Gwennen.
> Eye vedn gwrrez de gu Teez. Dandle peath an beaz.
> Fleaz hep skeeanz. Vedn gweel gu Seeaznz.
> Bur mor crown gy pedery. Pan dall gu gwary.
> Ha madra ta. Pandrigg Seera ha Damah.
> Narehanz moaz dan Cooz. Do cuntle gu booz.
> Buz gen nebbes lavirrians. Eye venjah dendel gu booz dillaz.

> [There are many wives worse than chaff,
> Better left than taken
> And there are many women like the bees,
> They will help their men to earn worldly wealth.
> Children without wisdom will do their whim,

But if they think what their play is worth
And take careful note of what father and mother did
They would not go to the wood to collect their food
But with a little labour they would earn their food and drink.][22]

At the same time, Thomas Tonkin collected songs and verses in Cornish. One of those collected was from Edward Chirgwin (c.1698), a Cornish version of the well-known folk-song 'Where are you going, my pretty maid?', where the male questioner propositions the girl. The eroticism of the middle section of the song is turned on its head by the girl at the end, when she requests that the father had better be a tailor to provide for her and the child:

Fatla gûra ve agaz gorra why en dowr,
    Gen agaz bedgeth gwin, ha agaz blew mellyn?
Me vedn sevel arta sarra wheage,
    Rag delkiow sevi gwra muzi teag.

Pen dre vedd why geil rag lednow rag 'as flo,
    Gen agaz pedn du, ha agaz blew mellyn?
E feera veath trehez, sarra wheag,
    Rag delkiow sevi gwra muzi teag.

[How if I put you on the ground,
    With your white face and your yellow hair?
I will stand up again, sweet sir,
    for strawberry leaves make maids fair.

What will you do for clothes for your child,
    With your black head and yellow hair?
His father will be a tailor, sweet sir,
    for strawberry leaves make maids fair.][23]

Meanwhile, Nicholas Boson wrote a children's story titled *The Dutchesse of Cornwall's Progresse to see the Land's End and to visit the Mount*.[24] The work was a compendium of Cornish folklore – part-real, part-imaginary – written in English, though containing some proverbs and sayings in Cornish. In terms of the overall continuum of the construction of Cornwall, Boson's narrative stands as something of a mid-way point between the work of Carew and Roscarrock, and that of the nineteenth-century folklorists such as Hunt and Bottrell. Our difficulty with this text is sorting out how much of the narrative is real, recorded observation and how much is embellished. The sometimes broken text also has links to future observers and how they came to perceive Cornwall, in that it is the journal literature of someone 'inside' Cornish culture of the period. One of the central characters of the text is Harry the Hermitt who 'in his state and gravity' attends the 'evenson at the chappell of Carnbre', and makes pronouncements in Cornish (Nages travith dale talues an bee /Bus gen dieu benegas do gweel gan crees [This world hath nothing worth our love/But to make peace with God above]). Although Boson tells of his Christian belief, Harry is also described by Boson as 'a great witch', a pagan capable of raising storms and other magical powers. Despite its origin as a story for Boson's children, paralleling the emergence of such travelogues about Cornwall, it still contains stunning imagery depicting Cornwall's position on the western coast of the archipelago:

> On one of the outmost rocks they espy'd a huge beast which they perceived to be a seahorse. Afar off they beheld a mermaid, & upon the right hand a Triton sounding his Trumpett attended with a great many Dolphins.[24]

Tritons and Dolphins were a long way removed from Boson's second major text of the period. *Nebbaz Gerriau dro tho Cornoack* [A Few Words About Cornish] was a much more down-to-earth piece of work, recording his observations (in Cornish) on the state of the language.[25] The treatise gives us much insight into the way Cornish was perceived at the time. Though it is often disparaging and critical, the overall impression is that Boson is frustrated since he wants Cornish to do more. His best known work, however, is a complete folk-tale known as *John of Chyanhor*, or *The Three Points of Wisdom*, a story with international equivalents, notably 'The Servant's Good Counsels'. It was written in Cornish some time between 1660 and 1700:

> En Terman ez passiez thera Trigaz en St. Levan; Dean ha Bennett en Tellar creiez chei a Horr.
> Ha an Weale a Kothaz scant: Ha meth a Dean Da an Wreag; mee a ved'n moze Da whelaz weale da weele; ha whi el dendal gose bounans obba.
>
> [In tyme that is passed, there Dwelt in St. Levan a man & woman in a place caled The House of a Ramm.
> And the worke did fall scare; & saith the man to his wife; I will goe to looke for worke to doe; & you can earne your living here.][26]

Only verses 1 to 14 survive, which were recorded by John Boson, but the whole story was recorded by Edward Lhuyd in his phonetic spelling system.[27] The tale revolves around three points of wisdom given to John after he takes employment with a farmer. John swops his year's wages of three pounds for the first valuable piece of advice from the farmer: 'Komer weeth na reo gara an vorr goeth rag an vorr noueth [Have a care you do not leave an old way for a new way]'. The second year at the farm, John again swaps his wages for a piece of advice; this time: 'Komeer weeth na Raw'y Ostia en chei lebma vo dean koath Demithez da Bennen Younk [Have a care you do not lodge in a house where an old man may be married to a young woman]', and in the third year, finally for 'Bethez gueskez duath, ken gueskel eneth, rag edda eu an guella point a skeeanz oll [Be struck twice before you strike once for that is the best point of wit of All]'. In journeying home, choosing the old road saves him from being set upon by highwaymen, and then not staying in a house where an old man lives with a young wife allows him to find the murderers of the old man, and, finally, thinking twice before striking once, prevents him from thinking his wife is being adulterous, finding that it is his own son who had been born to her shortly after he left.

More recently the folktale has been looked at afresh by Page, Gendall, and Murdoch. Page gives a thorough linguistic analysis praising its 'admirable construction', while Gendall argues strongly for the tale to be read with an awareness of the oral tradition in Cornwall, using evidence collected in William Bottrell's English version and the two different versions in Cornish.[28] Murdoch, meanwhile, asks if it is really a 'Cornish *Ruodlieb*', comparing Boson's seventeenth-century version of the story with the eleventh-century Latin poem *Ruodlieb* from southern Germany. Murdoch rightly sets the tale of John of Chyanhor in a wider European literary context, not least with regard to cognate versions of the tale in other Celtic countries. As Payton notes in his comments on Murdoch's theory, if Boson 'first heard the story in Cornish from his servants, then we have a picture of the last generations of Cornish speakers which contrasts strongly with their conventional portrayal (even by some Cornish revivalists) as socially and culturally marginalized illiterates'.[29] Such a theory however, would seem to support the continuing supposition of this study as to how multi-cultural and multi-faceted the themes of Cornish literature are, from the post-Roman period onwards.

Having asserted the wider components of the tale, we should also consider that it tells us much about Cornish society and its economy at this time. Instead of eking out a living in their area, Cornish people had to relocate to find work. The advice about not leaving the old road arrives at an interesting time, when Cornish roads were still considered – by English travellers at least – to be appalling. New routes of travel were beginning to be opened up, as we recognize in the travellers and diarists. The three merchants who travel on the new road have been to Exeter Fair, which suggests established economic and trading links with Exeter from west Cornwall, whilst the distrust of organized religion is here seen in the monk who plots with the young landlady to murder her old husband.

Thus, the tale should both be seen in the wider European and world context and in an era of changing economic and social conditions in Cornwall. The far-reaching nature of this is later encapsulated in a copy of a fascinating letter sent by William Gwavas in 1710, clearly to a group of Cornish speakers somewhere in America – addressing them and native American peoples, suggesting that Cornish language was travelling beyond Cornwall:

> An [Why] poble hui, en pow America, uncuth dho nei, huei deskaz dho gurria an Deu guir a'n nev ha'n doar Neb g'ryk an Houl, an Lur, ha an Steren Rag porth a'n Tiz war an Tir, ha g'ryk kynifara tra en Dallath ha Eu Deu, olghalluzek dres ol an Beyz. Bounaz hep Diueth. Amen

> [You people in the land of America, unknown to us, you have learnt to worship the true God of the heaven and the earth, Who made the sun, the moon, and the stars for the aid of the people on the earth, and made everything in the beginning and is God almighty over all the world. Life without end. Amen.][30]

Despite the enforced religion upon native Americans, the reality of this, of course, was that such correspondence fitted into the longer established continuum of Cornish literature travelling across the globe, as witnessed already by the growth of Arthuriana, Tristan and Isolde and medieval drama. In effect, such correspondence (though fragmentary) was just the latest incarnation of this continuum.

As Williams has shown, it was during this phase that Edward Lhuyd visited Cornwall.[31] Lhuyd was born in Shropshire of Welsh parents in 1660, and became Under-Keeper of the Ashmolean Museum, Oxford, in 1684, and then Keeper in 1691. Lhuyd was an ambitious scholar, and he took it upon himself to study and record the indigenous languages of Britain. The project was a fashionable one; the task immense. His eventual epic study – the *Archaeologia Britannica*[32] – began to be published in 1709, the year of his death. In order to complete his task, between 1679 and 1701, 'honest Lhuyd' as he was called,[33] toured all the Celtic territories, recording his observations upon philology, linguistics and antiquity, in a way helping to found the modern academic discipline of Celtic Studies.[34] With the specific case of Cornwall, Lhuyd wanted to know 'what remains of the British language, customs and names of places may be found there',[35] and planned to visit the group of scholars in Penzance, Newlyn and Mousehole. In particular, he was keen to visit John Keigwin whom he felt 'without any comparison the most skilful judge of our age in the

Cornish language'.[36] Lhuyd prepared for his visit by corresponding with Thomas Tonkin of St Agnes,[37] and eventually came to Cornwall in 1700, recording much important Cornish material during the four months of his stay. As well as the vocabulary he found and transcribed, he recorded poems and songs, and at St Just-in-Penwith, Lhuyd recorded the prophetic englyn – or triplet – offered to him by the parish clerk, given at the start of this chapter. Sir Jonathan Trelawny, the Bishop of Exeter, also gave Lhuyd three Cornish manuscripts for him to look over, which had been translated into English by Keigwin.[38] Lhuyd's detailed observations and now familiarity with Cornish also allowed him eventually to identify the Vocabulary found in the Cottonian Library, as Old Cornish.[39]

In some ways, the work of Lhuyd was marginalized by Cornish scholars of his age,[40] and later by those working within the Revival.[41] In one way, this was because his basis for Cornish was clearly modelled on Welsh. However, other ideological concerns have also left his poetic work marginalized. One of the most fascinating pieces from this period is Lhuyd's 'In Obitum Regis Wilhelmi 3tii Carmen Britannicum, Dialectu Cornubiensis; An Normann Poetarum Seculi Sexti [On the Death of King William III, a British Song in the Cornish Dialect according to the pattern of the poets of the 6th century]', a poem rarely anthologized or referred to. The poem was problematic because first of all, it fitted Lhuyd's sympathies as a Williamite (even though such elegies in different languages were popular during this period), and because in the Celtic Revival, any elegy which alluded to the success of King William trod on too many toes, since Revivalists affected Jacobitism. It celebrated Protestant glory, whilst aspects of the pan-Celtic revival were Celtic, Catholic and Legitimist-driven.[42] Doubtless it would have won the approval of Colonel Charles Trelawny, his brother Jonathan the Bishop, and the Cornish soldiers who fought for King William at the Battle of the Boyne.[43] Thirdly, the poem, though drawing on the tradition of the Cornish englyn verse form, was perhaps viewed as being too 'English' and 'modern' in its construction; that is, it was not 'Celtic enough':

> Gwlâz Kernow regollaz y gweraz;
> Rygollaz Enys Brethon y Threvdaz:
> Ha 'Rhedzians gwir Dadloyar brâz.
>
> Kosgardh an dowr, squattyow goz rwzow,
> Goz golow, goz revow, goz oll skaphow;
> Seith mledhan ne dhibryw vor-bozow.
>
> Kosgardh an Stên, rowmann goz bolow;

Gwlezow, ravow, palow, pigolow:
Komero' gostanow, marhow, ha kledhow.

[The Kingdom of Cornwall has lost its help;
The Island of Britain has lost its Patriarch;
And true religion, a great advocate.

Fellows of the water, scat your nets,
Your sails, your oars, all your boats;
For seven years do not eat sea-food.

Fellows of the Tin, abandon your mines;
Picks, shovels, spades, pick-axes:
Take shields, horses and swords.][44]

Lhuyd's achievement and depiction of the day-to-day experience of Cornish fishermen and miners however, was massive. The poem proved how Cornish could turn successfully to secular material, and how the language might develop in the future. Other poets were following Lhuyd's lead on this. As well as a metrically clever poem titled 'A Cornish Song, to the Tune of "The Modest Maid of Kent"' – celebrating a good price for tin and hoping for large shoals of pilchards[45] – John Tonkin of St Just-in-Penwith wrote a strikingly similar piece to Lhuyd's elegy titled 'Kanna Kernuack'. Again, because of its controversial subject-matter, referring to the Glorious Revolution and it achievements, it has been marginalized in the same way:

Mattern James rig quachas e stoppia
bus E na allja e theath tha gloppia
Eve rig quachas moaze tha an gwella ternuan
bus e gothas drez an ne wharn

Ha ul e poble poonias tha Gova
Hemma e bra gwarre why na gova
Ha e tha worthen eath e whonnen
rag cowas gen e gare Trip-Cunnen

[King James tried to stop him
but he could not trip him up
He tried to go in the best direction
but he fell over the downs

And all the people ran to
then that his brave play do you not remember
and went to Ireland himself
to speak with his friend TirConnell][46]

Other Cornish 'late' and 'revived' writings of the nineteenth century will be considered later, but one or two final observations upon the Cornish literature of this period are worth making at this point; particularly with regard to the story of Dorothy (or Dolly) Pentreath who died in 1777, and the state of Cornish in the aftermath of her death. As a number of scholars have described, Dolly Pentreath of Mousehole was one of the last speakers of Cornish to exist in the eighteenth century.[47] There has been substantial debate as to whether she was a monoglot Cornish speaker,[48] but in all probability since she was something of an attraction in the later years of her life, she would have had some knowledge of English. What is interesting about her is that numerous antiquarians, scholars and observers knew of her and projected, as Mitchell has shown, a particular image of this speaker.[49] Most of the 'legend' of Dolly Pentreath is enshrined in the writing of Daines Barrington,[50] who in pursuing the observations of his brother Admiral Samuel Barrington, came to west Cornwall in 1768 to see if anyone could still speak and write Cornish. Barrington found Pentreath – a fish jowster – who was 'maintained mostly by the parish, and partly by fortune telling and gabbling in Cornish'.[51] He presented his findings to the Society of Antiquities in 1775:

> I continued nine or ten days in Cornwall after this, but found that my friends, whom I had left to eastwards, continued as incredulous almost as they were before, about these last remains of the Cornish language, because (amongst other reasons) Dr. Borlase had supposed, in his *Natural History of Cornwall*, that it had entirely ceased to be spoken.[52]

Mitchell's detailed study of the external antiquarians like Barrington and internal ones such as Borlase, has gone some way to deconstruct the reasoning behind their observations, and shows how, in fact, objectivity about the shift in language usage during the latter years of the eighteenth century, was barely present. With such a premise, the quest for the last speaker of Cornish may be regarded as more of a frightening ideological exercise rather than a true study of the socio-linguistics of the period. Numerous other later speakers and writers have been discussed by several scholars – among them the Truro engineer named Thompson, John Nancarrow (who travelled to Philadelphia in 1804), W.J. Rawlings, John Davey, Jane Barnicoat, Ann Wallis, John Tremethack, Mrs Kelynack, Betsy Matthews and the St Ives policeman called Botheras.[53] There are also the curious two Cornish poems of Georg Sauerwein dating from c.1865.[54] One of the most important however, is the correspondence of William

R. Scadden delin.

DOROTHY PENTREATH of MOUSEHOLE in CORNWALL,
the last Person who could converse in the Cornish language?

Printed for I. Hinton, at the Kings Arms, in Paternoster Row.

10. Dolly Pentreath, engraved by Richard Scadden, 1781.

Bodinar, a Mousehole fisherman, who in 1776 wrote a letter to Barrington. It is perhaps one of the last known examples of Cornish prose from this period:

> Bluth vee try egance a pemp. Theara vee dean bodjack an puscas. Me rig deskey Cornoack termen me vee mawe. Me vee de more gen seara vee a pemp dean moy en cock. Me rig scantlower clowes eden ger Sowsnack cowes en cock rag sythen warebar. Na riga vee biscath gwellas lever Cornoack. Me deskey Cornoack moas da more gen tees coath. Nag es moye vel pager po pemp en dreav nye ell clapia Cornoack leben, poble coath pager egance blouth. Cornoack ewe oll neceaves gen poble younk.

> [My age is sixty-five. I am a poor fisherman. I learned Cornish when I was a boy. I went to sea with my father and five other men in the boat. I hardly heard a single word of English spoken in the boat for as much as a week. I never saw a Cornish book. I learned Cornish going to sea with old men. There are no more than four or five in the village who can speak Cornish now, old people eighty years of age. Cornish is all forgotten by the young folk.][55]

In completing this work in Cornwall, Lhuyd, Barrington, Borlase and other antiquarians of the age are a sort of curious synthesis of the literary energies of this period, since as visitors (with the exception of Borlase[56]) they fit the model of other travellers and diarists who were 'discovering' and 'recording' Cornwall, yet they also preface the work of the nineteenth-century Folklorists like Robert Hunt and William Bottrell. However, the antiquarians were not there in the same capacity as travellers like Celia Fiennes, Daniel Defoe or, later, John Skinner. Lhuyd and perhaps even Barrington had more in common with those indigenous Cornish writers and scholars of the age than the English, who had merely come to be curious – and in doing so, set forth another development of Cornish literature which was to have massive future ramifications.

We should ask why did this curiosity about Cornwall begin as part of the growth of modern tourism? As North has argued, there was no mechanism for making or maintaining roads; 'those who needed to travel transported themselves and their goods by horse or by water, with considerable difficulty'.[57] But by the seventeenth century a road system was starting to be in place, bringing with it travellers for both business and pleasure. No doubt the long war with France also encouraged the increase of 'holidays at home'; it certainly encouraged the realization that it was possible to undertake a Grand Tour without leaving the island or having to make oneself understood abroad, and in the process observe, record and celebrate 'Greater Britain'.

There is no better introduction to this period of English literary history in Cornwall than the proto-tourist account of Celia Fiennes, who made her 'Great Journey' from the River Tamar to Land's End in the autumn of 1698,[58] which in its way was a development of the work of other writers such as William Camden (1551–1623) and John Leland (c.1503–52), who, like her, were writing a form apt to a nation emerging into a consciousness of its own power and nationhood. As Colley has argued, a new British nation was being invented in the wake of the Act of Union between England, Wales and Scotland in 1707, in which diverse peoples of this Protestant culture were being forced into closer union.[59] They were reminded of what they had in common – rather than how different they were – and how men and women from varied ethnic and social backgrounds were given powerful incentives to be British. In the process, as Brayshay *et al* show, British identity came to be superimposed onto much older regional identities, one of which was Cornwall; and this ideological desire – emanating from England – finds expression in the travel writing of the age.[60]

Fiennes was among the first visitors to write about Cornwall, and her work starts a trend which was to last well into the late twentieth century. As an early travel writer, Fiennes writes in an engaging style, but her account perhaps lacks perspective and historical context. The Cornish sections demonstrate this. Few coaches made the journey into Cornwall at the end of the seventeenth century and so Fiennes had to travel on horseback into Cornwall. She crossed the Tamar by the Cremyll ferry, a wet and hazardous passage that took an hour and gave her a cold, then rode to Looe. From Looe she followed the 'main' road through Fowey and Par, 'over the heath and commons by the tinn mines' to St Austell, where she was much pleased with her supper, with her tart and Cornish cream, though not with the custom of the country, 'which is a universall smoaking; both men, women and children have all their pipes of tobacco in their mouths, and soe sit round the fire smoaking'.[61] Whilst she may have deplored the habits of the Cornish people, her description of tin mining is an admirable piece of reporting, demonstrating just how technically advanced Cornwall was at this relatively early time.[62] Additionally, she passes scores of mine shafts after leaving St Austell, some 'that were lost by the waters overwhelming them', crossed the Fal at Tregony and so reached Tregothnan, the home of her cousin, Hugh Boscawen, placed at the confluence of the Fal and Truro rivers. On the roof of the house she could see 'the Great Ocean which runs into Falmouth' and to the west 'the hills full of Copper mines'.[63] She went on and reached Land's End, scrambling over the rocks as far west she could, saw the 'Island of Scilly', fell in love with Truro, 'formerly a great tradeing town' but now 'a ruinated disregarded place', was awed by the 'great mountaine of Brown Willy', impressed by the Delabole quarries and from Stowe caught a glimpse of Lundy Island which her grandfather, William Fiennes, had captured from the Grenvilles during the Civil War.[64] It is a useful description of Cornish landscape and culture during the period, yet remains a highly subjective and personalised account.

Near to Fiennes' time was *A Tour Through the Whole Island of Great Britain* by Daniel Defoe (1660–1731).[65] It was published in three volumes 1724 and 1726, and was a remarkable survey of these islands. Although he travelled the length and breadth of the island, his *Tour* nevertheless indicates 'an Idea of England', in many ways highlighting the unionizing thrust over the Celtic countries that was English-led and English-determined.[66]

In the sections on Cornwall, Defoe contrasts the contemporary processes of early industrialization with the decay of preceding societies, as in his description of the apparently deteriorated stone circle at Boscawen Ûn:

> Between [Penzance] and St Burien stands a circle of great stones, not unlike those at Stonehenge in Wiltshire, with one bigger than the rest in the middle; they stand about 12 foot asunder, but have no inscription.[67]

For Defoe, Cornwall is a land of great contrast, but then he had an appreciation for both industrial development and sites of 'heritage'. Devastation at ancient ruins is then intentionally set next to images of modernity and development. As Rogers notes, Defoe repeatedly uses phrases such as 'the injury of time', 'time the great devourer', or 'ruins eaten up by time'; always noting transition,[68] and yet, only a page later, this decay is juxtaposed with the industrial activity on Bodmin Moor, where 'there are many tin mines'.[69] Defoe's work is also significant in its cynical integration of folk belief and legend ('I leave the ruins of Tintagel. . . and as for the story of King Arthur being both born and killed there, 'tis a piece of tradition'[70]), and the details of commercial life he discovered ('whereas the town of Truro lying far within, and at the mouth of two fresh rivers, is not navigable for vessels of above 150 tons').[71]

Defoe records nothing of Cornish language or literature, giving solid enough evidence of its widespread decline at this point. Defoe is not the unobservant Englishman either, since in the Scottish and

Welsh sections, he does write about Gaelic and Welsh respectively. Lhuyd had compared Cornish to Welsh and Breton which were still being spoken by all classes in their respective countries; Cornish's absence from Defoe's account demonstrates its status by this point. In terms of ethnic markers, however, Defoe does remark on hurling and wrestling still being seen as characteristic activities of the Cornish, but he labels hurling 'a rude violent play among the boors, or country people; brutish and furious, and a sort of evidence that they were, once, a kind of barbarians'.[72] We may object to the terms in which the Cornish are described here, but this barbarianism is matched with the awareness of a Cornwall marching quickly into the modern world. Defoe was fortunate, too, in the historical moment when he completed the Tour. In particular, the Cornish material offers the finest account of Cornwall on the eve of industrialization.

As roads and accommodation throughout Britain improved during the latter part of the eighteenth century (Exeter now took six days to reach from London instead of almost a fortnight),[73] 'Home travel' to the Lake District, the Wye Valley, Scotland, North Wales and Cornwall became a fashionable pursuit for the wealthier classes. Unlike Fiennes or Defoe, these travellers primarily sought 'the picturesque', although during that time this could refer to both antiquities and industry. Cornwall was of particular interest because of its exciting and immediate maritime culture and the development of deep metal mines. One of the finest examples of this form applied on Cornwall is John Skinner's 1797 travel diary.[74]

Much of Skinner's work is descriptive; he obviously took great interest in the histories of old buildings and landscape in general, but he also describes some of the activities and pursuits of the 'common people' of Cornwall. As Jones notes, Skinner is 'naturally class-conscious – at one point noting the ungentlemanlike appearance of certain naval officers in charge of French prisoners in Falmouth,'[75] but this seems more out of habit than malice. Skinner records Cornish industry of the period, and describes the techniques of pressing and packing pilchards with great detail.[76] Furthermore, he was delighted by the religious fervour shown by the Cornish people, and noted that it was almost unexpected since they were so far removed from religious instruction.[77] Skinner also made sketches of historic buildings and landscape and industrial features. Despite his interest in antiquities, his style is neither flowery nor ornate, and even over two centuries later, the account reads easily. Such interest in land and seascape, as well as the behaviour and customs of people, were to be highly formative in the writing appearing after this phase, as the Anglo-Cornish travelogue developed into the Anglo-Cornish novel.

Having considered the late renaissance of writing in Cornish, the failure of an Anglo-Cornish literature and the expansion of an English travel literature of Cornwall, we have covered much of the distinctive literary development of Cornwall during the seventeenth and eighteenth century, though a fourth transformation needs to be examined more closely, if we are to truly understand both this phase and subsequent phases of literary history in Cornwall. That transforming effect was Methodism. As Shaw and, later, Payton, have shown, the Anglican church, which had replaced Catholicism in Cornwall, was failing to adapt itself to the economic changes occurring.[78] In the copper-mining regions, the population of some Cornish parishes had doubled, and increased five-fold in others, resulting in severe social problems for those communities. The Anglican church could not cope, nor could it deal sufficiently with the spiritual needs of these new (often industrialized) communities.[79] In the growing order of industrialization, the church failed to negotiate a new consensus between itself and the people it was meant to serve. Rowe has argued that this old order

> . . . was out of place in a society that was becoming increasingly dependent on tearing from Nature riches hidden in the earth . . . [and that] the difficult and hazardous nature of mining predisposed men to believe that by their own efforts along they could win or conquer the bounties of God or Nature.[80]

Other problems were realised alongside this phenomenon. People no longer believed in the notion of predestination and questioned what Rowe calls 'their individual favour in the eyes of God',[81] believing instead that their efforts and labour (not to mention improving technical skills) could make a difference in their future happiness. Another concern which had been evolving throughout the eighteenth century was the fact that the Anglican church's clergy had become a highly distinctive social group, with their own codes and conventions, widening the gap between them and the 'common people'.[82] The cumulative effect of all these factors meant that new, industrialized communities in Cornwall were ready to accept the Wesleyanism when it came. It was a spiritual, ideological and social change which was to have a massive effect over the next two centuries upon the literary energies of Cornwall.

Charles and John Wesley first arrived in Cornwall in 1743, making their base in St Ives. There is not time here to go into the full history of their work, but suffice to say that their travels and encounters in Cornwall have become near-legendary.[83] There were highly publicised clashes with a number of churchmen, even though not all of them were against the Wesleys. Additionally, both supporters of the Wesleys and anti-Wesleyans often had run-ins with the law.[84] As their journals reveal, their preachings caused controversy, but their message and beliefs gradually began to win over mining and fishing communities, such as Gwennap, Crowan, Newlyn and St Ives.[85] It is clear that the Methodists appealed to a Cornish working-class audience, and despite unfounded accusations that they were 'Popish',[86] their evangelism succeeded. In some senses, their appeal worked in just the same way as the Mystery Plays had, since they offended the intellectual ecclesiastics. What Methodism did was to revive the very Cornish concept of what Rowe perceptively terms 'the belief in the congregation as a communion and as a community'.[87]

As early as 1746 Cornwall was one of the seven Methodist circuits of 'England' – a considerable achievement. We must however be sceptical over later observers' claims about the power of Methodist reform upon the Cornish.[88] Despite all the supposed sermons heard by smugglers, the activity was actually abated by the deployment of naval ships around the coastline, in the aftermath of the Napoleonic Wars. We must also be sceptical of how Methodism reduced the number of hurling games, wrestling matches and other 'physical' community events in the same period, supposedly viewing such activities as barbaric. In all likelihood, their reduction was more to do with Methodist events proving to be more important social counter-attractions for miners often facing shorter holidays. Likewise, wrecking, that was to become such a dramatic theme of Anglo-Cornish literature in future centuries, was not put to an end through Wesley's orations. Wreckers simply had a different notion of property than the state had. As Morley contends, it was the enforcement of the law that brought the decline in wrecking in the eighteenth century, rather than Methodism's rise and progress.[89]

One writer who provides an important link between the journals of the English visitors of the age, the ideology of Methodism and the full-blown forthcoming phase of Anglo-Cornish poetry and fiction, is Harry Carter.[90] Carter wrote his autobiography in 1809, and it details a period of south Cornish history at the end of the eighteenth century. The 'free trader' Harry Carter was a precision Methodist; he would have no swearing or unseemly talk on board his ship, and when living in enforced retirement at Roscoff in Brittany, he conducted services for the benefit of the Cornish smugglers in the town. 'The men took off their hats,' he noted in his diary, 'all very serious, no laffing, no trifling conversations.'[91] Thus Carter's autobiography is an odd mixture of adventure story and Wesleyan tract, though the two are not as much at odds as they first might appear to be. There is a sophistication in the narration and description which points to what was to come. Whether Carter felt growing confidence in a re-invented Cornwall is difficult to deduce, but it does seem from the text that he writes as one of the earliest examples of the Methodist-transformed modern Cornishman. That is why Carter's text is significant.

The narrative is exciting; it is, after all, the story of a smuggler's life and we first see a genuine attempt by a Cornish writer to reflect on experience; an experience which had certainly happened to other Cornish smugglers; in this case, Cornish people's fear of being caught smuggling and the experiences of capture:

> This was a strange seeing unto me, the first prison I ever saw the inside of, the hearing of so many iron doors opening, etc. So I was put up to the last floor in the top of that very high Castle, in a criminal jail, where there were a little short, dirty straw, etc. . . . but as the jailer left me, hearing the rattling of the doors, and the noise of the keys, I begun to reflect, where am I now? I shall shorley never come out of this place whilst the war lasts, shorly I shall die here, etc.[92]

Stylistically, the autobiography is laboured by modern standards, but it is symptomatic of the transition which was wrought by Methodism and by other social and economic changes that writers like Defoe and Skinner had observed. It is his honesty and directness that we admire in Carter, and his ability to reflect on and analyse his progress and achievements. This is a crucial and important new development in Anglo-Cornish writing, which would bear remarkable fruit over the coming century.

One other writer needs to be considered as the eighteenth century turned into the nineteenth century. As one of history's most famous Cornishmen, Humphry Davy is now celebrated for his invention of the miner's safety lamp in 1815 (actually of more use to coal miners than to the hard-rock miners of Cornwall). Although Davy, as Paris and King have shown, is best known as a scientist, chemist and inventor, he was also a poet.[93] Davy was born at Varfell, Ludgvan, near Penzance in 1778. His father was a wood-carver and hoped that his son might grow up to be a writer. The Cornish landscape proved to be hugely inspirational, and it was onto the natural environment around him that he welded his philosophy on life. The combination of these elements make Davy Cornwall's most important 'Romantic' poet.

Davy wrote the following untitled poem around 1795 while sitting in Ludgvan churchyard observing the tombstones:

My eye is wet with tears
For I see the white stones
    That are covered with names
    The stones of my forefathers' graves

No grass grows upon them
For deep in the earth
    In darkness and silence the organs of life
    To their primitive atoms return.[94]

It is by no means a perfect poem, but the intensity of such verse conveys something of a Cornishman's assertion of 'identity' with the depths of the earth, given that he is writing in the Romantic period. Individual experience of this kind formed the subject-matter for a number of poets of this period writing in English. Davy manages to sense in the Cornish landscape the transcendental; particularly in the poems written between 1795 and 1796, such as 'The Sons of Genius'.[95] Davy also began an unfinished poem on Mount's Bay, which gives a mythic edge to his childhood landscape, whilst championing a new Cornish historical imagination. Here, this is completed by a reinvention and a romantic account of the ocean and cliffs around Penzance; Bolerium being the Roman name for Land's End during the Iron Age:

On the sea
The sunbeams tremble; and the purple light
Illumes the dark Bolerium, seat of storms.
High are his granite rocks. His frowning brow
Hangs o'er the smiling Ocean. In his caves
Th'Atlantic breezes murmur. In his caves,
Where sleep the haggard Spirits of the storm,
Wild dreary are the schistine rocks around
Encircled by the wave, where to the breeze
The haggard Cormorant shrieks. And far beyond
Are seen the cloud-like Islands, grey in mists.[96]

As Pritchard notes, such poems emulate the style of Cowper, and in many ways are comparable to the earlier works of Wordsworth and Coleridge, both of whom he later met.[97] However, as Treneer has shown in her brief biography of the 'mercurial chemist', everything was in place, but he failed to develop his poetry any further, concentrating instead on prose and the travelogue.[98] We can only guess at the kind of impact upon the literary culture of Cornwall that Davy might have had, had he decided to pursue his interest in poetry rather than, like a number of other Cornishmen of the age, in science, mining and engineering. As it stands, Davy leaves us with a tantalizing

11. Sir Humphry Davy, engraved by E. Scriven from the painting by Sir Thomas Lawrence, original at the Royal Society, London.

picture of the makings of a brilliant potential Cornish poet of the romantic movement, still separated from Methodist experience and able to inject a revolt against classical English forms and conservative morality. And so, having seen how the 'songs of the western men' began to be murmured at the end of the eighteenth century in the prose writings of Harry Carter and the poetry of Humphry Davy, we next must hear their full-blown voices.

In the early nineteenth century, Anglo-Cornish literature initially took a populist turn. Whilst Carter was offering a questioning, Methodist-reformed, intensely personal prose, a new poetic development was beginning to emerge on the heels of Davy. Though English travellers continued to visit Cornwall, and write engaging accounts of its by now well-documented industrialization, the indigenous Anglo-Cornish writing again focused on the Cornish community in a way it had not done since before the Reformation. The form was not verse drama, but the ballad. It is the themes, content and forms of these ballads which show the signs of a confident Cornwall returning – in their puns, their developed sense of identity, and in their ability to poke fun at their countrymen and women. There is perhaps a need for greater awareness of the impact of popular writing upon people and their identities throughout history. Cornwall has generated many wandering balladeers throughout its history, though they appeared with a renewed vigour at the turn of the nineteenth century, as a literary phenomenon operating at the same time as the expansion of mining. As communities expanded and grew quickly, there was a need for additional entertainment and a new literature for one and all.

In part this role was fulfilled by the balladeers, and otherwise by the so-called 'droll-tellers'. As Weatherhill details, the concept of a droll-teller is a problematical one, since there are few records of when the term was first used, or what his or her precise role was.[99] We come to see it as a term applied to those persons who, in effect, worked as Cornish storytellers during this period, and whose narratives were later recorded and re-interpreted by early folklorists such as Hunt and Bottrell. To some observers, such as Deane and Shaw, the droll-teller and balladeer are one and the same person,[100] but this view is not always sustainable, and the two probably represented very different literary trends operating at the same moment in Cornish history.

The image of the balladeers of this period is of an itinerant lifestyle, wandering from village to village and town to town, where they would be welcomed at each house, and a meal and a bed always found for them. Val Baker, and Quayle and Foreman, each promote this image of oral tradition in the Cornish community,[101] and Deane and Shaw argue that, 'their rent was seldom more than a song or a story, perhaps with an odd-job completed as an extra token of gratitude'.[102] This is perhaps quite a romantic view of their lifestyle, and in reality, their lives must have been quite difficult. In fact, the balladeers were finding trade and audience in the newly-developed mining villages, and in the exportation of Cornish comic talent into England. It seems the Cornish balladeers had a considerable reputation in the south-west of Britain; and whilst travel allowed English visitors into Cornwall, it allowed the balladeers out.[103]

Deane and Shaw give details of several balladeers from the eighteenth and nineteenth century. One was Richard Nancollas, otherwise known as 'Rhyming Dick' who sang at alehouses and festivals both inside and outside Cornwall.[104] Another was 'Uncle' Anthony James, who worked primarily around west Cornwall singing well-known ballads as well as his own compositions. Billy Foss (or Frost) of Sancreed, wrote a number of different types of verse ranging from full-rhymed verses to epitaphs.[105] This example demonstrates the poverty of agricultural communities of west Cornwall during the period:

> As I traversed Boslow I saw an old cow,
> A hog and a flock of starved sheep;
> Besides an old mare, whose bones were so bare
> As to make its poor master to weep.
>
> No grass for the flocks, but a carn of dry rocks
> Which afforded an horrible sight.
> If you pass the way, you must do so by day,
> For you'd scat out your brains in the night![106]

Perhaps the most celebrated balladeer of this period was Henry, or 'Henna', Quick. Born in Zennor in 1792, he died there in poverty in 1857 at the age of sixty-five. During his life he was quite popular in west Cornwall. Quick wrote and distributed his own broadsheets and journals. An acrostic ends many of the balladeers' verses, and Quick was a master of them, often incorporating the most difficult names into his concluding lines. To a broadly illiterate audience, this must have seemed a clever and witty device, moving forward the complexities of simple ballads for working-class Cornish people.

A useful biography of Henry Quick has been written by P.A.S. Pool, who offers interesting insights into the social and economic background of Quick's verse.[107] According to Pool, Quick's father died in 1805, and the widow and son were left in poverty, unable to obtain any monetary support from the parish.[108] Despite his poverty, however, the success of his poetry led to his earning the title 'the Zennor Poet' and several likenesses of him were even distributed in west Cornwall during his life.[109] Pool argues that 'no-one could claim that Quick's work has any real literary merit or significance' and that most of it is 'deplorable doggerel'.[110] Pool was right on both accounts, but Quick is nevertheless significant in Cornu-English literature's development, and his doggerel, despite the hilariously contrived rhymes, is not always deplorable. The value of his verse, like that of the other early balladeers, lies in its depiction of life in Cornwall at the opening of the nineteenth century, and as a representative example of popular literary taste.

Quick's best work was his *Life and Progress*, a record of his own life. He was clearly a Methodist, and much of his work concerns Methodist themes. Pool sees Quick as believing Methodists to be 'the people of the Lord',[111] and Quick's work may stand as an indication of how influential Methodism was in St Ives and its surrounds during this period. His writing shows how well the forging of the British nation had worked, and how successfully England had extended its grip over Cornwall. If the place-names and culture of the rhymesters were resolutely Cornish, amongst the populace identity appeared to have aligned itself with England; the word 'Old' here shows how confidently Englishness had been embedded in the Cornish consciousness:

> Henry is my Christian name,
> And Quick of course by nature came;
> Old England is my native plain,
> God did create and me sustain.[112]

But it would clearly be wrong-headed of us to think that this meant cultural extinction for the Cornish. In fact, Quick's work shows that residual Cornishness was still felt strongly, but was being newly invigorated by modernity and industrial prowess. Quick's verse strongly reflects this paradox of continuity and alteration which the Cornish underwent at the turn of the nineteenth century. Although Pool laments that Quick did not write more about the folklore of the area, his appeal was as a populist poet, writing for a developing industrial Cornwall and including within his verse the fears of the people involved in that development and how the ideology of Cornwall was altering:

> The Cornish drolls are dead, each one;
> The fairies from their haunts have gone:
> There's scarce a witch in all the land,
> The world has grown so learn'd and grand.[113]

Quick was right to note how Cornwall was changing, but we perhaps can see he was being presumptive in viewing this culture as completely ending; for indeed it was to continue side-by-side with the

12. Henry Quick, the Zennor poet, drawn by R.T. Pentreath, published by J.P. Vebert, Penzance, August, 1833.

industrial culture, and was to undergo a succession of later preservations and revivals, commencing in his own lifetime. Quick's point may have been, however, how swiftly the concerns of Cornish people were altering to want literary depictions of economic and social change. Of this type, one of his most impressive poems is *The Death of Pascoe Semmens*, a man from the parish of Ludgvan, who was killed by lightning in a thunderstorm at Castle-Dennis-Downs. Others include verses on the sudden death of two poor miners in Wheal Vor mine (1829) and an account of the fatal accident and death of John Martins, a poor young man of the parish of Ludgvan who was crushed in the bowels of the earth, while attempting to run an old shaft in Wheal Tin Croft Mine (1836). In fact, mining imagery pervades his work. Of his parents, Quick wrote:

> My father laboured underground,
> Mother the spinning-wheel put round.[114]

Quick's humorous and sentimental work is important in its depiction of change. The Cornish had in one sense become 'tongueless' through their loss of the Cornish language, and the territory and people were subject to being constructed by successive sets of travellers keen to observe and record Cornwall.[115] However, despite the catastrophic effect of language decline, this did not prevent Cornish identity from being asserted; it merely altered. Additionally, elements of continuity from the previous century – particularly the more secular themes of Cornish texts, and the desire to use literary puns and devices within English – were not completely destroyed, but rather developed in new ways. However, the effects of industrialization, which were beginning to be considered in the writings of Fiennes and Defoe, not to mention Foss and Quick, come further to the forefront of our discussion when we consider the next phase of literary development in Cornwall.

NOTES

1. William Pryce, *Archeologia Cornu-Britannica* (Menston 1972 [1790]), p. 220.
2. John Whitaker, *Supplement to the First and Second Books of Polwhele's History of Cornwall* (London 1804), pp 41–2.
3. See Mark Stoyle, '"Sir Richard Grenville's Creatures": The New Cornish Tertia, 1644–46' in Philip Payton (ed.), *Cornish Studies: Four* (Exeter 1996b), pp 26–44.
4. See John Rowe, *Cornwall in the Age of the Industrial Revolution* (St Austell 1993 [1953]); Philip Payton, *The Making of Modern Cornwall* (Redruth 1992).

5. See Craig Weatherhill, *Cornish Place Names and Language* (Wilmslow 1995), pp 109–11.
6. Joanna Mattingly and June Palmer (eds.), *From Pilgrimage to Package Tour* (Truro 1992).
7. Emma Mitchell, 'The Myth of Objectivity: The Cornish Language and the Eighteenth-Century Antiquarians' in Philip Payton (ed.), *Cornish Studies: Six* (Exeter 1998), pp 62–80.
8. See 'The Embers' in Peter Berreford Ellis, *The Cornish Language and its Literature* (London and Boston 1974), pp 125–46.
9. See *Gwreans an Bys* MS Bodley 219, Oxford; Paula Neuss (ed. and tr.), *The Creacion of the World: A Critical Edition and Translation* (New York and London 1983); E.G. Retallack Hooper (ed. and tr.), (1985) *William Jordan: Gwryans an Bys/The Creation of the World* (Redruth 1985).
10. Brian Murdoch, *Cornish Literature* (Cambridge 1993), p. 76.
11. Retallack Hooper, op.cit., pp 107–8. This text uses unified spelling.
12. For strong evidence of this, see A.K. Hamilton Jenkin, *The Cornish Miner* (Newton Abbot 1972 [1927]), p. 42 and the observations of Richard Carew in F.E. Halliday (ed.), *Richard Carew* (London 1953), p. 88.
13. Retallack Hooper, op.cit., pp 175–6.
14. Harvey Fried (ed.), *A Critical Edition of Brome's "The Northern Lasse"* (New York and London 1980), p. 138. The Cornish translates to 'Fat (or big) head, will you be hanged?'.
15. The essay is in Davies Gilbert (ed.), *The Parochial History of Cornwall*, 4 (London 1838), pp 203–19.
16. Cited in W.Ll. Davies, *Cornish Manuscripts in the National Library of Wales* (Aberystwyth 1939), p. 10. This is a translation of the Latin preface of Keigwin's translation.
17. For detail on this group, see P.A.S. Pool, *The Death of Cornish* (Penzance 1982 [1975]); Murdoch, op.cit., pp 131–42.
18. Andrew Brice, 'The Exmoor Scolding' in *Brice's Weekly Journal*, 52 (1727).
19. Ellis, op.cit.; Pool, op.cit.; Murdoch, op.cit.
20. Pryce, op.cit., p. 225.
21. *Old Cornwall*, Winter (1938), pp. 169–74.
22. *Old Cornwall*, Winter (1948), pp. 268–73.
23. *Old Cornwall*, Summer (1947), pp. 210–13.
24. Oliver J. Padel, *The Cornish Writings of the Boson Family* (Redruth 1975), pp 8–14.
25. Ibid., pp 8–9.
26. Ibid., pp 24–37.
27. Ibid., pp 15–16.
28. John Page, *Jowan Chy an Horth Examined* (Redruth 1982), p. ii; Jan Gendall, 'John of Chyanhor & the Oral Tradition' in *The Celtic Pen* 1:4 (1994), pp 22–3.
29. Brian Murdoch, 'Is John of Chyanhor really a "Cornish Ruodlieb"?' in Payton (ed.), op.cit. (1996), pp 45–63. See Payton (ed.) (1996), p. 3.
30. *Old Cornwall*, Summer (1925), p. 17.

31. Derek R. Williams, *Prying into Every Hole and Corner: Edward Lhuyd in Cornwall* (Redruth 1993).
32. Edward Lhuyd, *Archeologia Britannica* (Menston 1969 [1707]).
33. Williams, op.cit., p. 5.
34. For comment on this, see Simon James, *The Atlantic Celts* (London 1999), pp 43–59.
35. Letter to Martin Lister, Oxford, February 18th 1691/2. See Williams, op.cit., p. 7.
36. Lhuyd, op.cit. (1969 [1707]), p. 222. For a response to this, see Alan M. Kent, *Dreaming in Cornish* (Liskeard 1998).
37. For the correspondence, see Pryce, op.cit., pp 227–38.
38. See M.G. Smith, *Fighting Joshua: A Study of the Career of Sir Jonathan Trelawny* (Redruth 1985), p. 155; Pool, op.cit., p. 21.
39. Pool, ibid., p. 23.
40. In Oliver Pender's 1711 correspondence with William Gwavas, Pender criticises Lhuyd's poem on the 'Death of King William III' as 'not worth the trouble of reading'. Pender prefers Gwavas' Cornish to Lhuyd's, commenting that the latter's Cornish was 'more like Welsh, what he did'. *Old Cornwall*, April (1926), pp 23–4.
41. Early twentieth-century Cornish language revivalists rejected Lhuyd's phonetic Cornish in favour of a medieval base for revived Cornish. For a defence of Lhuyd, see Richard Gendall, *1000 Years of Cornish* (Menheniot 1994), p. 7.
42. Tim Saunders, 'Cornish – Symbol and Substance' in Cathal Ó Luain (ed.), *For a Celtic Future* (Dublin 1983), p. 256.
43. Smith, op.cit., pp 119–20.
44. Pryce, op.cit., p. 233.
45. *Old Cornwall*, April (1930), pp 27–9.
46. *Old Cornwall*, October (1930), pp 41–2.
47. Ellis, op.cit., pp 115–24; Pool, op.cit., pp 25–6; Murdoch, op.cit., p. 3.
48. Ibid.
49. Mitchell, op.cit., pp 71–4. For another later example of the 'ennobling' of the Cornish, see W.H. Hudson, *The Land's End* (London 1981 [1908]), pp 95–112.
50. For Daines Barrington, see Ellis, op.cit., pp 115–6.
51. For 'On the Expiration of the Cornish Language', see ibid., pp 116–9.
52. Ibid., p. 117. For the work of William Borlase on Cornish, see *Antiquities Historical and Monumental of the County of Cornwall* (London 1754), pp 413–4.
53. See Mitchell, op.cit., Weatherhill, op.cit., pp 147–9; Ellis, op.cit., pp 125–46.
54. For Saurwein and Cornish, see Saunders, op.cit., p. 256.
55. *Old Cornwall*, Summer (1940), pp 306–8.
56. Borlase was from Cornwall.
57. Christine North, 'Travel in West Barbary' in Mattingly and Palmer, op.cit., pp 3–9.

58. Christopher Morris (ed.), *Journeys of Celia Fiennes* (London 1947).

59. Linda Colley, *Britons: Forging the Nation 1707–1837* (New Haven and London 1992).

60. Mark Brayshay (ed.), *Topographical Writers in South-West England* (Exeter 1992).

61. Morris, op.cit., pp 256–7.

62. Ibid., pp 257–8.

63. Ibid., pp 259–60.

64. Ibid., pp 261–8.

65. Pat Rogers (ed.), *Daniel Defoe: A Tour Through the Whole Island of Great Britain* (Harmondsworth 1971 [1724–1726]).

66. Morris, op.cit., p. 10.

67. Defoe, op.cit., pp 233–4.

68. Ibid., p. 31.

69. Ibid., p. 229.

70. Ibid., p. 243.

71. Ibid., p. 231.

72. Ibid., p. 243.

73. See F.E. Halliday, *A History of Cornwall* (London 1959), pp 279–80.

74. See Roger Jones (ed.), *John Skinner: West Country Tour: Being the Diary of a Tour through the Counties of Somerset, Devon and Cornwall in 1797* (Bradford on Avon 1985).

75. Ibid., pp 10, 78.

76. Ibid., p. 63.

77. Ibid., p. 68.

78. Thomas Shaw, *A History of Cornish Methodism* (Truro 1967); Payton, op.cit (1992). See also Peter Isaac, *A History of Evangelical Christianity in Cornwall* (Cornwall 2000).

79. Philip Payton, *Cornwall* (Fowey 1996), pp 213–8.

80. Rowe, op.cit., p. 67.2.

81. Ibid.

82. Ibid., p. 67.3. Rowe notes how in the clerical families such as the Collins, Borlases and Trists, caste stratification was developed by intermarriage.

83. See examples cited in Donald R. Rawe, *A Prospect of Cornwall* (Chapel Amble 1996), p. 147.

84. Rowe, op.cit., pp 67.3–.39. This gives a detailed account of religious change brought about by the Wesleys.

85. See Nehemiah Curnock (ed.), *The Journal of the Rev. John Wesley Vols 1–8* (London 1938).

86. This was unfounded, though in 1747 the Bishop of Exeter issued the first part of his 'Enthusiasm of Methodists and Papists compared'. See Rowe, op.cit., pp 67.14–.15.

87. Ibid., p. 67.18.

88. For an example of this argument, see Marjorie Filbee, *Celtic Cornwall* (London 1996), p. 133.

89. Geoffrey Morley, *The Smuggling War: The Government's Fight against Smuggling in the 18th and 19th Centuries* (Dover 1994).
90. John B. Cornish (ed.), *The Autobiography of a Cornish Smuggler (Captain Harry Carter, of Prussia Cove) 1749–1809* (Truro 1971 [1894]).
91. Ibid., p. 70.
92. Ibid., p. 7.
93. John Aryton Paris, *The Life of Sir Humphry Davy* (London 1831); Ronald King, *Humphry Davy* (London 1978).
94. Alison Pritchard (ed.), *The Poetry of Humphry Davy* (Penzance 1978), p. 1.
95. Ibid., p. 4.
96. Ibid., p. 5.
97. Ibid., p. 1.
98. Anne Treneer, *The Mercurial Chemist: A Life of Sir Humphry Davy* (London 1963).
99. Craig Weatherhill and Paul Devereux, *Myths and Legends of Cornwall* (Wilmslow 1994), p. iii. According to Henry Jenner, 'the word "daralla", a tale, is perhaps the origin of the word "droll"'. See Henry Jenner, 'Some Possible Arthurian Place-Names in West Penwith' in *Journal of the Royal Institution of Cornwall* (1912), p. 87.
100. Tony Deane and Tony Shaw, *The Folklore of Cornwall* (Totowa, New Jersey 1975), pp 145–51.
101. Denys Val Baker, *The Timeless Land: The Creative Spirit in Cornwall* (Bath 1973), p. 3; Eric Quayle and Michael Foreman, *The Magic Ointment and other Cornish Legends* (London 1986), pp 11–12.
102. Deane and Shaw, op.cit., pp 145–6.
103. This trend continued into the nineteenth century with Robert Maybee and C. Taylor Stevens. Both were popular outside of Cornwall. See P.A.S Pool (ed.), *The Life and Progress of Henry Quick of Zennor* (Redruth 1994 [1963]), pp 8–9.
104. Deane and Shaw, op.cit., p. 146.
105. See Weatherhill and Devereux, op.cit., p. iii.
106. Deane and Shaw, op.cit., p. 147.
107. Pool, op.cit.
108. Ibid., p. 6.
109. In 1842, an oil painting of Quick was completed. Ibid., p. 6.
110. Ibid., p. 7.
111. Ibid., p. 8.
112. Ibid., p. 11.
113. Ibid., p. 31.
114. Ibid., p. 11.
115. The travelogue was to remain a popular form in the nineteenth century. For a fine example, see Dinah Craik, *An Unsentimental Journey through Cornwall* (Penzance 1988 [1884]).

'The Songs of the Western Men': Paradigms of Identity and Continuity in the Literature of Nineteenth-century Cornwall, 1820–1890

'Goin' up Camborne 'ill, Comin' down,
Goin' up Camborne 'ill, Comin' down,
The 'osses stood still, the wheels turned aroun',
Goin' up Camborne 'ill. comin' down.'

> *Traditional Cornu-English Song,*
> early nineteenth century.[1]

'Let no hand of man
Destroy these stony prophets which the Lord
Has placed upon the tarns and sounding downs
With tones for distant ages.'

> John Harris, *Destruction of the*
> *Cornish Dolmen* (c.1874)[2]

Henry Quick could not have foretold how the poets of mid-nineteenth-century Cornwall were to provide such an outstanding vision of industrial confidence and revived identity. Two of those poets, Robert Stephen Hawker (1803–75) and John Harris (1820–84), are seen as central to nineteenth-century Cornwall and its poetic construction, and it is they who sing most loudly and most confidently 'the songs of the Western men (and women)' in poetry. Davy had suggested the romantic possibilities of the landscape whilst Quick had outlined the alterations in Cornish society, albeit with piety, resignation and a certain innocence, and had offered a projection of popular sentiment. Hawker and Harris were to develop this vision of Cornwall far further than Carter, Davy or Quick could have dreamed, though in remarkably different and divergent ways.

At this stage, Hawker upsets the continuity developing in Cornish literature in the work of Carter, Davy, Quick, and later, in the work of the Methodist-mining poet, John Harris. The apparent tangent that he takes, however, had several precedents before him. For instance, we may match Hawker with the direction earlier in history that Roscarrock takes in contrast to Carew, and though Quick understood the impact of industrial Cornwall, like Hawker he lamented the loss of an older culture. Later, Hawker was to be viewed as the antecedent of another phase of Cornish revival at the turn of the twentieth century. The reasons for Hawker's position and tangential move away from the Methodist mainstream of Cornish writing at this time, are related to his religious beliefs and his understanding of Cornish history, and these are worth exploring.

Hawker was a clergyman of the Church of England at Morwenstow from 1824 to 1874, a High Churchman, who was resistant to Puritan views and the growth of Methodism. Part of this resistance was geographical. In the early nineteenth century, north Cornwall had little linkage or similarities to the industrial areas of the south and west; its confidence and identity were based on the memory of the strength of Cornish Royalism of the area in the Civil War, when the Cornish defeated the invading Roundheads at Stamford Hill. It was not undergoing the same transitions as elsewhere in Cornwall. We may attribute much of Hawker's verse to the fact that here remained, in the nineteenth century, an older, spiritual pocket; a view offered in the 'footprints of former men in far Cornwall' ideology of his collection of prose writings. The Cornwall that Hawker wrote about may thus be seen in the light of a certain historical moment: John Wesley had never actually left the Church of England and had resisted increasing pressures to leave in his lifetime.[3] But after his death in 1791, the Wesleyans broke away from the Anglicans, and soon a growing number of sects were established, among them William Bryan's Bible Christians.[4]

Hawker was one of the foremost members of the Church of England, who, faced with the success of Methodism and Nonconformity, turned to the High Church ritualist party; he was eventually converted to Catholicism on August 15th 1875, just twelve hours before he died. As an Anglo-Catholic, Hawker found himself out of step with utilitarian Cornwall. As Payton has argued, 'Hawker's High Church, anti-industrial sentiments found little support and struck few chords in Cornwall at the height of its mining and engineering prowess'.[5] In his prose, Hawker writes depressingly of 'the existence of underground life'.[6] Linking Methodism to the mines, he talks disparagingly elsewhere of 'the merry minister of the mines, whose cure was honeycombed by the underground men'[7] and of how the jury in his story of *The Gauger's Pocket* were 'all bad rascals, tin-and-copper-men'.[8] Hawker was far from being the archetypal Cornishman of his age. As Todd has shown, that role was left to Davies Gilbert, the 'Cornish philosopher' who took an interest in antiquarian studies and had earlier published a version of the medieval passion poem *Passyon Agan Arluth*.[9] It was Gilbert, therefore, and men like him, who accurately reflected the concerns of mid-nineteenth-century Cornwall, and Hawker was obviously not sympathetic to the down-to-earth miners, engineers and technocrats flourishing elsewhere. Hawker's verse strongly alluded to what industrialists saw as a romantic view of previous ages while they favoured the triumph of industrialization and modernity over them; in doing so, matching how the majority of people viewed themselves and their culture.

But Hawker, as his major biographer and editor, Piers Brendon, has shown, was undeterred.[10] Critically, Hawker has been thought of as an isolated and eccentric figure, though the picturesque portrait drawn in Sabine Baring-Gould's *The Vicar of Morwenstow* (1875) of his 'commanding the devils' with 'Solomon's seal',[11] has since been modified by the researches of Brendon. Although he may have been eccentric, in fact Hawker struggled against the odds to carry out his pastoral duties in his poor and remote Cornish parish. He built himself a hut on the cliff tops from the timbers of wrecked ships and it was there he wrote much of his poetry. Much of Hawker's verse was inspired by the Cornish landscape and legends, and despite the mismatch of their moment of production to the technical age, they are among the finest examples of nineteenth-century Anglo-Cornish verse. In a number of his poems we see vigorous new life breathed into the Christian myths and pagan legends, the Arthurian story, the heroes and wreckers, the spells and curses of an older, pre-industrial Cornwall.

But this alone would give us a very limited reading of Hawker's poetry. In addition, he gives eloquent expression to real-life dramatic incidents which he himself had experienced, which were not dissimilar to those witnessed by Quick and the other balladeers: storms, ship-wrecks, local deaths and tragedies. However, in his work we do witness an aesthetic shift in Cornish writing emphasing the romantic coastline, which has since continued as a literary construct of Cornwall. No other early writer – indigenous or visiting – developed it quite so thoroughly as Hawker.

Hawker's most famous work is his 1825 poem, 'The Song of the Western Men', which according to Stanier and Brendon refers to a popular proverb which was known throughout Cornwall: 'And shall Trelawny die? Here's twenty thousand Cornish men will know the reason why!', created after the imprisonment of Jonathan Trelawny and six other bishops by James II, just after Monmouth's western rising of 1685.[12] This caused much resentment and discontent in Cornwall and it is this event, some century and a half earlier, which Hawker romantically evokes:

> A good sword and a trusty hand!
> A merry heart and true!
> King James's men shall understand
> What Cornish lads can do.[13]

Most historians now agree that the incident arose from the life of Sir Jonathan Trelawny.[14] At the trial of the bishops, Trelawny and the others were acquitted, but in reality there was no kind of Cornish rebellion, or even a threat of rebellion of the kind alluded to by Hawker. The poet was effectively re-writing history. That his version of history has remained in the popular consciousness is testament to his skill as a poet, and the fact that his revivalism, if not appreciated at the time, was later to come of age. 'Trelawny', as Polmear, and Clarke and Harry record, is now viewed as the Cornish national anthem – ironic, in the sense that though about a projected glorious moment in Cornwall's past history, it came to existence in industrial Cornwall. Paradoxically, 'Trelawny' became an expression of the self-confidence of Cornish industrial and post-industrial society.[15]

Thus, as a poet recounting and reinterpreting a pre-industrial age in an industrial one, Hawker has come to embody the essence of Cornish patriotism, and an incipient nationalism, as in another poem concerned with events in the Civil War, 'Sir Beville: The Gate-Song of Stowe'. Here, Hawker celebrates the Royalist leader – Sir Beville Grenville (1594–1643) – who lived at Stowe, and, as a hero, was still embedded in north Cornish folklore of the time. Hawker's verse is a carefully constructed testament to the linkage between Cornwall and the Crown, and hence of identity, distinctiveness and nationhood, which if not being removed from the verse of Quick and his fellow balladeers, was more subdued. Again, dissatisfied with the age he lived in, Hawker found a dynamic Cornish power and energy in Sir Beville:

> Trevanion is up, and Godolphin is nigh,
> And Harris of Hayne's o'er the river;
> From Lundy to Looe, 'One and all' is the cry,
> And the King and Sir Beville for ever.[16]

But Hawker's recreation of past Cornwall goes much further than this. He taps into numerous other significant threads in literary history. In 1863, after the death of his first wife Charlotte, and spurred by grief, and according to Brendon, stimulated by opium, Hawker composed what is viewed by both Brendon and Trewin as his masterpiece, 'The Quest of the Sangraal'.[17] Like Carew before him, Hawker had a strong interest in Arthurian legend, and whilst Carew had moved to a satirical vision of Tintagel in *A Herring's Tail*,[18] Hawker elected for a serious retelling using blank verse, but the poem has not received the attention it merits from mainstream English scholars. As Jenkins and Broadhurst show,[19] with the romantic revival of the early nineteenth century there began a new phase in the retelling of the Arthurian cycles, and Hawker entirely fits this development; he is its Cornish model. Rich men of the time built castles and staged feasts in medieval costume, and Britain as a whole – the forging of Great Britain complete – enthused over Arthurian legend with all the vigour of a wealthy and hugely self-confident society. Malory was republished from 1816 onwards, and Tennyson produced his first Arthurian poem, 'The Lady of Shalott', in 1832.

Thus, the far more likely reason for the poem's composition was fashion. Hawker, living near Tintagel, rooted to the area and having an interest in reviving earlier Cornish culture, was appropriate to assume the task of rewriting the story for the mid-nineteenth century. Its appreciation was probably found in the English critics and writers of the day, rather than in Cornish society. This is reflected in the praise given to Hawker. Brendon has detailed the comments of Longfellow who said that 'I have read Tennyson's "Holy Grail" and Mr. Hawker's "Quest", and I think the latter poem far superior to the Laureate's', and even Tennyson himself acknowledged, 'Hawker has beat me on my own ground'.[20] But this was not Tennyson's own ground; it was Hawker's. His version of events relies much on the biblical connection of the Holy Grail and the visitation of Joseph of Arimathea to Britain ('Bearing that awful vase, the Sangraal! The vessel of the Pasch'), but this is combined with a powerful new version of a Cornish King Arthur:

> [Arthur] spake – while Tamar sounded to the sea.
> 'Comrades in arms! mates of the table-round!
> Fair Sirs, my fellows in the bannered ring, –
> Ours is a lofty tryst!'[21]

Clearly, this matched perfectly the imperial fervour of a confident greater Britain, which had first begun to be constructed by statesmen a century before, and is also seen in the work of Defoe and other early English travellers. Again, this verse probably did not appeal to the majority in Cornwall, firstly because of its lack of connection to a real Cornwall increasingly concerned with the lasting effects of industrialization, and secondly because the industrial revolution had helped

Cornwall gain an important new identity. In addition, it was becoming increasingly swallowed within England, as economic, political, artistic and cultural forces reinforced dual identity (Hawker once refers to Cornwall as 'old and Celtic England').[22] Hawker's prophecy of Arthur's return may have seemed irrelevant or even dangerously confrontational.

Hawker's poetry was more complex and wide-ranging than simply recalling the glorious days of Arthur, however, yet this complexity has been missed by a number of observers, including Trewin, Thomas, and Redgrove.[23] To explore the politics of Hawker's verse further, we should look at history again. By the early nineteenth century emerging Methodist politics and subtle changes in the Cornish economy inspired many Cornish people to take advantage of opportunities overseas. A steady stream of emigrants left north Cornwall on their way to either South Australia or America – 'the next parish after Land's End' – as seen in 'The Cornish Emigrant's Song', where Hawker perhaps describes the naïvety of those hoping for a better life:

> And I will be the preacher,
>   And preach three times a day
> To every living creature
>   In North Americay.[24]

Thus the charge that Hawker's verse recalls only the glory days of Cornwall's past is untrue, for he ably describes one aspect of the reality of living in Cornwall in the early to mid-nineteenth century; perhaps here to make people think twice about the decision they were making.

Hawker's direct experience was with the agricultural poor, but the danger of the sea was another area of Cornish experience which impinged strongly on the subject-matter and concerns of his verse. It is often forgotten that whilst Cornwall was undergoing industrial development, large numbers of the community were employed in the fishing and marine industry. It was the experiences and dangers of nineteenth-century fishermen and mariners that Hawker voices, yet it is the poems of shipwrecks which carry most emotion. Hawker gave Christian burials to sailors who had been shipwrecked along the fearsome north coast; among those were the sailors of the Scottish brig *Caledonia*. The incident is re-interpreted in one of Hawker's most celebrated poems, 'The Figurehead of the *Caledonia* at Her Captain's Grave':

> We laid them in their lowly rest,
>   The strangers of a distant shore;

We smoothed the green turf on their breast,
   'mid baffled Ocean's angry roar;
And there, the relique of the storm,
We fixed fair Scotland's figured form.[25]

In addition to the poems of loss at sea, in Hawker we first see a completed manifestation of pastoral and landscape poetry about Cornwall, a trend that had started with some of the finer poems of Carew and Godolphin, but had never really found maturity in either Cornish or Anglo-Cornish writing until Hawker. The balladeers had considered the Cornish landscape, but it was never seen as striking or significant on its own; rather it had to be matched with an event or incident. Hawker is perhaps not the first Cornish poet to realize the significance and power of the Cornish landscape proper – that was Davy's role – but he is the first to write it, in a crafted, poetic way; in doing so, setting in motion a type of writing which was to continue to the present day. Unlike Harris, who was finding a Cornish Eden being re-invented with machinery and industry, Hawker was able to see a gentler, perhaps older Cornwall, and was again among the first to capture the synthesis in Cornwall between the Cornish people and their environment, the importance of that environment and the creator of that environment. This theme of the power – or, in Denys Val Baker's words – the 'timelessness' of the Cornish landscape re-emerges in a number of Hawker's poems, such as 'The Western Shore'.[26] A similar patriotic Cornish energy is found in 'The Tamar Spring'; Athelstan's divider still denoting difference for Hawker, or as he calls Cornwall in his prose writing, 'Tamar-land'.[27]

In their day, Hawker's poems would probably never have been considered particularly patriotic for the Cornish. Indeed, a patriotic or nationalist conception of Cornwall was not a construction which participants, activists or observers could easily apply to Cornish culture in the nineteenth century. This was ironical, since Cornwall was at the height of its industrial power, but its further assimilation into England, and the twin forces of Methodism and Liberalism, were to have a much larger effect on the shaping of Cornish spirit and identity during this period than any other movement, let alone the poetry of Hawker. However, in retrospect, we may see Hawker as an extremely important writer in shaping identity in Cornwall. Further evidence of this is found in his prose writings, as in his version of the life of Thomasine Bonaventure:

She comes of the burly Cornish kind, and they be ever rebels in blood and bone. Even now they be one and all for that knave Warbeck, who is among them in the West.[28]

And like this, his poetry was not of a kind which just glanced retrospectively at Cornish rebellions and residual elements of Cornish difference, the great age of Arthurian legend or the Cornish during the Civil War; and nothing patriotic would be stirred by them. Hawker aimed and claimed, in his reaction to the utilitarianism of his age, to present to the Cornish their collective past, which would allow them to understand their present and determine their future. In addition, he was no Celtic dreamer; despite his eventual conversion to Catholicism and apparent love of mystery, he was entirely in touch with the reality of life in rural Cornwall in the early to mid-nineteenth century. Hawker is thus a writer who does not fit the continuum of Cornish literature established in the latter years of the eighteenth century and continuing for much of the nineteenth. He was no less an important writer for it; in many ways fitting into the pattern of revivalism versus progression which had been established in Cornish and Anglo-Cornish literature as far back as the medieval period, the Renaissance and the seventeenth century. He was also, like John Harris, a precursor of a number of later important developments which he could not have foreseen.

John Harris is the Cornish poet who most typifies Cornish experience in the nineteenth century, and manages to capture that age in his verse. Harris had a completely different upbringing and education from Hawker, which resulted in another developmental phase of Anglo-Cornish poetry. Harris is generally viewed by observers such as Val Baker and Thomas as the most important poet of industrial Cornwall, and as a committed Methodist writer; thus earning him his reputation as the 'Mining-Methodist' poet of Cornwall.[29] But just as reading Hawker only as an Anglo-Catholic revivalist is too simple, the same must be said of Harris's over-emphasized Methodism and his depiction of industrial Cornwall, for both Cornishmen have elements of residual and emergent culture in their work, and neither can be adequately discussed by such sweeping assumptions. Their work must be seen in the light of the massive transforming effect of the nineteenth century upon Cornish experience.

Harris may seem less explicitly 'identity-conscious' in his verse than Hawker, but in terms of identity-formation, he has become increasingly important, in paralleling industrial romanticization in the twentieth century, and in particular mining as a symbol of Cornish identity and ethnicity. Aside from the usual concerns of Methodism, such as intemperance and war, Harris rarely criticizes any part of Cornish culture. Thus an initial polarity does emerge, since Hawker was explicit in his dislike of reformed Protestantism and what he considered to be the damaging effects of industrialization.

Following the pioneering work of D.M. Thomas, Charles Thomas, and Paul Newman, Harris has rightly been promoted from virtual obscurity into a major figure in Anglo-Cornish literature.[30] Most writers have described Harris' talent as somehow transcending the squalor of his early life, and the claim that in some way he was a poetic genius flourishing in, and somehow 'defeating', an industrial landscape. Yet this is a very limited view of Harris. He clearly fits our model of continuity in nineteenth-century Anglo-Cornish literature, as his work develops the poetic themes and concerns of the balladeers, containing within it the residual elements of sentimentality and piety in the face of larger adversity. In addition, however, Harris was part of a wider trend in British poetry, whereby indigenous poets of the age were reflecting upon their landscapes and writing verse extolling the virtues of their particular nation or region. In Cornwall, Harris was certainly not the only working-class poet struggling towards self-definition in this way; it is perhaps better and more accurate to see him as the figurehead of a large-scale and unprecedented, complex poetic movement in the Cornwall of this period. Harris' work seems increasingly to be viewed as the poetic triumph of industrialization in Cornwall, but there may be other equally valid readings of his work, as shown in the research of Symons, who asserts Harris' awareness of more explicitly Celtic, or rather 'non-English', structures and subject-matter.[31] Thus, to see only Hawker as the revivalist is a mistake; Harris certainly incorporates such elements into his verse.

Admirable biographies of Harris have been produced by Thomas, and Newman. According to Newman, Harris's life was the classic struggle against the harshest possible circumstances.[32] Born in 1820 on Bolenowe Carn, near Camborne, at the age of twelve Harris was sent to work down Dolcoath Mine. Married in the 1840s, he and his wife Jane Rule had four children. The death of his daughter Lucretia at Christmas 1855, was the subject of one of the most moving elegies written in the nineteenth century – 'On the Death of my Daughter Lucretia':

> And art thou gone so soon?
> And is thy loving gentle spirit fled?
> Ah! is my fair, my passing beautiful,
> My loved Lucretia numbered with the dead?
> Ah! art thou gone so soon?[33]

The second half of Harris' life was spent outside the mines as a Bible reader and comforter in Falmouth. He remained there until his death in 1884. Although Newman's excellent biographical work has provided the most comprehensive study of Harris's life, the poetry is not given enough of a Cornish context; therefore on occasions, Newman portrays the poet very much as an obscure yet interesting figure; still a sort of Cornish footnote in the greater picture of English literature. Such a reading fails to consider Harris' role in the continuum of specifically Anglo-Cornish literature. The exploration here should lead us to a more thorough understanding of the rest of the poetic movement of Cornwall in this period, culminating, under the editorship of W. Herbert Thomas, in the 1892 collection, *Poems of Cornwall by Thirty Cornish Authors*, and in other prose and fiction of the period.[34]

I have in this work argued for a close association between the generation of literature and the development of industry, and the specific case of how Cornwall's social, economic and political development has been consistently related to mining. That correlation must come ever closer in our reading of Harris, but it is not specifically the struggle of the young Harris in the depths of Dolcoath that needs re-emphasizing. Harris' poetry must be read in the context of the greater developments of mining, Methodism and Liberal politics which occurred in Cornwall during the eighteenth and nineteenth centuries. As Pollard and Payton have shown, these factors contributed to the continuation of Cornish cultural differentiation from the rest of Britain during this period.[35]

It is seldom acknowledged that Harris was the first British poet to thoroughly engage with the process of industrialization. In this context we may begin to re-evaluate Harris's work, as not only that of the poor, frightened boy working, as Newman writes, in a 'pitch-black hole full of dark and sweating shapes, smoke, explosions, curses and clanging machinery',[36] but as the first poet to begin to express and comment on the age of industrial progress. Once we depart from a somewhat hackneyed vision of Harris, we may begin to undertake a new, more important reading of his work.

Dolcoath shaft, where Harris worked with his father, was estimated to have some 75 miles of interconnecting passages. The activities of the industry within Dolcoath were to provide a fascinating environment, in which his Methodism and experience of underground mining could be synthesized together into a poetic, which was both fearsome, yet at the same moment enquiring – as in this section from one of Harris's most celebrated poems, 'Christian Heroism':

> Hast ever seen a mine? Hast ever been
> Down in its fabled grottoes, walled with gems,
> And canopied with torrid mineral belts,
> That blaze within the fiery orifice?[37]

113

13. John Harris, portrait photograph from Harris's *Wayside Pictures, Hymns and Poems*, London, 1874.

14.   Revd. Robert Stephen Hawker (1804–1875), portrait photograph by Thorn
of Bude, June, 1870.

The language of this poem expresses the fear and constant concerns of the mineral extractors. The downward push of the poem into the earth emphasizes the depth and heat of the mine, compared to a near image of hell, but also as a kind of new 'Eden', partly held naturally underground, and partly man-made. According to Newman, the poem was inspired by a real incident, about a miner who saved his colleague from death.[38] Unfortunately, such accidents were commonplace in the mines. Harris' poems are significant here because of their engagement with modern Cornwall; they deal not with Arthurian legend, saints, or the Civil War but with the effects of industrialization on individuals ('Gasping within its burning sulphur cloud,/Straining mine eyes along its ragged walls'); they gave concrete observation of Cornishmen's experiences underground ('The eternal echo of its emptiness') and have well-handled technical data ('Shrieking the well-known signal. He above/Strove but in vain, to put the windlass round').[39] In the verse of Harris we see a powerful identity-shaping process, with the Cornish at the height of their modern powers and prowess. Progress is a constant theme of Harris' verse. Sometimes, it is the new view of the earth revealed to him in the process of mining:

> Copper has colours different in the ores,
> As various as the rainbow — black and blue
> And green and red and yellow as a flower. . .
> Tin is more secret far, with duller eye
>   Oft hiding in the river's shingly bed. . .[40]

However, Harris also predicts Cornwall's industrial collapse ('Man's noblest works will fall,').[41] Images of change and alteration are frequent in all of Harris's verse. Even the titles themselves are explicit about the forces operating upon Cornish society. In one of his earliest volumes – *Lays from the Mine, the Moor and the Mountain* (1853) – we read poems titled 'The Strange Distribution of Worldly Wealth', 'The Parting Scene' and 'The Fall of the Old House', all showing in some way how the older order of Cornwall, if not actively crumbling, was being left behind.[42] Harris copes with hardship and both physical and spiritual change in a number of ways. The first was through Methodism. As Payton has observed:

> Offering practical help and moral support in this world, and anticipating the glories of that to come. . . [Methodism] encouraged a faith which equipped the individual to face the danger of a mine.[43]

Harris also resorted to memories of childhood and perceptions of childhood innocence. Here in 'Camborne' he displays an impressive

116

sense of place, people and time by focussing on the details of a shop window:

> [I gazed] at thy toy-shop windows, – gazed and gazed,
> Until I thought the little horses moved,
> And snapped their bitless bridles! then again
> Rubb'd both mine eyes to see the gingerbread,
> Like gilded soldiers marching on the stall,
> With lions, tigers, bears, and elephants. . .[44]

Although he also examines the landscapes of Land's End and Kynance Cove,[45] the key sense of place in Harris's poetry is provided by Carn Brea and his response to this landscape's particular history and mythical past offers us a more complex insight into Harris' poetic influences and concerns, and indeed the way he expresses Cornish experience at this historical moment. To Harris, Carn Brea was a mountain of history and romance. Harris was familiar with the writings of William Borlase, who had recorded its numerous prehistoric relics in 1754.[46] Borlase was a distinguished cleric who had studied the writings of William Stukeley concerning druids and stone monuments.[47] As Michell has shown, Stukeley was an imaginative antiquarian who, after surveying Stonehenge and Avebury, had declared them to be druidic temples.[48] This interpretation inspired many poets who desired to incorporate such concepts into their verse.

According to Piggott, and Matthews, there was also a distinctive revival of interest in druidry in the late eighteenth and nineteenth centuries; a time in which a number of books and treatises emerged which all claimed to have penetrated and understood the secrets of druidic culture, matching a philosophical quest in Britain to find an indigenous British mystical tradition.[49] Work by Edward Jones (1752–1824) and Iolo Morgannwg (1747–1826) began to spearhead a spiritual Celtic Revival and promoted a belief in the inherent spiritual power of the landscape.[50] Harris actively interprets these theories not, as Newman claims, in 'distant wizardry and mysticism',[51] but within the nineteenth-century Cornish context:

> How the great mountain like a rocky king
> Stands silent in the tempest. . .
> Carved by the Druid in the olden time,
> When men were wont to worship on his crest.[52]

In addition, in 1868 Harris developed his interest in this theme further when he wrote *Luda – A Lay of the Druids*, a post-Roman Britain epic, featuring a palmer, a Danish chieftain and an attractive Celtic maiden of Cornwall.[53] Harris offered the view that Christianity helped to reform ancient Pagan practices, a theme exemplified in the following sequence; a synthesis of Harris's knowledge of druidry, British ethnicity, and his belief in the power of Christianity:

> I gain'd the hill-top, saw its boulders bare
> Some worn by time, some carved by Druid art,
> Where oft perhaps the painted Briton prayed
> To Thor and Woden, offering human blood,
> When moral darkness filled our blessed isle,[54]

For Harris Carn Brea was a place of retreat; a place where, high above the noise of industry the miner could escape from underground life:

> No hiss of steam, no hammer's bang,
> Or anvil's ring, or bucket's clang. . .
> But solitude and silence lone,
> Sat musing on a seat of stone.[55]

However, it is in such poetry that we come to a more complex reading of Harris, for he was certainly influenced by the poetic and philosophical fashions of the age, far more than most critics have given him credit for. In addition, we can see that his subject-matter moves far beyond that of Dolcoath and its immediate surrounds. Harris is a much more complex poet than we might at first realize, and was interpreting many different levels of Cornish experience within his poetry. D.M. Thomas equates this depiction of experience with what he defines as Harris' 'inner landscape':

> a reconciliation of the social and lyrical impulse, the Augustan and the Romantic. . . He was being strictly accurate when he described himself, time and again, as a bard, with harp or lyre.[56]

In response to Thomas and Newman's biographical work on Harris, in 1995 Andrew Symons offered a different and more radical interpretation of the poet's work. Symons was at pains not to see Harris as 'a nineteenth-century regional poet, seeking to ingratiate himself with the English literary establishment', but as a dynamic exponent of what he terms a 'more ancient Celtic tradition'.[57] Symons argues that the elements of 'eulogy, lament, narrative, religion, morality and nature' so prevalent in Harris' work are specifically related to oral performance rather than a strictly literary tradition. Indeed, if we follow Symons' account, according to Anglo-centric criticism simplicity, sentimentality and melodrama are negative literary qualities, but such devices are essential in performance. Symons argues that this oral, or as he terms it, 'bardic' tradition was a distinctive quality of Methodist preaching, which would have been naturally reflected in

Harris' verse. We have seen in *Monro* that Harris perceived of himself as a 'bard':

> In adverse blasts his muse will trill the more.
> Earthquake and fire may not destroy his song.[58]

To Harris, bardship was where poetry and religion were fused. He considered his poetry to be God-given. Symons develops his argument further by drawing attention to the curious fact that an apparently uneducated Cornish miner could appreciate the work of Shakespeare. Symons argues that actually 'Shakespeare's language and rhythms were more accessible to Harris than [to] the literati' and that

> [t]he Camborne area would have become bilingual during Shakespeare's time, and knowledge of the King James Bible and the Prayer Book would have helped to preserve the language of that period down to and beyond the nineteenth century.[59]

Symons' argument is that Harris' debt to this period revolves around language. Harris' fusion of the literary and oral traditions matched Methodism's most dynamic phase from 1833 to the 1850s.

As the price of minerals collapsed and the exodus of the 1870s began, Harris' work responded by becoming, as Newman perceptively notes, increasingly 'negative, censorious and escapist'.[60] Harris' last work dates from 1884, and it was the opinion of A.K. Hamilton Jenkin, in *The Story of Cornwall* (1934), that 'by 1890 the glory of the industrial age had departed'.[61] By the 1870s at least Cornwall was fast becoming one of the first post-industrial regions of Britain. Although we should not underestimate Harris' position as a spokesman of working-class, industrial Cornwall, like R.S. Hawker, it is a mistake to see Harris as representing only one strand in Anglo-Cornish literature. We gain the best poetic depiction of nineteenth-century Cornwall by reading both, and observing their differences and similarities. Each, in his own way, has developed the work of the balladeers and has looked back to an earlier Cornwall. Both appreciate the Cornwall of the past, a Cornwall they themselves never knew. Hawker views Methodism and industrial Cornwall with scepticism and resignation; whilst Harris acknowledges and accepts spiritual and economic progress. These ideological conflicts, which we have established as being set up as far back in literary history as the difference between the writings of Roscarrock and Carew, are continued elsewhere in the nineteenth century. This polarity within poetry in Cornwall is later exemplified and developed by the work of a number of other writers.

A large number of poetic texts were produced in Cornwall in the nineteenth century, and sadly there is not the space here to consider them all. As literacy standards improved, a series of highly popular texts emerged from the middle of the nineteenth century onwards. They were really a development of earlier Cornish Almanacs and were marketed as 'Books in the Cornish Dialect'. These texts were written by a range of authors, yet they all displayed similar construction, subject-matter and style. Often, the volumes combined the short story with a selection of verse, depicting working-class Cornish people 'making good'. This genre more fully established the continuum of Cornu-English writing. A series of titles emerged, mainly published by Netherton and Worth of Truro. Included in this series were such titles as *Timothy Towser and Nineteen other Tales*, *A Cornish Love Story and Nine Other Tales*, *Dan Daddow's Cornish Comicalities*, *Zacharias Trenoodle and Alice Ann at the Fisheries* and *Billy the Goat and the Pepper Mine and Seven Other Tales*. These were all reprinted several times.

The leading writer of this genre was John Tabois Tregellas (1792–1863). As his publishers note, Tregellas possessed 'a singular faculty of representing with the most minute accuracy, those subtle distinctions of intonation and phraseology which are noticeable in Cornwall, even as between adjoining parishes',[62] but the emphasis on language alone provides only a limited reading of Tregellas's work; for within his prose and poetry, we have a fine record of the ideology of working-class people of Cornwall. The finest representative example of his work is the collection entitled *Cornish Tales*; the contents page itself gives a catalogue of the issues affecting Cornish society in the middle of the nineteenth century. Everything seems to be included; from mining to emigration, fishing to the organization of the Cornish economy from London:

> Tremuan – The St Agnes Bear Hunt – The Perran Cherrybeam
> – The Squire's Tame Conger – Hacky and Marky – California
> – Josee Cock – The Wounded Miner – Rozzy Paul and Zacky
> Martin – The London Director's Report – The Sea of Fire.[63]

In short, such volumes hold a high degree of interest, since they portray, like Harris and Hawker, the transformation of old Cornwall. Like *Cornish Tales*, most of the volumes also contained a glossary, suggesting that the texts had a wider circulation beyond Cornwall – fitting into the knowledge that the earlier balladeers had been very successful in England, though perhaps also indicating that already people were noticing that some usages were dying and that there was a need to preserve older language before it was lost.

Tregellas retains throughout his verse a notion of Cornish Celticity, even though the predominant tendency by now was to think of Cornwall as a somewhat strange and unusual part of England. He

120

notes the 'rash Celtic phase of the Cornish miner's character' and says that 'the Saxon element will not be found, even here'.[64] To assert this distinctive identity and claim of non-Englishness, Tregellas takes the reader through a series of humorous poetic episodes, which allow him to use dialect as a delineating device. Tregellas' power as a performance poet is exemplified in the story of Rozzy Paul and Zacky Martin, whose shared aim is to become Members of Parliament. The reader follows their journey to London to meet with Sir Walter Starling. In a sense, the writing is a nineteenth-century version of Andrew Boorde's observations on Cornishmen 'abroad' in England, but here, despite their own intellectual limitations, they end up the winners:

> "Es et a ticket – who can tell!
> Let's knaw the hes wuth – we may as well;
> But thee not I caant read nor spell,
> And ef we az this Lunnon crew
> They'll loff, and loff, that's all they'll do;
> And then again they are so wicket,
> They'd raather stail, than raid the ticket."
> So both agreed (to make it clear)
> They'd to an Inn and get some beer,
> And from *their ticket* pay their cheer.[65]

The same confidence is given to the Cornish characters of another representative example of the genre, *The Exhibition and Fourteen other celebrated Tales* (c.1851) by W.B. Forfar and others.[66] Forfar uses Cousin Jan as his central character in the narrative poems of this collection, having him meeting travellers, falling in love and finding 'keenly lodes' of tin,[67] though Forfar is, at times, more progressive in his verse forms and structure than Tregellas. Such an expression of Cornish experience is developed further in his verse dialogues, between the likes of 'Gracey Penrose and Mally Treviskey' over men's drunkenness. There is not the temperance address of Harris here; instead comes advice and practical measures for dealing with the problem:

> Never mind it Un Gracey, – cheeld, put un to bed;
> He'll slaip oal the liquor away from his head.[68]

Sadly there is little information about the readership of such authors, but it seems likely that the poetry of Forfar and Tregellas was important in shaping popular imagination in Cornwall, and though lacking the descriptive power, or indeed the historical awareness, of Harris and Hawker, it was nonetheless an important literary phenomenon of the middle years of the nineteenth century, with parallels both before and after.

Whilst this form of poetry continued to be written well into the early years of the twentieth century – with very similar subject matter and form – other, more serious poets, were beginning to recognize, in the wake of Harris, the emergence during the end of the nineteenth century of an indigenous Anglo-Cornish poetry. This group looked towards Harris as their immediate mentor and inspiration for the way to write about modern Cornwall. This phase of writing occurred in the final third of the nineteenth century, beginning at around the same time as the split in Methodism, the collapse of the mineral economy and the increase of emigration from Cornwall. That said, as the populist interpretation came to be published in the work of Tregellas and Forfar, these poets actively tried to offer what was, in their view at least, a more 'genuine' and 'well-written' vision of Cornwall. Thus in 1892, the journalist W. Herbert Thomas compiled an important anthology of thirty Cornish authors titled *Poems of Cornwall*, which is the finest example of a collection of late nineteenth-century Anglo-Cornish verse.

Thomas sees the work as an attempt to 'issue a representative volume of Cornish poetry', which would have a 'wide circulation. . . among Cornish people home and abroad'.[69] There is certainly a sense running through the collection that it was intended to be purchased amongst those emigrants who wanted a 'spiritual' and lasting poetic reminder of their homeland, in case they did not return. Thomas couches this introduction in two illuminating phrases; Cornwall is described as the 'rocky land of strangers'; presumably a near-literal translation of Cornwall's name, but a re-assertion, as well, of Celticity and identity. This is followed by the more anglified inventionist concept of 'the life of the mining, seafaring, and other dwellers in "West Barbary"';[70] thus to English and Cornish readers Cornwall was still being promoted and interpreted as primitive, ungodly and barbaric, despite the supposed reforming activities of Methodism. These divergent views are reflected in much of the volume, opening up more explicitly the debate over colonialism and nationalism once more.

The collection begins with Thomas's own poem 'All Hail! Old Cornwall!', which works as a prelude to the rest of the anthology. Thomas was the son of a Cornish mine-smith at St Day, but he had also worked in San Francisco, so had seen Cornwall from within and outside of it. The poem is a very confident vision of Cornwall in the later years of the nineteenth century, celebrating both past and present achievement. Ancient Cornwall is glorified and given biblical allusion, whilst at the same time the colonial impact of England is subtly reiterated:

O Cornwall! On the scroll of history
    Thy name is writ in ancient characters,
Until we reach the veil of mystery,
    Where truth is hid, and speculation errs.
Aggressive nations cross'd the watery main
    To claim thy min'ral treasure for their prize;
And bloody battle-fields, and warriors slain,
    Awoke exultant shouts and heart-wrung cries.[71]

Unfortunately, the worst ravages of an intensely Methodist vision are also given in the verse of the Bodmin poet, Henry Sewell Stokes, and the Perranzabuloe poet, J.G. Ashworth. Higher quality material is offered by William Cock of Tuckingmill, whose poem 'To Cornubia' – dedicated to James Dryden Hosken (considered in Chapter Four) – appears as near-rousing an anthem as Hawker's 'The Song of the Western Men', offering a patriotic call:

Awake! O Cornubia! rouse thy slumb'rous frame!
    Tell Albion's sons thou has a mighty bard!
Make thou a way for his melodious strain,
    Whose song-wrapt soul the mystic muse doth guard.[72]

Whilst in Cornwall such volumes were finding publication and a popular readership, elsewhere in Britain and in the rest of the world, a number of plays were written which had a resolutely Cornish flavour about them. In part, this was the response of the populist dramatic community of nineteenth-century England to depict Cornwall as a place of adventure and myth, and also because Cornwall was seen as perfect for the construction of melodrama. Melodrama is sensational and romantic and as the process of romanticization of Cornwall developed, so did the English plays about Cornwall and the Cornish. In his *Collectanea Cornubiensia* George Clement Boase provides brief sketches of the drama of the nineteenth century.[73] Among the first plays of the era, he notes, are H. Pomeroy Gilbert's *The Cornish Brothers, or the Bride of Lisbon* (1872), G.W. Geoffry's *Queen Mab* (1874) and William Schwenck Gilbert and Arthur Sullivan's comic opera *The Pirates of Penzance, or Love and Duty* (1879), which opened in Paignton and New York on the same night.

It was, however, the 1880s that saw the pinnacle of popular English drama about Cornwall. Ironically, though this was the decade in which there was by now an acute depression in the tin and copper industries and emigration was taken to be a fact of life in Cornwall, English romanticization and interest in Cornwall's mining, culture and the ideology of smuggling, generated a considerable number of texts.

All of these texts helped to shape the nineteenth-century English response to Cornwall for that generation. Typical dramas of the early part of the decade were *Over the Cliff* (1884) by Alfred Farthing Robbins and *The Wreckers or Martial Law* (1884) by R. Dodson. The full-blown melodramas, however, emerged in the second-half of the decade, in part inspired by the huge success of *The Pirates of Penzance*. *Our Joan* (1885) by Herman Merivale and Cecil Dale was first produced by Rose Coghlan in the United States of America. In this play, Jane Trevenna is the daughter of a lighthouse keeper and the belle of a Cornish village. This decade also saw productions of *Ruddigore or The Witch's Curse*, written by Gilbert and Sullivan, which has its first scene as the village of Rederring in Cornwall, and Walter Parke and William Hogarth's comic opera *Gipsy Gabriel*, the whole of which is set in Cornwall. The year 1888 was the height of this form of dramatic production with three plays emerging: J. Carne Ross's *Forgery*, which was performed in London and Penzance that year, Frank Maryat's *Golden Goblin* – a story of wrecking – and T. Edgar Pemberton and W.H. Vernon's *The Loadstone*; the heroine is named Kate Trevenna and the whole play set in Cornwall. No matter how badly performed, such dramas were very important in imparting to audiences, in and outside of Cornwall, an awareness of their culture and identity, however misrepresented or melodramatically presented. However, the fact that these plays existed and that Cornish subject-matter was prevalent in the theatre of the age proves the influence and place of the Cornish as the 'industrial Celt' at the end of the nineteenth century.

The first half of this chapter has thus answered in some detail the question of how Cornwall was written about by poets and dramatists of the late eighteenth and nineteenth centuries. The picture is a complex one, containing divergent and convergent trends; the writers using industrial confidence and progress, Methodism, then later using emigration and the changing nature of Cornish identity as the main themes of their work. The poets, in particular, sang fully in nineteenth-century Cornwall and articulated sometimes complementary, sometimes conflicting images of Cornishness in their verse. However, elsewhere it was not poetry that illuminated Cornish experience, but the development of writing in prose.

Anglo-Cornish prose writing would be impoverished without the work of two writers of the mid- to late nineteenth century. They were not authors in the narrow sense, since Robert Hunt and William Bottrell worked rather as folklore collectors, recording, studying and rewriting the oral narratives of Cornwall; paradoxically at the zenith of its industrial progress. The oral narratives which Hunt and Bottrell collected had defined and affirmed Cornish identity for centuries – providing narrative continuity in an oral form for generations of Cornish people. The collections of folktales of Bottrell and Hunt are representative of a particular period of their re-telling and evolution; yet ironically their collation and 'written definition' encased the story by preserving it, rather than allowing the oral culture to continue to reshape it. Had Bottrell and Hunt not completed their task however, these stories might have been forever lost, and whilst now one particular version of the tale dominates, individuals and groups have been able to re-read and re-tell (if in a less 'genuine' oral way) the literary versions of these key Cornish stories.

The narratives within Hunt's *Popular Romances of the West of England* or *The Drolls, Traditions and Superstitions of Old Cornwall* (1865) and Bottrell's *Traditions and Hearthside Stories of West Cornwall* (1870, 1873 and 1880),[74] are therefore, extraordinary mythic representations of Cornish difference. Following readings of Hunt and Bottrell, first Deane and Shaw, and later Philip, have grouped the Cornish narratives according to Antti Aarne and Stith Thompson's *The Types of the Folktale* (1961) in an index of tale types, and using Thompson's *Motif-Index of Folk Literature* (1966), according to motif.[75] Whilst useful in allowing us to understand continuity and variation across the 'historic-geographic' spectrum of oral narratives recorded by Bottrell and Hunt, this method does little to help us understand their precise construction of say, Cornwall, Cornishness or Celticity. The tales do, however, clearly offer us a thorough record of past thematic continuities within Cornish writing, and via their recording became a source for those texts produced around the same period, and those which were to follow. Thus, the volumes of Hunt and Bottrell have become a central repository of texts, a kind of 'literary reservoir' of Cornish narrative and culture; touchstones for other retellings.

The collections of Hunt and Bottrell emerged as the academic discipline of Folklore was taking shape. Much of the impetus of the early folklore collectors was preservationist in intent, conducted with the belief that modernization was eliminating older 'traditional' prac- tices. At the same time, travel throughout the more peripheral regions of the British Isles became easier and quicker. This caused a change in enquiry to some extent; rather than resort to past textual evidence and other written sources, folklorists could now collect from real, live, informants. Celtic regions were seen as being ripe for enquiry by the early ethnographers. They were more 'backward' and so would thus yield a more 'genuine' crop of narratives. The backwardness was also read in 'racial' terms as well; that the descendants of the Celts were to be found in the more primitive racial groups existing within the British

15. 'The Giant Bolster', from frontispiece of Robert Hunt's *Popular Romances of the West of England*, London, 1865.

126

Isles. Research into the Celtic regions fell into two distinct groups: that completed by English scholars, and that completed by Celtic scholars. The political climate of the nineteenth century meant that the two groups had rather different research objectives. Celtic scholarship tended to be guided by emergent nationalist or proto-nationalist objectives of both preservation and revival; whilst English scholarship was conducted broadly in line with the popular estimations of Matthew Arnold, often credited with kickstarting 'English' interest in the Celtic renaissance, viewing the Celts as valuable and inspirational assets to Britain, but too passionate and troublesome to conduct their own affairs.[76]

Folkloric activity in Cornwall during this period has generally followed the pattern of this ideological split. However, this division had actually had a number of parallels already seen in Cornish literary culture. Roscarrock had worked as a hagiographical folklorist with a Catholic-Celtic agenda, whilst Carew, though recording Cornish folk-lore, saw future allegiance as being with England. Similarly, at the turn of the eighteenth century, Cornish scholars such as Keigwin, Boson and Tonkin, and Celtic scholars like Lhuyd actively sought to preserve, yet also to revive, Cornish language and literature. At the same time, other literary travellers recorded what they observed and what they were told. Thus the cycle of preservation and revival, paradoxically juxtaposed with external agendas of accommodation and allegiance to England, have long been a part of Cornish literary and cultural continuity.

Collectors, however, were not only operative in Cornwall during the middle of the nineteenth century. In the 1860s in Brittany, F.M. Luzel collected folktales from Armorica; in Scotland, Campbell of Islay completed a massive study of Gaelic culture as early as 1847, and Douglas Hyde completed his volume, *Beside the Fire: A Collection of Irish Gaelic Folk Stories* in 1890.[77] Collecting in Cornwall occurred com-paratively early; though in general this is not recognized. As evidence of the early impact of collection, the Rev. H.J. Whitfeld studied the Scilly Isles in 1852, 'a part of the kingdom which is seldom visited by tourists'.[78]

Hunt's text emerged first, even though he acknowledges a debt to the continuing work of Bottrell. As Pearson has shown, Hunt fits a certain model of literary figure whom we now associate with Cornwall in the industrial revolution, being both a scientist and artist.[79] The results of Hunt's collecting efforts were published in May 1865 and achieved immediate popularity, the two illustrations of the 'Giant Bolster' and 'A Flight of Witches' by George Cruickshank (1792–1878) adding greatly to its prestige. Cruickshank was known to the nineteenth-century public for his association with the writings of Charles Dickens. No doubt Cruickshank's association with the volume was an important indication of its significance as a collection – the publishers even going so far to include a letter from the illustrator explaining why he had drawn the Giant Bolster in such a way.

Hunt himself noted that stories – such as that of Hender the Huntsman of Lanhydrock – he had collected in 1829 had been forgotten. Thus it is evident that he produced his collection just in time to preserve a major part of Cornwall's heritage. Aside from the narratives themselves, which it would be impossible to detail here, the most interesting aspect of Hunt's volume is its introduction. Hunt acknowledges that part of the reason for the narratives disappearing are 'the constantly-repressing influences of Christian teaching' and 'the advances of civilization',[80] which strikingly parallels Scawen's argument two centuries before on the decline of Cornish.[81] Hunt also believes that 'Cornwall has, until a recent period, maintained a somewhat singular isolation'.[82] Perhaps the most important assertion made in Hunt's introduction comes from his notion of what we may term a 'greater Cornwall', reaffirming the limiting effect of Athelstan's original definition of the land of Cornwall and the Cornish people; justifying his choice of title for the entire collection:

> I found that the traditions of Devonshire, as far east as Exeter – the tract of country which was known as 'Danmonium', or even more recently as 'Old Cornwall' – had a striking family resemblance. My collection then received the name it bears, as embracing the district ordinarily known as the West of England.[83]

Hunt thus proves himself to be a unique figure; since though operating more as an English scholar, given his mining background, he had a near-indigenous insight into the place and purpose of the narratives he collected; whilst at the same time defining, at least, in an antiquarian sense, the difference of Cornish narrative.

In opposition, yet towards the same purpose, Bottrell defines himself as 'an old Celt'.[84] Bottrell's researches were more comprehensive than Hunt's, yet he perhaps had less ability than Hunt to make the narratives 'live' in the literary sense. His effort towards publication was also greater, taking some ten years to produce all three volumes. Bottrell's focus is west Cornwall, yet his actual studies encompass a wide area, stretching as far eastwards as Ladock in mid-Cornwall. Bottrell defines the geographic area where the tales are located as 'one of the most secluded and unknown parts of England',[85] though he notes the distinction between narratives of the coast and those found on the agricultural and mining hinterland. Whilst Hunt grouped his stories according to theme, here Bottrell tells them as they relate to a geographical journey westwards; thus, his first volume begins in Portreath, ending near Land's End. By the end of the third series, longer narratives were more difficult to collect, and so he also included relevant, yet perhaps more fragmentary material on 'Midsummer Customs' and 'Cornish words still in use'.[86] Typical of the style of the longer narratives is *Tom and the Knackers*, at once defining identity by its use of dialogue, place and established Cornish folklore of mining spirits – the Knackers – now more commonly known as knockers:

> Tom Trevorrow! Tom Trevorrow!
> Leave some of thy fuggan for Bucca,
> Or bad luck to thee, to-morrow![87]

Having viewed the development of these texts by Whitfeld, Hunt and Bottrell, it is now worth considering further the consequences of their gathering as publications. For one thing, there was a specific period in which this folkloric recording occurred. Paradoxically it was taking place at the same time as the confident industrial march towards progress and alongside the further development of Methodist activity in Cornwall. The stories themselves were proudly recording a world which few expected ever to see again. Simultaneously, another antiquarian, William Copeland Borlase, wrote *Nœnia Cornubiœ*, his 1872 study of the archaeology of Cornwall. By 1880 the last of the major collections had been published, though it was clear that Cornish self-confidence was not quite what it had been some twenty years earlier. The volumes thus assumed a new role in redefining industrial Cornwall's experience in addition to the ancient heritage. M.A. Courtney's *Cornish Feasts and Folklore* published in 1890 and William Copeland Borlase's *The Age of Saints*, offered final nineteenth-century recordings of ancient Cornwall, but it was becoming clear that preservation was not enough.[88] The Cornish having lost cultural confidence once again towards the end of the nineteenth century, new work would have to take a different direction, towards self-determination.

Thus, as well as providing a central repository of Cornish narratives, which could be re-told and used by novelists and poets in the Cornish context, towards the end of the nineteenth century and at the turn of the twentieth century, the collections were to help pioneer a new breed of overtly nationalist Celtic collectors with the emphasis on promoting indigenous culture for the sake of revival rather than preservation. The beginnings of this Celtic revival, working in tandem – and sometimes at odds – with a concept of Cornwall at the English literary margins will be considered more fully in Chapter Four. Yet these collectors were directly to influence other modes of literary production in mid-nineteenth-century Cornwall and it is thus to a new form for Cornish writing – the novel – that we shall next turn, to show how Cornwall was conceived in fiction in the nineteenth century.

This section focuses in cultural terms on a particularly powerful achievement of nineteenth-century narratives about Cornwall: as Ermarth argues in her analysis of the novel in history, its construction of history 'as a social common denominator'. As Ermarth perceptively states, "In' history, all sorts of social problems become susceptible to recuperation, restoration, revision, repair.'[89] Nineteenth-century Anglo-Cornish fiction exemplifies this kind of revisionist mechanism, where past constructions of Cornwall were given a narrative 'make-over' in order to make them acceptable, entertaining and, sometimes, morally correct for the age's readership; a reader that was present both in and outside of Cornwall. The elements of this revisionist approach were varied. Sometimes they were central, as in mining and Methodism; on other occasions they involved activities which were actually on the fringe of earlier Cornish society, but were deemed apt for incorporation into the fiction; for instance the particular themes of smuggling and wrecking. Cornish 'order' – both personal and social – were given exaggeration, alteration and amendment to suit present needs. Thus Cornish history and identity came to be viewed in a certain ideological light by readers; a light which would set the trend of fiction for the next century. To apply Ermarth, Anglo-Cornish novels became 'experimental laboratories for defining and exploring a new construction of corporate order'.[90]

Initially, I shall try to trace the development of the Anglo-Cornish novel in the nineteenth century; its beginnings, influences and achievements. The section then moves from the beginning to the end of the period between 1860 and 1890, in order to locate certain pressure points at which narrative developed new formations, with specific regard to two novels: *Deep Down: A Tale of the Cornish Mines* (1869) by R.M. Ballantyne and *Tin* (1888) by Edward Bosanketh.[91] This section necessarily assumes the definition of Cornish history as a particular kind of formality, not fully explained until the third section, which discusses the conventions so much at the heart of the Anglo-Cornish novel of the nineteenth century that we continue to take the conventions for granted, despite their extraordinary artificiality.

By artificiality, I mean that some of the late nineteenth-century interpretations of Cornwall by mostly visiting writers, and indeed by some indigenous writers, were not necessarily an accurate (in so far as any fiction can be accurate) account of the Cornish experience of both the present, and of the recent past. Thus, in several representative fictions of the period, icons and symbols, historical, spiritual and social changes in Cornwall, were actively manipulated and re-cast, providing a concept of 'Cornwall as a fiction' – a microcosm of space and stereotype – at the same time creating a somewhat false miniature cosmography, paradoxically heightening Cornish awareness of difference. This re-casting process was shaped by two related, yet contradictory processes: firstly, the Cornish themselves demanded affirmation of their myths and history (in no small part shaped by Whitfeld, Hunt and Bottrell), their symbols and substance – smuggling, wrecking, mining, Methodist reform, Jewish/Spanish blood-line – of their achievement and identity at this point in their history. Secondly, visiting writers were writing exactly what the emerging tourists expected the ideology of Cornwall to be. Ironically, this process was happening just after the peak of industrial confidence, with numerous families in Cornwall experiencing the effects of emigration, and whilst Methodism moved into a state of fragmentation.

The late arrival of the novel on the Cornish literary scene tells us something important about the genre and its readership: for the first time, widespread literacy was allowing more individuals to seek enjoyment from the written word. In addition, the novel is, above all else, a form of literature which looks at people in society. Most novels are concerned with ordinary people and their problems in the societies in which they find themselves. In the nineteenth century, the novel became the supremely confident form for the consideration of an increasingly complex world. Seemingly then, one might expect the novel to have developed earlier in Cornwall than elsewhere in Britain, seeing that Cornwall had already become an increasingly complex, industrial society. Indeed, its poets had already began to explore this – its benefits, problems and dislocations – so why did the novel arrive so much later? One reason was that nowhere else in Britain had Methodism gained such respect and belief as in Cornwall; in part, because of the dangerous working conditions a large proportion of the population had to endure. Thus, an essentially religious view of life was maintained a long time into the nineteenth century, whereas other parts of Britain, which had not undergone earlier religious reform, were becoming increasingly dissatisfied. Hence, the novel in Cornwall does not really begin to emerge until the second half of the century, when doubts about the cohesion of Methodism began to be expressed, when there was renewed confidence in tin, and when Cornwall had survived the 'reforming thirties' and the 'hungry forties'.

There are, in terms of continuity, however, some precursors of the form that we may identify, and can here reiterate. The depth and complexity of both biblical and medieval Cornish society and characterization were at least, in part, covered by the Mystery Plays – in essence dramatized narrative for the populace of specific communities. *The Black Letter Pamphlet* may similarly be regarded as one of the earliest fictions of Cornwall. Harry Carter's autobiography of his life as a smuggler, then his later acceptance of Methodism, stands as one of the earliest forms of an education novel. Furthermore, some of the moral short stories offered by John Harris in his poetry collections, and the populist, if clumsy, prose writings of Tregellas and Forfar also show the signs of the emergent novel. In some cases though, the novel was to be a form in which a kind of populist Methodism tried to deny the incoherence of the faith; this phenomenon lasting well into the twentieth century.

Thus, three different literary trends inform the development of the novel and lead to its eventual rise in Cornwall. Firstly, there was the survey or travelogue, begun by Carew, developed by Fiennes, Skinner and Defoe, and retained throughout the eighteenth and nineteenth century, gradually incorporating less topographical description, and more folklore and anecdotal material. In part, this was sustained by the visits and travels of English writers throughout the nineteenth century. Secondly, emergent in the writings of Davy, Quick, Hawker and Harris was the longer narrative poem, but verse, as Harris found mid-way through his career, was swiftly becoming an outmoded form for a detailed construction of industrial experience. Thirdly, despite its accommodation into England, Cornwall had retained its Celticity – or rather reinvented it as befitting its industrial aptitude – and as Whitfeld, Hunt and Bottrell recorded, Cornwall had retained a sense of itself as a site for narrative in its folk-tales. The delineation of these, the experiences of industrial progress and reformed Protestantism, and where these interact and intersect, resulted in a great expansion of literature – in the form of the novel.

This expansion was also initiated by the increasing number of visitors to Cornwall who recorded their travels during the nineteenth century. It would certainly seem that few important figures in the literary world omitted to make at least one pilgrimage to Cornwall, both because of its Arthurian connections and because mining looked an interesting narrative site. This is partially reflected in the work of Baker Peter Smith, whose relatively early *Trip to the Far West* reported upon a 'pedestrious Excursion through various parts of Cornwall' in September 1839.[92] The text both reinforced the perceived peripherality of Cornwall, whilst also examining its difference from England. Other similar texts followed. Wilkie Collins' *Rambles beyond Railways* describes a walking tour Collins and the artist, Henry C. Brandling, made in 1850. Collins then incorporated, to good effect, the cultural geography of west Cornwall that he had observed on this trip for his novels *Basil* (1852) and *The Dead Secret* (1857).[93]

However, a number of other nineteenth-century novelists were aware of the potential of Cornwall. Charles Kingsley's *Westward Ho!* (1855) was written at the English-Cornish border, so, as Chitty has argued, this part of north Cornwall and the heroic Grenvilles of the Civil War – much alluded to in the poetry of Hawker – feature in the novel.[94] His 1857 novel *Two Years Ago* is a probable response to what Rowe and Andrews describe as the 'great epidemic of cholera' spent on the village of Mevagissey in 1849.[95] In Kingsley's novel, Mevagissey is named Aberalva, and the fiction captures much of the intensity of the outbreak.

Elsewhere the fiction considered the industrial landscape and processes. R.M. Ballantyne used Botallack Mine as the model for *Deep Down: A Tale of the Cornish Mines* (1868) while staying at Penzance.[96] *Tin* by Edward Bosanketh is similarly set in the fictional towns of Redbourne (St Just) and Camruth (Penzance), and is a novel of legality, exploring the deception and fraud behind the mining companies. In the same area, James Francis Cobb's *The Watchers on the Longships* (1876) is set a century before and demonstrates the importance of history in fictional constructions of Cornwall.[97] An increasing number of Cornish novels appeared towards the end of the nineteenth century, many with the flavour of the sea; partly produced by the decline of mining and the emigration process, and partly through the increasing construction of Cornwall as a holiday destination. These novels include F. Frankfurt Moore's *Tre, Pol, and Pen* (1887) and Sabine Baring-Gould's *The Gaverocks* (1887) and *In the Roar of the Sea* (1892). Typically these texts combined imagery of the ravaging effects of the ocean patterning human emotions and activities both at sea on and shore. Elizabeth Godfrey's fiction, *Cornish Diamonds* (1895) – one of the superior texts of this genre – is set on the English border, where the dramatic maritime theme is enhanced by a cliff rescue.[98] As we shall see, these texts were, in part, the forerunners of the historical romances of Cornwall of the twentieth century, the populist fictional construction of Cornwall at the turn of the century, and perhaps, some of the final serious attempts to assert Methodist values within a fictional format.

Our attention now focuses upon two constructions of Cornwall which emerge from distinctive pressure-points in Cornish history, developing for the first time a complete fiction of the mining industry in Cornwall. *Deep Down: A Tale of the Cornish Mines* (1868) is perhaps a specific moment in Cornwall's history, where instead of constructing a journal of his experiences while travelling in Cornwall, the author decided to use these experiences to form the basis of a fiction. Twenty

years before, the best writing about Cornwall could be found in the
Reverend C.A. John's *A Week at the Lizard* (1848),[99] a record of that
area's landscape, nature and community; the 'notes in Cornwall taken
a-foot' then succeeded by the 'quasi-novel' account found in Wilkie
Collins's *Rambles beyond Railways*. In this way alone, *Deep Down* is a
pioneering and very important work in Anglo-Cornish literature's
development, but it was also the first novel to explore both an earlier
historical moment and the real impact of industrialization in the
Cornish context. Ballantyne's novel emerges just after a period when
there was a marked decline in the output of Cornish copper. Tin
prices also fell through the mid-1870s. In the popular imagination,
however – whether in Cornwall, or elsewhere in Britain – mining
remained central to Cornish identity, and no sooner had the mines
started to close, than they were already subject to an understandable
process of romanticization. Despite the decline, the mines of Cornwall
were world-famous; another reason for the novel's emergence.

Deep Down acts as the forerunner for a great deal of fiction about
Cornwall which was to follow in its wake. In his preface, Ballantyne
shows the difference between this and the earlier accounts of the
mines by insisting that this 'is not a record of facts, but a story founded
on facts'.[100] His device for completing this is the fictionalized account
of a mine doctor, named Oliver Trembath, who returns from his
studies to work at Botallack. Into this narrative, Ballantyne manages to
incorporate the emergent typical 'Cornish' subject-matter of smuggling and wrecking, but in doing so, succeeds in convincing the reader
of the reality and importance of these activities in west Cornwall, not
in the middle of the nineteenth century, but at the turn of the
eighteenth. The story is set at the pinnacle of Cornwall's industrial
prowess in the early nineteenth century, yet the narrator magically
transports us to the present, where we learn of 'the Prince and
Princess of Wales descending this deep burrow under the sea in the
year 1865'.[101] The prowess is mainly achieved via Ballantyne's
fascination with Botallack mine itself, and how extraordinary a work
of engineering it is. It is 'grand in the extreme', holding 'engines with
all their fantastic machinery' and 'wheels and chains, fastened and
perched in fantastic forms in dangerous-looking places'.[102] The text is
crammed with technical data, though this is not obtrusive; rather, it
shows how Ballantyne convinces us that if people can go this 'deep'
under the ocean to mine for metals, then there is no stopping them.
The idea of immense depth is foregrounded throughout, from:

> Thus down, down, he goes, sinking his shaft and driving his levels
> on – that is, always following – the lode *ad infinitum*.[103]

As in Harris, the harsh conditions are not criticized; only described. Ballantyne explains how 'sturdy urchins. . .' were 'proud as peacocks' to be accompanying their father down the mine at an early age and details their 'bosoms swelling with that stern Cornish spirit of determination to face and overcome great difficulties'.[104] Ballantyne's novel is perhaps best seen in this context; of the Cornish being supremely confident in their identity and place in the scheme of things ('As far as I have seen, there does not appear to be a more free, hearty and independent race under the sun than Cornish miners'[105] and 'To work went Maggot and Trevarrow and Zackey on their new pitch like true Britons').[106] Yet, though this is asserted, Ballantyne also manages to give a sense of transition. Trembath provides fictional comment on touring artists (like the painter – Henry C. Brandling – who accompanied Wilkie Collins), when the hero notes 'What a splendid country for a painter of cliffs!' and how he cannot yet see why 'all the world has not fallen violently in love with furze-clad moorland and rugged sea-cliffs', but his very acknowledgement of the process shows how convenient travel had become and how near was tourism's obsession with Cornwall; Ballantyne records this moment of change.[107]

A further example of Ballantyne's acute awareness of the culture he was depicting is the invention of the traveller George Augustus Clearemout, who offers the opinion that 'the mines of Cornwall have ever been a subject of deep interest to me, and the miners I regard as a race of men singularly endued with courage and perseverance'.[108] Clearemout's intentions appear reasonable, but Ballantyne's creation of this London traveller show a wider Cornish mistrust of interference from those outside Cornwall over the running of the mines, and the profits to be made from them. It is Clearemout who lies about his original intentions and organizes a bogus share opportunity, which almost results in the closing of Botallack.

The issues of shares, fraud and mining companies comes more to the forefront of a later fiction of the mining industry. *Tin* by Edward Bosanketh (Richard Edward Boyns) emerges some twenty years after *Deep Down* and is the finest example of an indigenous Cornish novel of the nineteenth century; all the more significant for the scandal which surrounded its production and reception at the time. As Justin Brooke outlines:

> When 'Tin' appeared in May 1888 it caused a sensation. In contrast to the single paragraph it usually gave to new publications, the Mining Journal devoted two pages to extracts, for the book, although described as a novel, was all about real people in mining and banking whom the Cornish reader and people in the mining industry could recognize without difficulty.[109]

In short, *Tin* was a dangerous text because, unlike *Deep Down*, it cut too close to the bone – specifically the financial proceedings behind the scenes of a number of Cornish mines. The action in the novel is based on actual happenings between about 1880 and 1883, when Banker Boyns ('Charles East' in the novel) disappeared over a dividend and liquidation scandal.[110] The importance of *Tin* in Cornwall's literary development is that it developed the Cornish industrial novel by proving that a complex story of legality and economics could be as gripping as that of the experiences of the underground miners themselves. *Tin* is one of the finest examples in Anglo-Cornish literature of the social production of art, for its text is deeply rooted in the materialism of its moment of construction. It is a sophisticated expression of the complexity of nineteenth-century Cornwall, and at the same time actively asserts a critique of both the organizational procedures of mining and the interests of English (London-based) shareholders, and their neglect and lack of knowledge of how Cornish mining actually works; as in the doctor's criticisms of the way committees run mining:

> A manager must have free scope to develop a mine after his own fashion, and if it is necessary, in order to double the quantity of tin next month to raise none this month, let him alone to do as he thinks best. . . Committees are the curse of mining.[111]

Despite its overall less adventurous narrative, *Tin* did give a complexity to the subject-matter of writing concerned with Cornwall. Between Ballantyne's *Deep Down* and Bosanketh's *Tin*, several other mining novels appeared, written by travellers recognizing the narrative possibilities of Cornwall. Perhaps the other best known text is the story of Hugh Trelawney in *The Master of the Mine* by the Scottish novelist, Robert Buchanan (1841–1901), written three years before *Tin*.[112] Yet despite the fact that the majority of these industrial novels were written by non-Cornish authors, they did have a certain realism, principally because a number of mines were still active, and because though all the narratives (with the exception of *Tin*) were set a century before, the ideology of present-day mining could easily be projected back to the 'glory days', in order to formulate fundamental ideas of identity and social cohesion.

This technique was applied elsewhere to less successful effect by other visiting writers. It is the impact of this construction of Cornish history that I would next like to explore. The process of the romanticization of Cornwall contained several principal elements. Poetic interpretations demanded a re-engagement with the Arthurian, the druidic or bardic heritage, enlisting a redefined Celtic sensibility

dependent upon a growing romanticization and mythological projection of past Cornwall. There was also a growing sense and active
assertion of Cornwall's past 'barbarism', constructed via its by now
legendary tales of wrecking and smuggling, allied to Cornish perseverance and determinism. Ironically, this construction of Cornwall was
pulling in the opposite direction from the reality of experience for a
large number of the Cornish population. Having been industrial
'cocks of the walk' for some century and a half, Cornwall was now
finding this identity eroded. It was a victim of unemployment and
emigration, and an uncertain future. It would be fair to say that most
Cornish people accepted the fictional construct of their past, because
in some measure it helped them to define 'who they were' and 'where
they were going' at the end of the nineteenth century. If the picture
they saw immediately around them was depressing, at least a projected fictional history, however unrealistic, gave them hope and a
confidence for the future.

This artificiality is to be noted in a number of other late nineteenth-
century texts. James F. Cobb's *The Watcher on the Longships* (1876)
describes itself from the outset as 'a tale of Cornwall in the last
century';[113] thereby defining its historicism and what the text attempts
to create in the mind of the nineteenth-century reader. Cobb's novel is
artificial, concerned as it is with exaggerated accounts of wrecking and
smuggling, but in the process it contains a particular form of projected
Cornish activity which was then taken for granted by the reading
public; thus still defining and enhancing Cornish difference. Certainly
smuggling itself has been part of the continuity of subject-matter of
Cornish literature since Carew, and later Carter; Cobb merely
embellishes its values and activities further. The reality of smuggling in
the seventeenth and eighteenth centuries is actually negated, but a
myth of lifestyle, dialogue and narrative can be constructed, which is
long-lasting and easily sustainable. Cobb entirely believes that
Methodism reformed smuggling activity:

> In no part of England was the preaching of John Wesley more
> crowned with success than in Cornwall: men who had been
> eminent for fighting, drinking, and all manner of wickedness, now
> became eminent for sobriety, piety, and all manner of goodness.[114]

Yet historically, smuggling and wrecking were stopped by govern-
mental crack-down on the perpetrators rather than by simple spiritual
reform. Thus, Cobb's novel encompasses and develops a myth of
Cornwall which in reality never occurred. However, the artificiality
of this myth allows Cobb to develop the conventions of the Cornish
novel. The hero, Owen Tresilian, is first torn between swearing to his

wife upon her death-bed that he will never be involved in wrecking or smuggling again, and his own knowledge that such activity had been helpful when 'his wife's health had been failing, when his children had been crying for bread, when fishing had failed'.[115] To his wife, wrecking is the 'curse of the land',[116] but Cobb sets up an opposition in the text which sees it as a necessary evil; when the reality was that smuggling and wrecking were part of Cornish experience and survival, and that Methodism was unlikely to reform them. Cobb writes the text in such a way that the superior reader of the nineteenth century can look back and observe how awful things were then. A text like this is actively reformulating fundamental ideas of Cornish identity, nature and society for its nineteenth-century readership. A fine example of this is how the local squire's privileged son, Arthur Pendrean, is every inch an eighteenth-century icon of Cornishness learning 'all the wild legends of the country' and there was not 'a mine in the neighbourhood he had not gone down'.[117] Yet he disappoints his father when he becomes interested in Methodism, eventually becoming the rector of St Sennen. It is here, in observing the proliferation of wrecks upon the coast, that Pendrean then decides a lighthouse must be erected; much against the wishes of the local wreckers. It is the reformed wrecker, Owen Tresilian who assists Pendrean with his vision. Tresilian is Cobb's projection of the spirit of nineteenth-century Cornwall back into the eighteenth, a time when Cornish identity was less well-defined and confident. To this extent, Cobb continuously refers to how difficult times were then – 'The nation was constantly at war' and 'rebellions and mutinies were frequent' – so as to reinforce his belief in the myth of Methodist reform.[118]

A myth with firmer evidence emerges in F. Frankfurt Moore's *Tre, Pol and Pen*; that of the confident Cornishman at sea. When Trevilian's son Philip is press-ganged into the Navy, we are uncertain how he will fare, particularly when the crewmen discover he is a Methodist, but in the mythic construct offered by Cobb, we are confident he will succeed, because there is a mythic eternal and poetic relationship between the Cornish and the ocean itself. In conflict with the French, Cornish heroism wins through, even when Philip's ship, *Redoubtable*, begins to sink. Because he has belief in God he will survive. As a juxtaposition to this Methodist stance, the text then offers the reader a catalogue of Cornish icons. Cobb describes a smugglers' cave ('This was one of those low, narrow, winding caverns, to be found in most of the rocky cliffs round our shores')[119] and the Methodist activity of opening the Bible at random, putting the finger on the page and reading the text on which it rested ('Here, indeed, was comfort! It seemed as if God Himself was speaking to her out of the sacred book').[120]

Emergent in Cobb's novel are the beginnings of a literary fixation (in part also observed in the work of Bottrell) on the notion of west Cornwall being somehow more Cornish than the rest of Cornwall; since geographically it was more isolated, it had retained the language longer, it held more ancient sites and was the most westerly part of mainland Britain, and therefore somehow more 'different'. Cobb develops this myth in *The Watchers on the Longships* by the obvious placing of the lighthouse – in the extremity of British culture – on the Longships rock; but also through his general depiction of Sennen and west Cornwall where civilized order seems more difficult to maintain, suggesting a greater 'barbarism' and residual volatile Celticity amongst those who have not been converted by Wesleyism. This construct, emergent here, is found in other fiction of the age, and that which was to follow. It is therefore in texts such as Cobb's that this vision of eighteenth-century Cornish order comes to be foregrounded; the lighthouse is not only a physical symbol of modernity for guiding shipping, but also the 'lighthouse' offered by the morality of a unifying Methodism, Cornish-style – a myth perpetuated by Cobb during the very phase of its disintegration.

Though Methodism is not emphasized in *Armorel of Lyonesse* by Walter Besant (1836–1901), his ambitious novel of 1890 does demonstrate a number of conventions which we have continued to take for granted, again despite their artificiality. This time, even greater isolation and difference are achieved, since the novel is set on the Isles of Scilly, or in mythic terms, the residual landscape of Lyonesse. Thus, not only is the narrative in the far west, but it is both a construct of Cornwall and of the country of Lyonesse. Scilly *is* and *is not* a part of Cornwall, attesting to itself its own peculiar, but related history to Cornwall. The principal artificiality established in the novel is how Armorel Rosevean – one of the last inhabitants of the island of Samson – is to have her life and peace disturbed in the shape of a young artist from the mainland. This disruption from outside is a theme of most Celtic literatures; the disruption coming from the dominant neighbouring culture. Thus, the artist is at once a symbol of the proto-tourists or the travellers who were beginning to paint their vision of a Cornwall and Scilly, and those 'others' from outside who upset the seemingly age-old balance and cycle of life, demonstrating via this intrusion the complexity and difficulty of living in the modern world. Here, Besant interestingly tries to offer an indigenous female's experience of such changes.

Besant subtitles the work 'A Romance of Today', indicating a combination of the ancient, Arthurian connection of Lyonesse with the modernity of present. Unlike Ballantyne's or Cobb's, the novel is contemporary; seemingly there is less of a need to interpret history there, since it is already more primitive and isolated, more 'western', and in this construct, more Celtic to begin with. To convince the reader of this exotic quality, Besant writes of how the next nearest lands are 'the broad mouth of the Oroonooque and the shore of El Dorado'.[121] The novel opens with a dramatic rescue of two men from London, who are caught out by Scilly's tides. One of them, Roland Lee, is the artist. Besant shows that they are a different kind of visitor to Cornwall; not, as Lee comments, 'a Plymouth tripper'[122] – showing how well-advanced tourism was on the islands by the end of the nineteenth century.

However, though it is couched in the transformatory effect of tourism which Besant had experienced on Scilly, he cannot resist – probably purely on fashionable grounds – incorporating smuggling and wrecking ('a ship's lantern on between the horns of a cow'[123]) into the narrative, and like Cobb and Ballantyne recalls its myth and its literary construct as a symbol of Cornish culture. Again, a polarity is established in the narrative between Scilly as a 'land of enchantment' and the proliferation of smuggling in the previous century.[124] Another problematical myth is perpetrated by Besant: Armorel has dark hair, eyes and skin, and he continuously asserts the possibility – in the eyes of the Englishman at least – of her having some Spanish blood. In her modesty, attire and ethnic 'darkness', she is the emergent quintessential Cornish heroine of late nineteenth-century fiction.

Yet also encoded within the text is the effect of what visitors will do to the Scillonian – and by extension – Cornish landscape and culture. Besant also notes how widespread the flower farms are ('Somebody discovered that the early spring flowers, which begin here in January, could be carried to London and sold quite fresh').[125] Besant's text thus asserts, in a thoughtful way, the problems of tourism for culture, landscape and community. A microcosm of this is the way Lee enforces his reading preferences upon Armorel as she 'cannot speak the language of Society'[126] – but as the pair fall in love, Armorel is unable to resist the lure of modernity and fashion away from Samson. However, Armorel's synthesis with modern culture is assured only on her terms, when she discovers a substantial inheritance from her family's wrecking and smuggling past. This leads her to leave Scilly and enter London society where her beauty gives her success as a model and as an actress. Again, the whole text is a piece of wish-fulfilment, since so few real Cornish women would have had this opportunity, and when Armorel does escape the poverty of the islands, she eventually returns, filled with ideas of reform, to ensure a higher standard of living for the islanders – and a life together for her and

Roland Lee. The reality of the age was somewhat different. Under emigration, the wish to return to Cornwall would not always have been so easily guaranteed; thus the myth created here is one of the poor Cornishwoman finding marriage and happiness with the outsider, whose union is matched by a spiritual connection with the landscape and place of Scilly or Cornwall itself; but in actual fact, this union was paralleled by an increasing tourist culture and multiculturalism. Thus here, though Besant tries to depict the marginality of Scilly, the overall effect is more problematical since, in broad terms, English culture was rapidly connecting and adapting it to its own needs.

Thus, fictional visions of Cornwall in the nineteenth century were very much at the mercy of the historical moment and the materialism surrounding them. As cultural sites, they are markers in a growing and complex exploration of Cornishness in a century of rapid change. Being written ironically just past the point of Cornwall's high watermark of industrial activity, they nonetheless celebrate that achievement and provide a fine delineation of Cornish identity and, ultimately, difference from England. The expression of that identity and difference is broadly constructed in two ways; either it is formulated from direct experience at the moment of production, as in *Tin* or *Armorel of Lyonesse*; or else it offers versions of past identity constructed with the agenda of the present, perhaps most remarkably seen in *The Watchers on the Longships*.

Parallels are to be found in both the poetry and drama of the period. In constructing his paradigm of Cornwall, Harris chose to site it within his bardic and druidic heritage; Hawker, meanwhile, elected for Arthurian legend and the Civil War. These dilemmas of interpretation and affirmation, truth and artificiality, did not end here however. The decline of mining, the confusion over Methodism's direction, and emigration, actually co-incided at the turn of the twentieth century with the beginnings of mass tourism, an English literary fixation upon Cornwall as a place of marginality, and another phase of Celtic Revivalism with the explicit aim of resurrecting Cornish for spoken and written purposes. It was the interaction of these elements which was to lead to the most dynamic phase yet of Cornwall's literary development.

NOTES

1. James Hodge, *Richard Trevithick 1771–1833* (Princes Risborough 1995 [1973]), p. 44. The events commemorated in this song took place on

Christmas Eve 1801 when Trevithick tested his steam locomotive in
Camborne. The author is unknown.

2. Cited in D.M. Thomas (ed.), *Songs from the Earth: Selected Poems of John Harris, Cornish Miner, 1820–84* (Padstow 1977), p. 119.
3. See John Rowe, *Cornwall in the Age of the Industrial Revolution* (St Austell 1993 [1953]), pp 67.24–.35.
4. See Thomas Shaw, *The Bible Christians* (London 1965).
5. Philip Payton, *The Making of Modern Cornwall* (Redruth 1992), p. 129.
6. J.C. Trewin (ed.), *Robert Stephen Hawker: Footprints of Former Men in Far Cornwall* (London 1948 [1857]), pp 39–40.
7. Ibid., p. 65.
8. Ibid., p. 91.
9. A.C. Todd, *Beyond the Blaze: A Biography of Davies Gilbert* (Truro 1967).
10. See Piers Brendon, *Hawker of Morwenstow* (London 1975a), (ed.) (1975b) *Robert Stephen Hawker: Cornish Ballads and Other Poems* (St Germans 1975b).
11. See Tor Mark Press (ed.), *A First Cornish Anthology* (Truro n.d.), p. 39.
12. Peter Stanier, *Cornwall's Literary Heritage* (Truro 1992), p. 18; Brendon, op.cit. (1975b), p. 14.
13. Ibid., pp 13–14.
14. M.G. Smith, *Fighting Joshua* (Redruth 1985); Philip Payton, *Cornwall* (Fowey 1996), p. 167.
15. See K. Polmear, 'Cornish Christmas Music' in Myrna Combellack-Harris (ed.), *Cornish Studies for Cornish Schools* (Redruth 1989), pp 83–89; Jerry Clarke and Terry Harry (eds.), *Tales of Twickenham* (Redruth 1991), p. 24.
16. Brendon, op.cit. (1975b), p. 49.
17. Ibid., p. x.
18. See F.E. Halliday (ed.), *Richard Carew* (London 1953), pp 281–99.
19. See Elizabeth Jenkins, *The Mystery of King Arthur* (London 1975), pp 182–215; Paul Broadhurst, *Tintagel and the Arthurian Mythos* (Launceston 1992), pp 57–73.
20. Brendon, op.cit. (1975b), p. x.
21. Ibid., pp 54–5.
22. Trewin, op.cit., p. 100.
23. Ibid., pp ix–xiii; D.M. Thomas (ed.), *The Granite Kingdom* (Truro 1970), pp 9–15; Peter Redgrove (ed.), *Cornwall in Verse* (Harmondsworth 1983 [1982]), pp x–xii.
24. A.L. Rowse (ed.), *A Cornish Anthology* (London 1968), p. 6.
25. Brendon, op.cit. (1975b), p. 40.
26. Ibid., p. 30.
27. Trewin, op.cit., p. 5.
28. Ibid., p. 62.
29. Denys Val Baker, *The Spirit of Cornwall* (London 1980), p. 70; Thomas, op.cit., pp 12–14.
30. See Thomas, ibid.; D.M. Thomas (ed.) op.cit. (1977); Charles Thomas, *John Harris of Bolenowe: Poet and Preacher 1820–1884* (Cornwall 1984); Paul

Newman, *The Meads of Love: The Life and Poetry of John Harris (1820–84)* (Redruth 1994).

31. Andrew C. Symons, 'John Harris – A Weaving of Traditions' in *An Baner Kernewek/The Cornish Banner* 82 (1995), pp 11–12. See also John Hurst, 'Mine, Moor and Chapel: The Poetry of John Harris' in Ella Westland (ed.), *Cornwall: The Cultural Construction of Place* (Penzance 1997), pp 40–52.
32. Newman, op.cit., pp 1–46.
33. John Harris, *Wayside Pictures, Hymns and Poems* (London 1874), p. 142.
34. W. Herbert Thomas (ed.), *Poems of Cornwall by Thirty Cornish Authors* (Penzance 1892).
35. Payton, op.cit. (1996), p. 198; Sidney Pollard, *Peaceful Conquest: The Industrialization of Europe 1760–1970* (Oxford and New York 1981).
36. Newman, op.cit., p. 11.
37. John Harris, *Lays from the Mine, the Moor and the Mountain* (London 1853), pp 42–3.
38. Newman, op.cit., p. 141.
39. Harris, op.cit. (1853), p. 40.
40. John Harris, *The Mountain Prophet, the Mine and Other Poems* (London 1860), pp 57–8.
41. John Harris, *A Story of Carn Brea, Essays and Poems* (London 1863), pp 231–2.
42. Harris, op.cit. (1853), p. 84, p. 104 and p. 124.
43. Payton, op.cit. (1996), p. 217.
44. Harris, op.cit. (1853), p. 113.
45. John Harris, *The Land's End, Kynance Cove and Other Poems* (London 1858).
46. See P.A.S. Pool, *William Borlase* (Truro 1996).
47. See Stuart Piggott, *The Druids* (London 1968), pp 146–50.
48. John Michell, *The New View over Atlantis* (London 1972), pp 13–58.
49. Stuart Piggott, *Ancient Britons and the Antiquarian Imagination: Ideas from the Renaissance to the Regency* (London 1989), pp 123–59; John Matthews (ed.), *The Druid Source Book* (London 1995), pp 85–90.
50. Matthews, ibid., pp 102–22.
51. Newman, op.cit., p. 24.
52. Harris, op.cit. (1863), p. 53.
53. John Harris, *Luda: A Lay of the Druids* (London 1868), p. 2.
54. Harris, op.cit. (1863), p. 33.
55. Ibid., p. 8.
56. Thomas, op.cit. (1970), p. 13.
57. Symons, op.cit., p. 11.
58. John Harris, *Monro* (London 1879), p. 63.
59. Symons, op.cit., p. 11.
60. Newman, op.cit., pp 92–111.
61. A. K. Hamilton Jenkin, *The Story of Cornwall* (London 1934), p. 107.
62. John Tabois Tregellas, *Cornish Tales* (Truro c.1863), p. 4.
63. Ibid., p. vii.
64. Ibid., p. 4.

65. Ibid., p. 118.
66. W.B. Forfar, *The Exhibition and Other Cornish Poems* (Truro c.1891), p. 11.
67. Ibid., p. 58.
68. Ibid., pp 80–1.
69. Thomas, op.cit. (1892), preface.
70. For 'West Barbary', see Bernard Deacon, 'The hallow jarring of the distant steam engines': Images of Cornwall between West Barbary and Delectable Duchy' in Westland, op.cit., pp 7–24.
71. Thomas, op.cit. (1892), p. i.
72. Ibid., p. 80.
73. George Clement Boase, *Collectanea Cornubiensia* (Truro 1890), p. 1374.
74. Robert Hunt (ed.), *The Drolls, Traditions, and Superstitions of Old Cornwall* (London 1865); William Bottrell (ed.), *Traditions and Hearthside Stories of West Cornwall* (Penzance 1870–1880). Hunt records many legends and stories of Cornwall in these collections. Interestingly, he records numerous Jewish-Cornish connections. This is deconstructed by various scholars in Keith Pearce and Helen Fry (eds.), *The Lost Jews of Cornwall* (Bristol 2000).
75. For application of Antti Aarne and Stith's Thompson's indexes on Cornish folktales, see Tony Deane and Tony Shaw, *The Folklore of Cornwall* (Totowa, New Jersey 1975), pp 205–9; Neil Philip (ed.), *The Penguin Book of English Folktales* (Harmondsworth 1992), pp 313–48.
76. See Matthew Arnold, *The Study of Celtic Literature* (London 1867).
77. See F.M. Luzel, *Folktales from Armorica* (Felinfach 1992 [c.1870]). For commentary on Campbell of Islay, see Duncan and Linda Williamson (ed.), *A Thorn in the King's Foot: Stories of the Scottish Travelling People* (Harmondsworth 1987), pp 13–15. For Douglas Hyde, see Sean O'Sullivan (ed.), *Folktales of Ireland* (Chicago 1966), pp v–xxxii.
78. H.J. Whitfeld, *Scilly and its Legends* (London 1852), p. ii.
79. See A. Pearson, *Robert Hunt, F.R.S. (1807–1887)* (Penzance 1976).
80. Hunt, op.cit., p. 24.
81. For William Scawen's essay, see Davies Gilbert (ed.), *The Parochial History of Cornwall, 4* (London 1838), pp 203–19.
82. Hunt, op.cit., p. 25.
83. Ibid., p. 28. By 'Danmonium', presumably Hunt meant 'Dumnonia'.
84. Bottrell, op.cit. (1870), p. i.
85. Ibid., p. iii.
86. Bottrell, op.cit. (1880), p. 179 and p. 185.
87. Bottrell, op.cit. (1873), p. 187.
88. Among these were William Copeland Borlase, *Nænia Cornubiæ: The Cromlechs and Tumuli of Cornwall* (Felinfach 1994 [1872]); Margaret Courtney, *Folklore and Legends of Cornwall [Cornish Feasts and Folklore]* (Exeter 1989 [1890]), and William Copeland Borlase, *The Age of Saints* (Felinfach 1995 [1893]).
89. Elizabeth Deeds Ermarth, *The English Novel in History: 1840–1895* (London and New York 1997), p. vii.

90. Ibid.
91. R.M. Ballantyne, *Deep Down: A Tale of the Cornish Mines* (London 1868); Edward Bosanketh, *Tin* (Marazion 1988 [1888]).
92. Baker Peter Smith, *Trip to the Far West* (London 1839), p. v.
93. Wilkie Collins, *Rambles Beyond Railways* (London 1948 [1851]), *Basil* (Oxford 1990 [1852]), *The Dead Secret* (London 1929 [1857]).
94. Charles Kingsley, *Westward Ho!* (London 1906 [1855]). See Simon Chitty, *Charles Kingsley's Landscape* (Newton Abbot 1976).
95. Charles Kingsley, *Two Years Ago* (London 1902 [1857]). See John Rowe and C.T. Andrews, 'Cholera in Cornwall' in *Journal of the Royal Institution of Cornwall* 8 (1974), pp 153–164.
96. R(obert) M(ichael) Ballantyne (1825–94) began his career with *The Coral Island* in 1857. In search of authentic background he travelled widely, working at various occupations, including mining.
97. Francis F. Cobb, *The Watchers on the Longships* (Redhill 1948 [1876]).
98. See Sabine Baring-Gould, *The Gaverocks: A Tale of the Cornish Coast* (London 1887), *In the Roar of the Sea* (London 1892); Elizabeth Godfrey, *Cornish Diamonds* (London 1895). Other texts of the period were M. Filleul, *Pendower: A Story of Cornwall at the time of Henry the Eighth* (London 1877); James Baker, *By the Western Sea: A Summer Idyll* (London 1889).
99. C.A. Johns, *A Week at the Lizard* (Felinfach 1992 [1848]).
100. Ballantyne, op.cit., p. iii.
101. Ibid., p. 55.
102. Ibid., pp 54–5.
103. Ibid., p. 59.
104. Ibid., p. 72.
105. Ibid., p. 173.
106. Ibid., p. 240.
107. Ibid., p. 155.
108. Ibid., p. 128.
109. See Bosanketh, op.cit., p. i.
110. The complexities of this incident are argued by Brooke, ibid., pp 143–60. A second edition was reprinted only in 1988.
111. Ibid., p. 7.
112. See Robert Buchanan, *The Master of the Mine* (London 1885).
113. Cobb, op.cit., p. ii.
114. Ibid., p. 14.
115. Ibid., p. 13.
116. Ibid., p. 11.
117. Ibid., p. 19.
118. Ibid., p. 40.
119. F. Frankfurt Moore, *Tre, Pol and Pen* (London 1887), p. 191.
120. Ibid., p. 197.
121. Walter Besant, *Armorel of Lyonesse: A Romance of Today* (Felinfach 1993 [1890]), p. 2.
122. Ibid., p. 16.

123. Ibid., p. 401.
124. Ibid., p. 22.
125. Ibid., p. 49.
126. Ibid., p. 72.

'Lyonesse' meets 'A Cornish School'?: English Literary Margins and Celtic Revivalism, 1890–1940

When I set out for Lyonesse,
    A hundred miles away,
    The rime was on the spray,
And starlight lit my lonesomeness
When I set out for Lyonesse
    A hundred miles away.

Thomas Hardy, *When I set out for Lyonesse* (1870)[1]

Defunct Cornish dialect has no literature to show, and therefore is not concerned in the special Celtic revivals characteristic of the literature in the other dialects.

Magnus Maclean, *The Literature of the Celts* (1902)[2]

Exactly how Cornwall, and Cornish identity, were written about in the late nineteenth and early twentieth centuries has much to do with a series of collisions and meetings between two separate yet inter-connected literary groups, operating inside and outside Cornwall. In several ways, this contestation over the literary construction of Cornwall was nothing new: the debate between the visiting writer's view of Cornwall and that of the indigenous writer was further pushed into the limelight, as well as the debate over which language should be used: Cornish or English. It was a contestation which stretched back into the medieval period, and was first crystallized in the differing perspectives of Renaissance Cornwall presented by the Catholic, folkloric, hagiographical writings of Nicholas Roscarrock and the embracement of English by Richard Carew. The meeting ground between 'English' literary texts imagining Cornwall and those from indigenous Cornish and Cornu-English writers grew wider in the eighteenth century, with English culture apparently gaining the 'upper hand' in the nineteenth century.

147

As a number of observers have shown, it was, however, to be framed and constructed differently in the early twentieth century.[3] 'Lyonesse' was a convenient concept for the English novelist and poet, Thomas Hardy, which he applied to his modern vision of Cornwall.[4] Hardy, Virginia Woolf and D.H. Lawrence, were the leading lights amongst a group of early twentieth-century English writers who were finding in Cornwall's apparent marginality an ideology congenial to them. It gave them 'inspiration', had a Celtic 'primitivism' and offered an early 'alternative' lifestyle on the periphery of the island of Britain. In turn, these writers were joined by other writers from outside Cornwall who did not treat Cornwall as merely an interesting place of difference, where it was convenient to write, and which was convenient to write about. Rather, they synthesized their own identities with Cornwall's and developed innovative writing which was clearly observing and depicting Cornwall with a more effective sense of reality than the modernist 'big guns' such as Hardy, Woolf and Lawrence. Among this group we might include Eden Phillpotts, Leo Walmsley, Charles Lee and Daphne du Maurier.[5] Finally, there was a third significant group; those writers whom the controversial columnist Argus of the *The West Briton* labelled a 'Cornish school', in that they were all indigenous Cornish authors writing a literature which showed great potential, as impressive as that in England or Ireland,[6] and there are reasons as to why that particular school failed to develop. However, even in its embryonic form, the school was highly significant. Works that can be placed in this category include the proto-historical romance of Silas and Joseph Hocking, the feminism of Salome Hocking Fifield, the proto-nationalism of Edwin Chirgwin (writing in Cornish) and James Dryden Hosken, and the major Anglo-Cornish writer of this period, Arthur Quiller Couch.

Despite their alignments and meetings, all of these writers were producing texts in a radically different climate from that of the nineteenth century. A revival of pre-industrial Cornish identity, which had philosophically been on the cards throughout the nineteenth century, was about to take place.[7] The collusions, collisions and sometimes even rejection of such a phenomenon, were to have a profound influence on the direction of Cornish and Anglo-Cornish literature until World War Two. This chapter will be an exploration of meetings between the three groups of writers sited within the meeting ground of Celtic Revivalism and the English literary margins.

In the late nineteenth century, the first wave of a consciously contrived 'Cornish Revival' could be observed, even though previous centuries had actually seen similar efforts of preservation and regeneration, though as Deacon and Payton assert:

This was a conscious project on the part of a small fraction of the Cornish middle class to solve the problems caused by the collapse of industrial Cornwall. Instead of focusing on the lost glories of steam-engine technology, this group began to look to a past when Cornwall was unashamedly 'different' and more 'Celtic', ignoring the more subtle difference of a discredited popular culture. To do so, they had to go back at least to before 1537, preferably to the fourteenth century, when a large proportion of the Cornish people were Cornish-speaking, when its churches were Catholic, and when the Duchy was the central political institution.[8]

In such ways, the 'Cornish Revival' of this period looked back to the period when the Cornish Mystery Play cycles were performed and when Cornwall had a 'real' medieval literature, somehow 'unpolluted' by instrusions of English. As this book has shown, the reality was somewhat different in the aftermath of the medieval period; and had the Revivalists of this period looked more closely, they might have seen that whilst Cornish language textual production did decline, in other cases a kind of 'creolization' of Cornish and heightened use of Cornu-English register increased. Thus, though the Revival of this period looked very much at the eighteenth and nineteenth centuries as periods of decline, the past might have been more productively read in terms of linguistic shifts. Cornish difference was nonetheless still articulated through both language and literature. Such a paradigm on the part of the initial activists in language 'recovery' was symbolized, at least in part, by early rejection of the late Cornish texts and by the revived language being founded upon a firm medieval base, and secondly by the Revivalists' broad demeaning and rejection of Cornu-English as a signifier of identity.

Among the major literary figures operating collectively as part of this Revival were Edwin Norris, Robert Williams, Whitley Stokes, Frederick W.P. Jago and the Reverend W.S. Lach-Szyrma.[9] These figures then inspired Henry Jenner (1848–1934) to publish, in 1904, his *Handbook of the Cornish Language*. He asks:

> Why should Cornishmen learn Cornish? There is no money in it, it serves no practical purpose. . . The question is a fair one, the answer is simple. Because they are Cornish.[10]

There has been a great deal of scholarly analysis examining the elitist, academic, middle-class ideologies of the early Cornish Revival.[11] The bulk of the scholarship has commented that the early aims of this Revival had very little meaning for the majority of the Cornish population. As Deacon and Payton conclude:

149

> With hindsight, this could hardly have been further from the
> radical Liberal, Methodist, rugby-watching working-class culture
> that Cornish popular identity was based upon. Nevertheless. . .
> largely because of Jenner's advocacy, Cornwall [was accepted]
> into the Celtic Congress around the same time. The Cornish
> Revival had arrived.[12]

Though Deacon and Payton were right to assert this, unlike Wales
and Brittany however, which were also during this period exploring
their historical Celticity and linguistic difference, Cornwall lacked the
institutional infrastructure, which might have contributed to an earlier
dispersal of the Revivalists' agenda. There was no institute of higher
education in Cornwall which might have facilitated cultural exchange
between different groups working within the social and cultural landscape. Indeed, this was why it was so easy for a scholar such as Magnus
Maclean to make such sweeping and negative assumptions about
Cornwall.[13]

From the turn of the century until after World War Two, an
interesting Celtic Revivalist project thus emerged in Cornwall, which
was to have an immense impact on Cornish literary production of this
period. From 1920 to 1935 Revivalists developed (in the absence of a
university or similar) institutions which they envisioned would become
their vehicles for gaining popular support. In 1920, Robert Morton
Nance started the Old Cornwall Societies, which he evolved from
existing antiquarian groups throughout Cornwall. The aims of these
were to 'gather the fragments' of Cornish culture in order to serve as the
foundation for a revitalized, distinctively Cornish, future Cornwall.
Then in 1928, Nance and Henry Jenner, with the help of the Welsh
Archdruid, initiated a Cornish Gorseth, which like its Breton and Welsh
counterparts was to promote achievement and research into Cornish
language, art and literature. By 1933, more radical Cornish language
elements of the movement formed *Tyr ha Tavas* (Land and Language), a
proto-nationalist organization devoted to promoting Cornish cultural
distinctiveness through the spoken and written revival of Cornish.[14]

These organizations were influential in some respects but out of
touch in many others. Although the Revivalist project was masked as
predominantly cultural in nature, in fact, underlying many of the
cultural concerns were deeper social, political and economic issues.
The notions of separateness and nationhood which Revivalists
espoused greatly affected literary production of the period. We can
discern commmon themes and images in parallel strands of emergent
writing in revived Cornish, Cornu-English and Anglo-Cornish.

These events in the early part of the the twentieth century have
continued to profoundly affect literary production in Cornwall,

16. Old Cornwall Societies, St George and the Dragon, St Ives, c.1924. *From left to right*: A.K. Hamilton Jenkin (Turkish Knight), Phoebe Nance, R.J. Noall (Father Christmas), Bernard Leach (Doctor, in top hat), Michael Cardew, R. Morton Nance (St George), others unidentified.

17. Gorsedd: Henry Jenner (1848–1934), perhaps at a Welsh Gorsedd.

although there have been difficulties. In hindsight, it becomes clear that the early Revivalists aimed to straddle too many separate strands of cultural and political life in Cornwall, and this sometimes dissipated their literary energies. Often, with some notable exceptions, there seemed to be a greater emphasis on 'cultural performance' and the explicit project of linguistic game-playing than literary production. Such early events were to have repercussions, and certainly this has been a contributing factor as to why the Gorseth in particular is deemed to be somewhat out of touch with much of Cornish society; a criticism levelled at the ceremony since its inception. Additionally, from the outset the Cornish Gorseth was still controlled and unduly influenced by the Welsh Gorsedd, with its own particular agendas which were not always appropriate to a Cornish context. Thus, the Cornish Gorseth in many ways was created in a glorious invented Brythonic mythos of cultural unity, subservient to the Welsh Gorsedd, and which bore little resemblance to a specifically Cornu-centric world perspective. Although these criticisms have always been levelled at it, the Gorseth, and the cultural of literary production surrounding it, have continued through the twentieth century.

The Cornish Gorseth and the attendant Celtic Revival in Cornwall were one response to a multi-faceted change in Cornwall's cultural continuum. At the other end of Cornish society, the industrial infra-structure had already collapsed and this brought with it emigration, unemployment and poverty. Payton has viewed this period as the 'Great Paralysis',[15] and Cornish society, as Payton and Deacon observe, increasingly had to 'make do'.[16] Yet despite this apparent paralysis, working almost in tandem with the aims of the Gorseth there was a cultural project devoted to the 'literary re-construction' of Cornwall. Remarkably, this project was a partnership of two separate literary groups, one Cornish and the other from outside, whose objectives in writing about Cornwall were entirely different, and yet whose interests, subject-matter and forms were at this crucial point colliding, and would eventually, in the overall continuum, become congruent.

This 're-construction' of modern Cornwall went wider than the field of literature. It also affected other artforms, which certainly then fed back into the writing. Of prime importance were a number of artistic communities developing from the 1880s onwards at Newlyn and Lamorna, and also later at St Ives.[17] In 1932 the Minack Theatre was opened and aided the reconstruction of Cornwall as a romantic Other, which dominated the visual arts during this period, and was beginning to emerge in some of the prose texts of the period as well. The Minack was conceived as a theatre 'very un-English and exotic', as it is perched on a cliff-top and decorated with Celtic and Classical architectural features, yet these features actually reinforced its English conceptual origins. This, combined with the artists' interest in the Penwith hinterland, with its megalithic monuments, made sure that the romantic vision of Celtic Cornwall came to the fore, in its way linked, but at this stage, unknowingly so, to the work of the Revivalists.

As a number of observers have argued, the resultant collective impact of this re-construction is found in the emergent tourist industry.[18] Aware of the re-construction of Cornwall around it, the Great Western Railway marketed its own vision of Cornwall, in posters and promotional literature, using both the visual images of the Newlyn School and the folklore of Cornwall collected by Bottrell and Hunt, reinforcing romantic conceptions of Cornwall as home of legend-producing superstitious Celts.[19] Payton and Thomas have shown the significance of the Great Western Railway's advertisements, locomotive names and general ideology in establishing an effectively imperial relationship between centre and periphery, as well as reinforcing Cornish difference.[20] Malcolm Chapman and John Lowerson have individually summarised the process of outsider constructions colluding with insider meanings in the creation of 'Other'-driven Celtic identities, Lowerson specifically in the Cornish context, describing developing 'Celtic tourism'.[21] The unequal power relationship between Cornwall and England produced the effect of the Cornish cultural élite promoting proactively the 'Other'-driven constructions of Celtic Cornwall generated at the centre, not out of a spirit of deference, but one of resistance and reassertion of identity. It is this meeting ground that we consider next.

In its effort to promote Cornish literature and literary production, Cornish Gorseth organizers honoured a number of writers with bardships in their earliest ceremonies, among whom were Arthur Quiller Couch and John Dryden Hosken.[22] One of the aims of the Cornish Gorseth at this time was to encourage and support Cornish literary production. Gorseth organizers believed that this would be one of the primary distinguishing features between the Cornish and Welsh Gorsethow. At the Gorseth in 1932, five bards were admitted by examination for their knowledge of the language, a system of bardship which is still highly contested. Two of them were to become important figures in the Revivalist movement – A.S.D. Smith (who was later to write his 8,000 line poetic re-telling of Tristan and Isolde in Cornish during World War Two) and E.G.R. Hooper. A third, Edwin Chirgwin (1892–1960), was to become one of the most important new poets of 'revived' Cornish literature for such works as 'An Jynjy gesys dhe goll (The Deserted Engine House)', 'Den

153

Hanternos (At Midnight)', 'An Velin Goth (The Old Mill)' and here 'Gorthewer (Evening)':

> A-ugh an bron y-teth yn hell an lor
> Ha powes whek wor all an bys a-goth,
> Yma y'n ebron haneth steren-goth
> Ha golow-lor a-gram a-hes an dor.

> [Above the hill slowly the moon goes up
> and sweet response falls upon all the earth
> in the sky tonight there is a shooting star
> and all along the ground the moonlight creeps.][23]

'Gorthewer' is a significant piece, since it demonstrates the meeting ground of English literature and Cornish Celtic Revivalism. The poem is in Unified Cornish, yet the structure of the poem – a sonnet – is resolutely English. Though Chirgwin's work is not well-known in Cornwall, and ignored by Celtic academics, his importance must not be underestimated. He knew that Cornish literature did not have the range of verse forms which Welsh had, and was also aware of Cornwall's earlier accommodation. Thus in a single poem he synthesizes the discordancy of Cornish literary development since the Renaissance into a reconstructed poetic form. 'An Jynjy gesys dhe goll (The Deserted Engine House)' uses a verse form which is present in the medieval literature, but the subject matter is post-industrial.[24] Yet, despite the industrial collapse and the subtext of the Cornish 'making do', the poem's lament of economic loss is paradoxically opposite to the linguistic and poetic gains elsewhere.

Chirgwin had the confidence to know his verse was going in the right direction and we may rightly call him the pioneer of modern verse in Cornish. Although Smith was writing, his major poetic efforts were to emerge slightly later. As a parallel to Chirgwin's work in Cornish, the figure who was supremely important in shaping Anglo-Cornish poetry in this period was James Dryden Hosken, who in his day was rated as a major Anglo-Cornish poet. Originally a postman from Helston, Hosken was virtually self-taught and wrote over a considerable period of time, from the beginnings of industrial collapse, to the period of the establishment and growth of the revival. In its earliest phase, Hosken's writing looked outside Cornwall rather than within it. He was interested in the culture of ancient Greece and wrote a number of plays set there, including *Phaon and Sappho* and *Nimrod*,[25] yet it is possible to trace Hosken's poetic development from a kind of naïve romanticism of place, through his frustration over Cornwall's culture, to a full-blown nationalism, and confidence in his, and his territory's, identity.

When one begins to understand his poetic development, one begins to see why Hosken stood in Boscawen Ûn as part of the first Cornish Gorseth. Hosken selected his verse forms and his inspiration from the English poets of the nineteenth century, though as the reconstruction of Cornwall began, his verse started to pattern this development. His earliest work can perhaps usefully be compared to the romanticism of Davy, but in material such as 'Song', the Cornwall evoked is one of collapse and decay:

> Sink gently in the silent sea,
> Die slowly, slowly in the west.[26]

Hosken was, however, an extremely innovative and important proto-nationalist poet. His work throws much light on the cultural concerns of this period, and how Cornwall's split literary personality – on the one hand, 'Celtic Revivalism' and on the other 'being part of the English literary periphery' – came to be foregrounded. Hosken succeeded in breaking up the outworn conventions of Anglo-Cornish poetry in the post-John Harris phase, by moving its subject-matter in a more political direction, and by writing about everyday activities and concerns in Cornwall. Whilst being resolutely Cornish, he was also a learned poet, who knew how to manoeuvre inside the European poetic continuum; which is the first time a Cornish writer began to reassess his role within wider European literature. This is perhaps most felt in his 1902 collection, *Poems and Songs of Cornwall*, where Hosken understands the Cornish experience and begins to realize what has happened to a number of aspects of Cornwall's economy, culture and history. This is reflected in the following stanza from the poem 'One and All', which displays a confidence in confronting Cornwall's post-industrial experience and in shaping its future:

> Now hear me all the Cornish clan,
> Each Grammar Grace and Uncle Jan,
> Who sprang from that first Cornishman
>   Who long ago
> Could sling a Giant like a can
>   O'er Plymouth Hoe.[27]

This confidence is repeated in poems such as 'Visions of Cornish Moor', 'Phran of Goonhilly', 'Porthleven', 'Lyonesse' and 'Carminowe and Goomhylda'. Hosken's poetic ability meant that the romantic Celtic emphasis of his verse was often synthesized with images of industrial, modern Cornwall to a greater degree than the work of the other Revivalists. In 1928, Hosken's work was collected into a volume and here, Hosken's realization of Cornwall's difference is often articulated in a type of proto-nationalism, exemplified in 'The Land of the West':

> She hath an ancient story,
>   And stricken fields of fame,
> A bright historic glory,
>   A halo round her name.[28]

Thus, in Hosken and Chirgwin, we see fine examples of how, after industrial collapse, both poets re-aligned themselves. Initially, they found themselves lamenting the void of economic and cultural activity that Cornwall had become. However, by aligning themselves with the Revivalists, they found they were, in remarkably similar ways, able to transcend this sense of having to 'make do with their lot'. They had begun an explicit re-definition of poetry in Cornish and a proto-nationalist Anglo-Cornish poetic which were selecting some aspects of English accommodation begun in the Renaissance, and were rejecting others. A nationalist poetic could truly be said to be emerging at the same time as other socio-political movements in Cornwall.

At the same time, Cornu-English verse took a different direction. In the nineteenth century and to an extent, earlier centuries, Cornu-English expression had been a proud and convincing assertion of identity, carrying with it a confidence and superiority. But as the industrial base collapsed, this Cornu-English voice collapsed with it, and such writing became more reflective of the working-class 'making do' culture. The jokey, happy-go-lucky Cornish narratives and verse of Tregellas and Forfar gave way to more introspective reflection on the harshness of life in post-industrial Cornwall, which was never glamorous and most often depressing. This cheerless view is particularly reflected in the early Cornu-English writings of Jack Clemo, both in his autobiography *Confession of a Rebel*,[29] as well as in his short stories, such as *Mrs. Strout's Match-making*, later collected into *The Bouncing Hills*:

> Tom Gumma screened hisself by the shrubs overhanging a corner outside the last house o' Pengooth churchtown, and listened. Twad'n the first time he'd hide around thikky place, but he'd never waited there feeling so wisht as he did now. 'Twas early afternoon of a December day, very cold and gloomy, and Tom did'n expect to hear nothing what would bring sunshine to un.[30]

Clemo, for much of his writing career, was fervently anti-Celtic Revivalism and anti-nationalist.[31] In addition to *The Bouncing Hills*, his Cornu-English writing featured in such annuals as *Saundry's Almanack*, *Netherton's Almanack* and the *One and All Almanack*. In their way, these stories and others like them within the Almanacks formed the basis of popular literature in Cornwall during this period. They were still the direct successors to the narratives of Tregellas and Forfar, yet were pulled culturally in the opposite direction to other aspects of Cornwall's literary revival. Other literary insights into the poverty of this region and others in Cornwall are found in A.L. Rowse's *A Cornish Childhood*, and Marshel Arthur's *The Autobiography of a China Clay Worker*.[32]

Not all Cornu-English writing followed this route, however. The re-emergence of popular balladry in the china clay mining region expressed the frustration of working conditions and associated poor pay. Though the clay workers' concerns were far removed from the idealism of the Revivalists, there is certainly a sense within these works that, though having to struggle to exist, the working class of mid-Cornwall was beginning to assert a confident identity once again. As I have shown elsewhere, there was much activity in the china clay industry in 1912 and 1913, when workers struck unsuccessfully for union recognition, wage rises, and an eight-hour day.[33] The events of the dispute are well-preserved in the ballad 'The Cornish Clay Strike: The White Country Dispute', narrated from the point of view of an unskilled labourer:

> Perhaps it's interesting and I guess that you would like
> to hear an account of the Cornish Clay Strike.
> Well, the men at Carne Stents were first to down tools,
> And for taking that action were counted as fools.[34]

Its sixty-four stanzas reveal how the strikers were eventually brought to order by a police contingent from South Wales. The breaking up of the clay-workers' picket was particularly brutal, and resulted in the near death of some of the strikers.

Payton has argued that the collective use of Cornu-English was a 'mechanism to express introspection' and that 'the choice of dialect as a medium suggests an exclusive self-sufficiency, signaling the Cornish as *cognisente* and almost deliberately excluding the outsider, a means of social commentary in which language clearly defines ownership'.[35] It was this ownership which determined literary expression for the working classes within the almanacks and local newspapers – narrative about working classes in Cornwall – written by the Cornish for the Cornish. Perhaps mistakenly, whilst Cornu-English proved to be the most effective badge of Cornishness for the populace in the late nineteenth and early twentieth centuries, the Revivalists chose the more overtly 'Celtic' symbolism of Cornish language as the badge of difference; thus at this crucial moment of reconstruction, failing, and limiting the expression of the Cornish working classes, since it repressed their voice. The Revival eschewed Cornish dialect of English as a marker of Cornishness, when comparatively it was as close to a delineator of difference as Scots is in the Scottish context. Looking back, this might have been a crucial moment in Cornwall's literary, political and cultural development, but instead of foregrounding it, dialect was pushed sideways. Dialect symbolized an industrial age perceived to have been conducted entirely in English, of tugging forelocks to English masters, ignorant of true Celticity. The Cornish language revived that true Celticity; this, despite the fact that Cornu-English was spoken far across the globe, from South Australia to California and carried with it an internationally renowned badge of identity and respect.

However, a crucial moment for the mobilization of popular Cornish culture was thus lost, and even at the turn of the millennium such a misunderstanding is still prevalent. Cornu-English has been side-lined in Cornish culture as the medium solely for innuendo and humour[36] and, in outside writers' perceptions, left to the old retainers or simple characters.[37] Ken Phillipps, however, understood the true importance of Cornu-English for defining and asserting individuality when he commented that 'dialect could acquire a certain prestige. . .valued as a blend of shibboleth and talisman, to prove one's identity. . .'[38]

Early on, one of the central Revivalists, Robert Morton Nance understood the value of Cornu-English in promoting a distinctive Cornish identity. According to Williams, in 1906, after moving to Nancledra, Nance wrote and produced a series of plays in Cornu-English. *The Cledry Plays* series were later staged at St Ives Arts Club, and their success directly led to the formation there, in 1920, of the first Old Cornwall Society.[39] All three plays: *Duffy: A Tale of Trove*, *Sally's Shiners: A Droll of Smuggling Days* and *The Kite in the Castle: A Legend of Lamorna* have a very similar structure, combining a guise-dance format with very basic musical accompaniment. Nance's explicit aim appears to have been to put into a popular dramatic format some of the folklore of west Cornwall, expressed in Cornu-English, as typified by Joan the housekeeper:

> Aw! 'Tes a wisht poor ould piliack I've come to be, sure 'nough – what weth the wan eye clain gone, and t'other jist upon, my woorkin days es most awver![40]

Yet for all the play's linguistic realism, Nance obviously felt that dialect was not the appropriate linguistic form to assist with the revival of Cornish culture, even though for the period, its demarcation of identity was more extreme and 'non-English'. Perhaps his misgivings are also expressed in the way some of the characters are stereotyped and the way dialect seems appropriate only for comic 'feastentide entertainment'.[41] His real ideological path seems more accurately recorded in one of the prologues – 'The tongue of our forebears cherished / Is lost from our living speeches'.[42] Although Nance's plays were more confident in their construction of Cornwall, and carried with them less introspection than, say, the stories of Clemo, the plays now remain an interesting vestigial part of Cornish Revivalist activity in this phase, since clearly had Nance and the other Revivalists better promoted Cornu-English alongside Cornish language, the Revival might have achieved more popular success in a shorter period of time.

Elsewhere, the cultural introspection of this period between 1890 and 1930 continued in Anglo-Cornish literature, and is perhaps best illustrated by the work of several novelists whose only way of dealing with this despair was a reassertion of faith in Methodism, expressed in a popular format, with the explicit aim of convincing the readership that this patience and forbearance in the face of adversity would eventually bring them eternal joy. These writers had a knowledge of Cornish identity and difference, but were expressing that difference via a form of 'pulp Methodism' for a mass audience. One writer of this genre is the Devon-based Eden Phillpotts (1862–1960), who, though not Cornish himself, manages to achieve a complex depiction of north Cornish society in the early twentieth century, in his novel *Old Delabole*, first published in 1915. The novel is an intimate glimpse into the Delabole community, focusing on a series of relationships centred on the Methodist chapel and the slate quarry. A landslip within the quarry threatens to ruin a good stope of slate, and make many of the men of the village unemployed. However, the characters' innate belief in the power of their faith and in doing the right thing means that unemployment and poverty are at least temporarily prevented. The opening descriptions of the north Cornish landscape are far removed from the idealized images of the railway companies of the age. Instead, this is a deprived and seemingly hopeless landscape, where men and women battle with the elements on a daily basis:

> There is a land that borders the Atlantic and stretches for many a league against the setting sun. You may regard this far-flung coastline of the West Country as nothing but a bleak and inclement region of undulating hills, that are lifted some hundred feet above the sea, to repeat monotonously and tyrannously their contours, to extend for mile upon mile, featureless, pitiless, despotic.[43]

The lives of the characters of the novel are parochial and limited, but Phillpotts convinces the reader of their reality, and the resigned circumstances they live in. Their hamlet is 'created by one industry' and 'since Tudor times the slate of Delabole has come to market';[44] thus exemplifying all the criticism of the lack of economic diversification in Cornwall. Yet this belief in their industry walks side-by-side with their faith. This is reinforced by the wild prophecies of the old retainer Grandfather Nute, whose wild fire-and-brimstone nineteenth-century Methodism ('If you believe in God, you be bound to believe in man. If you believe in man, you be bound to believe in the Devil'[45]) fails in this new age. The central character, Thomas Hawkey, has 'the love and lore of slate in his blood' but has to weigh up the benefits of staying in economically devastated Cornwall, or travelling to 'the great slate quarries of Pennsylvania where many hundred of Cornishmen prospered'.[46] Hawkey elects to stay, but not only has to question his economic reasons for remaining in Cornwall, but also his spiritual ones. Phillpotts takes Hawkey through a series of near-biblical challenges, to the edge of his faith – and the quarry landslip – but ends the novel with his faith intact.

But identity for the people of Delabole stays strong. Edith Retallack knows 'Cornwall is the freest county in England'[47] and throughout the novel, dialect is used as a positive badge of difference; perhaps because Phillpotts was less connected to aspects of the Revival. However, whilst on the one hand the novel is re-asserting a construction of Cornish difference, Phillpotts is unable to see a future for that difference without its allegiance to Methodism. Cornwall as the 'freest county' is only free because of this.

The kind of fiction which Phillpotts was writing – a continuation of mid-nineteenth-century Methodist literary 'rearguard action' – had been shaped in the latter part of that century by three other Cornish novelists: Silas Kitto Hocking (1850–1935), Joseph Hocking (1860–1937) and their sister, Salome Hocking Fifield (1859–1927). The Hockings were a Cornish literary phenomenon and in the opening years of the twentieth century – as far as the sale and reading of popular literature in the rest of Britain was concerned – these writers presented the widely accepted construction of Cornwall. Silas Kitto Hocking, in a writing career that stretched from 1878 to 1934, produced almost one hundred novels; Joseph Hocking, writing between 1887 and 1936 equalled his brother's output, and Salome Hocking Fifield produced ten prose works between 1884 and 1903. The three novelists captured many of the cultural, economic, religious and political changes which were occurring in Cornwall, Britain and Europe. In doing so, the Hockings present the reader with a complex and changing construction of Cornwall: from the closing years of industrialization to industrial collapse and decay, to emigration through tourism and Celtic Revivalism, to an awareness of Cornwall's new position – after 1890 – on the literary margins of England. For whilst the Revivalists pushed their assertion of a new construction of Cornwall based on a Catholic-Celtic construct, the Hockings – from Methodist stock – advocated Protestantism with conviction in all their novels.

The Hockings' novels are highly formulaic, but their fictions never existed in a vacuum. Rather, the novels were directed to a specific cultural and historical context – aiming to put people on the straight and narrow path via their 'moral' or 'uplifting fictions' in a strikingly similar way to the later poems and fiction of John Harris. However, the Hockings developed the nineteenth-century Anglo-Cornish novel considerably. Both Silas' and Joseph's early fiction sits well within the category of the nineteenth-century sentimental novel.[48] There then followed an adaptation of this often religious form employing the colour of industrial regions (usually Cornwall, or the north-west of England).[49] A more refined version was the novels which were written after the industrial base collapsed and the Hockings' own travels, so that their fictions took on more global issues of economic collapse, emigration, diasporas and war. There were, though, the vestigial remains of the sentimentality, sanctimoniousness and sermonizing.[50] Their novels conclude in Joseph's later work with the full-blown historical-romantic thriller, which in part forms the blue-print for the fiction to emerge in the mid-1930s and the interface with World War Two.[51]

Typical of the conservative ideology of the Hockings' work in general is Joseph's 1897 novel *The Birthright*, which contains a fictional account of John Wesley's travels throughout Cornwall in the middle of the eighteenth century. Here, they were being retold for a Cornwall having to 'make do' with Wesley's message and be thankful for what it had. Joseph, perhaps predictably, devotes part of the novel to the taunts Wesley received in Falmouth in 1745:

> Others shouted, 'Ef we can git to un, we'll kill un. We doan't want no Canorum; we doan't want no new sort ov religion. We like our beer and wrastlin', we do'.[52]

Unlike those looking to Brittany and to the medieval period of Cornwall's history for cultural redetermination, Joseph has no time for Catholicism, which he felt was completely out of step with the direction of industrial, educated and progressive Cornwall. This is best put in Joseph's 1911 novel *The Jesuit*, where the Cornu-Irish hero, Kerry, stays in a 'Catholic' village ('In spite of the natural beauty of the place, ignorance, squalor, and thriftlessness prevailed everywhere').[53] Joseph's commitment to Methodism is re-emphasized time and again in his fiction, by reverting to a 'golden age' around 1800. In the novel *Not One in Ten* (1933), the central theme is the union of the three Methodist churches (Wesleyan, United and Primitive) which took place at the Royal Albert Hall that year and which many Cornish people attended, in part trying to assert once more Methodism's unified future.[54]

The formulaic novels of Silas and Joseph Hocking present an interesting construction of Cornwall at the turn of the twentieth century. Typically, the plot runs as follows: the scene is unspecified Cornwall, using real geographical names mixed with the implausible (for example, Treviscoe, a real inland china clay village, mutates to Trevisca Bay), whilst the male protagonist is in love with an inaccessible female. He often leaves the community – as in Silas's *A Desperate Hope* (1909) – and becomes a 'Cousin Jack', experiencing much hardship and numerous difficulties, but he will return a better man and Methodist for his endurance.[55] Virtually all the novels culminate in marriage, in which the traumas of the past are negated. It is thus easy to see why this kind of text appealed to a newly literate working-class audience, both in and outside of Cornwall. Such novels reflect the dreams and ambitions of that audience: for those inside Cornwall, the novels offered a more prosperous future; for those outside, with Cornwall's romanticization ever increasing with the tourist industry, the fictions were set in a landscape and a community redolent of romance, holidays and a certain indefinable Celticism – an Otherness of experience.

Though in the Hockings' fiction Cornwall is rarely constructed as a small nation, as in the Revivalist ideology of their peers, Cornwall's difference is to be perceived. Dissimilarity from England, and distinctiveness, are central concepts within the narratives. In the 1928 novel *The Broken Fence*, an argument over a piece of land provokes the following depiction of Cornish temperament; with shades of perhaps the clayworkers' strike of the previous decade, or possibly even earlier Cornish rebellions:

> That night about eleven o'clock a crowd gathered in the Fore Street of Carloggas. . . No one spoke. They waited in close formation till the church clock had finished striking eleven. Then they began to march towards the 'downs'. Tramp, tramp, they went to the tune of:
>> 'And shall Trelawny die
>> Then twenty thousand Cornish men
>> Will know the reason why.'[56]

However, the reality was that Cornwall itself was changing immeasurably. It is with *Nancy* (1919) that Silas first considers the theme of tourism and sets a novel in Quayporth, a fictionalization of Newquay. The central character's dream ('the smell of the sea, the tang of the gorse')[57] is again shattered by rapidly expanding tourism:

> As a lad I rambled all over this countryside. Quayporth, by the bye, is a blot upon the landscape. The glorious cliffs have been spoiled by jerry-builders. . . The town is positively hideous. . . I could have wept when I arrived after twelve years' absence.[58]

Thus, in the 1920s, Joseph had began to take on board some of the arguments promoted by the Revivalists, as in this remarkable sequence from *The Sign of the Triangle*:

> Everything connected with Cornwall was of interest to him. It was true he had never visited the county in his life. Yet he always regarded it as his home country. . . Up to a few centuries before, Cornwall had practically been a nation, and had been far removed from the life of England. Perhaps that is why Cornwall was as much a country as Scotland or Ireland or Wales, and why the true Cornishman was always so proud of his country.[59]

Yet Joseph was powerless to take this aspect of his writing any further. Revered by the Cornish and by the wider British populace, and ignored by the Revivalists, he was caught between success and revivalism. Despite achieving a prose which, for the first time, expressed such nationalism, being a successful popular writer and ex-Methodist minister meant that he would have difficulties shaping these beliefs any further, in an age when nationalism was under fire in Ireland. In particular, nationalism, as in Cornwall, had aligned itself with Catholicism. However, Joseph's lasting contribution to twentieth-century Anglo-Cornish literature was his vision of historical romance, and a case may be argued for the assertion that he established the prototype for a genre which was to regain a new energy in the late twentieth century. Joseph helped to establish the genre by taking his cues from the revisionist strategies of some of the other nineteenth-century novelists writing about earlier periods of Cornish history, but also supplying them with an easy set of morals for a popular readership.

The fiction of Salome Hocking Fifield, whilst containing some elements also found in her brother's novels, was, in fact, rather more open and fluid in thematic terms. Her work may aptly be described as proto-feminist, in that her fiction tells events from working-class Cornish female perspectives. In this way, Salome remains an important pioneer. Her 1866 novel *Norah Lang: The Mine Girl*, drew on her experiences of the Terras tin-mining region, asserting the place of women and women's work on the apparent fringes of the mining community: Norah is to be found working at her 'recks' (a table on which tin is cleaned).[60] However, *Some Old Cornish Folk* (1903) is now Salome's most remembered creation. The book is a collection of stories devoted to interesting characters, folklore and ways of life which she felt were disappearing. In fact, this text had a closer alignment with aspects of the Cornish Revival, recording as it does old ways of older members of the mid-Cornwall community. In the introduction to the work, Salome explains how only after leaving Cornwall did she realize how 'quaint' were some of the characters she had known from her childhood; her task being to preserve 'zum of the ould people' and record Cornu-English dialect, which again she saw as the primary linguistic method of distinguishing the Cornish. The social evidence of the book is made complete by its consideration of Cornish identity itself:

> There is no-one who loves a humorous, well-told story more than a Cornishman. It does not matter even if the story tells against him; if it is kindly done, he will enjoy it. But once let him think (if you are a stranger) that you are laughing at him, and he will withdraw himself inside his shell as completely as a snail when his horns are touched.[61]

Thus, though not writing as much material as her brothers, Salome managed to respond more consistently to the concerns of contemporary Revivalism; yet the importance and place of her brothers in developing a popular and world-wide conception of Cornwall through the latter years of the nineteenth and the early years of the twentieth centuries should not be ignored. Indeed, in many ways, Silas and Joseph stand at the height of literary success in Protestant, industrial Cornwall, always meeting the demands of either a Cornish readership 'making do' yet looking for a golden age of Methodism, or else an outside readership, observing in Cornwall a construction of historical romance, paralleling the development of mass tourism.

These debates over industrialism, tourism and Methodism between 1890 and 1930 were also to be central to the work of Arthur Quiller Couch (1863–1944). Quiller Couch is the writer who represents the closest meeting (from the Cornish perspective at least) of Cornish Revivalism and the English literary establishment, and yet even this was not without problems. He was a mover and operator in both worlds, working in the Revivalist movement inside Cornwall (he encouraged debate over the cultural and economic direction of

Cornwall, crucially founding *Cornish Magazine*, whilst at the same time writing fiction and poetry with resolutely Cornish themes), and yet was also a player on the world-stage of 'English'.[62] Like Dryden Hosken, Quiller Couch helped to draw together and re-synthesize the two strands of Cornish culture which had been in polarity since the Renaissance. He was also, like the Hockings, a very popular novelist and poet, offering those inside and outside Cornwall his construction of community, people and ideology – and so was the most culturally all-encompassing writer of the age. His achievements were to have lasting effects on the future direction of literature in Cornwall. Quiller Couch was educated at Clifton and Oxford, where he began writing parodies under the pseudonym 'Q' which he used all his life. His prolific literary career opened with the publication of an adventure novel, *Dead Man's Rock* (1887), after which followed a vast output of criticism, novels, short stories, verse, anthologies and literary journalism.

Like many antiquarians and writers Quiller Couch became a member of Cowethas Kelto-Kernewek (Celtic-Cornish Society), but he was never involved in explicitly nationalist activity. Although his fiction and poetry were resolutely Cornish, he was never a Revivalist in the way that James Dryden Hosken was. As a symbol of this uncertainty about the 'backwards-looking' aspects of the Revival, his response to the suggestion that an aim might be to resurrect some of the medieval Mystery plays was that 'the audience would have to be play-acting even more strenuously than the actors'.[63] Yet there was no doubt that Quiller Couch was committed to developing culture and economy in the aftermath of de-industrialization. In the mid-1890s he initiated a debate concerning tourism and the economic development of Cornwall in the *Cornish Magazine*. Quiller Couch's own position was ambivalent; he believed the future lay with mass tourism, but he asks for 'respect' for both the tourist and 'our native land as well'.[64] In fact, his own phrase, 'The Delectable Duchy', was particularly effective in marketing Cornwall in a new era of mass tourism.[65] Here again, we see the processes of collusion between insiders and outsiders in forming images of Cornwall. As a cultural critic, Quiller Couch's role between 1890 and 1930 was central. He foresaw Cornwall's unstoppable progression to a post-industrial economy, and as was fashionable among his class, opted to synthesize that with limited Revivalist activity. In this sense, Quiller Couch's place in the Cornish literary continuum ran back to Richard Carew, who embraced a similar ideology in his age.

Typical of the early phase of Quiller Couch's construction of Cornwall is *The Astonishing History of Troy Town* (1888), perhaps his best known novel.[66] The title of the volume comes from the traditional

18. Sir Arthur Quiller Couch, from the portrait by William Nicholson, 1934, in the possession of Jesus College, Cambridge.

Cornish use of 'Troy Town' to describe a place of happy confusion. The novel constructs a Cornwall facing much change, and it is the processes of that transition which cause the confusion. The small but select middle-class circle of Troy Town are incredulous concerning the arrival of the Honourable Frederic Goodwyn-Sandys and his wife from England. At the same time, Mr Fogo, who seeks the life of a recluse in deepest Cornwall, is also arriving. Travel to the 'periphery' has initiated this development and the balance of Troy Town's society is upset. Yet though Quiller Couch locates the action in a joyful and comic vision of Fowey, the plot is redolent of the massive changes occurring to Cornish society, as traditional methods on the periphery were beginning to be seen by the centre as quaint and thus attractive. Quiller Couch was writing this process. Similar images of transition are to be found in Quiller Couch's other novels: among them *The Splendid Spur* (1889), *The Ship of Stars* (1899), *Hetty Wesley* (1903), *Sir John Constantine* (1906) and *The Mayor of Troy* (1906).[67] The novels detail convincing portraits of Cornish maritime society at the turn of the century.

Throughout his writing career, Quiller Couch was taking an ever-increasing part in Cornish public affairs, particularly in education and politics. His experiences as a member of the Cornish education committee are reflected in his novels (especially *Shining Ferry* (1905)) and other writings,[68] and his political activities appear sporadically in his stories and sketches. As Garry Tregidga has shown, politically Quiller Couch promoted an image of Cornwall which was Anglican and Liberal, and just as capable of home rule as the Irish.[69] Although he was a Liberal, Quiller Couch disliked Methodism, ironically at a time when, despite actual decline, it was being reasserted by the Hockings; and in which the ethos of Catholicism was being asserted by those from within the Revival itself.

As a poet, Quiller Couch had a deep sense of history and his personal relationship with it. His family hailed from Polperro, and experiences of visiting nearby Talland Church inspired his work. Quiller Couch, like Dryden Hosken, used couplets to explore Cornish experience:

> By Talland Church as I did go,
> I passed my kindred all in a row;
>
> Straight and silent there by the spade
> Each in his narrow chamber laid.[70]

Elsewhere, Quiller Couch was able to use classical imagery in his exploration of a particular aspect of Scillonian landscape to powerful and convincing effect, as in this sonnet. Here nineteenth-century romanticism is reworked into a more complete image of distinctiveness on the British periphery:

> But I must wake, and toil again, and pray:
>   And yet will come but rarely, and at whiles,
> The shout and vision of the sea-gods grey,
>   Stampeding by the lone Scillonian isles.[71]

An understanding of Cornwall, and how Cornwall might be constructed within both the Anglo-Cornish fiction and poetry of the period, belonged to Quiller Couch, but Charles Lee (1870–1956) had an eye equal to 'Q', for how both Cornish characterization should be presented and how Cornu-English dialect should best be used. Lee was a Londoner, but in 1893 he went to live in Newlyn.[72] Though not a native, Lee was one of the most successful re-creators of Cornish life in fictional form. He stayed in several places in Cornwall, during which time, in his own words, he was 'a chiel among ye takin' notes'.[73] Lee was an exceptionally keen observer – he accurately recorded Cornish speech patterns and the ways in which he used them in narrative read authentically. By the end of the nineteenth century, he had written three novels: *Paul Carah Cornishman* (1898), *The Widow Woman* (1899) and *Cynthia in the West* (1900).[74]

The Widow Woman, one of Lee's most important novels, presents an accurate construction of what life was like in a fishing community in west Cornwall at the end of the nineteenth century. In the novel Mrs Pollard defies the social and cultural conventions of the fictional town of Pendennack by trying to choose a new husband after she has been widowed, and accordingly pays the price. In this way, Lee explores the pattern of Cornish life which, at the turn of the century, was still conditioned by Methodism, a world in which Cornish women held little social power. Val Baker suggests that some critics at the time blamed Lee for using 'too facetious a form of humour to hold up the action' of his narratives[75] – but perhaps those critics failed to under-stand Lee's portrayal of Cornish difference. Lee's observations may appear coarse, but they are nonetheless accurate, as in the pithy philosophy of Uncle Hannibal, in *The Widow Woman*:

> 'When a chap an' a maid to come together, chap shuts his eyes tight; maid aupens hers a bit wider. How should a chap look to have a chanst? Man's human, but woman's woman – 'at's what I'd say in my smart way.'[76]

There is no doubt, however, that Lee's work contains some of the finest writing in Cornu-English and has recently been re-evaluated by some commentators.[77] A consensus seems to have emerged which locates Lee's work as central to the definition of Cornish experience between 1890 and 1940. Principally, this was achieved by his out-standing use of biting Cornish humour, coupled with his conclusion that Cornu-English was a fine delineator of Cornish identity. All his fiction asserts strong and resilient Cornishness in the face of constant adversity, though Lee rarely made any explicit connection to Cornwall's Celticity. Rather, within his work he appears to take this for granted, as is proven in a sequence from the Mawgan-in-Pyder section of his *Journal*, where he writes of 'the Cornishman's love of abstract argument – surely a rare trait among peasantry outside Celtdom'.[78] Yet though a synthesis with aspects of the Revival is never fully articulated in Lee's work, ironically, had the Revivalists promoted Lee's work, he might have been viewed as their finest champion of difference.

Sadly, after 1911, Lee did not publish any more novels. Quiller Couch writes that probably the 'ill-success of *Dorinda's Birthday* may have discouraged Mr Lee, "too quick to despair", from further writing'. Ironically, Quiller Couch described the novel as a 'master-piece'.[79] Lee was a writer from the outside, but his observations set the standard for how Cornwall would need to be approached by those attempting to deal with its difference in any literary form. Though in many ways more an Englishman who believed that in Cornwall he had found an ever-present source of interesting, and somewhat comic material, he nonetheless well knew Cornwall's specific identity and moved some considerable distance in coming to understand its differ-ence. In this way, Lee was an important visiting novelist who syn-thesized the English margins with indigenous Cornish experience. In so doing, he found and explored the meeting of this peripheral literary activity and its coalition with elements of Revivalism. Certainly, Lee shows an awareness – in both dialect and comedy – of how Cornwall expressed itself and how it defined itself in his vision of working-class order and disorder.

Lee's reputation was reasonably large within Cornwall, yet other writers who are now central within the canon of specifically English literature were also coming to Cornwall – redefining their construc-tions of the territory as Celtic Other. Thomas Hardy first came as a young architect in March 1870 to supervise the restoration of St Juliot's Church, near Boscastle.[80] However, upon his arrival he began to write his personal vision of the more widely re-constructed roman-ticized Cornwall which was already underway by other writers, revivalists and tourist operators. Remarkably, his idiosyncratic vision of Cornwall has by its nature, and because of other cultural processes surrounding his work, drawn critics such as Beard to comment on how Hardy should be read in response to the 'especial nature of Cornwall' and as Cornwall 'appeals to the modern artist. . .' because there he can escape 'the selfish structure of society and. . . wars that he can do nothing to prevent'.[81] Hardy was a romantic writer, though the observations of Beard and others have not fully explained how Cornwall and Cornish identity are portrayed in his work; rather they have romanticised the effect of Cornwall on Hardy.[82]

The novelists and folklorists of the nineteenth century had already demonstrated the romantic possibilities of myths and legends against the background of dramatic landscapes and seascapes. As Phelps notes, for the poet Hardy, the romance of place was to become inseparable from his intense love affair with Emma Lavinia Gifford.[83] Hardy managed to write of his experiences on what he considered to be the margins of Britain at the turn of the century, whilst at the same time combining this with a growing awareness of, and interest in, the territory he names 'Lyonesse' as he grew more interested in the wider Celtic Revivalism and Arthuriana of the period. When Hardy arrived in Cornwall in 1870, Boscastle was, by English standards at least, a remote part of Britain. Forty years later he sat down and wrote poetry about his time there. In Cornish folklore Lyonesse was the Atlantis-like submerged region between west Cornwall and the Isles of Scilly. However, Hardy, who was based in north Cornwall, uses the mythical concept of Lyonesse to stand for the whole of the territory. Out of that earliest visit were born some of the most passionate love poems written in English, almost all of them directly relating this intense relationship to a construction of Cornwall. This is exemplified in the opening lines of 'Beeny Cliff', where the 'otherness' of Cornwall and the couple's relationship is synthesized together:

> O the opal and the sapphire of that wandering western sea,
> And the woman riding high above with bright hair flapping free –
> The woman whom I loved so, and who loyally loved me.[84]

According to the critic Simon Tresize, Cornwall played a vital role in the life of Thomas Hardy.[85] In the 1895 preface to his Cornish novel *A Pair of Blue Eyes*, Hardy refers to the 'vague border of the Wessex kingdom. . . which like the westering edge of modern American settlements, was progressive and uncertain'.[86] This is an interesting definition of territory, drawing us back as it does to Hunt's 'Greater Cornwall' whilst at the same time delineating and defining English or Wessex territory from somewhere else. Thus Hardy's Cornwall had two elements – sometimes the marginal, to use Tresize's useful term

'Off Wessex', but perhaps more importantly the far-off land of Lyonesse. His analogy also suggests that Hardy's Cornwall is to some extent mythic and this mythos is reinforced by Hardy's blending of the real and unreal. As Tresize notes, in his two major prose works set in Cornwall, *A Pair of Blue Eyes* (1873) and 'A Mere Interlude' (1885), Plymouth and London (places obviously not in Cornwall) retain their real names, but the place names of Cornwall have been recombined which has the effect of shifting the action from real to unreal place as in St Lances (Launceston) or Castle Boterel (Boscastle).[87] The peripheralism and Celticity are then reflected in the characterization and ideology of both texts.

A Pair of Blue Eyes was published in a period where fishing and farming in Cornwall were undergoing further depression, and yet travel to Cornwall was becoming easier. The narrative of this novel is completely embedded in this shift of circumstances for Cornwall, where, as Hardy sees it, the romance of life on the harsh and economically starved periphery of Britain is beginning to be negated by the arrival of the railway and better communications. It is the train which carries the central characters Henry Knight and Stephen Smith (an architect) to Cornwall, yet it also carries the dead heroine Elfride. Hardy describes the Cornwall of *A Pair of Blue Eyes* in terms that suggest a 'repressed side' of Britain, what Tresize terms 'the unconscious whose fountain of energy should not be ignored by the smug centre'.[88] The north-Cornish cliffs hold 'the ghostly birds, the pall-like sea, the frothy wind, the eternal soliloquy of the waters' and 'the place is pre-eminently (for one person at least) the region of dream and mystery'.[89]

Whilst biographical material is advantageous on some level, such scholarship does not begin to confront the important issues in Hardy's place in the construction of late nineteenth-century Cornwall. The text, meanwhile, shows that the food offered at the Swancourt family house is traditionally Cornish ('Cold fowl, rabbit-pie, pasties')[90] but all the while the railway encroaches on Hardy's conception of an ancient landscape, as the centre puts out its feelers to the periphery, seemingly taking Cornwall towards further assimilation into England. However, this cultural integration is paralleled by a process whereby characters' emotions or extreme situations are projected onto or are demonstrated by the romance of the Cornish landscape; for example when Henry Knight is unable to climb back up the cliff again.[91] Such situations of heightened drama combined with rugged landscape were to become a defining feature of future romance set in Cornwall.

A similar construction was to appear in the little known short story 'A Mere Interlude' which was first published in 1885, and is a short, but highly significant representation of a nineteenth-century Cornwall in transition.[92] The incredible coincidences may be seen as typically Hardyesque and threaten to undermine a reading which reveals more about Cornish difference, but in studying it, we can see that many of the incidents happen as they do precisely because of circumstances and changes in Cornwall. Baptista – of 'the Lyonesse Isles' – starts the narrative as an exile, working away from Scilly, as a teacher. But she is dissatisfied with her 'English' existence in Lower Wessex and is tempted to return to the periphery by an offer of marriage. As in *A Pair of Blue Eyes*, train transport makes events in the story possible; Baptista's journey by train to Penzance is 'hot and tedious' but less tedious, we might argue, than it would have been a few years earlier, when such a journey would have taken a week or so. The train also allows her and Charles to travel quickly to Trufal (Truro) to get married, and later for her to attend his funeral at Redrutin. In short, the railway was changing the very representation of Cornwall. We learn of the boxes of flowers and vegetables grown in Lyonesse, and then sent up the line to London. Yet at the same time as this modernity and progress is emphasized, Hardy has recourse to older symbols of Cornwall's past. The men of Pen-zypher were 'loading and unloading as in the time of the Phoenicians'; difference is again asserted by Hardy's image of the 'western Duchy', and Cornish identity is emphasized by use of distinctive dialect.[93] There is only small mention of other industry in Cornwall aside from tourism, and this is reflected in Baptista's intended husband, David Heddegan, when even he tries to fit in with this new tourist outlook ('an apartment with a good view').[94] Baptista's punishment and blackmail are brought about by her collision with the effects of modernization. At points, she longs for the simplicity of life on the islands, but technology and the effects of tourism interrupt this.

These two concerns of Hardy's – the ancient and the modern – are perhaps emphasized in the context of his final Cornish text. The period 1920–30 – Hardy's last decade – was 'the highpoint of Arthurian fever in Cornwall'. Charles Thomas neatly summarizes events of this era:

> Papers on Arthurian topics dot all the issues of the Cornish journals, and an Arthurian congress was held at Truro in 1930, organized by the Revivalist J. Hambly Rowe. Pamphlets like Dickinson's *The Story of King Arthur in Cornwall*, started endless reprinting.[95]

At this point it is perhaps worth noticing how Arthuriana comes to exemplify specific ideological differences between Cornwall (and

Wales) and England. For Victorian and Edwardian England, King Arthur had come to symbolize everything that was powerful and majestic about the age – Arthur, in painting and literature, had been transformed into a champion of Englishness.[96] Yet the same was not true in Cornwall, where an alternative reading of Arthur still persisted, and which was re-asserted by the emergent ethos of Celtic Revivalism. Here, for Revivalists, Arthur was the bastion of resistance against Anglo-Saxon intrusion; he was a Celtic Warrior King who stood for both the identity of past Cornwall (espoused in his spirit contained in the Cornish chough) and offered hope for a 'revived' Celtic nation in the future.[97] Indeed, for them Cornwall had been the genesis of the legend, and thus all other pan-European constructions – from the French Romances through Malory, to Tennyson and the Pre-Raphaelites, had a Cornish beginning.

It is against this background that there appeared Hardy's verse drama *The Famous Tragedy of the Queen of Cornwall At Tintagel in Lyonesse* (1923). The play appears to resemble classical Greek drama in structure, including as it does unities and a chorus. Yet wider British folk drama is also recalled by the sub-title 'Arranged as a play for mummers. . . In one act, requiring no theatre or scenery'. Whilst this may bring to mind lost secular Cornish drama of the medieval period, it also closely resembles Robert Morton Nance's attempted resurrections of Cornish mumming traditions in *The Cledry Plays*. Some critics, such as Phelps and Millgate, have noted how the two Iseults may be seen to represent Emma and Florence, Hardy's two wives.[98] Tristan asks the Queen of Cornwall to recognise his marriage to Iseult, and we should mark Hardy's construction of Celtic independence, in the epic way the ancient native monarchy of Brittany is presented:

> My daughter,
> The last best bloom of Western Monarchy,
> Iseult of the White Hands the people call her –
> Is thine.[99]

The importance of the play in the continuum of writing about Cornwall is that it constitutes Hardy's prime expression of his vision of Lyonesse. Hardy drew on a number of medieval and nineteenth-century sources for his version, including A.C. Swinburne's *Tristram of Lyonesse* (1882).[100] Meanwhile in Cornwall, according to Thomas, Arthuriana had reached its zenith

> . . .with the arrival from the north of Frederick Glasscock, custard millionaire and philanthropist. . . and the construction of King Arthur's Hall in the village. It is still there, the size of a

small abbey with some of Britain's finest 20th-century stained glass windows by Veronica Whall, and William Hatherell's ten oil paintings of Arthurian scenes. The Fellowship of the Knights of the Round Table was founded, on the highest moral principles.[101]

We can therefore see that Hardy's construction of Cornwall altered considerably during his writing career. First, it represented a place of romance, which provided the basis for one of the finest syntheses of love and landscape written in the twentieth century. As Hardy came to understand his 'Lyonesse' better as a novelist, he seems to have realized more fully than in some of his 'English' novels, how different its culture was. This brought about a more complete understanding of Cornish difference. This greater understanding was manifested in the poetry written after Emma's death, and in his Arthurian drama; one of the closest meetings yet of an English writer upon the periphery encountering a wider Celtic Revivalism in the early twentieth century.

Other reasons brought a series of significant literary figures to Cornwall during the early part of the twentieth century. Among them was D.H. Lawrence (1885–1930). As both Tease and later Maddox have demonstrated, Lawrence's period in Cornwall established a set of precedents for artistic and writing behaviour on the periphery of Britain.[102] In coming to Cornwall in 1917, Lawrence was seeking – unlike Hardy, but like those of the artistic community of west Cornwall – a geographical and cultural Other; a place far removed from the hurried pace of metropolitan England, where 'normal' rules could apparently be contested and recast. This is hardly any different from those who have flocked to Cornwall to escape urbanity throughout the twentieth century by constructing alternative lifestyles.[103] Lawrence's attitude to Cornwall was complex. He certainly believed in its Celticity and its ancientness, promoting a physical and essentialised 'Celticity' which was central to Cornish Otherness, and this is reflected in the characterization of his fiction. *Kangaroo* (1928) is a complex novel mingling political outbursts with observant evocation of Australian life and landscape. However, Chapter 10, 'The Nightmare', is a fictional-ization of Lawrence's own experiences in Cornwall and his con-frontations with authority there. Lawrence's hero in the novel is Richard Love Somers, who is a writer. At one point Somers makes some disturbing observations on the links between religion and race:

> The old Celtic countries have never had our Latin Teutonic consciousness, never will have. They have never been Christian, in the blue-eyed, or even in the truly Roman, Latin sense of the word.[104]

Interestingly Lawrence recognizes the imperial act of the English upon the Cornish, and gives it sustained and serious treatment in the novel. Yet Lawrence also comments on Cornish identity as he saw it, characterising their world-view as somehow distinctive and separate from the norms of English society:

> Right and wrong was not fixed for them as for the English. There was still a mystery for them in what was right and what was wrong.[105]

It was perhaps these qualities which first attracted him to live in Cornwall, understanding that the Cornish were different and that the community might quench his need for spiritual fulfilment. However, according to the novelist Helen Dunmore,[106] Lawrence and his German wife had a difficult time in Cornwall, since they arrived during World War One.[107] However, despite his love-hate relationship with Cornish Celticity and the Cornish themselves, it does not detract from Lawrence's central position in helping to reconstruct in a widely read forum a notion of Cornwall as a world apart and the Cornish themselves as a kind of separate race from the English, in spite of the process of modernization. Although Lawrence's stay at Higher Tregerthen, Zennor, was relatively brief, it nevertheless was time enough to allow him to form a complex reaction to the Cornish people; his views altering as his experiences of the locals became more hostile:

> I don't like the people here. They ought to be living in the darkness and warmth and passionateness of the blood, sudden, incalculable. Whereas they are like insects gone cold, living only for money, *for dirt*. . . The Cornish have had a harsh, unprotected life and in order to survive they have had to withdraw into their shells – this often seeming, to an outsider, self-centred.[108]

Lawrence was to encounter other ethnicities later in his career, as he travelled to Mexico, France and Italy, and though we may question some of his more racially-contrived observations, the fact is characterization of Cornish identity as introspective is not without merit or understanding. Profoundly similar and equally disturbing observations of this kind are made by W.H. Hudson in *The Land's End*, a natural history of the area and an early twentieth-century ethnography of the Cornish, whom he describes as reminding him of an 'orang-utan' and who have 'monkey-like arms'. Paradoxically, like Lawrence however, Hudson's observations on difference could also be acutely accurate: a Cornish fisherman is described as 'big' and 'stolid. . . a claypipe in his mouth, perfectly unmoved, like a post.'[109]

175

Yet for both Hudson and Lawrence, Cornwall offered alternative experience. In such a territory a kind of new world order could be constructed and was apparently within reach:

> '[T]here is a little grassy terrace outside and at the back the moor tumbles down, great enormous grey boulders and gorse. . . It would be so splendid if it could come off; such a lovely place; our Ranamin'.[110]

The concept of a 'Ranamin' – Lawrence's utopia – in this Celtic Other which first attracted Lawrence to Cornwall, was also attracting other writers, at once part of the meeting process of a wider Celtic Revivalism with the margins of English culture. Virginia Woolf (1882–1941) was writing as a contemporary of Lawrence in much the same area in Cornwall around St Ives Bay. Woolf spent a much greater time than Lawrence in Cornwall and as Judith Hubback notes, she was personally very deeply affected by her experiences.[111] She lived in St Ives at a house owned by her father, the critic Leslie Stephen. The stunning view of Godrevy Lighthouse inspired the 1927 novel *To the Lighthouse*.[112] Although the novel is set in a fictional Hebrides, the true inspiration was clearly the cultural geography of St Ives Bay. Her conceptualization of Cornwall is steeped in images of the elemental and romantic (shaping independently a trend which as I have shown links with both the Anglo-Cornish novels of the previous century and with the fiction of Thomas Hardy):

> The romance of Cornwall has once more overcome me. I find that one lapses into a particular mood of absolute enjoyment which takes me back to my childhood. How I wish you were here – as only the Cornish bred see its stupendous merits.[113]

During the period that Woolf was writing, Cornwall was becoming home to a number of visual artists and writers all attracted to Cornwall's difference; this was occurring parallel to the Revivalists' promotion of Cornish difference in other cultural and political arenas. However, it seems that although these writers from outside and those of the Cornish School (the majority writing in English and Cornu-English, yet some also producing an emergent – but limited – modern Cornish literature) were writing independently with no sense of a greater movement, their collective activities made a new image of Cornwall in early twentieth-century literature.

Among those active in making this new image of Cornwall was the Yorkshire-born novelist, Leo Walmsley (1892–1966). Set in the 1930s, *Love in the Sun* (1939) is the story of a writer chasing and eventually finding a 'New Age' experience in a remote but beautiful creek in

South Cornwall.[114] The novel is a fictionalized account of Walmsley's own life, and demonstrates the actions of a class and a type of people migrating to Cornwall during the economically depressed years of the 1930s. The narrator and his wife, Dain, leave behind their tight-knit and disapproving community in Yorkshire to move to the Cornish town of St Jude, where it would appear that (in deep contrast to, say, the observations of Charles Lee) 'morality' is somehow more fluid. There is even a sense that the community is almost used to those seeking an alternative lifestyle coming to them from England. Walmsley's Cornwall, in which the narrator arrives, is apparently exotic, different and a kind of 'new Eden'; the characters feeling the depression of the north falling away from them.

The couple set up home with little money and no belongings in a derelict army hut on a beautiful Cornish estuary. While the narrator writes the book that will, he hopes, pay off his debts and make their fortune, they live off the land and sea in a near-Robinson Crusoe manner. At points, Dain comments, 'Let's be a Swiss Family Robinson. Let's imagine we've been shipwrecked'.[115] Walmsley emphasizes their isolation as well; Dain and the narrator are not only at the periphery; they are on its fringe as well by living away from the town. Removed from worldly affairs (the growing military build-up and conflict in Europe) they find complete contentment and satisfaction in this Cornish context, of the kind Lawrence desired. Walmsley creates his retreat along the banks of the River Pol, but one can see how already the town of the 1930s had altered since the opening decades of the twentieth century. Now, there is a 'residential area of hotels, boarding houses and villas' ending 'near the sea in public pleasure gardens, with a golf course extending along the coastline',[116] whilst St Jude's previous role as an important port and ship-building centre has declined:

> There was no activity in the harbour, and apart from three large cargo steamers moored close to the farther shore of the estuary, no ships. The steamers had evidently been laid-up for a considerable time.[117]

Yet while the depression in Cornish industry is noticed by the narrator in his sanctuary, it is not about to ruin his retreat. On finding St Jude in Cornwall he feels he has entered a 'foreign country'.[118] In many ways, Walmsley's text is a description of people reacting against the centralization and industrialization of England, and moving to Cornwall for a 'greener', simpler and more satisfying lifestyle. Put another way, whilst Walmsley was understanding Cornwall's difference and the identity of Cornish people, his narrator becomes the first character, to use a current neologism, to *downshift*. Cornwall's Celticity, however, takes a back seat when compared to its isolation and beauty, for those are the two main motivators here. Despite the initial hardship the narrator and his wife suffer, eventually the film-rights of one of his books is bought and their financial security is guaranteed. This is significant since it establishes a kind of individual working in Cornwall during this period, whose finances are intrinsically caught up with the centre, but who is happy to live in a Cornish Otherworld – a trend which continued throughout the century. Walmsley's novel does not engage with any issues of explicit Celtic Revivalism. Rather, the narrator is the Englishman who has moved to the periphery, par excellence. However, it is the wider revivalism of Cornwall's Celticity, most obvious in this sense of Romantic Other, which is emphasized in the text; and there is a direct analogy throughout between Cornwall's exoticism and places far distant. For the English writer 'on the fringe of Britain', Cornwall was exotic enough.

Though writing several years later than D.H. Lawrence, Daphne du Maurier (1907–1989) also fits the model of the writer from outside, who came to Cornwall seeking her own personal Ranamin. However, unlike Lawrence, as a number of critics have shown, the work of du Maurier has endured internationally in shaping overall perceptions of Cornwall.[119] Beginning in the 1930s, du Maurier wrote a number of novels which became so popular that she is now nearly synonymous with Cornwall. Her construction of Cornwall as a place of romance amidst wild landscape was immensely commercially successful and ideologically influential.[120] Related to this, has been a growing myth regarding her lifestyle, sexuality, politics and how her texts are intrinsically related to these.[121] This kind of exploration has moved away from the fictions themselves and developed into a kind of 'cult-of-personality' criticism, which fails to recognize the historical moments of the texts' creation – and which also fails to consider issues of continuity with other Cornish texts, and to go beyond an 'assumptive' and limited reading of Cornish difference and identity. However, this picture is beginning to change, and some critics are beginning to ask more difficult questions of du Maurier's work, paralleled by a move away from her reductive 'popular' position towards being seen as a central writer in the extended canon of English Literature.[122]

Du Maurier was not the only writer who came to Cornwall during the 1920s and 1930s. As I have shown, a series of writers came to the territory for a wide variety of reasons. All, to some extent, encountered the indigenous Celtic Revivalism, and all, whether unknowingly or deliberately, helped to shape a reconstructed Cornwall. Du Maurier – writing at the end of the third decade of the twentieth century – found herself in the perfect position to write a kind of reconstructed historical/romantic novel, since the groundwork of the ideological reformulation of Cornwall, which had begun in the late nineteenth century and which, in part, had been further laid by the Revivalists, had constructed in the public imagination a particular ideological, social and political conception of Cornwall and Cornish identity. At this stage, du Maurier herself was not aware of this, but the wider cultural movement had created the right circumstances for the positive reception of her writing. Put another way, the meeting of Celtic Revivalism and the image of Cornwall taken to the rest of the world by visiting writers and artists had established Cornwall as a place of Otherness, of romance, of Celticism and Arthuriana, which was at once peripheral, exciting and sometimes dangerous.

This view of Cornwall had been shaped at the turn of the century by the Hockings, but there was also in the wider readership a residual awareness of the mining adventure novels from the previous century. This was then combined with the developments of the opening years of the twentieth century. Whilst with a cursory eye du Maurier might seem an early exponent of the genre of historical romance, that was actually a type of fiction which was to emerge in the post-World War Two period. It was certainly influenced by du Maurier's achievement, but we must see her as something rather different. Du Maurier's narrative is sophisticated and macabre as well more complex than many standard post-war Cornish romances, a category in which she is sometimes placed. Ella Westland has identified this quality and notes that, 'The loveliest places in "du Maurier country" are not the safest refuges'.[123] Such narratives are all found in her novels of this period, such as *The Loving Spirit* (1931), *Jamaica Inn* (1936), *Rebecca* (1938), *Frenchman's Creek* (1941), and *The King's General* (1946).[124]

Du Maurier was born in London and educated in Paris, though her family could be traced to Brittany.[125] Her first novel, *The Loving Spirit* was published in 1931 and shows a woman's concern with three generations of her family. The work is based on the lives of the ship-building community which also formed part of Walmsley's fiction. Two non-Cornish novels followed,[126] but her fourth fiction was to provide one of the most lasting literary constructions of Cornwall of the twentieth century. *Jamaica Inn* swiftly became a bestseller in Britain. The popularity of the novel and the cult of du Maurier have ensured the Inn's continuing success as a tourist destination.[127] Events, characters and locations within the text have now passed not only into Cornish folklore, but the wider world's construction of Cornwall. Du Maurier could not, of course, have realized the future cultural ramifications of the text. Her 1935 view of it is given in the author's note at the beginning of the novel, stating that:

179

> In the following story of adventure I have pictured it as it might
> have been over a hundred and twenty years ago; and although
> existing place-names figure in the pages, the characters and
> events described are purely imaginary.[128]

The central character is the orphaned Mary Yellan who, leaving
the very different landscape of Helford, goes to live with her aunt at
Jamaica Inn, Bolventor, on Bodmin Moor. Her Aunt Patience is a
'poor tattered creature. . . dressed now like a slattern, and twenty
years her age'[129] and appears to be bullied by her husband Joss
Merlyn, who is revealed to be a smuggler and a murderer. Val Baker
argues that atmosphere is created in *Jamaica Inn* by its sense of 'other-
worldliness' and by 'stressing the unease'.[130] He accentuates this
argument by quoting du Maurier's portrayal of the landlord Joss
Merlyn:

> His frame was so big that in a sense his head was dwarfed, and
> sunk between his shoulders, giving that half stooping impression
> of a giant gorilla, with his black eyebrows and his mat of hair.[131]

This description is derogatory in its depiction of the Cornishman.
He is 'ape-like' and the imagery is written to make him look
Neanderthal, closely paralleling the ethnographic observations of
Hudson. Val Baker calls it 'writing that is larger than life – and
therefore eminently suited to a Cornish novel', presumably because
Cornwall is larger than life.[132] More likely du Maurier creates Joss
Merlyn in this way because she wants to show him as being a fearsome
character to Mary Yellan, but also because the description is trying –
albeit in a crude way – to put across a sense of greater primitivism and
pagan-ness as a way of accentuating ethnic difference. This difference
is further marked in the villainous albino vicar of Alternun, Francis
Davey – the smugglers' ringleader – who feels he comes from long
ago 'when the rivers and sea were one, and the old gods walked the
hills'.[133] The fact that in characters like Merlyn and Davey the two are
merged suits du Maurier's purpose, yet ironically this primitivism and
pagan behaviour of the Cornishmen is what made Cornwall what it
was to the popular readership – reinforcing identity. However a
duality emerges in du Maurier's response to the Cornish in novels like
Jamaica Inn. Mary Yellan represents the other view of the Cornish –
she can be resourceful, cunning and beautiful. Her Celticism is not
'primitive'; it is modern, inquiring and non-threatening, and a good
deal closer to working-class sentiment in real 1930s Cornwall.

By creating such a narrative, du Maurier fashionably presents
Cornwall as pagan, exotic, wild and marginal and is emphasizing the
difference between the periphery and metropolitan 'England'. Thus

the fiction encompasses an idea of Cornwall as an ancient, wild and marginal land with a separate identity, using this image to provide the setting for melodrama and romance, with an erotic undercurrent. Such romances created the picture of a different community whose attraction sprang from the reader's nostalgia, and which reaffirmed the concept of Englishness in the south-east of England, but which also, albeit in a romantic and melodramatic way, defined Cornwall's difference. This was how much of du Maurier's construction of Cornwall worked, and though it might seem a long way removed from the reality of language and literary revival in Cornish, it assisted the English readership, at least, in redefining Cornish dialect and differ-ence, and gave demarcation to a particular territory, part of the overall Revivalist agenda. Therefore, even though du Maurier's work may seem to be in complete opposition to the culture and literature of the Revivalists, it actually helped to define some of their objectives, which politically were becoming more problematical, in a Cornwall rapidly heading toward 'south-west' regionalism, but whose identity and difference were kept alive in the consciousness of middle England.

Du Maurier's fifth, Freudian-themed novel, *Rebecca* (1938), displays similar characteristics. The opening is now world famous: 'Last night I dreamt I went to Manderley again'.[134] The story is about a young inexperienced girl newly married to a wealthy widower named Max de Winter. He is obsessed by his first wife's death, the Rebecca of the title. The obsession is heightened by the hostility of the housekeeper of Manderley, Mrs Danvers, who was obviously very fond of the first Mrs de Winter. This time the definition of Cornish difference is not established by the moor, the smugglers or by an inn, but rather by Manderley itself, symbol of this Otherness – of a culture that in 1930s middle England was beginning to crumble, but which might still be found in exotic and wild Cornwall:

> Time could not wreck the perfect symmetry of those walls, nor the site itself, a jewel in the hollow of a hand.[135]

The same conceptualization process is to be found in the novels following *Rebecca*, where the behaviour of men and women on the periphery is presented as more extreme, more wild, more romantic. *Frenchman's Creek* (1941), set at the time of the Restoration, quickly set the cultural geographic context: 'When the east wind blows up Helford river. . .'.[136] Here, a pirate anchors his ship *La Mouette* (The Seagull) in secret in 'Frenchman's Creek', and falls in love with Lady Dona. The creek has a 'strange enchantment',[137] a kind of Celtic pulling power upon both the characters and readers; the Celticity of place also reinforced by the 'French' pirate, who is actually a Breton –

du Maurier fictionally asserting the links that the Revivalists suggested. The Cornishman Godolphin calls him 'a low sneaking foreigner, who. . . knows our coast like the back of his hand, and slips away to the other side, to Brittany, before we can lay our hands on him', and later Dona hears a 'patois she could not follow – it must be Breton'.[138] Early in the novel her encounters with the Cornish form a kind of personal dislocation, which make her realize more clearly the separateness of the culture she has re-entered:

> She had forgotten the Cornish people spoke in so strange a way, foreign almost, a curious accent. . .[139]

History continues to be a fine place for du Maurier to demonstrate the independence and distinctiveness of Cornish culture, which despite her apparent distance from wider Revivalism, du Maurier seems, as her work develops, to begin to understand. *The King's General* (1946) is du Maurier's epic Cornish novel, and shares with aspects of the Revival an interest in Cornwall's role in the Civil War, where territory was as important as the actual defence of the King. In the previous century, Hawker had poetically celebrated the patriotic Cornish during the Civil War, and here the novel contains all the great Cornish families of the period, such as the Arundells, the Trelawnys and the Trevanions. Her depiction of the Civil War was paralleled at the time of writing by World War Two, a time when Britain appeared to be united. Nevertheless du Maurier still promotes Cornish difference in this text:

> We are each one of us suspicious of our neighbour. Oh brave new world! The docile English may endure it for a while, but not we Cornish. They cannot take our independence from us, and in a year or so, when we have licked our wounds, we'll have another rising, and there'll be more blood spilt and more hearts broken.[140]

Alison Light has explained an even more radical view of du Maurier, which has ramifications within the development of her writing about Cornwall, and underpins some of the above comments. Light convincingly argues that we cannot make sense of du Maurier's conception of Englishness – and therefore within her fiction of a residual Cornish identity – between the wars, unless we recognize 'how much ideas of national identity were bound up with notions of femininity and private life'.[141] She argues that in du Maurier's fiction can be traced the making of a conservative national temperament which is simultaneously protective yet progressive. Light views du Maurier as an example of 'romantic Toryism', 'one which evokes the past as a nobler, loftier place where it was possible to live a more expansive and exciting life'.[142] Yet it is not this that is remembered in du Maurier's construction of Cornwall; rather, according to Light, it is the 'unruly and ungovernable', which she found attractive about Cornwall to begin with.[143] Ironically, it was this very 'lack-lustre present' that the bulk of Cornish people were living through.[144]

Though initially there is a distance between the Revivalists and du Maurier as novelist, as her career progresses we notice an ideological shift. As I have argued elsewhere, du Maurier's increasing public persona as a recluse is patterned by her increasing awareness of how tourism, and indeed the conception of 'du Maurier country', had destroyed her own reasons for settling in Cornwall in the first place.[145] In other words, her fictions had become 'literary monsters' that she was no longer able to control, and which were, in essence, helping to cause the destruction of the very Cornwall she had conceived within them. When she came to write *Vanishing Cornwall* in 1967, she expressed grave doubts over both tourism and mass migration from England,[146] and though there she still shows some ignorance about Cornish history ('[Cornwall] never in olden times, produced a living culture')[147] she also describes 'that stalwart band of Cornish nationalists Mebyon Kernow' and how 'Cornish individuality and independence' can be preserved.[148] Indeed, it is a little known fact, but a very telling synthesis of the cultural understanding du Maurier had achieved by the end of her life, that she became a member of Mebyon Kernow. Her meeting with Celtic Revivalism took a long time to be merged, but a degree of unity was eventually achieved.[149]

This shift in du Maurier's consciousness, and assimilation into the wider Cornish Revival, happened later, but it is nonetheless significant to discuss at this point. This ideological shift is readily identifiable much earlier, with the novel *Castle Dor*, published in 1962. It was begun by Arthur Quiller Couch, and after his death his daughter Foy, a friend of du Maurier, asked her to complete the novel.[150] Thus there was continuity to this earlier phase through the shared authorship, yet also, since the novel took as the basis for its plot the story of Tristan and Isolde, it provided continuity from other earlier tellings, locating the tale in a specific Cornish geographical context, whilst also making links to a still growing world-wide fascination with all aspects of Arthuriana. The novel gives a nineteenth-century context to the Tristan and Isolde narrative. Here, the wife of an innkeeper and a Breton onion-seller re-invent the parts of Tristan and Isolde in the nineteenth century, whilst King Mark becomes the landlord of the Rose and Anchor at Troy (Fowey).[151]

What is clear is that by 1962, du Maurier had become more actively engaged with Cornish culture, moving from Light's 'romantic Toryism' to something more significant. This is manifested in the characterization of the Breton scholar Monsieur Ledru who, whilst the narrative is being enacted in the nineteenth-century setting, travels the countryside around Fowey, studying relics and fragments of earlier Cornish culture. Among these are the Tristan stone, and Castle Dor hillfort itself, the possible site of Mark's south Cornish castle. Ledru meticulously considers all the evidence; then exclaims, '*Voyons*, let us reconstruct! Those old romancers exaggerated by custom, but they built on fact'.[152] This call to 'gather the fragments' is from the symbolism of the early twentieth-century Revival, and du Maurier's sentiment is in line with it.

Secondly, this ideological shift is also prevalent in her 1972 novel *Rule Britannia*, where the narrative is far removed from her earlier work. The text details the change in her concerns and sympathies, and predicts many of the political concerns of the late twentieth century. The extraordinary story is of Britain leaving the European confederation and joining the United States in a new alliance. Far from its being an alliance, America assumes the dominant role and attempts to subdue the country. The Cornish population rebels, and American Marines land in Par Bay. Far from moving to a Revivalist position, here du Maurier constructs the Cornish along the lines of radical nationalism. The Cornish rebellion against the American oppressors is most felt in an outbreak of anarchy on the streets of Cornwall, now home to an occupying army:

> Following the explosions in the Falmouth area, there have been two more, one near Camborne and a second in the clay district, a mile from Nanpean. . . It is believed that Celtic factions amongst the population are taking this opportunity of giving vent to their dissatisfaction with the Coalition Government. . .[153]

In such a way, the text actually becomes a call for devolution, its title a rallying message to the 'ancient Britons'. Du Maurier invokes the importance of the Welsh and the Cornish in the defence of Britain throughout history, and thus justifies their rebellious position in this future dystopia. On Thanksgiving Day, as Britain submits to American control, the Prime Minister speaks to those 'countrymen who live in the west country and who, because of their place of birth, imagine themselves to be different from the rest of us'.[154] Later, in a call to arms, one of the rebels, a Welshman named Willis comments:

> 'Welsh nationalism and Scots nationalism have been irritants in certain governmental circles for many years now, we all know

that, but the Cornish are, shall I say more secretive behind the usual open front. They are strong underground, very strong indeed. But with mining stock that's natural isn't it?'[155]

He later tells Mad that he would have her 'speaking Cornish, Welsh and Gaelic in the manner born',[156] this time specifically to retain identity and secrecy in the face of the invasion, since the Americans construct the United Kingdom in only 'English' terms. The notion that du Maurier, therefore, failed to engage in any aspect of the Cornish Revival is mistaken. Though she was initially naïve in her depiction of Celtic peoples, her later work demands to be read with an understanding of her eventual alignment with wider Celtic Revivalism.[157]

Du Maurier had continued to write throughout World War Two, but the conflict temporarily put a halt to any further Revivalism. The Nazi occupation of Europe had meant that popular opinion eschewed any involvement in nationalist movements in Britain; whilst Cornish identity once again invested itself in a wider English identity to counteract the expansion of a Hitler-led Germany throughout Europe. Devolved identity to the periphery of Britain seemed to be the last thing on the territory's mind, with the collective political emphasis on 'pulling together', yet Cornwall was in a strange predicament. It was on the one hand at the frontier of the conflict, as it had been in the Renaissance with the Spanish threat. Cornwall was the German army's next step. On the other hand, the war ensured that Cornwall, once again, had to resume its established historical role as an 'English county'. It became one of the safest places for the child refugees of the large English cities to be sent, though paradoxically that process helped a generation of English people to understand more closely the difference of Cornish identity.

And yet it is fair to say, approaching, as du Maurier was, a greater understanding of Cornish historical continuity and difference, that the meeting ground between the indigenous writers and those from outside had been destroyed again after a wider Celtic Revivalism had actually caused them to converge and make borrowings from one another. This phase of Cornish literature between 1890 and 1940 had been characterized by a linking and rejoining of two formerly separate literary traditions which had been established at the Renaissance. The phase had also brought about a new awareness of the continuity of Cornish writing. This was shaped in no small part by a growing band of Revivalist poets, such as importantly Edwin Chirgwin and A.S.D. Smith, but also by a substantial number of Breton and Welsh linguistic hobbyists from outside Cornwall effectively playing semantic 'dungeons and dragons' with the language. The subject-matter was also limited, almost trying too hard to fit into a pan-Celtic or even Cornish continuum; the poetry's central themes being Christian, Arthurian, Royalist or simplistically patriotic.[158]

Cornish literary culture is thus a tenuous, and at times, highly tested tradition which re-invents itself for each era, and for new consumers of that literature. The way both Celticity and the Tristan and Isolde narrative were re-interpreted are fine examples of this process occurring. The Cornish School proposed by the columnist Argus almost reached fruition. Indeed, in the Anglo-Cornish context, we might well argue that there was a school, as influential and shaping of Cornish literature as the artists' colonies of west Cornwall. It could not develop, because as yet, despite the wider Celtic revival, the grass-roots cultural Revival was still limited, and the Cornish were still having to 'make do'. In addition, for the school to have fully flourished would have taken a linking of Cornish and English to a new level of sophistication, and despite the inclinations of the Revivalists, from both the Cornish and Cornu-English groups, the cultural machinery and institutions were not yet in place. One other crucial failure should perhaps be noted here: the Revivalists' overall dismissal of Cornu-English as a badge of identity. Recognition should, however, be given to those writers who contributed to the realization of Cornwall's Celticity during this phase. Though often only making fleeting visits within the continuum of writing about Cornwall, writers like Hardy, Lawrence and Woolf all helped with the reconstruction of Celtic Cornwall by becoming intimately involved with its landscape, its communities and people, and noting within them a difference from England, and a continuing resistance to the moment of accommodation in the Renaissance. Writers like Lee, Walmsley and du Maurier contributed to that difference, constructing literary representations of Cornwall in distinctive, and in the specific case of the later du Maurier, more nationalistic terms.

The next phase of Cornish writing from 1940–1980 was to be its most sophisticated yet, but it was also to be its most problematical. The near-harmony created first by the collision, and then the later combination of inside and outside writers in reconstructing Cornwall was never to be quite the same again. Though by no means a black-and-white division, a number of highly individualistic writers by the end of World War Two had each begun to construct his/her own, very personal, and sometimes English-accommodated vision of Cornwall, which defined and shaped Cornish identity in new ways – and which appeared ideologically quite different from the call for Cornish Home Rule and the Revivalists' objectives of the previous decades. Secondly, as a number of observers have argued, there followed marked changes in the political, sociological and psychological make-up of the territory of Cornwall, as more Cornish people moved out to find work and education, whilst more people from other territories came to Cornwall to live – still with an ideological conception of the Cornish lifestyle which had been formulated in the opening decades of the twentieth century.[159] This near-fixation on Cornwall's romance and its continued development into a Celtic, New Age and Pagan centre caused a series of new writers to expand the genre of historical romance, and to develop writing within what one may term an 'alternative' tradition. The literary construction of Cornwall was about to enter a less cohesive, but still highly dynamic new phase.

NOTES

1. See James Gibson (ed.), *Chosen Poems of Thomas Hardy* (Basingstoke 1975), p. 46. This poem was not published until 1914.
2. Magnus Maclean, *The Literature of the Celts* (London 1902), p. 249.
3. See Denys Val Baker, *A View from Land's End* (London 1982), pp 76–128; Alison Light, *Forever England: Femininity, Literature and Conservatism between the Wars* (London 1991), pp 156–207 and Philip Payton and Bernard Deacon 'The Ideology of Language Revival' in Philip Payton (ed.), *Cornwall Since the War* (Redruth 1993a), pp 271–90.
4. See Simon Tresize, '"Off Wessex", or a Place in the Mind' in Melissa Hardie (ed.), *A Mere Interlude* (Penzance 1992), pp 27–36. A useful map of Hardy's Cornwall is offered in Thomas Hardy, *A Pair of Blue Eyes* (Harmondsworth 1986 [1873]), pp 42–3.
5. See Denys Val Baker, *The Spirit of Cornwall* (London 1980), pp 66–86.
6. 'Notes by Argus' in *The West Briton* February 6th 1902, p. 3. The article is too long to give in full but Argus mentions how the Cornish School is 'full of promise in the production of new writers, whose stories have been most highly spoken of by the viewing fraternity' and that 'we may be justifiably proud of the increasing wealth of literary merit which we are gradually accumulating'.
7. Edwin Norris records that he heard an old man recite the Creed in Cornish just prior to 1860. For numerous other examples, see Peter Berresford Ellis, *The Cornish Language and its Literature* (London and Boston 1974), pp 125–46.
8. Bernard Deacon and Philip Payton, 'Re-inventing Cornwall: Cultural Change on the European Periphery' in Philip Payton (ed.), *Cornish Studies: One* (Exeter 1993b), p. 72.
9. Edwin Norris, *The Ancient Cornish Drama* (London and New York 1968 [1859]); Robert Williams, *Lexicon Cornu-Britannicum* (Llandovery and

London 1865); Whitley Stokes, 'The Passion: A Middle Cornish poem' in *Transactions of the Philological Society* 1–100 (1860–1); Fred. W.P. Jago, *The Ancient Language and Dialect of Cornwall* (Truro 1882), *An English-Cornish Dictionary* (New York 1984 [1887]); W. Lach-Szyrma, 'Last Relics of the Cornish Tongue' in *Folklore, and the Folklore Society* (c.1880). For Lach-Szyrma's correspondence with Henry Jenner, see *The Jenner Papers*, RIC, Box Eight.

10. Henry Jenner, *A Handbook of the Cornish Language* (London 1904), p. xi.
11. See for example, Amy Hale, 'Rethinking Celtic Cornwall: An Ethnographic Approach', pp 85–99; Amy Hale, 'Genesis of the Celto-Cornish Revival? L.C. Duncombe-Jewell and the Cowethas Kelto-Kernuack', pp 100–11; Ronald Perry, 'Celtic Revival and Economic Development in Edwardian Cornwall', pp 112–24; Garry Tregidga, 'The Politics of the Celto-Cornish Revival, 1886–1939', pp 125–50, all in Philip Payton (ed.), *Cornish Studies: Five* (Exeter 1997).
12. Deacon and Payton, op.cit., pp 72–3. For Cornwall's acceptance into the Celtic Congress, see Peter Berresford Ellis, *The Celtic Dawn* (London 1993), pp 73–86.
13. Maclean, op.cit., pp 248–9.
14. For a detailed analysis of this period, see Amy Hale, *Gathering the Fragments: Performing Contemporary Celtic Identities in Cornwall* (Ph.D University of California, Los Angeles 1998). For a less critical history of the Cornish Gorseth, see Hugh Miners, *Gorseth Kernow: The First 50 Years* (Penzance 1978), pp 11–27.
15. Philip Payton, *The Making of Modern Cornwall* (Redruth 1992), p. 119.
16. Deacon and Payton, op.cit., p. 68.
17. See Caroline Fox, *Stanhope Forbes and the Newlyn School* (Newton Abbot 1993); Tom Cross, *The Shining Sands: Artists in Newlyn and St Ives 1880–1930* (Tiverton 1994), Austin Wormleighton, *A Painter Laureate: Lamorna Birch and his Circle* (Bristol 1995). For a history of the St Ives School, see Marion Whybrow, *St Ives 1883–1993: A Portrait of an Art Colony* (Woodbridge 1994).
18. Peter Laws, 'The Cornish Riviera – Architects and Builders Provide the Necessary Ingredient' in Joanna Mattingly and June Palmer (eds.), *From Pilgrimage to Package Tour* (Truro 1992), pp 10–13.
19. The Great Western Railway Company, *Legend Land* 3 volumes (London 1922–1923).
20. Philip Payton and Paul Thornton, 'The Great Western Railway and the Cornish-Celtic Revival' in Philip Payton (ed.), *Cornish Studies: Three* (Exeter 1995), pp 83–103. See also Chris Thomas, 'See Your Own Country First: The Geography of a Railway Landscape' in Ella Westland, *Cornwall*, pp 107–28.
21. Malcolm Chapman, *The Celts* (Basingstoke 1992), p. 214; John Lowerson, 'Celtic Tourism: Some Recent Magnets' in Philip Payton, *Cornish Studies: Two* (Exeter 1994), pp 128–37.
22. See Miners, op.cit., p. 55.

23. Poem cited in Ellis, op.cit. (1974), p. 163. For other poetry, see Edwin Chirgwin in *Kernow* and *An Lef Kernewek*. Chirgwin was published regularly in these magazines. See also Tim Saunders (ed.), *The Wheel: An Anthology of Modern Poetry in Cornish 1850–1980* (London 1999), pp 98–103.
24. Ellis, op.cit., pp 164–5.
25. W. Herbert Thomas (ed.), *Poems of Cornwall by Thirty Cornish Authors* (Penzance 1892), pp 69–70.
26. Ibid., p. 71.
27. James Dryden Hosken, *Poems and Songs of Cornwall* (Plymouth 1906), pp 32–5.
28. James Dryden Hosken, *Shores of Lyonesse: Poems Dramatic, Narrative and Lyrical* (London c.1928), p. 121.
29. Jack Clemo, *Confession of a Rebel* (London 1949).
30. Jack Clemo, *The Bouncing Hills* (Redruth 1983), p. 17.
31. See Clemo, op.cit. (1949), p. 121. Aligning himself with the Cornish writer John Rowland, Clemo agreed in 'our dislike of. . . the pathetic pretentiousness of Cornish "Nationalists", leaders of the Gorsedd and *Tyr ha Tavas* movements'.
32. A.L. Rowse, *A Cornish Childhood* (London 1982 [1942]), pp 7–100; Marshel Arthur, *The Autobiography of a China Clay Worker 1879–1962* (Cornwall, 1995). See also Jack Clemo, 'The Clay Dump' (1951) in Denys Val Baker (ed.), *Cornish Short Stories* (Harmondsworth 1976), pp 11–12.
33. Alan M. Kent, 'The Cornish Alps: Resisting Romance in the Clay Country' in Westland, op.cit., pp 53–67.
34. Restormel Arts Clay Stories Project, *Tales from the White Mountains* (St Austell 1993), p. 43.
35. Philip Payton, *Cornwall* (Fowey 1996), p. 252.
36. For example see Alan Pearson (ed.), *Cornish Dialect: Prose and Verse* (Cornwall 1982); Michael Tangye, 'The Wrasslin' Match' (1994) in *An Baner Kernewek/The Cornish Banner* 79 (1995), pp 19–20; C.N. Henwood, *Tales written in Cornish Dialect* (Newquay n.d.); Doris Heard, *The Spare Room and other Cornish Tales* (Redruth n.d.)
37. See 'Jud' in Winston Graham, 'Ross Poldark: a novel of Cornwall 1783–1787' in *The Poldark Omnibus* (London 1991 [1945]), pp 38–9; and 'Yan', in Enid Blyton, *Five Go Down to the Sea* (London 1990 [1953]), p. 53.
38. K.C. Phillipps, *A Glossary of Cornish Dialect* (Padstow 1993), pp 1–2.
39. Derek R. Williams, 'Robert Morton Nance' in *An Baner Kernewek/The Cornish Banner* 88 (1997), pp 14–18.
40. Robert Morton Nance, *The Cledry Plays: Drolls of Old Cornwall for Village Acting and Home Reading* (Penzance 1956), p. 9.
41. Ibid., p. 3.
42. Ibid., p. 8.
43. Eden Phillpotts, *Old Delabole* (London 1915), p. 1.
44. Ibid., p. 5.
45. Ibid., p. 15.
46. Ibid., p. 7.

47. Ibid., p. 51.
48. For examples of this phase, see Silas Kitto Hocking, *Sea Waif: A Tale of the Cornish Cliffs* (London 1882); Joseph Hocking, *Jabez Easterbook* (London 1890).
49. See Silas Kitto Hocking, *Tales of a Tin Mine* (London 1898); Joseph Hocking, *The Birthright* (London 1897).
50. See Silas Kitto Hocking, *The Broken Fence* (London 1928); Joseph Hocking, *What Shall it Profit a Man?* (London 1924).
51. Joseph Hocking, *Mistress Nancy Molesworth* (London 1898).
52. Joseph Hocking, op.cit. (1897), p. 129.
53. Joseph Hocking, *The Jesuit* (London 1911), p. 149.
54. Joseph Hocking, *Not One in Ten* (London 1933).
55. Silas Kitto Hocking, *A Desperate Hope* (London 1909).
56. Silas Kitto Hocking, op.cit. (1928), pp 119–20.
57. Silas Kitto Hocking, *Nancy* (London 1919), p. 80.
58. Ibid., p. 14.
59. Joseph Hocking, *The Sign of the Triangle* (London 1929), p. 38.
60. Salome Hocking Fifield, *Norah Lang: The Mine Girl* (London 1886).
61. Salome Hocking Fifield, *Some Old Cornish Folk* (London 1903), p. 171.
62. 'Q' was given the bardic name *Marghak Cough* (Red Knight). See Miners, op.cit., p. 55; Arthur Quiller Couch founded *The Cornish Magazine* in 1895; he also edited the anthology *The Oxford Book of English Verse (1250–1900)* (Oxford 1900). See also F. Brittain (ed.), *Q Anthology: A Selection from the Prose and Verse of Sir Arthur Quiller Couch* (London 1948), pp v–xiv. For a useful biography of Quiller Couch, see A.L. Rowse, *Quiller Couch: A Portrait of 'Q'* (London 1988).
63. See Arthur Quiller Couch, *From a Cornish Window* (Cambridge 1928 [1906]), p. 268.
64. Arthur Quiller Couch (ed.), *The Cornish Magazine* 1 (1895), p. 236.
65. Arthur Quiller Couch, *The Delectable Duchy* (London 1915), p. 3.
66. Arthur Quiller Couch, *The Astonishing History of Troy Town* (London 1983 [1888]).
67. Arthur Quiller Couch, *The Splendid Spur* (London 1889), *The Ship of Stars* (London 1899), *Hetty Wesley* (London 1903), *Sir John Constantine* (London 1906), *The Mayor of Troy* (London 1906)
68. Arthur Quiller Couch, *Shining Ferry* (London 1905).
69. Tregidga, op.cit., p. 138.
70. See Brittain, op.cit., p. 60.
71. Ibid., p. 63.
72. See K.C. Phillipps (ed.), *The Cornish Journal of Charles Lee, 1892–1908* (Padstow 1995), pp xv–xvii.
73. Quoted in Val Baker, op.cit. (1980), p. 71.
74. Charles Lee, *Paul Carah Cornishman* (London 1898); 'The Widow Woman' (1899) in Arthur Quiller Couch (ed.), *Cornish Tales by Charles Lee* (London 1941), pp 13–107, *Cynthia in the West* (London 1900).

75. Quoted in Denys Val Baker, *A View from Land's End* (London 1982), p. 73.
76. Lee in Quiller Couch, op.cit., p. 41.
77. K.C. Phillipps admires Lee for his 'fluent polish' and notes that his technique was 'masterly'. A Charles Lee Society exists.
78. In Phillipps, op.cit., p. 99.
79. See Quiller Couch, op.cit. (1941), pp 8–9.
80. See Denys Kay-Robinson, *The First Mrs Thomas Hardy* (London 1979); Michael Millgate, *Thomas Hardy: His Career as a Novelist* (London 1971).
81. See Elizabeth Beard, in Denys Val Baker, *The Timeless Land* (Bath 1973), p. 27.
82. See Roger Ebbatson, *The Evolutionary Self: Hardy, Forster, Lawrence* (London 1982); Trevor Johnson, 'Time was Away: A Pair of Blue Eyes and the Poems of 1912–13' in Hardie, op.cit., pp 37–55. See also Val Baker, ibid. (1973), p. 27, and Evelyn Hardy, *The Countryman's Ear and Other Essays on Thomas Hardy* (Padstow 1982), pp 15–23.
83. Kenneth Phelps, *The Wormwood Cup – Thomas Hardy in Cornwall: A Study in Temperament, Topography and Timing* (Padstow 1975), pp 1–42.
84. 'Beeny Cliff' in Gibson (ed.) op.cit., p. 74.
85. Tresize, op.cit.
86. Thomas Hardy, *A Pair of Blue Eyes* (Oxford 1987 [1873]), p. 3.
87. Tresize, op.cit., p. 29.
88. Ibid., p. 35.
89. Hardy, op.cit. (1987 [1873]), pp 47–8.
90. Ibid., p. 53.
91. Ibid., p. 271.
92. The story first appeared in the *Bolton Weekly Journal*, dated as October, 1865.
93. See 'A Mere Interlude' in Thomas Hardy, *The Distracted Preacher and Other Tales* (Harmondsworth 1979), p. 104, p. 115 and p. 124.
94. Ibid., p. 118.
95. Charles Thomas 'Hardy and Lyonnesse: Parallel Mythologies' in Hardie, op.cit., p. 16.
96. See Christine Poulson, *The Quest for the Grail: Arthurian Legend in British Art 1840–1920* (Manchester 1999); Fran and Geoff Doel, Terry Lloyd, *Worlds of Arthur* (Stroud 1998), pp 105–33.
97. See Jas. L. Palmer, *The Cornish Chough through the Ages* (Penzance n.d.); Henry Jenner, 'Some Possible Arthurian Place-Names in West Penwith' (Truro 1912). One of the final exaltations made by Cornish Gorseth bards is 'Nynsyu Marow Myghtern Arthur [You are not dead King Arthur]'.
98. See Phelps, op.cit., pp 101–10; Michael Millgate, *Thomas Hardy: A Biography* (Oxford 1985), pp 550–55.
99. Thomas Hardy, *The Famous Tragedy of the Queen of Cornwall* (London: Macmillan 1923), p. 39.
100. For A.C. Swinburne's Tristan and Isolde, see D.M. Thomas (ed.), *The Granite Kingdom* (Truro 1970), pp 19–23.

101. Thomas in Hardie, op.cit. (1992), pp 18–20. In this essay Thomas offers a brilliant account of Arthuriana in Cornwall.

102. Geoffrey Trease, *The Phoenix and the Flame* (London 1973), pp 119–21; Brenda Maddox, *The Married Man: A Life of D.H. Lawrence* (London 1995), pp 243–51.

103. The solar eclipse of August 1999 brought about a similar quest for spiritual reawakening in Cornwall.

104. D.H. Lawrence, *Kangaroo* (Harmondsworth 1975 [1923]), pp 263–4.

105. Ibid., p. 262.

106. Helen Dunmore, *Zennor in Darkness* (Harmondsworth 1994). This is a fictionalization of Lawrence's time in Cornwall.

107. See also Roger Slack, 'D.H. Lawrence: Recollections and Poetry' in Hardie, op.cit., pp 63–73; Paul Delany, *D.H. Lawrence's Nightmare: The Writer and His Circle in the Years of the Great War* (Hassocks 1979); C.J. Stevens, *Lawrence at Tregerthen: D.H. Lawrence in Cornwall* (New York, 1988).

108. Cited in Val Baker, op.cit. (1980), p. 72.

109. W.H. Hudson, *The Land's End* (London 1981 [1908]), pp 96–7.

110. Cited in Val Baker, op.cit. (1980), p. 73.

111. See Judith Hubback, 'Women, Symbolism and the Coast of Cornwall' in Westland, op.cit., pp 99–106.

112. Virginia Woolf, *To the Lighthouse* (Oxford 1992 [1927]).

113. Cited in Val Baker, op.cit. (1980), p. 74.

114. Leo Walmsley, *Love in the Sun* (London 1983 [1939]).

115. Ibid., p. 32.

116. Ibid., p. 7.

117. Ibid., p. 10.

118. Ibid., p. 9.

119. For a useful biography, see Judith Cook, *Daphne: A Portrait of Daphne du Maurier* (London 1992). See also Piers Dudgeon, *Daphne du Maurier's Cornwall: Her Pictorial Memoir* (Chichester, 1995); Stanley Vickers and Diana King (eds.), *The du Maurier Companion* (Fowey 1997).

120. For example, see 'Du Maurier land' in Val Baker, op.cit. (1973), pp 40–52; Martyn Shallcross, *Daphne du Maurier Country* (St Teath 1987); James Mildren (ed.), *The Cornish World of Daphne du Maurier* (St Teath 1995). See also Great Western/Arrow Books, *Daphne du Maurier: Du Maurier's Cornwall* (1996) – promotional tie-in with train tickets during summer 1996; Daphne du Maurier Festival Committee, *The Daphne du Maurier Festival of Arts and Literature Programme* (St Austell 1997); John Marquais (ed.), *The Cornish Paradise of Daphne du Maurier* (Falmouth 1997).

121. Among the books which have contributed to this myth are Margaret Forster, *Daphne du Maurier* (London 1993); Martyn Shallcross, *The Private World of Daphne du Maurier* (London 1993); Oriel Mallet (ed.), *Letters from Menabilly* (London 1993); Flavia Lang, *Daphne du Maurier: A Daughter's Memoir* (London 1994).

122. See 'Daphne du Maurier's romance with the past' in Alison Light, op.cit., pp 156–207. Helen Hughes, 'A Silent, Desolate Country': Images of Cornwall in Daphne du Maurier's Jamaica Inn' and Harold Birks, 'Jamaica Inn: The Creation of Meanings on a Tourist Site' in Westland, op.cit., pp 68–76 and pp 137–42.
123. Ella Westland, 'The Passionate Periphery: Cornwall and Romantic Fiction' in Ian A. Bell (ed.), *Peripheral Visions* (Cardiff 1995), p. 167.
124. Daphne du Maurier, *The Loving Spirit* (London 1992 [1931]), *Jamaica Inn* (London 1992 [1936]), *Rebecca* (London 1992 [1938]), *Frenchman's Creek* (London 1992 [1941]), *The King's General* (London 1992 [1946]).
125. See 'A family link with the Celts' in Marquis, op.cit., p. 7.
126. These novels were *I'll Never be Young Again* (London 1932), *The Progress of Julius* (London 1933).
127. For more on tourism, see Birks, op.cit.
128. Du Maurier, op.cit. (1992 [1936]), p. 3.
129. Ibid., p. 19.
130. Val Baker, op.cit. (1980), p. 67.
131. Du Maurier, op.cit. (1992 [1936]), p. 18.
132. Val Baker, op.cit. (1980).
133. Du Maurier, op.cit. (1992 [1936]), p. 243.
134. Du Maurier, op.cit. (1992 [1938]), p. 5.
135. Ibid., p. 6.
136. Du Maurier, op.cit. (1992 [1941]), p. 7.
137. Ibid., p. 8.
138. Ibid., p. 34 and p. 47.
139. Ibid., p. 22.
140. Du Maurier, op.cit. (1992 [1946]), p. 12.
141. Light, op.cit., back cover.
142. Ibid., p. 156.
143. Ibid., p. 157.
144. Ibid., p. 156. See examples of lack-lustre Cornish lifestyles detailed in Jack Gillespie (ed.), *Our Cornwall: The Stories of Cornish Men and Women* (Padstow 1988).
145. Alan M. Kent, *Wives, Mothers and Sisters* (Penzance 1998), pp 35–41.
146. Daphne du Maurier, *Vanishing Cornwall* (Harmondsworth 1972 [1967]), pp 197–99.
147. Ibid., p. 200.
148. Ibid.
149. See Forster, op.cit., p.372. Forster writes how 'an invitation to join the Cornish Nationalist Party was therefore exactly in tune with her thinking, and she accepted at once. . . She wrote to Foy that she was thinking of wearing the Party's black kilt and quite fancied 'blowing up bridges' should the need arise. . . She was happy and proud to think she belonged to a "rebel" organization'.
150. Ibid., pp 225–34. Du Maurier and Quiller Couch had been long-standing friends, she first visiting 'Q' in the early 1930s.

151. Arthur Quiller Couch and Daphne du Maurier, *Castle Dor* (London 1994 [1962]), pp 15–83.
152. Ibid., p. 70.
153. Daphne du Maurier, *Rule Britannia* (London 1992 [1972]), p. 109.
154. Ibid., p. 251.
155. Ibid., p. 280.
156. Ibid., p. 281.
157. See also Daphne du Maurier, *My Cousin Rachel* (London 1992 [1951]), *The House on the Strand* (London 1992 [1969]), for the transitional stages of this ideological shift in her perception of Cornwall.
158. See Tim Saunders (ed.), op.cit. This useful volume shows the early progression of 'revived' verse in Cornish. For a critical appraisal of such verse, see Brian Murdoch, *Cornish Literature* (Cambridge 1993). The rare hand-coloured magazine *An Houlsedhas* produced by Robert Walling during World War One also offers an interesting picture of Cornish language activity during this phase. See Tim Saunders, 'Cornish – Symbol and Substance' in Cathal Ó Luain (ed.) (Dublin 1984), p. 256.
159. See Bernard Deacon, Andrew George and Ronald Perry, *Cornwall at the Crossroads* (Redruth 1988); Payton, op.cit. (1993).

'My room is a bright glass cabin . . .': Imagining Identity in Modern Cornish Literature, 1940–1980

My room is a bright glass cabin,
    All Cornwall thunders at my door,
And the white ships of winter lie
    In the sea-roads of the moor.

    Charles Causley, *The Seasons in North Cornwall*[1]

Easy to cry: 'And shall Trelawny die?
Impossible to ask: 'And shall Cornwall die?
And count on forty Cornishmen to know the reason
    why.

Hugh MacDiarmid, *Cornish Heroic Song for Valda Trevlyn*[2]

The Launceston-born writer Charles Causley, writes the above lines at the end of his poem, 'The Seasons in North Cornwall', so suggesting the urgency and power of modern Anglo-Cornish literature in the period 1940 to 1980. Causley, one of the most significant Cornish writers of the period, creates a confident and sophisticated metaphor describing how difference has persisted, and is still to be found in mid-twentieth-century Cornwall now imagining itself in the post-war period. The second quotation is from a visiting writer, Hugh MacDiarmid, who in his re-working of Hawker's 'The Song of the Western Men', nevertheless understood Cornish identity and nationalism in the face of much upheaval and transition. Though the Anglo-Cornish novel continued in the aftermath of du Maurier's global success, it was mainly to be in poetry that these writers constructed their interpretation of Cornwall. No longer operating in unison (like the earlier Revivalists and to some extent the nineteenth-century novelists), these writers were to imagine Cornwall along highly individualistic lines, yet all, to some extent, were to comment on the political, economic and social changes which occurred in Cornwall during this phase.

195

Instead of being merged into a wider Great Britain, in the immediate aftermath of World War Two, and despite the fact that the energy of Cornish Revivalism had become somewhat dissipated, Causley and his generation were still able to write of a Cornwall confidently asserting its identity in new and varied forms, whilst ironically within a 'Great Britain' keen to further homogenize. The homogenizing process undoubtedly percolated into the work of some writers, yet was strongly resisted by others. Understanding the processes of resistance and of the differing ways in which resistance was offered will be central in any analysis of Cornish, Anglo-Cornish and Cornu-English literature between 1940 and 1980. With this in mind, it becomes clear that during this phase writing in and about Cornwall was subject to a range of competing discourses, seeking to understand the direction of the community. This leads to particular imaginings and constructions when a literary culture is self-evidently committed, as a number of these writers are, to the promotion and development of distinctively Cornish structures and relationships. Such writers were exploring the sense of difference amongst themselves, and a wider Cornish difference from post-war England. It is also clear that as social mobility became more prevalent, Cornwall increasingly had a wider multiplicity of cultural expression. That is the aim of this chapter: to explore how Cornwall wrote about – and imagined – itself between 1940 and 1980.

Cornish writing during the post-war period took place against a backdrop of great economic and political change.[3] There were wider alterations in both British and wider European economies, often driven by centralist policies. After World War Two, the Cornish Revival became more overtly political. In 1951 Mebyon Kernow was formed, Cornwall's first explicitly nationalist political party, which both highlighted Cornish socio-economic issues and strove to promote and maintain Cornwall's Celtic culture. Although the party has yet to register significant electoral gains, it has consistently acted as a fairly successful pressure group, constantly drawing Cornish matters to the fore.

Perhaps the most fruitful time for Cornish nationalism was during the 1970s, during which Mebyon Kernow made its most significant electoral gains. The nationalist movement itself became more radicalized with the formation of the splinter Cornish Nationalist Party in 1975 calling for more direct action, whilst other activists attempted to restore Cornwall's Stannary Parliament. Cornish identity issues also became more popularized with the election of MP David Penhaligon in 1974 who became a well-known champion of Cornish identity.[4] The increase of interest in Cornwall's Celtic character took place in the context of wider popular interest in Celtic cultures throughout Britain, both inside and outside Celtic territories. In addition to political initiatives stressing devolution and self-determination, it was a time of Celtic-inspired cultural innovation, ranging from dance and music to, as we shall see, literature.

As well as the political, economic and social conditions of the age, three literary developments are crucial to understanding the development of this phase of Cornish literature. First, there was the significant role played by the literary magazine, the *Cornish Review*, edited by the author Denys Val Baker; secondly, there was the continuation of a very small-scale, yet highly influential set of magazines publishing material in Cornish; and thirdly, the growth and development of indigenous Cornish publishing houses wanting to promote and publish Cornish material. It is these three literary developments which aided the resistance against a wider cultural movement aiming to further integrate Cornwall into the 'West Country'. Although an explicitly nationalist literature was not being written initially (that was to emerge later), it nevertheless was one which was to dramatically shape and construct images of Cornish identity, in often quite dissimilar ways which, when put together, contributed to the greater wider redefinition and imagining of Cornish identity in the post-war period. That identity was actually dissimilar to what was originally being constructed by the Revivalists prior to World War Two, and in some specific cases it involved, as one might expect, during and after the war, a greater collusion with English accommodation.

Yet, despite this residual accommodation, enough writers were still writing strongly about Cornwall and Cornish identity with a high degree of awareness of its historical difference and their place in the continuity of the culture. However, in the post-war era there was no longer the meeting ground of the writers from outside and the earlier Revivalists, as a result of shifts in the economic and cultural position. Nevertheless, images of Cornwall were still being as strongly defined as ever. It was certainly a changed Cornwall. The centre of industry had shifted from the Redruth/Camborne area to the china clay mining region of St. Austell, and the territorial and cultural integrity of Cornwall seemed more under threat. This particular cultural climate made for a series of changes in literary representations of Cornwall which were to last until the end of the twentieth century.

One of the most influential writers and activists on the literary scene during the post-war period of Cornish literary history was Denys Val Baker (1917-84).[5] From the 1940s onward Val Baker's output was phenomenal and his influence on Cornish cultural development remarkable, even if his romantic interpretation of the territory sometimes intruded on his sharper awareness of the cultural politics of Cornwall. Aside from his obvious love of Cornwall he had a talent for organizing and bringing together the various writers and artists working together during the late 1940s and 50s. He once commented: 'I had met so many writers and painters and other people busily creating that it began to seem to me a crime there was not a printed vehicle for their views and ideas'.[6] It was this lack of an artistic forum that caused him to develop the seminal publication *Cornish Review* of which ten issues were published between 1949 and 1952. Among the early writers and artists who contributed were Ben Nicholson, Peter Lanyon, Sven Berlin, Guido Morris, W.S. Graham, Jack Clemo, Robert Morton Nance, A.L. Rowse and the poet Arthur Caddick. The *Cornish Review* served as an important outlet for these talents, and also provided (then and now) a snapshot of creative activity in Cornwall during that period.

In addition to editing *Cornish Review*, Val Baker himself continued with his own literary career, at one point returning to London, but also writing *Britain's Art Colony By the Sea* (1959) and *The Sea's in the Kitchen* (1962), which were sympathetic portraits of a kind of 'Cornish Bohemia'.[7] Then, at the end of the 1960s, the *Cornish Review* was re-launched. The contribution of the magazine in its comparatively short lifespan in defining and shaping the post-war voice of Cornu-English literature was highly significant, however, and it nurtured and shaped a generation of writers.

It is perhaps also worth considering here the on-going continuity of Cornish literature, which in many ways had been eclipsed by the dominance of the Anglo-Cornish texts. However, as a number of observers have argued, Cornish literature had continued to be produced by a small but dedicated set of writers in the post-war period, for an audience almost exclusively composed of those people involved in the continued revival of Cornish.[8] Conceived at the time as marginal, hobbyist and even 'fringe', their work was, as Tim Saunders has shown, to have an important shaping effect.[9] As with Anglo-Cornish and Cornu-English literature, the principal mechanism for literary production was the magazine. As far back as 1934, the poet and language activist A.S.D. Smith had founded *Kernow*, a monthly magazine published entirely in Cornish. Some of the medieval texts were reprinted and altered into Unified Cornish (part of the Revivalists' ideological project and still being worked through). The magazine also published original work, but Cornish was only to be used in literary forms and imagery approved of by those conducting the business of revival. The trend set here (and in the earliest revived Cornish magazine *An Houlsedhas* from World War One) was in essence 'regressive'; the work explicitly 'Celtic' and envisaging itself as a continuation of the medieval tradition. This was to prove to be a restricting factor in the overall development of Cornish literature in the twentieth century (one, as we shall see later, which at last is beginning to fall away). As Saunders shows, these ideologically-restricted, yet nonetheless influential writers included Edwin Chirgwin, A. St. V. Allin-Collins, Phoebe Nance, Francis Cargeeg, Henry Trefusis and Michael Cardew. This set the trend in production in Cornish until the outbreak of World War Two.

After the war, Cornish writing was infused with a younger genera-tion of writers. In 1952, Richard Gendall's *An Lef* [*The Voice*] emerged, continuing the trend from the pre-war period. To learners, speakers and writers of Cornish, *An Lef* and its successors (such as *An Lef Kernewek* [*The Cornish Voice*] and *Hedhyu* [*Today*]) were highly important texts, taking the first tentative steps of a rejuvenated Cornish poetic.[11] However, they were still consumed by only a limited audience and relied on the Cornish 'cultural archetypes' established by the earlier Revivalists. Gendall, however, should be praised for his innovation, since he was leading a more progressive outlook on the language. He has became one of the most influential poets, scholars and songwriters in Cornish.[12] *An Lef Kernewek* ran until 1982 and continued to publish some of the best Cornish writing to emerge in the post-war period. Though there was a difficulty in breaking the ideological mould of the Revival, we should not underestimate the achievement of this maga-zine, since the Cornish language was (unlike in millennial Cornwall) considered still very peripheral. Among the writers featured were Gendall himself, Richard Jenkin, Tim Saunders, Wella Brown and N.J.A. Williams (activists who have continued to shape Cornish lan-guage and literature).

Some of the Cornish language writers, however, became increas-ingly dissatisfied with the direction taken with the revival of Cornish and its rather (in their view) retrogressive values, and inability to deal with contemporary and more political subject-matter. The result of this shift in ideology by some of the writers was a satirical magazine titled *Eythen* [Gorse], edited by Tim Saunders and Anthony Snell.[13] *Eythen* was produced between 1976 and 1980 and was an important departure in the Revival, since it was stylistically more sophisticated, and appealed to younger writers and readers. There was and still is however a good deal of establishment resistance to their critiques. As an example, despite Saunders' fluency and talent as a poet, he was made a bard of the Gorseth only as late as 1998. Given the somewhat restricted cultural view of the earlier publications, Saunders and Snell's progressive approach may now be seen as the best direction Cornish literature could take at that time.

In 1977, Graham Sandercock introduced *An Gannas*, a monthly magazine in Cornish, which is the longest running periodical in Cornish. Its content is broadly designed for learners, but also includes poetry and short stories.[14] *An Gannas* modelled itself on the format of the earlier publications, but it did bring to the foreground writers and scholars such as Jowann Richards and Ray Edwards. New writing in Cornish over the post-war period has had, for the most part, to operate on an amateur and poorly-funded basis; the publications run by a small but dedicated group of Cornish writers. It is this kind of growth, coupled with the annual Gorseth poetry competitions, which have, in many ways, shaped much of the verse and narrative in Cornish which has emerged in the post-war period.[15] Though there have been sporadic and sometimes sustained attempts by individuals to 'modernize' the literature, for the most part the writing failed to develop beyond the initial thematic and structural concerns of the Revival before World War Two. On the plus side, however, the Cornish Revival slowly but surely was beginning to assemble a small, yet distinctive collection of literature in the post-war period, which was internally and externally read. Whilst both *Cornish Review* and the various publications of those writing in Cornish continued to be published, another magazine also continued to sustain and support Cornish Literature. This was *Old Cornwall*, the magazine of the Federation of Old Cornwall Societies, which never quite regained its 'cutting edge' ethos of the pre-war period, but continued to publish both Cornish and Cornu-English literature.[16] It was, by now, very much a residual cultural document, though it remained an important publishing vehicle for those, by now older, writers involved with the Revival. Finally, after the decline of the indigenous publishing houses of the nineteenth century producing popular writing for the working classes in Cornwall, for much of the early twentieth century Cornwall suffered from a lack of indigenous publishers. In an early attempt to subvert the dominant grip larger Anglo-centric publishers had gained over Cornish writing by the post-war period, as Payton has shown, a number of Cornish publishing houses – D. Bradford Barton, Lodenek Press and Dyllansow Truran – produced more Cornish material, as part of the wider Revivalism of the period.[17]

From Cornish language to Cornu-English literature, Dyllansow Truran in particular, has attracted some of the most important shapers of modern Cornish identity. Among those who wrote for Dyllansow Truran and who is one of the most important figures in imagining modern Cornish identity is A.L. Rowse (1903–1997).[18] Rowse is a complex figure within Anglo-Cornish literature, who throughout various phases of his writing career has demonstrated allegiances to and with English culture, both stylistically and ideologically, yet has continued to demonstrate within his own work a sophisticated portrayal of the Cornish situation and Cornish identity. As Ollard shows, part of this disparity in his persona and writing has arisen through his own education and circumstances.[19] Rowse's work demonstrates many characteristics of Cornish independence and difference to Anglo-centric values, but was too embroiled in mainstream English culture to fully articulate popular Cornish nationalism. That said, Rowse created a body of writing which offers a thorough exploration of one form of Cornish identity from the early 1940s to the 1990s.[20]

In addition to his work as a poet and short story writer, Rowse was also a distinguished historian and scholar of the Renaissance, as well as of the Cornish. Rowse completed the first detailed study of Renaissance Cornwall in *Tudor Cornwall* in 1941, and also researched the role of the Cornish in North America.[21] In a number of ways, Rowse was in the direct line in Cornish writing stretching back to Quiller Couch (who assisted the young Rowse) through Carew, to scholars such as Trevisa. Like Quiller Couch, Rowse divided his time between Cornwall and the English academic establishment he was attached to, and tried hard to synthesize the two worlds. Rowse was also active politically during his life, standing as the Labour candidate in the Falmouth-Penryn constituency in the 1931 election, though he was later to champion Margaret Thatcher.[22]

A Cornish Childhood (1942) is one of the best examples of how Rowse balanced his Cornishness and the pressures he consistently felt to conform.[23] *A Cornish Childhood* is a picture of a working-class family 'making do' in a close clay mining community near St. Austell. It is not only a personal story; it is also a commentary on many of the issues shaping Cornwall such as Liberal politics, and the continuing phenomenon of emigration.[24] Here, Rowse captures the peculiar effect of emigration on the Cornish and its peculiar paradoxes. In Cornwall emigration both reinforced Cornish networks and generated the ability to work anywhere in the world, but the distance from the English centre remained:

> At home people knew what was going on in South Africa often rather better than what was happening 'up the country': the journey across the seas to another continent was more familiar than going very far 'up the country', say as far as London.[25]

In this work Rowse also meditates on his Cornishness. He considers himself '100 per cent Cornish', though he admits he has a very 'un-Cornish cast of mind'.[26] Rowse is critical of 'Anglo-Saxon idealism with its attendant hypocrisies', but seems more positively inclined to the 'certain disjunction between intellect and emotion' which he describes as being Celtic and 'un-English'.[27] Much of the unexplained in his existence is interestingly put down to his 'Cornishry'. Rowse integrates this with the beginnings of reflection upon the continuity and the meeting ground of English and Cornish literature. His conclusions here define the sense of identity that Rowse and a number of other Cornish writers in the post-war period seem to be experiencing:

> English literature and English writing are essentially middle-class. The conventions and assumptions and canons of writing are those of a great corporation to which I do not belong. . . My own use of language is freer, more unconventional, looser, with inaccuracies and solecisms which I am often aware of and deliberately employ, if they give greater naturalness and spontaneity and vigour.[28]

Rowse's comments are almost an agenda for Anglo-Cornish literature in the period between 1940 and 1960, though he himself was intensely aware of the difficulty of that process, as well as the centralism and class-orientation of literary production which he constantly faced, and found so disheartening. His frustration over how his own identity, and that of others, had to change is related to these issues, yet he was still intensely aware of his important role as a writer and how he had managed to challenge some of the clichés of 'Cornishry', which the Cornish themselves had continued to use in defining their identity. Rowse confronts the very icons of Cornish identity in order to move it on:

> Nobody has done more to celebrate the Cornish past and make it intelligible to and valued by English readers than I have done, certainly in my generation. Yet there is little enough appreciation of that in Cornwall, and when I consider the type that is dominant in the county – conventional, narrow, nonconformist, hypocritical, uncivilized – I am perpetually irritated by it.[29]

Rowse's most successful prose form was the short story (a form quite rare in the Cornish literary continuum until this phase), and he assembled several collections during this period; his narratives were often anthologized.[30] However, Rowse's ear for dialect was not as well defined or as genuine as that of the earlier writers such as Quiller Couch and Lee. In *A Cornish Childhood*, he confesses that he had a 'complex about Cornish dialect', because the education system he was entering was forcing him to standardize his speech and to use received pronunciation. Otherwise, he comments that he would have been 'infallibly barred', and here one begins to understand the cultural pressures Rowse had to cope with.[31] And it was symbolic of the wider linguistic pressures that the Cornish, and a number of other groups within Britain, were forced to live under, when regional voices and accents were inappropriate for those who wanted – using the Cornish idiom – to 'get on'. Rowse's decision to adapt was representative of the experiences of many a Cornish person of this period. In Rowse's case, the conformity allowed him to complete much needed scholarship upon Cornwall, but it came at a cost for the majority of the Cornish population – because Cornu-English, since the death of Cornish, was the most popular badge of identity. Rowse was aware of this issue – indeed it suffused many aspects of his poetry – yet because of his cultural circumstances and society's wider discrimination, he could not alter this position. His problem was not helped by the marginalization of Cornu-English within the Revival itself, which was still promoting in its magazines a vision of a modern Cornish society which had Cornish as its central linguistic pillar.

Cornu-English was nevertheless important within Rowse's narratives. 'The Curse Upon the Clavertons' (1967) is a historical tale set in the 'higher quarter' clayland of mid-Cornwall at the turn of the century. The story follows the business dealings of Thomas Claverton and how he exploited the abilities of William Slade, a man who 'd'knaw clay'.[32] Claverton is a man too big for his boots, whose desire to amalgamate smaller mining operations into a near-monopoly (around the period of the 1913–14 clay strikes) causes his downfall. The story depicts the changes occurring within the clay-mining industries of the post-war period which was marked by the merging of hundreds of smaller companies into a conglomerate. In this story, Rowse had identified the wider transition occurring in Cornish society; that in its need to modernize, to conform, to update, Cornwall was in a perceived danger of sacrificing its difference. Here Rowse identifies this dilemma – which is really the dilemma of modern Cornwall, and indeed most European societies of the late twentieth century.

In his lifetime, Rowse also produced a considerable number of poetry collections, and this work forms a debating ground for his changing and complex perceptions of Cornwall and Cornish identity.[33] His construction during this early time appears to have been predominantly modelled on the Anglo-Irish influence with its ideology representing simple, rural, Celtic life, as well as a certain mystic melancholy, and upholding an idealized philosophy of life. This is most prevalent in poetry such as 'The Old Cornish Woman by the Fire', 'At Duporth' and 'Saturday at Truro'.[34] Another early poem ('The Snake') pays tribute to D.H. Lawrence,[35] yet Rowse's construction neither sits within the desire for a Celtic Other of the visiting poets and novelists, nor the realism of the other Cornish writers of the early twentieth

19. A.L. Rowse as a boy with his grandparents (photo: H.Gibbs, St Austell).

Souvenir Programme   *Price two shillings*

20.   Gwen Wood's cover design for the 1951 Cornish Drama Festival souvenir programme.

21. Jack Clemo and mother, tempera and pastel portrait by Lionel Miskin, 1958.

THE

3s. 6d.

CORNISH REVIEW

EDITED BY DENYS VAL BAKER

Number Two   Summer 1966

22. Denys Val Baker's immensely influential *Cornish Review*.

century. The reality was that Rowse was radically reforming Cornish poetry, by understanding Cornish difference without resorting to the image-base of Dryden Hosken, Chirgwin or other poets involved more explicitly with the Revival. Neither was it explicitly Cornish in its metaphors, though this might have much to do with Rowse's own poetic accommodation into an apparently all-embracing English literature. Much of his poetry remains locked into describing a kind of wider Cornish arcadia; less directly inspired by those in the Revival, but providing a continuity back to Davy, Godolphin and Carew.[36] We may go further, and even suggest a direct continuity between Rowse and such medieval scholars as Trevisa and Roscarrock. Identity would not have to assume the symbolism of the Cornish Revival either; Rowse felt himself beyond that, and to an extent, he was correct. His poetry would transcend that, and yet it failed to capture popular Cornish identity of the period in the way that the works of Causley or Clemo were to do.

Rowse's construction of Cornwall is multi-faceted. A kind of Hardyesque longing is discernible in poems like 'The Road to Luxulyan' and 'Trenarren Waiting',[37] but is most exemplified by 'How Many Miles to Mylor?' – an exile's longing for home, and an obvious theme of any post-emigration literature from Cornish writers.[38] This is matched elsewhere into a coming-to-terms with the consequences of Cornish economic experience in 'The Old Cemetery at St Austell', and the certainty that there would be absolutely no return to industrial greatness after World War Two:

> [T]hey are all fled over the seven seas:
> Ruin descended on the mines and these
> Men were driven forth to earn their bread
> In America, Australia, Africa.
> These are our exiles: they have left their bones
> In foreign soil, under other stones.[39]

Cornish identity is further constructed in poems such as 'Home-Coming to Cornwall: December 1942', where Rowse explores how his community responds to his position as an academic, and how often those who have left Cornwall for life in England are criticized the most, for not 'toughing it out' like the rest. Thus in a poem which finds Rowse perhaps imagining one of the anonymous early writers, or maybe even Carew – 'that older poet/Search still for Arthur's grave in this waste land/Where Fragments of forgotten peoples dwell' – the very same people criticize the way he has had to alter his accent and persona to fit into English academia, whilst at the same time, Rowse invests so much emotional and poetic energy in a Cornish landscape and culture which he so clearly loves and feels patriotic about.[40] The love-hate relationship which Rowse had with Cornwall could not be solved, because for much of his life he was drawn between two cultures. Because of the way British society demanded greater homogeneity, Rowse was unable to resolve the tension. The expression of Cornish identity in Rowse's work comes at an ideological cost, as in 'Leaving Cornwall: Autumn 1944':

> And I have come
> Out of Cornwall, out of the kingdom of the *cliché*,
> Out of the region of misunderstanding, out
> Of the dark realm of suspicion and misapprehension. . .[41]

Rowse, as in his prose writings, was expressing the genuine concerns of a generation of Cornish people, who in order to be educated, to develop in their professions, would have to reconcile their Cornish identity to a wider academia, a wider South West, or even a Greater Britain; in which Cornish identity was something to be suppressed, something ignorant and primitive, something which Rowse and others had to shake off, even though it was deeply and passionately felt inside. His response to Cornwall is developed to new levels in his Cornish poems of the 1970s and 1980s, where the love-hate relationship is mellowed by a lifetime's deeper understanding of Cornwall's history and distinctiveness.

However, Rowse would not go much further into actively making known his allegiances or political views on Cornwall in later life, despite a clear acknowledgement of Cornish nationalism, and close relationships with those individuals involved in the struggle for Cornish self-determination.[42] Perhaps Rowse's most important poetic achievement is his epic poem 'Duporth' (1981), where, towards the end of his poetic career, he appears to have become more critical about how Cornwall had altered in the post-war period; in so doing, telling the folklore and history of the south Cornish coast. The poem goes beyond this, however, to become Rowse's finest understanding of the twentieth-century Cornish situation. There is a more critical eye, which juxtaposes Cornish history with the post-war economic direction. The poem climaxes with the news that Duporth's majestic scenery is to be changed by the ugly faces of modernity and tourism:

> In a time when the people have never had it so good:
> The ancient granite piers, pink-coated cement,
> Beckon the roadster to – a Butlin's Camp.[43]

As it is, 'Duporth' is Rowse's finest poetic achievement by the breadth of the imagery and detailing of Cornish history, and should be commended to any reader cynical about Rowse's work, who feels he is still somehow dismissive of the Cornish issue. Clearly Rowse was aware of the work of the Revivalists in publications like *Old Cornwall* and *Cornish Review*, where many of the ideological questions over Cornish culture were being addressed, but he did not engage with them frequently enough for the Cornish Revivalists to champion him. Because Rowse was never an overt nationalist or even Revivalist in the way that his predecessors (Dryden Hosken or Quiller Couch) were, he was unable to lead Cornish poetry forward to depict questions of identity in the way that was needed, given the historic circumstances and the incorporation of Cornwall into the 'South West' of England.

Rowse is typical of post-war writers in Cornwall. Writers operating in the Cornish context in the post-war period are the product of the economic separation of Cornwall into small town units, to which Ronald Perry has drawn attention, which works against the formation of artistic 'schools' (west Cornwall may have been one exception).[44] This is not necessarily regrettable. It may be that at this stage of its development as a society, with all the dramatic socio-economic change that has been experienced in Cornwall after World War Two, Cornwall was becoming a potent breeding ground for individual and distinctive visions of Cornish difference rather than of writers creating from a shared vision.

Thus, whilst Rowse articulated the Cornish experience of exile and the continuing difficulties of both personal and community accommodation with England in the twentieth century, another very different construction of Cornwall and Cornish identity is to be found in the writings of Jack Clemo. Clemo is almost mythic, and is often represented as a near-Miltonic, blind and deaf poet, who writes only of the china clay landscape near St Austell.[45] He is viewed as 'hermit mystic' rather than an artist. This is a mistaken view, which distracts from Clemo's position within the Cornish literary continuum, and actually denies the influence of his work. Clemo has had a far more important shaping effect on Anglo-Cornish literature, and gives us a sense of continuity from as far back as the medieval period. As well as providing what Andrew Symons labels one of the most 'authentic voices' of modern Cornish writing,[46] he also developed the Anglo-Cornish novel and short story to new levels of realism.

Clemo (1916–1994) attended Trethosa Village School, but was largely self-educated.[47] His autobiography, *Confession of a Rebel* (1949) traces the development of a boy reared on the edge of 'making do' poverty in an area where the expanding china-clay extractive industry was altering the landscape. As a young man, he had suffered partial, then total and permanent, deafness. From childhood he also knew periods of intermittent blindness, and eventually, in 1955, when aged thirty-nine, he lost his sight too.[48] His father, Reggie Clemo, had travelled, like many Cornishmen of his generation, to find work in North America which led, in Clemo's mother's opinion, to an immoral life.[49] After his father was killed in action in 1917, Clemo was single-handedly raised by his mother, Eveline Clemo, who was central in his development as a writer.[50] Clemo's early life was stereotypically Cornish in many ways, influenced as it was by Methodism, emigration and industrialism. It was also modern and many aspects of his Cornish context were also international: the one-parent family, alienation from organized religion, unemployment, problematic relationships and sexual curiosity. Clemo's driving force was a deeply religious and idio-syncratic sense of Christianity; details of which he describes in his 1958 theological book, *The Invading Gospel*.[51]

Clemo's vision of Cornish experience, like Harris' and Hardy's, is intensely personal. Clemo's writing career is generally assumed to have started with the publication of his novel *Wilding Graft* in 1948,[52] but the reality was that Clemo had been involved with the literary scene in Cornwall for a number of years prior to this, already having written a number of well-observed Cornu-English narratives.[53] Clemo had a distrust of Cornish Revivalist culture for much of his career; he considered it backward-looking, irrelevant and Pagan, though in 1970 accepted a Cornish Gorseth bardship.[54] He can never be described as a writer with nationalist convictions, though he is clearly aware of both his own, and Cornwall's, difference.[55] Indeed, he was not averse to calling himself Celtic and 'un-English';[56] perhaps the latter more accurately describing his vision. Within his prose writing, Clemo's assertion of identity, unlike the thrust of Revivalist culture, was focused upon Cornu-English and working-class experience: in its way more in tune with the popular construction of Cornishness in the mid-twentieth century.

The particular historical moment of the creation of Clemo's texts is important to consider. He was writing in a period of immense austerity and poverty,[57] and in an age in which the environmental consequences of the extractive industries in Cornwall were barely considered. On one level, he becomes their first critic; on another, their supporter. His spiritual inheritance is more complex, related as it is to the culture of Methodism and chapels which so infused life in nineteenth- and early twentieth-century Cornwall, but also to a certain Catholicism, which is certainly present in Clemo's work. In the 1940s Clemo developed his own Calvinistic belief system influenced by both Protestant evangelism and Orthodox spirituality. As Hurst comments, Clemo's nonconformity 'comes from a tradition central to the development of Cornish life', but ironically, given his pursuits, 'one which is usually uninterested in, or even inimical to, the arts.'[58]

Before Clemo gained recognition as a poet, his primary intention was to work as a novelist. He wrote several novels as a young man, though only two have been published. The first, *Wilding Graft* (1948), is a central text within post-war Anglo-Cornish literature, redefining the themes and characterization of the Cornish novel, and also offering a potent, disturbing realism. In essence, it was Cornwall's first modernist novel. This feel for Cornwall had begun to emerge in novels like *Out of this Fury* by A.W. Holmes,[59] but broadly, the hard-hitting vision of Cornwall had been late to arrive, since the bulk of Cornish writers operating between 1890 and 1940 had been more concerned with a reinvention of Cornwall as Celtic or as Celtic Other. *Wilding Graft* destroys that expectation in several ways. Primarily, the text moves away from the two established landscapes of Cornish writing – the coast and the tin- and copper-mining industries (which had come to the fore in the nineteenth century). Instead, it moves to the reality of working-class mid-Cornwall. Secondly, the achievement of the novel is Clemo's ability to evoke a convincing reality of a grim landscape in which the action is played out. The first glimpses the reader receives of it are far from the Cornwall of Leo Walmsley and the early fiction of Daphne du Maurier:

> His pace slackened perceptively as the huddled, shapeless white mass of Meledor claydumps jarred his vision above the frost-thinned scrub of downs.[60]

This is not the Cornwall of romance: there is a sense of discomfort in 'huddled' and 'shapeless'. It is the story of a clay-labourer, Garth Joslin, and his love for a fifteen-year-old London girl called Irma. She is driven from him by the scandal-mongers of a village community who cannot understand the nature of his spiritually intense love. This love takes place in a landscape which is hostile and unforgiving, full of suffering and tragedy ('[Seth Spragg] walked with a limp, never having recovered from an accident on Retew claywork two years ago when his leg was crushed by a skip wagon'[61]). Meledor also symbolizes the wider suffering of the world during World War Two. According to the observations of Lowman, *Wilding Graft* is a novel which attempts to depict the 'workings of grace' in human affairs in a way attempted by hardly any other British novelist this century.[62] The result is that Clemo's imagining of the Cornish landscape works as a metaphor for spiritual conflict. Lowman's critique of Clemo offers an important conceptualization of his work, though in our sense of the continuity of Anglo-Cornish literature, an embryonic sense of this is also found in the writings of John Harris and the Hocking family. Clemo is the continuum of that movement.

Though there is little construction of Celtic Revivalism within *Wilding Graft*, the novel does establish a new conceptualization of Cornish identity, which is explored in the merging of the higher spiritual with the industrial; and despite the fact that not all readers would identify or even sympathize with the spiritual level at which Clemo was working, a fictional text had begun to explore Cornwall in a way which connected with more of the emotional experiences of his generation. Clemo's sense of personal and wider cultural difference was to be expressed again in *A Shadowed Bed*, a novel completed in 1948, though not published until 1986.[63] In the preface, Clemo explains how this work also 'embodies the primitive clay-bed mysticism . . . in the gritty region of Cornwall which I describe';[64] a comment supported by the novel's opening: 'An excavator had crunched to and fro along the lane of the clay dump'.[65] This novel is the drama of one village, Carn Veor, in which an almost medieval imagination haunts a weird patch of the modern clay industry. The protagonist, Joe Gool, is a striking characterisation of the mid-twentieth-century working-class Cornish-man, where identity is projected onto industrial landscape:

> Joe Gool, who was working on the dam early in the afternoon, was not a paid labourer. He had come to the site when these men left it, and yielded to a whim, seeking some exertion before he met Bronwen Cundy. . . The stark, grey background suited him; he seemed to commune with the coldly volcanic clay world, knowing its vagaries and loving them.[66]

The text has a number of disturbing forces within it: Penroth pit's workers are apparently inhabitants of a mental institution, whilst the 'Pagan' standing stone at the end of Potter's Lane serves as a centre of evil, enabling Clemo to ask disturbing questions about Cornwall's pre-Christian past. Clemo may well be accurate in this depiction of Cornish identity, yet his own spirituality seems intolerant of others. The standing stone is tied inevitably with a murky and dangerous Pagan past, which Clemo intensively feels within his work, but which he connects always with the negative. The allegory takes on a cosmic significance as the lives of the villagers are changed by warring magnetic forces of good and evil. There is always the redemptive symbol of the clay – Christ – in the midst, however.

Unlike a predecessor such as John Harris, Clemo seems unable to reconcile the Pagan and Christian aspects of Cornish history. His is a highly individualistic view of Cornish culture, and one which was uncompromising. Clemo's unique style and vision established him as an important Anglo-Cornish writer, yet his popularity was restricted by the increase in interest in the Pagan and apparently more Celtic Cornwall of an earlier age. Similarly, in *Wilding Graft*, it is Griffiths' rejection of Christianity and his agnosticism which causes his life to go awry. This plot links Clemo directly with the moral fiction of the Hockings, and even to the earlier medieval literature in Cornish, where again a 'divine order' is being negotiated.[67]

Cornwall and Cornish identity (infused with Nonconformity) are central within Clemo's poetry. Yet for Clemo, his twentieth-century experience of Cornwall is completely intertwined with Christianity. The main themes of his poetry are the fall of humanity, suffering and redemption, and the sacrament of marriage. These themes are worked through in a Cornish context with the imagery of the clay industry as the central metaphor. Much of the poetry achieves its effect by uniting the spiritual and the material in both the language of his predecessors (solitude, stark, pledge) and that of the clay landscape around him (bedrock, pit, clayey). In the poem, which contextualises all the successive 'clay' poetry – 'Christ in the Clay Pit' – he asks 'Why should I find him here,/And not in church?'[68] The clay itself is symbolic of the flesh of Christ, and whilst to some people, the mid-Cornwall landscape may seem cruel and unrelenting, to Clemo the landscape is sensual:

> I feel exultantly
> The drip of clayey water from the poised
> Still bar above me, thrilling with the rite
> Of baptism all my own.[69]

The excavator of the clay landscape destroys the local environment, but here it becomes both a baptism and Christ's cross. As in all the early collections – *The Clay Verge* (1951), *The Map of Clay* (1961), *Cactus on Carmel* (1967) – there is concern with the formal reality of the Cornish landscape – lunar images to decribe pits, pyramids and breasts to describe tips.[70] It is Clemo's 'intimate landscape'.[71] He knows its power:

> Here on the sharp clay tip there broods
> Olympian thunder, bold and swift,
> Fiercest of all God's moods.[72]

Although Clemo's depiction of the mid-Cornish industrial land-scape is central to his poetry, it is not the only theme he explores. In his later writings he writes about incidents with wider appeal such as the Torrey Canyon oil tanker wreck off the Cornish coast.[73] Perhaps

Clemo's most typical poem of this 'broader' period of his writing is 'St Just-in-Roseland', inspired by a visit that he and his wife made to the Roseland peninsula churchyard. Here the poem takes the reader through several layers of Cornish identity, from the wild and exotic sense of the Other which had, in part, been created by the imagery produced by the Great Western Railway, the imagined primitivism of Cornwall, as well as the Age of Saints, connecting Clemo's work to a continuum beginning with Roscarrock:

> Roots of bamboo, eucalyptus, palm,
> Curl towards buried Cornish saints;
> Exotic leaves twang a jungle prayer
> Above the river-bed now drained at ebb-tide,
> Where boats lounge on mud-banks and wait
> For the gurgling inwash from Falmouth Bay.[74]

Clemo's last two collections are crucial in coming to a full understanding of his presentation of Cornwall and his own identity. Now travelled in Britain and Europe, he offers a wider reflective vision of the Cornishman outside his primary landscape, but occasionally returning to it. In 'Ironies of a Homecoming' from the volume titled *Approach to Murano*, Clemo remarks upon the 'Clay-tips again!' yet there is not the same consensus as before ('I no longer understand/The gaunt hills' lines of struggle.')[75] However, his Cornish consciousness is too embedded in Clemo for him ever to forget it completely:

> I plodded around Windsor Castle,
> Of all places – I who was born
> Under crusts of a drab trade, smoke-skewered,
> Clammy with kiln-stream,[76]

Inevitably, Clemo's geographical change in moving to Dorset in England with his wife was related to a spiritual and emotional shift away from what he later labelled 'cramped and austere concepts of truth'.[77] His final collection, *The Cured Arno*, shows how the symbol of Dante's river represents Clemo's 'cured ego', and there is more of a balance between Cornish and non-Cornish experiences.[78]

Clemo's verse has great power, but though he incorporated aspects of the Christian development of Cornwall, and to an extent the landscape of Cornwall, his writing and vision remained highly idiosyncratic and therefore rather inaccessible to many Cornish people who could not relate to his work. Clemo was too rooted in one landscape, in his own disabilities and his lack of connection to a wider Cornish identity, whether based in folklore, Cornish language or mining, to be a poetic champion for Cornwall during the post-war years. That champion was not to be found in mid- or west Cornwall, but perhaps surprisingly, on the border Athelstan had centuries earlier defined with England, in the town of Launceston. His name was Charles Causley.

Of all the post-war writers operating in the Cornish context, Causley (b.1917) is the poet who has been most successful in developing the sense of continuity in Cornish writing, in his choice both of subject-matter and form; he has also succeeded in his poetry in offering a positive and confident construction of Cornish identity, as well as a continued and well-articulated sense of difference. Causley, however, is not in any way a poet of nationalism; his Cornishness is defined in his poetry's rhythms and playfulness, and in his acute knowledge of Cornish folklore and narrative.

However, this has not prevented his work from also demonstrating some limited sense of dual identity: one moment being Cornish, the next English; principally arising from Causley's own personal history of naval service during World War Two, and the particular period in which he was writing – when despite his assertion of Cornish folk beliefs and traditions – the territory itself was being further integrated into England.[79] Like Rowse, and to an extent Clemo, Causley has had to negotiate these dual allegiances and testings of identity, which have so shaped literature in the post-war period. As with the other Anglo-Cornish writers of his generation between 1940 and 1980, there is a certain scepticism over the Cornish Revival and the regeneration of an indigenous Cornish literature. Causley rarely refers to these explicitly in his work, even though he offers a near-Revivalist interest in Cornwall's history and folklore, and infuses his poetry with words and phrases which are actually Cornish or are anglified versions of Cornish words. Causley's writing is thus a potent mixture of a number of aspects of Cornish identity, providing links to earlier literatures of Cornwall, whilst at the same time acknowledging the influence of English literature on his own writing.

Broadly independent of the Revivalist movement in Cornwall, Causley had written three plays by the outbreak of World War Two.[80] The war took him from Cornwall for the first time. His naval experiences provide the themes for much of his immediate post-war writing – *Farewell Aggie Weston* (1951), his first volume of poems, and the short story collection *Hands to Dance and Skylark* (1951).[81] Hurst comments that

> [i]t is as if the enlargement of experience given by his time in the
> Royal Navy, together with the background of voracious reading

215

of anything and everything available to him, combined to trigger the imagination that was to become an authentic (because it was unselfconscious and unassertive) voice of Cornwall.[82]

In *Hands to Dance and Skylark*, the stories 'Looking for Annie' and 'Mrs Lisboa' explore Cornwall during the years of World War Two. In the first story Causley is aware of 'being a Cornishman' and "belonged". . . to go to sea';[83] the writer is aware of a certain pre-destination in Cornish people to end up being connected with the sea and the ocean. Much underrated, these tales do much to explore Cornish culture during the war years. However, the distillation of Causley's years in the navy was his early poetry.[84] Causley writes often of the naval town of Plymouth. Plymouth, somehow, is a part of most Cornish people's existence: it is generally the first large English city they encounter, and for years, thousands of Cornish people have worked there. This experience, coupled with his position alongside the upper reaches of Tamar, gave Causley additional experiences of the 'borderland' – both in urban and rural contexts, and it had a significant shaping effect on his verse, and thus his construction of Cornish difference and identity.[86]

Frequently, Causley's influences are read by Anglo-centric critics as being typified by writers such as A.E. Housman and Robert Graves, and though these are important, rarely are Causley's Cornish influences considered.[87] In some respects, he lies at the mid-twentieth-century end of a continuum which began with the Cornish balladeers, though the religious elements of his writing can be linked back much further to Cornish medieval literature. Cornishness here is endorsed via narrative tradition (which itself has evolved from balladeering and droll-telling) evoking oral tradition rather than modernist poetic forms. In the preface to Causley's third poetry collection, *Union Street*, Edith Sitwell praised Causley for his 'strange individuality'.[88] Perhaps she was actually noting Causley's own different identity. However, while there has been much admiration and critical praise of his work, the political or cultural implications have rarely been addressed.[89]

Each volume of Causley's work contains a diverse mixture of poems on Cornish and non-Cornish themes, but there is often an additional group of narrative ballads on Cornish historical or legendary subjects. These are perhaps the most significant poetic indicators of his Cornish identity, and are important in that they have helped to popularize Cornish history and legendary material. His stories of Charlotte Dymond and Young Edgcumbe are two examples,[90] as is 'John Polrudden', a story which though dating from the Tudor period, still constitutes twentieth-century expression of Cornish adventure:

216

They saw his wine
His siver shine
They heard his fiddlers play.

'Tonight,' they said,
'Out of his bed
Polrudden we'll take away.'[91]

Causley's interest in folklore and mythology could be read as providing a direct continuity from the literary renderings of Robert Hunt
and William Bottrell, but also with the oral culture surrounding him.
Poems such as 'Christ at the Cheesewring', 'Ramhead and Dodman',
'The Young Man of Cury' and 'The Obby Oss' all take the reader to
remarkably Celtic spaces – standing stones, moorland, clifftops, festival
– which not only emphasise history and difference, but which as
magical realism, parallel constructions of the Celtic Otherworld which
mix the magical with the mundane.[92] In such ways, Causley was
meeting those writing within the Cornish Revival, but was operating on
a more sophisticated level. The poem 'Cornwall' reaches a fuller
expression of Causley's own Cornishness, and becomes the most
assertive of all his poems, pressing metaphorically for Cornwall to re-
establish itself and regain this fundamental and magical confidence; a
position completely in alignment with the Revivalists' new nationalism:

One day, friend and stranger,
The granite beast will rise
Rubbing the salt sea from his hundred eyes
Sleeping no longer.[93]

This is the closest Causley ever comes to this kind of sentiment, yet
his love of the territory is never in any doubt. Unlike Clemo, however,
Causley appears to have more time for the folklore and wider history
of Cornwall, and was more sympathetic to the magical themes found
in legend and folktale. Like Clemo (and unlike Rowse) he is at home
with Cornu-English; Causley is able to shift between dialect and
standard English with ease and he understands its importance in
defining popular identity. However, his use of Cornu-English is much
more indirect than Clemo's as he does not write it phonetically.
Nevertheless, the Cornish voice is quite evident here:

My young man's a Cornishman
He lives in Camborne town,
I met him going up the hill
As I was coming down.

And I shall give him scalded cream
And starry-gazy pie,

217

And make him a saffron cake for tea
And a pasty for by and by.[94]

Causley's ability here is to synthesize and popularize a number of symbols – both ancient and modern – of Cornish identity and experience. The effect of this is to provide a confident vision of the young twentieth-century Cornishman, transcending Perry's 'small-town' culture and unifying Cornish difference from the Tamar to Land's End; the very structure that was needed in the on-going reconstruction of identity. Cleverly, Causley integrates the medieval saintly tradition with that of nineteenth-century industrial activity, so that a post-modern depiction of Cornwall begins to emerge.[95]

Causley retained his magical realist interpretation of Cornish experience, but given his circumstances, and the lack of a more widely established sense of intellectual Cornish difference, his view of Cornish identity perhaps was disguised – possibly even anglified – to make it less radical than the sense of cultural nationalism which forms the backdrop to all his Cornish poems. Causley, whilst fundamentally achieving an important vision of Cornwall in his work, was culturally pulled both ways: in 'On the Border' he questions 'Is it Cornwall? Is it Devon?/Those promised fields, blue as the vine?'[96] This and other poems are the product of his borderland and naval experiences within the wider English effort to further assimilate Cornwall. In retrospect, his achievement in verse was his ability to subvert the wider cultural process, by an active assertion of a Cornish identity based upon childhood experiences, religion and folk belief.

Whilst writers like Causley, Rowse and Clemo continued to play 'the Cornish card' in and outside the territory during the 1960s and 1970s, Cornwall continued to attract a series of writers into the community, still seeking a Celtic Other, apparently distant from the materialism of England. Peter Redgrove's anthology, *Cornwall in Verse* (1982), encapsulates the response to Cornwall from a number of visiting writers, among them Redgrove himself, Peter Scupham, Patricia Beer, Penelope Shuttle, Frances Bellerby and Geoffrey Grigson; poets who have all constructed images of Cornwall within their work, and who, together, provide interesting insights into visiting writers' concerns with Cornwall in the post-war period.[97] However, for the most part, their writing has tended to steer towards depictions of landscape. Similarly, the poetry of Sylvia Kantaris and Zofia Ilinska use Cornwall as the incidental setting, rather than the essence of their work.[98]

Of all the visiting writers, however, one stands out as managing to capture – despite his background and lifestyle – a sense of Cornish identity in the face of profound post-war change. That writer is John

Betjeman. Betjeman (1906–84) was born in Highgate, but spent his childhood holidays in Cornwall. In particular, his poetry focuses on locations such as Trebetherick, Rock and Polzeath in north Cornwall, yet also manages to capture issues symptomatic of wider Cornwall between 1940 and 1980. He was particularly concerned with the impact of mass tourism. When he was made Poet Laureate in 1972, his position allowed his poetic construction of Cornwall to reach a wide readership. Several important issues emerge in Betjeman's writing on Cornwall. He was aware of his middle-class positioning, and wrote of the attitudes of the middle-class English to Cornwall, viewing it as simply a convenient playground, exotic, close to home and unthreatening. Paradoxically, this social awareness gave Betjeman better opportunity to comment on contemporary Cornwall than some of the indigenous writers of the period. As Hurst succinctly puts it:

> Betjeman is more explicitly concerned with 'the matter of Cornwall' and with what is happening to Cornwall than either Clemo or Causley – for whom Cornwall is the air they breathe, the assumed subject, rather than the concern.[99]

Therefore, in terms of the continuum of writing about Cornwall, Betjeman is a crucial figure, since he, more than any other poet criticized the direction that Cornwall was being forced to move in. In its own particular way, this was a significant part of the wider concern felt about Cornwall by Revivalists, nationalists and environmentalists alike in the post-war period. Perceptively, Betjeman realized that he himself was causing the destruction of Cornwall:

> The visitors come to Cornwall. I'm a visitor. We litter the cliff with our houses. We litter the cliffs with our shacks. When I was a boy, all this place was open fields. And Cornwall is older than the Cornish.[100]

Cornish saints and their lives remain an on-going thematic concern in Betjeman's poetry, linking him with early writers such as Nicholas Roscarrock, but also more recently with Hunt and Bottrell. Here in 'Trebetherick', memories of family holidays in Cornwall are woven into praise for St. Enodoc:

> Blessed be St Enodoc, blessed be the wave,
> Blessed be the springy turf, we pray, pray to thee
> Ask for our children all the happy days you gave
> To Ralph, Vasay, Alistair, Biddy, John and me.[101]

The saints of Cornwall are Betjeman's touchstone for promoting a type of spirituality that is apparently absent in the materialism of the post-war period. Collectively, poems such as 'Trebetherick' and 'Saint

Cadoc'[102] have helped to revitalize interest in the lives of Cornwall's saints, fulfilling part of the on-going fusion of Celtic Christianity and Celtic Neo-Paganism, which have both attracted many visitors and in-migrants. Betjeman's poems are unashamedly anti-metropolitan, and often long for an earlier, unspoilt Cornwall, that to which the Revivalists aspired and 'gazed' at. Taking Quiller Couch's earlier concept of the 'Delectable Duchy', Betjeman satirizes how vulgar and unrefined Cornwall has become (everything that also annoyed developing Cornish political nationalism):

> Here in the late October light
> See Cornwall, a pathetic sight,
> Raddled and put upon and tired
> And looking somewhat overhired.[103]

In his verse autobiography *Summoned by Bells* (1960) a similar concern can be noted. He recalls seeing how a local shoe-shop had adapted to tourism, selling 'dialect tales in verse/Published in Truro (Netherton and Worth)/And model lighthouses of serpentine'.[104] Betjeman was the poet who sounded loudly the alarm bell over how Cornish difference and identity might become 'over-hired', and reduced to 'serpentine lighthouses', even though he knew he had been part of the problem.

Another distinctive aspect of Betjeman's vision of Cornwall was his fascination with Cornish Christianity. Such poems allow Betjeman to explore how Christianity in its peculiarly Cornish forms has been expressed, and how that expression has shaped the identity of the Cornish. Even in the most mundane settings, Betjeman returns to and seeks spiritual experience in the Cornish setting. In *Summoned by Bells* he observes 'hills upon whose clinging side the farms/Hold Bible Christians',[105] – giving us a continuity from the Methodist morality in both fiction and poetry; whilst elsewhere he meets the supernatural face of Celtic Christianity, recalling his spiritual predecessors in 'North Coast Recollections':

> Here Petroc landed, here I stand to-day;
> The same Atlantic surges roll for me
> As rolled for Parson Hawker and for him. . .[106]

In such work, Betjeman allows the reader to understand the multitude of layers of Cornish spirituality and to understand the shaping force of such mysticism in Cornish identity, in its own way, stretching back to the Mystery plays of medieval Cornwall. Thus, Betjeman intensely understood the cultural pressures and spiritual changes which Cornwall was living under. In his well-known 1964 essay on

Cornwall, he explains the true characteristics of the Cornish people, who were increasingly becoming romanticized:

> The Cornish themselves are not dreamy and unpractical as the 'foreigners' sometimes suppose. Like most Celts, they combine a deep sense of religion with a shrewd gift for business.[107]

Betjeman's criticisms were disturbingly accurate. In being critical about the Cornish experience, Betjeman was writing progressive poetry; verse that was not afraid to confront the changing nature of Cornwall's difference and peripheralism. Indeed, similar arguments had been put forward by writers as diverse as Daphne du Maurier and A.L. Rowse. Furthermore, in the Cornish context, Betjeman also assumed the role of an early environmental campaigner and anti-developer; concerns which were to become increasingly to the forefront of the Cornish agenda after his death. Although a visiting writer imagining Cornwall often from outside, Betjeman nonetheless managed to interpret much of the wider doubt during this phase over Cornwall's future collective identity.

There were indigenous writers who were also beginning to offer new sophisticated representations of Cornish experience, which brought new constructions of Cornwall into collision with wider world movements in philosophy, psychology and the sexual revolution. D.M. Thomas may be the most daring of these. Thomas was born in 1935 in Carnkie, near the Camborne/Redruth mining area. He studied at Oxford, and later his National Service took him to Russia.[108] Thomas has written about the 'two emotional landscapes' of his world – Cornwall and Russia.[109] Though he is widely travelled, all the core ingredients of Cornish identity were present in his early life – mining, Methodism and the experience of emigration (Thomas' parents and older sister had lived in California before he was born). In his writing career, which began with a set of poems based on science fiction themes,[110] it is mainly his earlier work, during the 1970s and early 1980s which dealt with his imagined Cornwall. After the success of his Freudian novel *The White Hotel* (1981), he returned to Cornwall, though since then his writing has tended to consider more non-Cornish themes; the pyschological portraits and concerns with sexuality (established with his Cornish work) being applied elsewhere.[111] The early Cornish poems consider Thomas' central theme of sex and death, being worked through a series of narrative portraits of his family. In these poems, of all the poets writing during this phase, it is Thomas who best captures Cornish identity in the post-war period. His poetry is filled with empathy for the Cornish situation and he intimately understands the Cornish 'take' on life, via the people's 'natural' understatement:

'Goin' a' drop rain arr us?' – the sky
an enraged bladder. 'He've had a drop to drink'.
'I dear like a bit ride.'[112]

Such poems expressed Cornish people's residual sense of 'making do' despite never having it so good and living apparently in an era of increased wealth and consumer materialism. In addition, poems such as 'Ninemaidens', 'Botallack' (where 'The logan stone of me is here') and 'Meditation on Lines from the Methodist Hymnal' ('The granite shoulder of the penwith moor wears heather purple as the coat of Joseph of Arimathea') all show a sense of layering in Cornish experience, how not one layer of it can describe the totality of the identity.[113] Cornish experience (particularly spiritual experience) is complex and multi-layered, still on-going despite the modernization of the 1960s and 1970s. Thomas expresses Cornwall vividly through imagery, history and in language – his command of Cornish idiom and Cornu-English are direct and authentic, as in this section from 'Under Carn Brea':

Think of his dear mother, she could 'ardly stan', crawlin'
About on 'er 'ands and knees, I expec' she was,
Beatin' 'er 'ead n the ground, 'cause 'er *dear* Son. . .[114]

His imagery is intensely erotic, and sometimes disturbing, yet Thomas also manages to capture down-to-earth Cornish humour. This humour in fact becomes one of Thomas' ways of demonstrating Cornish difference – a technique which had its roots not only in the narratives of Tregellas and the other nineteenth-century 'dialecticians' but also in earlier writers such as Andrew Boorde.

Although Thomas is a thoroughly post-modern writer, he is still compelled by the notions of ancient landscape; standing stones and megalithic monuments are frequently the settings for his work. Here we see the ancient landscape of Pagan Cornwall infused with the erotic:

I am the men-an-tol, the wind's vagina;
I am the circle of stones grouped around grass.[115]

This was a new direction for Cornish literature. It is not necessarily that Thomas is among the first writers who grew up with Methodism to break from its strictures, but unlike any writer before him, he is comfortable expressing eroticism and Paganism freely in a Cornish context. Poems such as 'Penwith' and 'Ninemaidens' are close to the landscape and Pagan theme of Thomas' only novel with a Cornish setting, *Birthstone* (1980).[116] Set in late twentieth-century Cornwall, *Birthstone* contains Thomas' blend of fantasy, comedy, eroticism and magic. The novel concerns itself with a visitor, Jo, who is on holiday in Cornwall where she meets an American academic, Hector, and his mother, Lola. They endure a personal reawakening after they crawl through the hole at the centre of the men-an-tol. It is a temptation Jo and Lola cannot resist. Crawling through it is an ancient cure of all ills. The effects are not slow to occur. While Lola's decline into old age is reversed, her son's is greatly accelerated. Even when they return home, the birthstone's influence persists, and Thomas questions whether magical properties really exist, or whether the transformation is psychological. The novel therefore works as a Freudian fantasy set in a legendary landscape. Jo is forced to admit:

> I was even in touch with the lonely stone cottages. . . and the lives of the people who lived there, and of the dead whom they loved. I was in touch with the moor stones. They were flowering in my fingers.[117]

Such language is perhaps endemic of a particular kind of vision of Celtic Cornwall, which Thomas admirably writes here. Thomas is symbolic of how writers have tried to express the mix of eroticism, sexuality and Celticity which has come to be associated with the west Cornwall landscape in particular. Interestingly, Thomas' novel emerged at a point where west Cornwall (due to a combination of New Age interest in stone monuments, holy wells and folklore) had begun to develop, like Glastonbury, Stonehenge and Tintagel as an important Neo-Pagan centre within Britain. The novel was published as this development really begins to alter the socio-economic situation (not to mention spirituality), of the Penwith region.

Two of the main characters in *Birthstone*, Lola and Hector, are actually from the Cornish emigrant community in Grass Valley, California. Their addition to the text resonates with his own family background. Like Rowse, Thomas has an interest in the Cornish achievement abroad and is fascinated with the experiences and impact of emigration. One example is his poem 'A Cornish Graveyard at Keweenaw' about the miners in the Upper Peninsula of Michigan: ('And all in time who went on to unlock/Nevadan silver, Californian gold').[118] Thomas' portrayal of the lives and death of emigrants travelling to America indicates how real and compelling a theme this remains for the Cornish, even in the latter part of the twentieth century. Emigration was something which had affected most Cornish families in one way or another. It was, like Cornu-English, a defining trait of modern Cornish identity:

> And imagine what Liberty had hushed their dry
> Expanding stories awhile, their souls raw,

Their eyes bright moving west across the spectrum
Of hard rock, giving new land new energy.[119]

Other visiting poets and writers continued to be inspired by the romance of place in Cornwall. West Cornwall, and particularly the artists' communities which flourished there, continued to be an inspiration. The work of W.S. Graham is a prime example. Graham was originally from from Greenock in Scotland and came to Cornwall in 1943. The most influential factor in the development of his Cornish writing was his association with the modernist painters of the St Ives school of the 1950s, exemplified by Peter Lanyon. W.S. Graham, together with the work of Sven Berlin, promoted a small but significant St Ives school of writing. However, as Hurst has noted, 'the departure from Cornwall of Sven Berlin and the death of Peter Lanyon and Bryan Wynter broke off the impetus of a group which was becoming a powerful point of cultural take-off.'[120] Some of Graham's best poems are those based on his St Ives circle of friends; for example, the elegy for Peter Lanyon, 'The Thermal Stair', which in its imagery seems to entwine both pre- and post-industrial Cornwall:

The salt updraught slides off the broken air
And out of sight to quarter a new place.
The Celtic sea, the Methodist sea is there.[121]

His other Cornish poems are infused with a similar awareness of the experience of living in mid-twentieth-century west Cornwall, as St Ives became more and more associated with a particular kind of bohemian living and alternative culture in the wider British context.[122] Graham's association with this community and landscape generated a powerful poetic identity of Cornwall in his work, becoming perhaps the best synthesis of the 'written' and the 'artistic', forever associated with the work of the post-war St Ives creative community, now displayed in the Tate Gallery St Ives.[123]

The other Scottish writer whose poetry was highly significant in terms of his nationalist allegiances was Hugh MacDiarmid (1872–1968). Although he was technically a 'visiting' writer, MacDiarmid was remarkable in the expression of his Cornish nationalist sensibilities. MacDiarmid was a lifelong Communist and a pioneering Scottish nationalist. As both Bold and Berresford Ellis have detailed, MacDiarmid saw it as his personal task to 'work for the establishment of Workers' republics in Scotland, Ireland, Wales and Cornwall, and indeed, make a sort of Celtic Union of Socialist Soviet Republics in the British Isles'.[124] In the immediate aftermath of World War Two, he wrote a pioneering poem titled 'Cornish Heroic Song for Valda

Trevlyn'. Valda Trevlyn was MacDiarmid's Cornish-born wife, and his union with her brought him to a close understanding of Cornish difference, which is encapsulated in verse. The poem moves forward the response to Cornish ethnicity and heritage:

> I sing of Cornwall.
> Chip of Atlantis, that clings to England still,
> Alien in its traditions, utterly different. . .
> Cornwall and England, David and Goliath!
> Not the ideal but the actual Cornwall
> Full of the wandering abscess of English influence![125]

MacDiarmid continues to define and explore this 'wandering abscess' and how the Cornish should respond to it. The nationalist message is a hard-line one. Cornwall is 'caught in England's sarmentous toils', and MacDiarmid then acknowledges 'real' Cornwall – 'not of Lyonesse' – and proceeds to condemn English literary conceptualizations of Cornish identity – via the metaphor of King Arthur – finally offering a kind of confrontation which, from Cornish-born writers, would have seemed far too radical. Retrospectively, however, it is the very argument which much of late twentieth-century Cornish and Anglo-Cornish literature asserts. To conclude, MacDiarmid's belief is that the Cornish will achieve self-determination, conquering 'chaos', forming 'a new Creation', a phrase which explicitly provides a continuity from Cornwall's medieval literature and its separate political status.[126] Thus whilst Thomas was offering a more complex vision of both Cornish spirituality and emigration, MacDiarmid sought to shake the Cornish into a more overtly nationalist poetic. Though coming from very different directions, it was these themes which were to be taken up by poets and other writers toward the end of the century.

However, expression of Cornish identity was persisting elsewhere. Newlyn-born poet Frank Ruhrmund (b.1928), is a vastly underrated writer who embraced some of the changing thematic concerns of post-war Anglo-Cornish poetry.[127] In particular there is a sense of anger within his work at what industrial collapse and tourism have meant for Cornwall. Although Ruhrmund's poetry never moved explicitly towards consciously nationalist subject-matter, several writers have tried to move their work in that direction, and in so doing pioneered a new kind of Anglo-Cornish literature. On reflection, the early 1970s work of writers such as Arthur Caddick and Donald R. Rawe may now seem out of step with Rowse, Clemo and Causley. However, both Caddick and Rawe were radical writers aiming to combine a Cornish literary heritage with a political nationalism still relatively new and

sometimes naïve. It is by their skill and ability as writers and poets that
Caddick and Rawe gave voice to Cornish identity in a way which had
not been written before. Thus, whilst Thomas in the long term shaped
his work away from Cornwall, Caddick and Rawe more closely
focused their material on issues of Cornish identity, history and
culture. Their efforts were to have a profound effect on the next
generation of writers, and in taking the ideological steps which they
completed in their writing, they helped to re-cast the literary agenda
for Cornwall. Thus both Caddick and Rawe are highly significant
writers in the Cornish context, yet for different reasons.

Yorkshire-born Arthur Caddick (1911–87) came to Cornwall in
1945 and lived for thirty-six years at Nancledra. He was a regular
contributor to the *Cornish Review* and his poetry is ironic, sharp and
witty. *A Croft in Cornwall* (1968) is one of his significant early collections, though he continued to be productive until 1983 with *The Call of
the West*.[128] His explorations of the Cornish people and landscape are
some of the finest post-war poetry to emerge, though his work is not
particularly well known. His verse is characterized by scrupulous
craftsmanship and an awareness of the influence of the personal and
collective conscience of Cornwall. 'A Cornish Innkeeper' is one the
finest observations upon Cornish character and identity written
between 1940 and 1980:

> Mellow twilights would resound
> To his bass which led the chorus
> Of rich Cornish voices chiming
> As the dark brown ale was downed.[129]

One of Caddick's best poems is 'The Cornered Men', a work which
takes for its theme Cornish accommodation; how Cornwall's literal
translation becomes 'the horn of strangers'. Cornish people are
'cornered in', but this does not make them backward or primitive. In the
same poem, he comments ambivalently about the Cornish Gorseth.
While he appears to be critical, he also seems to admire their purpose:

> The academic and punctilious Bards
> Pray at the Gorsedd for [Arthur's] return.
> O gentle brotherhood! I think you hold
> A truth the nuclear wizards cannot learn.[130]

Despite widely satirizing the 'performance' of the revival, Caddick
actually asserted a more sophisticated form of cultural nationalism
during the era of the Cold War. It was a bold assertion of Cornish
identity, at a time when many of the early arguments over Cornish
'difference' were still being argued and contested. As Caddick's

construction of Cornwall became more sophisticated and he came to a closer understanding of the specific historical experience of Cornwall, he began to assert greater nationalist sympathies in his verse. 'The Ballad of Michael Joseph, The Captain of Cornwall' (1977) was a very important literary statement in a period in which the An Gof story was still seen as part of the 'nationalist fringe'. Caddick's poem tries to push Michael Joseph centre-stage; the text carrying a political vigour and language which seemed to carry on directly where MacDiarmid had left off:

> And when skeletons of children
> Crept around the blacksmith's forge
> With a wee bit crouse their begging
> Came a rising of his gorge –
>   Like the Great God Vulcan's gorge.[131]

Caddick gives the narrative a Causley-like rhythm, but it has a darker, more confrontational air to its verses. He criticizes the treatment of Cornwall by the English state, and the implication remains that the process did not end in 1497. In retelling the story, Caddick asserts his desire for the Cornish to gain political freedom juxtaposed with the historical events of the fifteenth century.

The work of Donald R. Rawe is bold and assertively Cornish, yet falls just short of expressing overt nationalism. To an extent, Rawe was in a difficult position as a writer initially operating in the post-war period. He was trying to redefine Anglo-Cornish literature, but his achievements were limited by a literary culture, both in Cornwall and England, where the kind of work he was daring to write about Cornwall, was still deemed inappropriate and somehow 'fringe'. It was not 'fringe'; it was rather that Rawe had set himself his own agenda about Cornish literature and, in doing so, moved it forward considerably. Rawe, who is of the same generation as D.M. Thomas, was born in 1930 in Padstow. Writing in the 1950s, under the pseudonym of Daniel Trevose, Rawe began his career as a novelist, with a novel following the adventures of a Cornishman in London during the post-war years. *Looking for Love in a Great City* (1956) is an important text in Anglo-Cornish writing since Rawe explores the feelings of a young Cornishman experiencing the possibilities of travel and displacement, not to mention exile, from Cornwall – a theme already central to Cornish writing, but about to be transformed once more by education and transport.[132] His short stories follow similar themes, and Rawe's highly evocative tales were included in most major Cornish anthologies. Among his most famous shorter narratives are 'The Deep Sea Dream' (1950) and 'Night on Roughtor' (1973). These narratives and those of the later volume *Haunted Landscapes* (1994) show a fascination with the macabre and supernatural in Cornwall.[133]

However, between 1965 and 1980, Rawe primarily became known for his ability as a dramatist and as a poet. Publicly, the drama came first, and despite the widespread publication of Rawe's poems in numerous magazines, journals and anthologies, a substantial collection of his verse has not yet been published.[134] An innovative dramatist, Rawe helped to reformulate theatrical conceptualizations of Cornwall during this period, and continues to write major plays on Cornish topics. Rawe's initial technique drew on elements of continuity from the medieval drama of Cornwall, with its populist, epic and humorous stagecraft. Rawe drew his material from Cornish hagiography, Arthuriana and folklore, writing scripts which fundamentally kept a Cornish character in speeches and lines, but in places also offered sections in Cornish. The first of these was *Petroc of Cornwall* (1970).[135] Inspired by the success of this, Rawe then wrote other texts suited to open-air theatre: *The Trials of St Piran* and *Geraint: Last of the Arthurians*.[136] Here the character Selyf confesses to his mother his fear for Cornwall's future:

> It seems that I alone can see what Cornwall needs if it is to be saved: a strong man at the head of a strong army: to awake from her long sleep and defend herself, or all will be lost between the Saxons on the one hand and mealy-mouthed altar-grovellers on the others.[137]

In such a way, Revivalist literature and literary performance were acquiring a more overtly political flavour. A BBC commentator of the period described a revived performance of *Beunans Meriasek* as 'nationalist', and at the same time a critic observed that Rawe was 'becoming synoymous with a Cornish National Theatre'.[138] What was clear was that Rawe's theatre was highly innovative. Unlike early Revivalist writers who tried to imitate Welsh and Irish verse forms (thus misunderstanding the Cornish literary continuum and also its unique Celticity), Rawe had identified the historical continuum of Cornish drama and developed his own model of it, synthesizing into the dramatic form the concerns of the Revival, such as saints, St Piran – rapidly assuming prominent status as the 'symbol' of nationalism – as well as the Arthurian heritage. This popular, outdoor, community concept of theatre was to be very influential in defining the future direction of Cornish drama (in particular the work of later companies such as Kneehigh, Miracle and Bedlam theatre), whilst also linking it to the past.

Other plays have followed, which have assumed less epic staging, and are more influenced by English drama in the post-war period.

Here, Rawe focuses his attentions on significant figures or moments of Cornish history. Thus Rawe dramatizes the life of *Hawker of Morwenstow* and later, *The Last Voyage of Alfred Wallis*.[139] *The Black Letter Pamphlet* also receives attention in Rawe's concern to assert the connection between past Cornwall and the present. His adaptation of the gruesome Penryn narrative, titled *Murder at Bohelland* provides continuity with the early modern period of Cornish history, whilst actively asserting the continuing presence of Cornish independence and difference.[140]

Aside from his work as a dramatist, Rawe has also worked as a poet, writing both in Cornish and English. Rawe's poems carry strong evocations of particular Cornish locations, and carry with them a keen interest in the spiritual nature of Cornish identity and experience. Rawe draws his subject-matter from all periods of Cornish history, often combining these in the same work, to show the longevity of Cornish culture. He prefers blank verse, though there is an acute sense of internal rhyme, as well as some keen observation of Cornish dialect and speech patterns. A thread of Celtic Christianity runs through a number of pieces, showing the integral connection of this spirituality to particular places. Typical are poems such as 'Warleggan', 'The Windows of St Neot' and 'The Angels of St Endellion',[141] which show Betjeman-influenced subject-matter. Elsewhere, Rawe matches the epic enquiry of his drama, which more thoroughly engages with a cultural-nationalist perspective in longer narrative poems, such as 'Journey to the North Coast'. Here he takes a kind of pilgrimage, travelling to where,

> Padstow men, their wives and children too
> Devote themselves to bring their Oss out on May Morning.
> Unite and Unite. *Gwary whek yu gwary tek.*[142]

In so doing, Rawe demonstrates Cornish difference and identity along the route, eventually realizing at Padstow the complexity of Cornish experience and how closely the poet and his spirituality are tied to the territory. Rawe's faith is equated with implicit political self-determination.

A similar poetic construction of Cornwall during this phase is also offered by Richard Jenkin (b.1925). A former Grand Bard, and long-time Cornish cultural activist, his vision is very much connected with the older iconography of the Revival,[143] yet his poetry, both in English (since 1945) and Cornish (since 1957) demands respect for its continued engagement with Cornish identity over the second half of the twentieth century. Whilst Jenkin sees himself as 'not so much a poet of Cornish themes as a Cornishman who is a poet',[144] he is also politically active and was a founder member of Mebyon Kernow. Thus his identity and difference are primarily asserted through language and construction, not always via content. In his Cornish poetry, more universal themes comes to the fore, though there is perhaps a pan-Celtic influence at work as well:

> Gyllys dhe-ves yu ef a gerys-vy.
> Eghan! A callen-vy y weles ajy
> Ow-'sedha unwyth arta ryp an tan.
> A, blew y ben o maga tu 'vel bran.

> [Gone away is he that I loved.
> Ochone! If only I could see him inside
> Sitting once more by the fire.
> Oh, the hair of his head was as black as a raven.][145]

Meanwhile in his Anglo-Cornish work, there is an assertion of continual but changing identity in the face of misinterpretation. Jenkin resists the romantic view of Cornwall. Poems such as 'Hurrah for the Tourist Trade' are more satirical in his open critique of mass tourism ('Fishers don't fish and farmers don't farm/They sell the mugs a piskey charm'[146]), whilst recently, Jenkin has turned his attention to further work in Cornish.[147] As in the case of Rawe, a volume of his collected poems is long overdue. But Jenkin, Rawe and Caddick, though traversing unchartered waters in Cornish, and moving the literary construction of Cornwall forward in highly significant ways, have been seen both by the Cornish and those observing from outside as still being marginal, sometimes too rooted in an older kind of Celtic cultural nationalism. Their work was still failing to capture the emotion of the populace, or to motivate the populace into greater awareness of their own territory and of their own ethnicity. This is not however, to detract from the quality of these writers' work. Rather it is to say that the culture needed time to catch up with them. By the end of the twentieth century it would happen, but in the interim, Cornwall had to be satisfied with a series of writers whose individual visions of Cornwall were highly distinctive, and where identity was shaped by particular regions of Cornwall or class experiences.

Several elements of the Cornish literary continuum can, however, be traced, and there is a sense that all the writers here connect directly with, or were influenced by those preceding them. The Revival itself, though gaining a broader political and cultural base, had produced a series of Cornish writers whose writings in Cornish were nevertheless seemingly still stuck in a classically Celtic or pseudo-medieval mode. They seemed more interested in telling of a once great Cornwall, now destroyed, than actively rebuilding a post-war culture. Undoubtedly, in the 1970s the on-going integration of all things Cornish into the wider 'Westcountry' conceptualization of Cornwall continued to subvert the efforts of those involved in the Revival, whilst Cornwall not only continued its role as a holiday destination, but was also becoming – as the comic strips of Posy Simmonds, and others, aptly demonstrate – a playground for the rich.[148]

Difference continued, however, to be strongly asserted throughout the literature of the period from 1940 to 1980 in new ways which were utterly 'un-English' and displayed some of the characteristics which were to offer a more radical and aggressive challenge to the historical invisibility of Cornish difference at the end of the twentieth century. Ironically, some of that difference had initially been asserted over the period 1940-1980 by those writers, who as Westland asserts had, parallel to the growth of mass tourism and the Celtic Revival, developed a construction of the 'romantic periphery' in the form of historical and romantic novels set in Cornwall.[149] The genre was to rapidly expand during the post-war period, mainly constructing an image and an idyll of Cornwall as seen primarily in the eighteenth and nineteenth centuries.[150] These texts formed a continuum from the romances, folk narratives and legends collected by Hunt and Bottrell, popular dialect narratives of the nineteenth century, as well as a combination of the texts developed by writers as diverse as the Hocking siblings, Daphne du Maurier and Leo Walmsley, but also by the developing paperback popular fiction market in Britain between 1940 and 1980.[151] It is tempting to be dismissive of these texts as offering false and oversimplified depictions of Cornish history and identity; but upon closer study, such texts, over time, have helped shape and form popular imagery of Cornish identity in the twentieth century. As Westland asserts, 'Passion and place are interdependent, bearing Cornwall along on two centuries of the Romantic reconstruction of love and landscape'.[152]

Paradoxically, however, though the texts have been extremely important in their construction of Cornish identity – particularly for non-Cornish readerships – their rise in popularity as literary depictions of Cornwall is now matched by an increasingly sophisticated Anglo-Cornish, Cornu-English and Cornish literature, which is beginning to tackle issues of nationalism, identity, difference and invisibility more consciously and assertively within the late twentieth-century Cornish context. Operating far more successfully as a school, and taking political changes towards devolution in Britain and Europe as applicable to Cornwall, these writers' aims have been to develop the literary energies of Rawe, Caddick and Jenkin, and even Betjeman and Thomas, several stages further, whilst not compromising the distinctive identities so present in writers like Rowse, Clemo and Causley.[153] Cornish literary culture at the end of the millennium is therefore a complex landscape, full of contrasting literary energies, which have much to say about the nature of Cornish difference and identity, whilst providing again a sense of continuity from the earlier forms, as well as new directions. The landscape is one in which all that had been read and seen before still exists and still influences, but it is also where *Poldark* meets those writers who are ready to reclaim the 'tongueless land'.

NOTES

1. Charles Causley, *Collected Poems 1951–1975* (London 1975), p. 44.
2. Michael Grieve and W.R. Aitken (eds.), *The Complete Poems of Hugh MacDiarmid* (Harmondsworth 1978), p. 707.
3. See Ronald Perry (1993) 'Economic Change and 'Opposition' Economics' in Philip Payton (ed.) *Cornwall Since the War* (Redruth 1993a), pp 48–83; James Whetter, *Cornish Essays/Scryvow Kernewek 1971–76* (Gorran 1977), pp 1–12.
4. See Annette Penhaligon, *Penhaligon* (London 1989).
5. For a useful biography, see Tim Scott, *The Cornish World of Denys Val Baker* (Bradford on Avon 1994).
6. Ibid., p. 29. See also Denys Val Baker (ed.), *The Cornish Review* (Series 1). (ed.), *The Cornish Review* (Series 2). Published by Porthmeor Press. Relaunched by Val Baker and Ken Moss in the spring of 1966. A further 27 issues were published.
7. Denys Val Baker, *Britain's Art Colony by the Sea* (Bristol 2000 [1959]); *The Sea's in the Kitchen* (London 1962). See also Scott, op.cit., p. 70.
8. See Peter Berresford Ellis, *The Cornish Language and its Literature* (London and Boston 1974), pp 177–212; Brian Murdoch, *Cornish Literature* (Cambridge 1993), pp 145–50; Richard G. Jenkin, 'Modern Cornish Literature in the 20th Century' in *The Celtic Pen* 1:3 (1994), pp 3–5, 'Cornish Literature in the Twentieth Century' in Eurwen Price (ed.) (1997) *Celtic Literature and Culture in the Twentieth Century* (Bangor 1997), pp 5–11.
9. Tim Saunders (ed.), *The Wheel: An Anthology of Modern Poetry in Cornish: 1850–1980* (London 1999).
10. Ibid.
11. See Richard Gendall (ed.), *An Lef* (pre-1953); E.G.R. Hooper (ed.), *An Lef Kernewek* (post-1953); Richard Gendall (ed.), *Hedhyu*. *Hedhyu* ran from 1956–8.
12. See the feature on Richard Gendall in Craig Weatherhill, *Cornish Place Names and Language* (Wilmslow 1995), pp 168–70.
13. See Tim Saunders and Anthony Snell (eds.), *Eythen*.
14. See Graham Sandercock (ed.), *An Gannas*.
15. Saunders, op.cit. (1999).
16. See *Old Cornwall*.
17. See Philip Payton, *Cornwall* (Fowey 1996a), p. 286.

18. In *An Baner Kernewek/The Cornish Banner* 73, Rowse features within the 'Parade of Cornish Heroes', p. 1.

19. Richard Ollard, *A Man of Contradictions: A Life of A.L. Rowse* (London 1999).

20. For the range of Rowse's work, see A.L. Rowse, *Matthew Arnold: Poet and Prophet* (London 1976), *The Little Land of Cornwall* (Gloucester 1986), *The Controversial Colensos* (Redruth 1989). See also selected bibliography in Ollard, op.cit., pp 336–8.

21. See Rowse, *Tudor Cornwall* (Redruth 1990 [1941]), *The Cornish in America* (Redruth 1991 [1969]).

22. Ollard, op.cit.

23. A.L. Rowse, *A Cornish Childhood* (London 1982 [1942]). For an interesting comparison, see the work of Anne Treneer. Treneer details mid-Cornwall between 1891–1947. See Patricia Moyer and Brenda Hull (eds.), *School House in the Wind: A Trilogy by Anne Treneer* (Exeter 1998).

24. For background on these, see Garry Tregidga, 'The Politics of the Celto-Cornish Revival, 1886–1939' in Philip Payton (ed.), *Cornish Studies: Five* (Exeter 1997); Philip Payton, *The Cornish Overseas* (Fowey 1999).

25. Op.cit., p. 35.

26. Ibid., pp 60–1.

27. Ibid., p. 168.

28. Ibid., p. 107.

29. Ibid., p. 214.

30. See for example, A.L. Rowse, 'The Stone that Liked Company' in Val Baker (ed.), *One and All: A Selection of Stories from Cornwall* (London 1951), p. 69. For other typical Rowse stories, see A.L. Rowse, *Cornish Stories* (London 1967).

31. Rowse, op.cit. (1982 [1942]), p. 106.

32. A.L. Rowse, 'The Curse of the Clavertons' (1967) in Denys Val Baker (ed.), *Cornish Short Stories* (Harmondsworth 1976), p. 72. Compare Rowse's use of dialect with one of the perceived dialecticians of the period, H. Lean, *A Continuation of Short Cornish Dialect Stories; Books 1–5* (Camborne 1951–1956), *Richard Harvey, The Smart Boy and other Stories* (Falmouth n.d.).

33. See A.L. Rowse, *A Life: Collected Poems* (Edinburgh 1981), for demonstration of Rowse's poetic development. See also Andrew Symons, 'The Poetry of A.L. Rowse' in *An Baner Kernewek/The Cornish Banner*, 73 (1993) p. 11.

34. Ibid., p. 6 and p. 11.

35. Ibid., p. 10.

36. Richard Carew, in particular, seems to pervade *A Cornish Childhood*. Rowse uses several quotations from *The Survey of Cornwall*.

37. Rowse, op.cit. (1981), p. 31 and p. 33.

38. Ibid., p. 27.

39. Ibid., p. 95.

40. Ibid., pp 134–6.

41. Ibid., p. 173.
42. Rowse's poetry continued in the 1990s to be published in *An Baner Kernewek/The Cornish Banner*. The editor, James Whetter is the chairman of the Cornish Nationalist Party and the magazine is the 'voice' of that party.
43. Rowse, op.cit. 1981, p. 371.
44. Perry, op.cit., pp 25–29.
45. See 'Jack Clemo's Clay Country' in Peter Stanier, *Cornwall's Literary Heritage* (Truro 1992), pp 19–20.
46. Andrew Symons, 'Clemo: The Authentic Voice' in *An Baner Kernewek/The Cornish Banner* 78 (1994), pp 9–10.
47. Sally Magnusson, *Clemo: A Love Story* (Tring 1986), pp 13–25.
48. Jack Clemo, *Confession of a Rebel* (London 1975 [1949]).
49. Magnusson, op.cit., details how Eveline Clemo 'painted him a picture of what real squalor was like and warned him of the dangers of sexual excess'. Clemo comments that his mother revealed 'the ugly secrets which she had kept for nearly twenty years', p. 36.
50. See Eveline Clemo, *I Proved Thee at the Waters: The Testimony of a Blind Writer's Mother* (Ilkston n.d.); Magnusson, op.cit., pp 26–39. Clemo's wife, Ruth, has also greatly influenced his work. See Jack Clemo, *The Marriage of a Rebel: A Mystical-Erotic Quest* (London 1980)
51. Jack Clemo, *The Invading Gospel: A Return to Faith* (Basingstoke 1986 [1958]).
52. Jack Clemo, *Wilding Graft* (London 1983 [1948]).
53. These were collated later in Jack Clemo, *The Bouncing Hills* (Redruth 1983).
54. See Clemo's doubts over the Cornish Revival and the Gorseth in Clemo, ibid., p. 88 and p. 121. See also Clemo, op.cit. (1980), pp 139–40.
55. Clemo was a regular contributor to *An Baner Kernewek/The Cornish Banner*.
56. In Clemo, op.cit. (1986 [1958]), p. 85, he describes himself as a 'fervid Celtic poet'. In Clemo, op.cit. (1975 [1949], p. 225, he views himself as 'un-English'.
57. See Clemo, ibid. (1975 [1949]), pp 44–57.
58. See John Hurst, 'Literature in Cornwall' in Payton, op.cit. (1993a), p. 295.
59. A.W. Holmes, *Out of this Fury* (London 1944).
60. Clemo, op.cit. (1983 [1948]), pp 7–8.
61. Ibid., p. 17.
62. P.L. Lowman, *Supernaturalistic Causality and Christian Theism in the Modern English Novel* Ph.D (Cardiff 1983), pp 572–618.
63. Jack Clemo, *The Shadowed Bed* (Tring 1986). See also Hurst, op.cit. A third novel is to be published in 2000.
64. Ibid., p. 7.
65. Ibid., p. 11.
66. Ibid.
67. For Clemo's connection to Harris, see Jack Clemo *Approch to Murano*

(Newcastle upon Tyne 1993), p. 28. For the Hockings, see Jack Clemo, op.cit. (1975 [1949]) pp 69–70; Jack Clemo *Selected Poems* (Newcastle upon Tyne 1988), p. 116.

68. Clemo, op.cit (1988), p. 21.

69. Ibid., p. 22.

70. Jack Clemo, *The Clay Verge* (London 1951), *The Map of Clay* (London 1961), *Cactus on Carmel* (London 1967).

71. Clemo, op.cit. (1988), p. 45.

72. Ibid., p. 30.

73. Ibid., p. 84.

74. Ibid., p. 92. For other poetry of this 'broader' period, see Jack Clemo, *The Echoing Tip* (London 1971), *Broad Autumn* (London 1976) and *A Different Drummer* (Padstow 1986).

75. Clemo, op.cit. (1993), p. 19.

76. Ibid., p. 33.

77. Ibid., p. 6.

78. Clemo, *The Cured Arno* (Newcastle upon Tyne 1995), p. 16.

79. In an article, Causley comments how 'it was a matter of chance that he was born a Cornishman rather than a Devonian'. See Jan Beart-Albrecht in *Artswest* October (1989), pp 22–5.

80. Charles Causley, *Runaway* (London 1936), *The Conquering Hero* (London 1937), *Benedict* (London 1938).

81. Charles Causley, *Farewell, Aggie Weston!* (Aldington 1951), *Hands to Dance and Skylark* (London 1979 [1951]).

82. See Hurst, op.cit. (1993), p. 293. See also Causley's comments in Geoffrey Summerfield (ed.), *Worlds: Seven Modern Poets* (Harmondsworth 1979), pp 17–31.

83. Causley, op.cit. (1979 [1951]), p. 38.

85. See Causley, op.cit. (1951), *Survivor's Leave* (Aldington 1953), *Union Street* (London 1957), *Johnny Alleluia* (Crediton 1961).

86. See Charles Causley *The Spirit of Launceston: A Celebration of Charles Causley's Poetry* (Launceston 1994).

87. See a number of the arguments presented by contributors in Harry Chambers (ed.), *Causley at 70* (Calstock, 1987).

88. In Causley, op.cit. (1957), p. i.

89. For this type of criticism see Michael Schmidt, *50 Modern British Poets* (London 1979), pp 291–96; Neil Philip, 'The Magic in the Poetry of Charles Causley' in *Signal* September (1982), pp 139–51.

90. See Causley, op.cit. (1975), pp 120–23 and pp 193–197.

91. Ibid., p. 186.

92. Ibid., p. 124, Charles Causley *Figgie Hobbin* (Harmondsworth 1985 [1970]), pp 48–9, *The Young Man of Cury and other Poems* (London 1991). See also *Collected Poems for Children* (London 1996) and *The Merrymaid of Zennor* (London 1999). Ramhead is now usually spelt Rame Head.

93. Causley, op.cit. (1975), p. 49.

94. Ibid., p. 231.

95. This imagining of Cornwall has continued in Charles Causley *Secret Destinations* (London 1984) and *A Field of Vision* (London 1988). Since this time Causley has not published any new adult collections. For a useful examination of Causley's work, see John Hurst, 'A Poetry of Dark Sounds: The Manuscripts of Charles Causley' in Philip Payton (ed.), *Cornish Studies: Seven* (Exeter 1999), pp 147–64.

96. Causley, op.cit. (1975), p. 258.

97. See Peter Redgrove (ed.), *Cornwall in Verse* (Harmondsworth 1983 [1982]).

98. Sylvia Kantaris, *Dirty Washing: New and Selected Poems* (Newcastle upon Tyne 1989); Zofia Ilinska, *Horoscope of the Moon* (Padstow 1992), *Address of Paradise* (Padstow 1996).

99. Hurst, op.cit. (1993), p. 297.

100. John Betjeman, *Betjeman's Cornwall* (London 1984), p. 20. See also Candida Lycett Green (ed.), *John Betjeman Letters, Volume One: 1926–1951* (London 1994); (ed.), *John Betjeman Letters, Volume Two: 1951–1984* (London 1995).

101. John Betjeman, *Collected Poems* (London 1988), p. 53.

102. Ibid., p. 81.

103. Ibid., p. 306.

104. John Betjeman, *Summoned by Bells* (London 1960), p. 40.

105. Ibid., p. 33.

106. Betjeman, op.cit. (1988), p. 135.

107. See John Guest (ed.), *The Best of Betjeman* (Harmondsworth 1978), p. 195.

108. See D.M. Thomas, *Memories and Hallucinations* (London 1988).

109. See the Preface to D.M. Thomas, *Selected Poems* (Harmondsworth 1983), p. vii.

110. D.M. Black, Peter Redgrove and D.M. Thomas, *Penguin Modern Poets 11* (Harmondsworth 1968).

111. D.M. Thomas, *The White Hotel* (London 1981). For an example of Thomas' wider canvas of writing, see *Eating Pavlova* (London 1994). However, in May 2000, in a radio interview for BBC Radio Cornwall, Thomas has talked of a return to more specifically Cornish themes such as rugby. His novel *Charlotte: The Final Journey of Jane Eyre* (London 2000) has Cornish sequences.

112. Thomas, op.cit., p. 54.

113. Ibid., p. 58; p. 48 and p. 49.

114. Ibid., p. 63.

115. Ibid., p. 47.

116. D.M. Thomas, *Birthstone* (London 1980).

117. Ibid., p. 85.

118. Thomas, op.cit. (1983), pp 60–1.

119. Ibid., p. 61.

120. Hurst, op.cit. (1993), p. 302.

121. See W.S. Graham, *Collected Poems 1942–1977* (London 1979), p. 155.

122. See Denys Val Baker, *The Timeless Land* (Bath 1973) pp 14–24.

123. Michael Tooby (ed.) *Tate St Ives: An Illustrated Companion* (London 1993).

124. See Alan Bold, *Hugh MacDiarmid: The Terrible Crystal* (London 1983); Peter Berresford Ellis, *The Celtic Dawn* (London: 1993), pp 96–7.

125. Grieve and Aitken (eds.), op.cit., p. 706.

126. Ibid., p. 708.

127. Frank Ruhrmund, *Penwith Poems* (Padstow 1976), *Brother John* (Penzance 1985).

128. Arthur Caddick, *A Croft in Cornwall* (Marazion 1968), *The Call of the West* (Nancledra 1983). For a biography, see Eric Hirth, *Never Sit Down in the Digey!: The Life and Times of Arthur Caddick* (Helston 1991). See also Catherine Brace, 'Cornish Identity and Landscape in the Work of Arthur Caddick' in Philip Payton (ed.) *Cornish Studies: Seven* (Exeter: 1999), pp 130–46.

129. Caddick, op.cit. (1968), p. 55.

130. Caddick, ibid., p. 58.

131. Arthur Caddick, *The Ballad of Michael Joseph: The Captain of Cornwall* (Penzance 1977), p. 2.

132. Daniel Trevose, *Looking for Love in a Great City* (London 1956).

133. Donald R. Rawe, 'The Deep Sea Dream' (1950) in Val Baker (ed.), op.cit. (1976), pp 193–201, 'Night on Roughtor' in Val Baker (ed.), op.cit. (1980 [1973]), pp 73–88, *Haunted Landscapes: Cornish and West Country Tales of the Supernatural* (Portloe 1994).

134. Rawe is widely published. See for example Bill Headdon (ed.), *Cornish Links/Kevrennow Kernewek* (Tunbridge Wells 1995), p. 57. He is also a significant children's writer. See Alan M. Kent, 'At the far end of England. . .: Constructions of Cornwall in Children's Literature' in *An Baner Kernewek/The Cornish Banner*, 98 (1999), pp 16–21.

135. Donald R. Rawe, *Petroc of Cornwall* (Padstow 1970). This was performed at Piran Round, near Perranzabuloe in 1970.

136. Donald R. Rawe, *The Trials of St Piran* (Padstow 1971), *Geraint: Last of the Arthurians* (Padstow 1972).

137. Rawe, ibid. (1972), p. 6.

138. See Val Baker, op.cit. (1973), p. 54 and Paul Newman, 'The Plays of Donald Rawe' in *Cornish Review*, 24, Summer (1973). See also Donald R. Rawe (ed.) *A Cornish Quintette: Five Original One-act Plays* (Padstow 1973).

139. Donald R. Rawe, *Hawker of Morwenstow* (1975), *The Last Voyage of Alfred Wallis* (1994).

140. Donald R. Rawe, *Murder at Bohellend* (1991)

141. These poems are from an unpublished collection of Rawe's work given to the author. Two of Rawe's poems in Cornish are published in Saunders (ed.), op.cit.

142. Ibid.

143. Jenkin now edits the Cornish language magazine *Delyow Derow*. The

magazine's ideological stance is symbolized by an image of a phoenix, emblazoned with *Dasserghyn* ['Resurgence'].

144. Recorded in a letter to the author, April 13th 1996.
145. An unpublished poem.
146. An unpublished poem. One of Jenkin's poems is published in Saunders (ed.), op.cit.
147. See 'Lef y'n Nos' in *Delyow Derow* 15 (1996), p. 5.
148. See 'Tresoddit' in Posy Simmonds, *Mrs Weber's Diary* (London 1979), pp 36–7; Donald R. Rawe, *A Prospect of Cornwall* (Chapel Amble 1996), pp 210–11; Deacon, George and Perry, op.cit.
149. See Ella Westland (1995) 'The Passionate Periphery: Cornwall and Romantic Fiction' in Ian A. Bell (ed.), *Peripheral Visions* (Cardiff 1995), pp 153–72.
150. See Bernard Deacon, 'Cornwall: Popular Culture and Guide Book Heritage' in Colin Robins, *Merlin's Diner* (Tiverton 1992), pp 83–6.
151. For the development of popular fiction in Britain, see Christopher Pawling (ed.), *Popular Fiction and Social Change* (Basingstoke, 1984).
152. See Westland, op.cit. (1995), p. 159.
153. See Alan M. Kent, 'Smashing the Sandcastles: Realism in Contemporary Cornish Fiction' in Bell, op.cit., pp 173–80, 'One and All: Unity and Difference in Cornish Literature' in Price, op.cit., pp 12–23; Payton, op.cit. (1996a), pp 285–6; Rawe, op.cit. (1996), pp 217–8.

'Kernopalooza!': Romancing and Reclaiming the Tongueless Land in Contemporary Cornish Literature, 1980–2000

Pyw a'byow ann bedh y'nn rose
heb hanw, heb maen, heb fos,
dow vîl seson ow Kwortos?
Pyw a'byow bedh penn ann hynz
ma y'kan hen govow y'nn gwynz?

[Whose is the grave in the heath, without name, without stone, without wall waiting for two thousand seasons? Whose is the grave at the end of the road where ancient memories sing in the wind?]

Tim Saunders, *An Ros Du [The Black Heath]* (1997)[1]

The country was named, by the ancestors of those who still venture among its aborigines, *Cornu Weahlas*, The Horn of Strangers, for the land tapers like a Cornucopia towards the golden sunsets in the western sea, and the language of the inhabitants was unintelligible to the interlopers.

N.R. Phillips, *The Horn of Strangers* (1996)[2]

Whilst the writers operating within the period 1940–1980, taken as a whole, expressed important new imaginings of Cornish identity, only a few of them were really operating in any kind of unison. That was to change remarkably towards the end of the century, when there seemed more of a collective literary response to the increase in awareness of Cornish identity issues in the face of globalization. We thus note the return of a resurgent and confident voice in contemporary Anglo-Cornish, Cornu-English and Cornish literature, which was seeking to

239

reclaim the too often 'voiceless' or rather – in the phrase of the traditional *englyn* – 'tongueless' land of Cornwall. Nowhere was this confidence more explicit than in Westcountry Carlton Television's eclectic Cornish language programme *Kernopalooza!* which with its innovative approach in mixing traditional notions of Cornish Celticity with contemporary themes, images and music, served as a media event which reflected the multitude of voices and ways of expressing identity which were available in Cornwall at the end of the millennium.[3] In many ways the show provided a critique on narrow, dated Revivalist constructions of Cornish as rarified and antiquarian, and was also a response to how Cornwall fitted into a global culture – it was the Cornish variant of the popular 1990s travelling American youth cultural festival *Lollapalooza!*[4] It was such a performance of eclecticism which paralleled what Cornwall had become – where past con-structions of Cornwall were either re-worked, re-synthesized or turned upside down, and where Cornish culture could work more effectively within global media. The latter had been an enormous problem for Cornish culture during the twentieth century, but as more individual and distinctive cultures asserted their difference, Cornwall could do the same. Cornwall found itself in a position (still continuing) whereby its 'Celticity' was, for the first time, its trump card.

As we have seen, it was only in the eighteenth century, after the collapse of the Cornish language, that Cornwall temporarily lost a confident literary voice. With the regained industrial identity of the late eighteenth and nineteenth century, a new literature emerged. However in the twentieth century there had been a slow-burning fuse of growing Cornish awareness. This was a new response to Cornish experience and new cultural politics – radically different from any that had preceded it – unafraid to confront issues of oppression and historical invisibility. These were re-emergent themes from the Revival onwards, but which, despite the effort of writers such as Donald R. Rawe, Arthur Caddick and Richard Jenkin, had never been fully assimilated, or foregrounded, until this comparatively recent phase.

Circumstances were now allowing this construction of Cornwall to be written and read, though it is important to note that whilst the reclamation process was under way, an equally important romanti-cization of Cornwall, which as this book has shown, had begun much earlier in Cornish history, was still being asserted. This romanticiza-tion was contributing to late twentieth-century Cornish eclecticism (in the form of continuing historical romantic novels, tourist literatures and in film and television), but the picture, as we shall see, is perhaps more complicated than it first might appear. We should be wary of dismissing this romanticization, since remarkably it was to come into contact with the emergent nationalist literature, in the cultural space brought about by increased Cornish 'solidarity' toward not only erosion of identity but, rather more, new assertions of it. Put together, all of this was paralleling other changes in Cornwall which had been aired for much of the post-war period, but were gaining new momentum in the years between 1980 and 2000, in which Cornwall was ever more confidently and strongly asserting its difference and separate identity on a hitherto unexpected scale. This was sometimes protracted and painful, but there were few who could deny that this process was taking place.

Cornwall was emerging as a territory with a new consciousness and belief in itself, and that it was in a state of cultural, political, social and even literary ascendancy. As Payton has argued, this 'resurgent Kernow' was, in essence, a 'microcosm' of wider political processes, which were mirrored elsewhere.[5] Jeremy Boissevain has noted that throughout western Europe at the close of the twentieth century, there was a dramatic rise in the attempts of territories and ethnicities to defend and assert their identities.[6] Although globalization of culture is one factor, others include structural unemployment, tourism, second-home ownership and a wider societal idealisation of the past; all of which have taken their toll on Cornwall over the twentieth century.

Defence and assertion were expressed in a variety of ways. Firstly, there were the 'traditional' performances of Cornishness inherent in older festivals such as the Helston Furry Dance, Trevithick Day and Padstow's Obby Oss.[7] There are also a growing set of revived or new festivals which were part of the reaction of the indigenous Cornish to the possibility of full English assimilation. Among these are the Lowender Peran Celtic Music and Dance Festival at Perranporth, the Golowan Festival at Penzance, Tom Bawcock's Eve at Mousehole, Bodmin Riding and Heritage Week and St Austell's White Gold week.[8] In addition, there have been larger-scale festivals attracting world-wide attention such as the Daphne du Maurier Festival of Literature and the Arts at Fowey, and the International Celtic Film and Television Festival, held for the first time in Cornwall at St Ives in 1997.[9] In the 1980s the holding of the Elephant Fayre, and the later Treworgey Tree Fayre in East Cornwall sought to offer popular music and 'alternative' or 'New Age' festival culture in a Cornish context.[10] This has been further advanced in the 1990s by the Headworx World Championship Surfing festival at Newquay as well as the proliferation of raves and dance events which regularly take place in Cornwall.[11] Despite some objections and reservations, the establishment in 1993 of the St Ives Tate Gallery, and related events such as the Quality of

Light festival, have made a major cultural impact upon Cornwall, and upon the arts in a Cornish context.[12]

Elsewhere such assertions of identity were expressed by 'Trelawny's Army', the rugby supporters who in the late 1980s and 1990s travelled to Twickenham to watch the Cornwall rugby football team's performance in the County Championship finals.[13] A similar, yet more powerful performance of identity came in 1997 when from May 24th to June 21st, the organization 'Keskerdh Kernow/Cornwall Marches On' recreated the 1497 Rebellion with a group of some twenty-six marchers walking the 370 miles from St Keverne to London.[14] The march culminated in hundreds of Cornish men and women walking with St Piran's flags, banners and all manner of Cornish paraphernalia – ranging from kilts and bagpipes to Celtic knotwork t-shirts and mining helmets – through Greenwich Park to Blackheath. With their cry of 'Oggy! Oggy! Oggy! Oi! Oi! Oi!, Kernow bys Vykken, Proper Job!' the marchers embodied popular Cornish sentiment, reflected in widespread media coverage and interest 'at home'. Symbolized by these events, there is therefore an on-going Cornish movement to continue to assert Cornish identity into the new century, resisting all attempts of assimilation. Related to this, as several scholars have shown, has been the re-emergence of Cornish identity within the diaspora, particularly in Australia and North America, but also within territories such as South Africa and Mexico.[15] Such groups not only negotiated their own identities in these multi-cultural territories, but also responded to events in Cornwall.

One of the problems of Cornwall's recent development has been the absence of institutions. Given the lack of a university and the historically decentred population distribution, it has been hard for Cornwall and those pushing for a stronger assertion of Cornish identity to function in larger groups. This altered in the late 1970s and 1980s with the formation of several organizations intent on providing an institutional base to unite those working with a similar cultural (not to mention political) agenda. Several smaller pressure groups emerged arguing for recognition of Cornish language and culture, problems with the Cornish economy and revising views of perceived Cornish 'backwardness'.[16] Their success has been mixed, and yet clearly the trend was pushing for more institutional support and development of Cornish culture.

The rise of Celtic spirituality in the 1980s and 1990s was also a crucial shaping factor on literary production. Much of this new wave was reliant upon established conceptualizations of Cornwall as a place of 'Romance' on the periphery, and the by now familiar presentation of Cornwall as a utopian Celtic Other or, in D.H. Lawrence's term,

'Ranamin'. Celticity was no longer a specifically ethnic concept. Immigrants who related to green, anti-metropolitan alternative sentiments believed that Celticity was also their birthright as the Celts were the original Britons. This was a reaction to perceived Anglo-Saxon linked traits of materialism, rationality and development. The result for Cornwall was that Celticity became a contested notion and was claimed by Neo-Pagans, Celtic Christianity and the Cornish.[17] John Lowerson has identified the place of Cornwall in this new spirituality of Britain:

> In the spectrum of modern Celticism, Cornwall has come almost
> to represent a British Tibet; distant, valued by outsiders and
> threatened by an occupying power.[18]

A number of enduring sub-cultural activities in Cornwall continually re-inforce and promote this 'alternative' construction of Celticity. Possibly the most contentious has been the persistence of New Age Traveller communities which have settled in Cornwall, drawn to the territory for the reasons outlined above but coming into conflict with the ethnic Cornish over land usage. Secondly, there was the build-up, event and aftermath of the 1999 solar eclipse, which highlighted contestation over space, place and culture. Promoters linked the the 'Celtic' mystery of the eclipse with alternative Celticity, neo-tribalism and popular music – but there was much Cornish reaction against this construction. Thirdly, there is on-going debate over industrial landscapes, which by some groups were seen as undesirable, but were increasingly being preserved by the Cornish as structures which reflected their identity. However, more recent work by Amy Hale has suggested that the argument over sites and spirituality is complex and that neither can it be defined only within a narrow field. Hale argues for the interconnection of several diverse yet complementary activities – Neo-Paganism, the Gorseth, nationalism, industrial heritage, Christianity, folklore, festival – which have sustained a continuous yet changing performance, symbolizing what is Celtic in Cornwall, but which is continually vied for between groups which have more in common than they first think.[19] This interconnection was to be reflected in much of the literature of this period.

Such politicization of ancient and industrial landscapes drew in all sorts of conceptualizations of Cornwall, from the imagery of *Poldark* to that of the Cornish Revival, from metal mining to Celtic Studies. All this is at the same time demonstrative of the new synthesis of Revivalist and popular culture in Cornwall. The Revivalist symbolism of St Piran's flags and caps and sweatshirts emblazoned with 'Kernow', sit alongside the traditional black and gold of jerseys at County

Championship rugby matches. At Newquay, meanwhile, Celtic knot-work decorates surfboards and clothing, whilst Celtic-rock groups play working-men's clubs of the china clay district. These crossovers – part of the overall *Kernopalooza!* culture – are important both for Cornwall and Cornish writers because they represent a more self-confident combination of hitherto disparate symbols in the drive towards a more forceful assertion of Cornish identity. This is happening in tandem with a greater politicization of the Revivalists' earlier cultural aims.

All these developments and contestations between economic, political, social, cultural and spiritual activity form the complex background to literary production and reception in Cornwall over the past two decades. The emergent literary culture is extremely confident, distinctive, yet also very diverse. One might expect here some confident championing of particularly nationalist writers who have integrated the politicization of the Revival into their writing. There are writers who do that, but other writers and their writing remain equally significant at this point in Cornish literary history. Equally, it is comparatively easy to set up a form of opposition between those writers of some kind of 'realist' Anglo-Cornish tradition and those writers who steer towards historical romance, or even Neo-Pagan literatures.[20]

Though this opposition is present, it is not altogether the exact division that some observers see.[21] It is true that several contemporary writers have set themselves up to produce a polemic against those writers who have, in the past or presently, presented a non-realist vision of Cornwall. However, more scholars and writers now acknowledge the fact that the writing of historical romance has been highly effective in offering to Cornish and non-Cornish readerships particular images of Cornish identity, history and difference, whilst also offering a continuum from numerous aspects of both structure and theme from Cornish literary history.[22] Therefore they must not be dismissed out of hand, nor for offering inexact visions of Cornishness – when their narratives have actually contributed to the perpetuation of difference since 1940. In their way, they are as much a response to the re-assertion of popular Cornish identity as anything else, and because 'romance' and the 'romance of place' are particularly important conceptualizations in the Cornish literary continuum. 'Romance' and 'romance of place' were present in the earliest narratives of Tristan and Isolde,[23] and are present here also.

The reason why Cornwall between 1980 and 2000 still lies at the centre of historical romantic fiction is complex, but important to unravel, if we are to argue that this construction is as significant in defining Cornwall's difference and identity as any nationalist/realist literature. It is equally important to demonstrate issues of continuity between these texts and those preceding them if we are to understand the development of writing about Cornwall. As Westland and Deacon have shown, much of the early association of Cornwall with romance derives from the ideology of the European Romantic Movement, beginning in the 1790s. By this time it was not necessary to leave the island of Britain to find a dramatic and exciting landscape, which would inspire the imagination. Cornwall quickly assumed status as one of these locations.[24] There was at the same time a frequent, yet ultimately flawed, conceptualization that Cornwall was the land of 'West Barbary', a territory containing savage and violent wreckers and leaders of riots, though contrary to this, Cornwall was actually progressing technologically and developing its maritime trade.

However, as Westland has argued, 'Later, as dangerous coastlines and seas became the rage – and as Cornwall's economic and naval importance declined – the country at the Land's End became a repository for romantic images'.[25] This conceptualization was further enhanced by a number of cultural trends; the landscape attracted nineteenth-century Arthurian poets like Tennyson and Swinburne; and by the first Celtic revival of the mid-1800s. This view of Cornwall was later developed by the imagery of the Great Western Railway, and more recently by Neo-Pagan tourism at ancient sites. Thus Westland concludes that,

> [t]oday it looks as if the romantics have conclusively won the battle for the periphery. . . Cornwall can bear the weight of all these romantic associations because it is a mentally manageable region. Tapering off into the Atlantic, it promises an agreeable wildness and remoteness. Cut off by the Tamar from England, it claims an independent history and tradition, offering Celtic depth without inconvenient breadth.[26]

Thus the romantic construction of Cornwall relies on its peripheral status, and even its claim of nationhood, yet as Westland also asserts, the conceptualization is additionally based on the combination in Cornwall of the industrial and the ancient; one of the leading larger structures found in the Cornish literary continuum:

> Its industrial history presents stark and simple contrasts between poor miners and rich capitalists; there are none of the obvious problems of comprehension posed by large cities and their complex past and continuing industrial present. The mining era in Cornwall is fixed in time, represented by ruined chimneys and engine-houses in areas now recovered by moorland. Paradoxi-cally, more distant peoples seem palpably close; the untrained eye

sees traces of Iron Age farms in the fields and weekend hikers walk the ramparts of Castle Dor.[27]

In Cornwall then – because of its peripherality – it takes little effort to combine the romance of one with the other, but at the same time offering readers a sophisticated construction of Cornish society and environment which had yet to be spoilt by the concerns of environmentalists, where, as I have argued in a study of the developing genre of romance of the china clay district, 'the industrial and rural are still in happy union', where in 'a landscape's ruination. . . a pervading sense of reminiscence and sentimentality is brought back'.[28] These factors therefore distinguish Cornish historical romance from that of other emergent territories,[29] whilst at the same time paradoxically offer positive images of Cornish experience which is different than that to be found in 'middle England' past or present, or even in the Cornish present. An 'emotional geography' has been established in Cornwall by a series of writers since the Romantic Movement, though the culmination of that process is remarkably active in the period between 1980 and 2000, where a series of what we may generically term 'historical romantic' novelists have presented a particular set of narratives about Cornwall, which have assisted in late twentieth-century definitions of Cornish identity and difference.

One of the most compelling and popular constructions of Cornish identity and difference has been the characterization and themes of the *Poldark* novels. By 1990, Winston Graham had completed the eleventh and concluding book in the *Poldark* series of historical Cornish novels. Titled *The Twisted Sword*, and covering the years 1815–16, this fiction completed a remarkable achievement in contemporary Anglo-Cornish literature, which had begun in 1945, with the publication of *Ross Poldark*, a novel set in the period 1783–87.[30] The intervening years had seen the publication of nine other Poldark novels and in the 1970s, two BBC television series.[31] *Poldark* therefore set the benchmark for the long Cornish romantic saga, yet is a significant set of texts in Anglo-Cornish literature for several reasons. First of all, the *Poldark* series was highly innovative, in writing of a particular period of Cornish history when there was a rise in Cornish confidence as the territory industrialized. Many of the central characters of the fictions, including both Ross Poldark and George Warleggan, demonstrate considerable awareness of their Cornishness, against the backdrop of significant world events, such as the American War of Independence and later, the Battle of Waterloo. Secondly, unlike many of the historical romances which followed the *Poldark* chronology, the novels are realistic in that they show the interrelationships between different classes in Cornish society, and demonstrate the precariousness of the mining industry itself, and for all their awareness of the wider world stage, Cornwall does not actually feature as a periphery. It is as if the centre of life has shifted westwards. Therefore, for a Cornish readership and audience, the novels, then later the television episodes, presented a construction of Cornwall which they had hitherto not experienced. Importantly, within *Poldark*, heroism and romance under Cornish conditions were made plausible and admirable.

Thirdly, as Nickianne Moody has shown, *Poldark* and 'Poldark's Cornwall' came to be significant for British culture as a whole, because of a particular set of cultural conditions which amplified the appeal of the texts and their appeal to popular imagination.[32] Moody perceptively argues that the continuing success and interest in *Poldark* has been stimulated by factors such as the potential revenue generated by nostalgia, heritage tourism and the on-going relationship between the texts and successive audiences. *Poldark* has evolved like no other Cornish text – producing a national cultural phenomenon, from an early popular print quartet, to television series, to extended saga, to video, to a life beyond page and screen in the appreciation society organized by the Poldark consumers.[33]

There may even be a case, as argued by the historian David Cannadine, for constructing Ross Poldark as a post-war settlement hero, who provides jobs for the redundant and prospects to improve health and housing;[34] the Cornish hero thus becoming a British hero:

> 'Savages! They think because they are done up in their finery they are almighty civilised people, but they're savages. And worse they treat their animals better than they treat their labourers. One day the knives will be out and then God help them.'
> 'And whose side will you be found on, Ross!?'
> 'Not on the side of the gentry you can be sure of that. I despair of my own class sometimes.'[35]

At the same time, Ross challenges the assumption of Welsh and English copper refiners that the Cornish are unlikely to develop their own smelting plants. Using the cover of a cost book company, Ross buys enough copper to subvert the English and Welsh dominance of the market, handing the real profit in copper-mining back to the Cornish; in the process upsetting the monopoly of the Warleggans. As Moody argues, 'the motivating force of Graham's novels is not always its love story but often the developing feud between the social climbing George Warleggan and the would-be paternal capitalist Ross Poldark'.[36] The rivalry between the two families continues in the other novels which followed.[37]

There are numerous threads of continuity between the *Poldark* series and earlier fiction. The family rivalry and arguments amongst the Cornish are derived from a continuum beginning at least with the Hockings and going back to the Renaissance with *The Black Letter Pamphlet*, whilst the characterization of Ross – as the returning exile aiming to do his community right – is a familiar enough motif of industrial and post-industrial Cornwall. Additionally, Poldark's rise from mining into politics was a familiar career path for numerous Cornishmen over the years, linked to his liberal conscience, which if not making the *Poldark* series typical Romances, have made Ross the typical Cornish hero. Demelza, meanwhile, redefines a construction of the Cornish heroine from humble origins who 'made good', and who despite her initial primitivism – framed in her inability to speak standard English ('Well, I ain't got what I went fur. And Luke's clo'es is all slottery.'[38]) and her making of mistakes – retains, after early reform, a high moral position within the narrative.

Symbolized by Demelza and Jud, but also the other working-class characters, identity in *Poldark* continues to be defined by Cornu-English, the linguistic badge of industrial Cornwall, though as Graham's understanding of Cornwall became more sophisticated there are new touches, suggesting a re-engagement with aspects of the Revival beyond industrial prowess, observed in the lines one character speaks with Ross:

> 'They are always called Wheal, aren't they? What does it mean?'
> 'Not always, but usually. It is from the Cornish, *huel*, meaning a hole.'[39]

Since *Poldark* first began, a series of writers have constructed similar visions of Cornwall during the late eighteenth and nineteenth centuries, parallelling a growing industrial heritage industry, seeing value and sentiment within a contested Cornish landscape.[40] The space is therefore not only fought over by planners and tourism officials but also by novelists. The *Poldark* legacy has set the agenda for other novelists such as Victoria Holt and Mary Williams, and later David Hillier and Malcolm Ross.[41]

Almost equalling the fictional and televised success of *Poldark*, as well as its active engagement with Cornish experience, is Susan Howatch's *Penmarric* (1971).[42] *Penmarric* was televised shortly after Poldark, and is considered an important Cornish romantic novel. Yet though, in a number of ways, *Penmarric* completely fits the genre – in its characterization, the themes of inheritance and betrayal and the symbolic Penmarric House itself – the text, as Christine Bridgwood and Ella Westland have argued, actually denies many of the conventions and reassurances of Cornish romance.[43] The importance of the House may be traced back to the Manderley of Daphne du Maurier's *Rebecca*, yet the conventions of its exciting peripheral location are denied. Penmarric is a 'bleak ugly mansion' sited upon 'ugly black cliffs', a place of sombre and brooding heartache. Trapped at Penmarric, Janna, one of the novel's five narrators, stares out 'at the rain slewing into the stormy sea'.[44] Instead of romance being accentuated by the place, there is uneasiness and a more realistic consideration of Cornish experience.

The story takes the reader from young Mark Castallack's first realization that he is in love with the woman who has been his father's mistress to a horrifying encounter in a Brighton hotel between his two families, legal and illegitimate. Torn between their allegiance to rival mothers, the children develop youthful antagonisms which in time are transformed into bitter hatred and rivalry. Thus the Cornish land-scape – of stark moors, precipitous cliffs and treacherous surfs – is symbolic of this bitterness, yet also the real experience of living in the harsh west Cornwall landscape. On this level, *Penmarric* is a historical romance which steps across boundaries, and begins to subvert the stereotypes of the genre.

Paradoxically, on another level, *Penmarric* did set a further con-vention, for Cornish historical romance to be set in a later period than the opening years of the nineteenth century. The sweep of *Penmarric* takes place between 1890 and 1945, paralleling precisely the age of Celtic Revivalism and the growth of the Cornish periphery as a loca-tion for writing and 'escapism'.[45] Industrial Cornwall was collapsing, and yet for successive novelists the period 1890 to 1940 could be seen as romantic, since Cornwall was seemingly still separate from the upheavals of the rest of the world. This was also the age of Daphne du Maurier, whose novels had inspired much of the later fiction, and it seemed appropriate to begin to set romance in a period of history which was just beginning to disappear out of living memory.[46] Elizabeth Ann Hill's *The Driftwood Fire* is typical of this emergent sub-genre, with a story set in 1930s Cornwall. In the growing tourist centre of Trezawne, a visiting artist, Hal Pentreath finds his love divided between Anne Trevena and Peggy Angilley, whilst they still celebrate 'Midsummer Eve with fire in the old Celtic way'.[47] Despite modernity and social sophistication, the older Celtic festivals still have a place and importance in determining the romantic outcome. In its own very different way Susan Hill's *Mrs de Winter* is also a response to the demand for fiction of this period and the trend to sequelising of classic novels, in its continuation of du Maurier's *Rebecca*.[48]

Cornwall from the end of the nineteenth century to 1940 also forms the background to Anita Burgh's Cornish trilogy *Daughters of a Granite Land*.[49] Here, Cornish difference and identity are foregrounded and are strong, despite world events and two World Wars. The central heroine, Alice Tregowan, is confident of her Cornishness – 'I'm a daughter of a land of granite. It gives us a very special strength, you see. . .'.[50] Similarly, Gloria Cook's writing moved forward in time to the early half of the twentieth century. *Trevallion* is set in the immediate aftermath of World War One, whilst *Kilgarthan* is set at the end of World War Two.[51] Rosemary Aitken's novels *The Girl from Penvarris* and *The Tinner's Daughter* also construct forward-looking families, operating mines at the turn of the century, despite industrial collapse and emigration;[52] the latter being one of the few Cornish experiences to yet be touched upon, with the exception of Daniel Mason's *Cousin Jack*.[53] It would seem that despite the economic and political changes enforced on Cornwall to make it part of an English region, and to even 'destroy' its Celticity, popular readerships preferred that the changing, yet persistent experience of Cornish difference continued.

Much of the response to this early twentieth-century Cornwall by writers such as Rosamunde Pilcher, Jean Stubbs, Mary E. Pearce and Katherine Sinclair[54] is encapsulated in the publisher's blurb for Susan Sallis' *Summer Visitors* (1988):

> Madge was four years old when she first saw the Cornish sea and fell in love with it, and it was there that her family grew and suffered and loved. It was there she and her mother went to recover from a heartrending family tragedy – there she was forced reluctantly into marriage – there she fell into a wild and passionate wartime love.[55]

Despite the seemingly endless proliferation of such novels, the Anglo-Cornish historical romantic novel has proven itself to be a very adaptable and dynamic genre, demonstrating that both *Poldark*-style heroes and heroines of the tin- and copper-mining industries, and those of the early twentieth century, could sustain Cornish identity. Rowena Summers in *Killigrew Clay*, *Clay Country* and *Family Ties*, Mary Lide in *Tregaran* and E.V. Thompson in *Ruddlemoor*, not to mention the earlier fiction of Rumer Godden in *China Court*,[56] saw the romantic potential of china clay mining in the early part of the twentieth century.[57] During *Killigrew Clay*, conventions of romance are used to maximum effect. In this sequence, used as a prologue, we learn how Ben and Morwen meet at midnight by the Larnie Stone (a fictional version of the Hensbarrow Longstone). This marvellously chimerical section epitomizes Cornwall's importance in historical romance as a place of difference, mystery and unconventional behaviour:

> They were here, beneath a great yellow moon, beside a standing stone with magic powers. A trysting place. . . and this was

Cornwall, where anything was possible. And ancient ways were
stronger than the laws of etiquette at that moment. . .[58]

With a clayworker's strike quelled and the father's rage abated,
Morwen and Ben are united and begin a 'new dynasty', yet 'Fate's not
done with them yet'.[59] In the sequel, Morwen is now mistress of
Killigrew House, but there are problems: her love for Ben is just as
strong as his for her, but at first they are unable to conceive. In the
final chapter, the birth of the son occurs on the same night as the end
of the Crimean war. The clay people's Celtic otherness is expressed:

> The celebration fire still burned brightly as dusk began to enhance
> the moorland scene. The flames leapt skywards, and townspeople
> far below stood outside houses and taverns and looked upwards to
> enjoy the spectacle. And many wished they had been born with the
> same lack of inhibitions as the clay folk.[60]

The china clay mining zone is not the only place to undergo a
romanticization process. Other writers – such as Sam Llewellyn and
Jim Crace – coinciding with a revival of interest and tourism there,
saw the potential of the Scilly Isles for romance.[61] Sheila Reddicliffe
has not only shifted the location of the romance to the Tamar
borderland, but also moved the romance to the medieval period,
culminating in a historical depiction of the 1497 rebellion.[62] Likewise
in a similar meeting ground between historical romance and nationalist writing, J.P. Mustill's *Summer Needs No Brightening* told the events of
1497 from the perspective of one of An Gof's captains.[63] Joanna
Hines' *The Cornish Girl* is set against the background of the Civil War
and presents a strong picture of Royalist, and paradoxically therefore,
'independent' Cornwall against Parliamentarian England.[64] Thus
romance and reclamation are actually merging and are closer than
some observers may think.

The successor to Graham's legacy, yet also the most dynamic
example of the changing nature of the genre, is the fiction of E.V.
Thompson, one of the most prolific historical romantic novelists in the
period 1980 to 2000. Since 1977 with his award-winning novel *Chase
the Wind*, Thompson has contributed to the continuum of historical
romance set in Cornwall, and the presentation of Cornish characters
overseas – as part of the colonization process, in military operations,
and in emigration.[65] Though Thompson has on several occasions
shifted the focus of his writing to other parts of Britain,[66] there has
been a consistent return to fiction about Cornwall.[67] Thompson
exemplifies the potential of the genre; his early texts concerned with
the fortunes of the Retallick family were set in the east of Cornwall,[68]
then with fishing communities and the Cornish overseas, and more

recently with new centres of romantic construction such as the mid-Cornwall china clay landscape and to social upheaval and changes associated with the opening years of the twentieth century.[69]

Ella Westland has asserted that both Winston Graham and E.V. Thompson's fiction are seen by readers as 'more factual' than other romances at the end of the twentieth century. Part of the reason for that, according to Westland, is that a novel like *Chase the Wind* 'structurally subordinates romance to realism'.[70] In the case of this novel the love story between Josh Retallick and Miriam Trago is displaced by the detail which Thompson gives to militant trade unions, the mining industry and issues surrounding Methodism – in effect particular historical symbols of Cornish difference. We may go further than this, however, and conclude that the reason readers find Thompson 'more factual' is because there is a more refined understanding of Cornish experience and therefore of Cornish identity. The fiction's success is not entirely dependent on the readership always 'identifying' with one or two particular characters, but rather the experience of learning about Cornish historical difference in a palatable and popular format. Additionally, Thompson's Cornwall is never immediately focused in the west of the territory – apparently more peripheral, more Celtic, more remote and wild. Instead, Thompson engages with the reality of the development of industry and communities within nineteenth-century Cornwall. He often moves his fictions to hitherto unexplored regions. His fictional construction of the Caradon mining community was highly original, acknowledging also the interrelationship between that part of Cornwall, the Stannary culture of west Devon, the River Tamar and the city of Plymouth.[71]

Thompson therefore has throughout his fictional construction of Cornwall offered several engagements with issues of difference and identity, whilst also continuing numerous themes and concerns of the Anglo-Cornish novel. Thompson is possibly the most well-known novelist of the genre operating in Cornwall, and though the texts have changed a good deal since Graham's original *Ross Poldark* novel, it seems unlikely the historical romantic construction will disappear. Rather, it may even be accentuated still further, in different locations and time periods, fitting fashionable nostalgia or particular heritage concerns. Far from dismissing these novels in their articulation of Cornwall and Cornish identity, perhaps there is a need to celebrate their achievement in the establishment of difference, and in their development of a continuum of response both to 'landscape' and 'romance' in Cornish literary history which is difficult to deny.

The Cornish writer N.R. Phillips is one novelist operating in the period between 1980 and 2000 who is more sceptical of the romantic construction of the territory. Phillips, in his aim as a writer to help reclaim the 'tongueless land', parodies the genre of historical romance, which to him, and other writers, is distant from the Cornwall they were experiencing, and gave a selective or even incorrect view of Cornish history and identity:

> '"And the handsome young squire . . . shook his black tousled locks . . . and broke into a canter . . . his dark brooding eyes . . . flashing us a haughty glance . . . as he descended the rugged track . . . past the eerie old tin mine . . . to the dark brooding house on the sea-dashed cliffs." Have you read it?'
> 'Many times.'
> 'And under many titles,' I said.[72]

For Phillips, such romanticization of the Cornish landscape and culture needed to be satirized and denied if Anglo-Cornish literature was to progress beyond such conventions and regain a new consciousness of Cornish identity based on a synthesis of Revivalist and popular Cornish culture. The development had been on the cards during the 1970s, but it took Phillips' novel *The Saffron Eaters* (1987) to set a new agenda for Anglo-Cornish literature and what it could write about. Phillips (b.1930) came from a St Ives fishing family, who over the post-war period had seen the sharp decline of their industry, as well as the continuing cultural development of St Ives as an artists' colony and a popular holiday destination.

Taking its title from Cornish people's food-ways, but also from the exotica of the Lotus Eaters, the novel is set in a fictional vision of St Ives. That it is St Ives is never mentioned, though the geography of the text leads the reader to believe that it can be nowhere else. Phillips' intention was to evoke the sentiments of Cornish people who resented the erosion of their communities and culture by the incursion of holidaymakers and 'foreigners', yet who paradoxically, for economic reasons, are inexorably themselves drawn into the world of bed-and-breakfast, beach cafés and trips around the bay. Phillips' recognition of this process is important, since he notes the high degree of 'pull factors' and collusion with the holiday industry that the Cornish themselves have constructed. In doing so, Phillips appears to say, they lose something of themselves, but the process is unavoidable and unstoppable. The theme is shaped by the opening chapter of the novel, which dislocates the reader's sense of the 'timeless' and picture-postcard views of unpolluted Cornish beaches and ocean:

> They fished it out with a stick and laid it on the sand, standing in reverence before the great condom before taking it to a tidal pool in the rocks and floating it in the clear salt water.

'Must have been made for a bleddy elephant,' said Tim.
'See the bleddy g'eat ring on 'n,' said Steve.[73]

Phillips moves the reader far away from romantic texts in one way, outlining the consequences of uncontrolled sewage effluent – a very topical issue in Cornwall in the period between 1980 and 2000 – whilst at the same time demonstrating the real consequences of romance on the periphery; that instead of finding crabs and sea anemones in rock pools, the Cornish children find used condoms. This swing between realism and romance is found throughout *The Saffron Eaters*. The narrator, Shimshai, whose identity is kept secret until the final page, observes all the events of the novel, understands the dislocating process of growing up in Cornwall and the separate identity he feels.

Phillips demonstrates continual understanding of the difference between Cornwall and England throughout the text, expressed in a series of carefully written comparisons, sometimes asserting identity via physical appearance ('A black-bearded man, quite short for an Englishman, quite tall for a Cornishman'); other times through Cornu-English ('Many theer?' she asked. 'A brear few.'), yet this demarcation of identity also goes beyond this, to individual Cornish towns related to specific industries and callings.[74] Yet though this realism and complex understanding of Cornish identity pervades the text, distinguishing it from Romance, the themes and constructs of Romance are still located within it, as the incoming artist Cleo comments:

> 'The landscape seems restless, seems full of suppressed energy, as if it hasn't fully developed yet. Yet it all looks so old and timeless.'[75]

Phillips was not completely able to break free from the romantic construction of the Cornish experience. The social realism of the novel and its admirable depiction of identity is, in the end, undermined by Cleo – the outsider – who seduces Steve into a relationship which is completely defined by the conventions of Romance. In essence, their relationship is built on a knowledge of each being the exotic other. Cleo finds in Steve a primitivism, which is connected to the landscape and 'timelessness' of Cornwall; whilst Steve finds in Cleo a freedom and sexuality which is impossible to find within the chapel-going and saffron-eating fishing community. As Westland has convincingly argued:

> Their passion is physical, bringing two beautiful bodies together to swim naked in the sea and make love on the cliff-top; it is also

imbued with the spiritual aura prescribed by romance, upholding the lovers and soul mates and affording Cleo the greatest compliment that a Cornishman can bestow, apotheosis into an honorary Celt.[76]

But this 'apotheosis' is only temporary. Cleo as outsider disrupts the value system, and must in the end be expelled. It is not an option for Steve to leave, and so it is Cleo who, despite her love of passion on the periphery – and even Phillips' recognition of the process – must leave. However, it is to Phillips' credit that Cleo, unlike in other Romances, is not depicted as finding lasting love in Cornwall. Phillips expresses the reality – that such a relationship will end because Cornwall is only romantic in the short term. The reality of living on the periphery is established by other events in the novel – such as the struggle to survive and earn a living from the fishing or from the tourist industry. Phillips' reclamation of the 'tongueless' land is therefore complex. It is imbued with a political awareness of the process of subjugation which Cornwall has been under for a number of years, and the need to fight against it, yet also a residual notion of the conventions of Romance, which in the end are shattered. Phillips' assertion of identity and difference are to be praised, for he remains one of the first writers to establish a new awareness of Cornishness at the end of the twentieth century; the continuity of the novel from other texts is expressed in its collusion with the conventions of romance, as well as in its awareness of the real Cornwall, which only writers such as Charles Lee and Jack Clemo had earlier expressed.

Almost a decade later, Phillips wrote a sequel to *The Saffron Eaters*, *The Horn of Strangers* (1996) which was much less of a lament for what had been lost, and demonstrated the previously 'destroyed' Cornish fighting back against changes enforced upon them from various outside agencies. In the novel we see Phillips widening the net of reclamation in his fight for Cornish self-expression. Realizing the difficulty and limitations of writing a novel in Cornish alone, instead he teases the reader with lines before each chapter (*An Pen wyth*. The very end. . .).[77] Elsewhere, more aggressively than in *The Saffron Eaters*, the text is littered with lines of late Cornish. Crucially, Cornish is integral, and multi-voiced; not ghetto-ised.

The 'strangers' of the novel come out most obviously in the ethnic struggle between the Cornish and those from outside wishing to develop the community, in the manner outlined by socio-economic commentators of the period.[78] Yet the struggle is also prevalent in the Cornish themselves. Aside from Barny, the other Cornish characters are too afraid to confront the political and cultural imperialism placed on their lives – in so doing, becoming 'strangers' to one another, and sealing their fate in a 'tongueless' future. It is only in extreme circumstances, such as the loss of a fishing vessel, that this fragmentation is reunited. The Cornish characters that Phillips offers are heightened versions of Cornish culture between 1980 and 2000, yet the fictional effect brings forward once subservient views into prominence; the horn he blows is a reactionary one, dedicated to a working through of romance, to reclamation of Cornu-English and Cornish literature for the Cornish.

As Payton asserts, 'although still echoing elements of that fatalistic edge recognizable in early twentieth-century Cornish fiction', the work of Phillips and others was demonstrating 'something like a unity of theme and purpose', suggesting that in the literary reaction to all the changes that had overtaken Cornwall between 1980 and 1997, there was a 'new coalescence – a Cornish school in the making'.[79] Characteristic of this new Cornish school was the increased politicality of the writing, as well as what Hurst defined as 'a shared sense of a Cornwall that is lost' and an acknowledgement of 'a complicity by the Cornish themselves in its loss'.[80] Phillips was thus part of a small but significant group of Anglo-Cornish and Cornu-English novelists who emerged in the late 1980s and early 1990s, dedicated to establishing a new kind of literary construction of Cornwall, which would deny the conventions of romance and assert the reality of late twentieth-century Cornish experience. Among these novelists is Myrna Combellack.

Combellack's 1989 novel *The Playing Place – A Cornish Round* is a striking example of how the continuum of Cornish literature is expressed. Combellack chooses a playing place – the theatre space of the Cornish medieval dramas – as a counterpoint to development and change for the worse. The novel – written in full Cornu-English – portrays the break-up of a community under the forces of modernity. The havoc that results from the process of globalization strikes at the very heart of Cornish 'high cultural' experience – the sacrosanct playing place. The playing place is more Celtic since it was there when Cornwall spoke Cornish, and therefore is of high symbolic value:

> Here, watched over by the parish church of St Coen on the east, and by the Steam Engine public house on the north, the darkened arena awaited the mowers for the tea-treat, for the annual play, for the wrestling match, and for the summer bonfire – as it had always done.[81]

Yet, as we can see, Combellack synthesizes this with symbols of Cornish identity throughout history; thus matching Cornish society itself, which was increasingly willing to accept previously distinctive and separate symbols as part of the same cultural heritage. The merging, then, of the memories of industrial Cornwall with the traditions from medieval Cornwall would make the Cornish stronger in the reclamation process and the assertion of the community against outside development. But the negative picture Combellack presents is unrelenting. The Cornish are attacked linguistically, culturally and politically, and despite the villagers' resistance, the plan to develop an estate of bungalows (of the kind attacked by John Betjeman) is doomed to failure.

Hurst suggests that Combellack recognizes that 'Cornwall's destiny lies in defining a relationship with the mainstream of British and European culture that recognizes Cornwall's distinctiveness without asserting its apartness'. Again, this awareness of Cornwall's status within the European continuum parallels the growing assertion by politicians and cultural activists of Cornwall within the European community in an effort to gain greater awareness from Brussels (if not from Westminster) of Cornish difference. Combellack's novel there-fore is an ambitious attempt to unite several threads of Cornish history and indeed the Cornish literary continuum, encompassing both pre-industrial, industrial and post-industrial Cornwall, against the background of a push towards making the Cornish experience central within Europe, rather than assumed peripherality. Combellack there-fore denies the conventions of romance and strongly reclaims the tongueless land in a sophisticated narrative.

Alan M. Kent's novel *Clay* (1991) differs from *The Playing Place* and *The Saffron Eaters* in having a more elaborate structure that makes possible a dialogue between Cornwall's past and its present. As Hurst explains,

> Kent uses the fictional device of a journal of a seventeenth-century clerk to the Parish of St Dennis to counterpoint the reality of the clay country before the discovery of china clay. Already, however, the clerk and his vicar sense a doom hanging over the land as technology begins to develop – the doom which works its way out in the cataclysmic climax of the novel as the land, ravaged by technology and greed, wreaks its own terrible vengeance. In this sense the novel constitutes not so much a lament for a lost Cornish civilization as an evocation of the potential catastrophe of civilization itself in the face of unbridled technology.[83]

Like Jack Clemo, Kent makes sure from the outset that the Cornwall he constructs is not the coast, but the industrial interior; the landscape of the bulk of Cornish people, who could not afford to live on the coast:

> This was the clay land. Somewhere else. This was no Cornwall. Cornwall was golden sand, azure seas and picture postcard harbours. Cornwall was a world away. A world away where things were done differently: prettier than this.[84]

Though the novel connects with the continuum of Anglo-Cornish fiction by delivering a fatalistic Hardy-esque ending, other issues of continuity appear in the work. In an epigram, Kent asserts that, 'When we do not know the truth, we invent stories. Stories last longer than lives. This is one of them', and throughout there are connections made to the oral continuum of Cornish culture.[85] The novel begins with a retelling of Robert Hunt's account of St Austell's clash with the Devil atop Hensbarrow Downs and culminates in the recurrence of the shower of blood, predicting disaster.[86] Folklore and folktale therefore are significant in the narrative, and are seen as core ingredients of Cornish identity, yet the stories are not the sanitized tales of tourism. Instead,

> Hensbarrow is a place of legend – not legends of King Arthur or any of those other airy fairy Cornish legends. Those legends are dead, but the legends on Hensbarrow live. They live in the present and can kill.[87]

Tom Cundy the china clay elder, to whom the hero Ben Sexton goes to hear such stories of the past, becomes the droll-teller from the Cornish literary continuum, so further narratives and secrets are revealed culminating in a set of magical books holding the secrets of the moor which have been passed down and recorded. Identity is revealed through Cornu-English and through employment. The china-clay industry, dominating communities and the landscape of mid-Cornwall, becomes symbolic of the Cornish experience and the reason why mining is so important in determining and defining identity. Thus, whilst identity and difference are not expressed in Revivalist terms, they are located within popular identity of the mid-Cornwall region. Continuity is provided by the text's link with the novels of Jack Clemo, though Kent's narrative lacks the Christian basis of Clemo's earlier explorations of the region. Kent asserts an imagining of this post-modern Cornwall, but there were not enough novelists constructing a Cornwall dissociated from the Revival and the traditions, or Cornish itself, expressing the real Cornwall of those uninvolved in this reclamation process. It would seem that if the Cornish novel is to progress beyond its self-definition and recognition of past historical invisibility, it needs to turn its subject-matter onto the 'Cornwall of Now', of the young, and stop lamenting what is lost.

Elsewhere, a more rigorous polemic paralleling the work of the novelists was being assembled, to counteract and contest Romantic Cornwall and 'du Maurier country'. Unexpectedly, this polemic was to emerge in poetry. Poets with nationalist convictions throughout the period from 1940 to 1980 had found their work marginalized and neglected in favour of those poets whose themes were rather more individualistic and celebratory. However, a small but significant group of poets had begun to express concerns over the lack of a truly nationalist poetry and wanted to write poetry which would help to undermine Anglo-centric views of Cornwall, giving Cornish people and others a greater understanding of their historical subordination and repression, and also to celebrate their ethnicity as a modern European region.

The movement was unexpected not only in the quantity and range of material produced but also the re-emergence of a series of other poets writing in Cornish who had helped to shape the earlier poetry, but had failed to take their poetry beyond the limited circulation of Cornish magazines. In particular, the group formed in the early 1990s composed of Bert Biscoe, Alan M. Kent and Pol Hodge – known as Berdh Arnowydh Kernewek/Modern Cornish Poets – was instrumental in providing the necessary kick-start to this movement, also facilitating a climate of expression for the wider exposure of established Cornu-English poets like Donald R. Rawe, Bill Headdon, Ann Trevenen Jenkin, and also a new flourish of work in Cornish, with Tim Saunders and Richard Gendall leading the way. The aim of this movement was therefore to celebrate the continuum of Cornish literature, but also to critique English hegemony. This group was far more politically committed than previous poets, and not afraid to express that commitment within their verse. Meanwhile, the social, political and economic environment had constructed a set of conditions which made their voices highly significant, more acceptable, and more 'in tune' with other changes and developments in and outside of Cornwall. The changes outside of Cornwall included, as A. Robert Lee, and Mike Storry and Peter Childs have asserted, a growing recognition of a 'multicultural' Britain, and a greater awareness, as Hans-Werner Ludwig and Lothar Fietz recognize, of the importance of 'non-metropolitan perspectives' and poetry's role in the 'self-definition of communities'.[88]

The poets were not only politically committed, but also recognized the importance of not ghettoising poetry and their post-modern reassertion of Cornish identity within that genre. This meant that these poets took their work to groups beyond those immediately concerned with the Revival. The renewed emphasis on the group being

259

part of a continuity of Cornish and Cornu-English literature meant that cultural identity could be strongly asserted by showing past themes and forms of writing, and re-engaging with them. All of these concerns are present in the poetry of Bert Biscoe (b.1952). Biscoe's verse has been important in shaping the new cultural politics of Cornwall. As a cultural activist, Biscoe had long been engaged in an assertion of Cornish identity within both a British and European context. Biscoe's poetic development has thus witnessed an exploration of landscape and culture, in the poems from his early collection *Accompanied by Larks* (1991),[89] to the beautiful craftsmanship of regularly read pieces such as 'The Mermaid's Song'. Here, Biscoe's recognition of industrial collapse and the paralysis which affected the territory is acknowledged, but this only heightens his belief in the ascendancy and rise of a confident Cornish identity, based in a post-modernist coalescence of the industrial with the folkloric:

> By the gate of a second home gravelled track,
> In a black plastic garbage sack,
> Sad Kernow wrapped.
> O Cousin Jack! The spinning wheel's unoiled clack
> Rings around your poor bal knack't.
> But hark, there by the crumbling stack
> A song of summers' burned heather black.
> Why Kernow,
> lift flooded hearts and smile a crack!
> That song is ours. . .
> that Mermaid's back![90]

Elsewhere, Biscoe uses the Cornish literary continuum to assert his voice, recognizing the importance of figures such as R.S. Hawker and the Cornish Revival in general.[91] His poetry draws much on eighteenth- and nineteenth-century Cornish imagery, reflected in many of the poems within his most recent collection, *Words of Granite*. This confidence and belief is given best expression in his satire on Cornwall's obsession with tourism – 'Wheal Ice Cream' – where 'these days the ore is won in our trade/From buses rolled down motorways'.[92] There is no doubt that Biscoe's voice is one of the most confident in contemporary Anglo-Cornish poetry.

Kent, already active as an Anglo-Cornish novelist, initially chose to locate his poetry within popular culture; his 1994 volume titled *Grunge*, demonstrating how a worldwide musical and fashion trend from Seattle, a peripheral city of the USA, had been interpreted and reconstituted in a Cornish context, where the 'grunge' ethos had been dictated by Cornwall's Neo-Paganism, alternative and surf culture. As well as this, there were reflections on his experiences of the china clay landscape and his childhood:

> The scramble course needed no marking. It was age-old.
> Set apart by granite's time and tyre lines
> As powerful as holding as any ancient ley.[93]

Kent's second work, however, was a much more active political engagement with Cornish experience at the end of the twentieth century. In *Out of the Ordinalia* (1995), the *Ordinalia* cycle is the starting point for a long poem, written entirely in five hundred rhyming couplets.[94] Fashioned from the suffering of the individual feeling an exile in his own territory, Kent's questioning brings about conversations with friends, family, the English, as well as his fourteenth-century mentor – the ghost of 'Glasney' – the original writer of the Mystery plays. Each couplet is given a translation in Cornish, and they were labelled with a year between 1497 and 1997; thereby demonstrating to the reader the co-dependence and interrelationship between the two languages in Cornwall, and also the immense period of time in which Cornish identity and distinctiveness had been asserted. The subject-matter travels through Arthurian, medieval, industrial and Revivalist constructions of Cornwall, synthesizing often disparate and separate Cornish material into a whole.

Kent's poetry demonstrates a number of the themes inherent in this new Cornish poetry of what Rawe called 'protest and patriotism', yet whilst his work moves towards a confident expression of Cornish identity, using new verse forms and styles, ranging from neo-classical to a new assertion of Cornish dialect, other poets have also altered the profile of Cornu-English poetry. Amongst those are Bill Headdon, Harry Hickey and Ann Trevenen Jenkin.[96] The vista would not however be complete without recognizing the important contribution made by K.C. Phillipps (1929–1995), who between the mid-1980s and 1995 made a significant impact on the development of Cornish writing. Phillipps was instrumental in re-establishing the importance of Cornu-English as a symbol of Cornish identity, through both his own poetry and his regular appearance on BBC Radio Cornwall. He had also been highly influential as a critic for several of the newer writers and publishers. Phillipps' Cornu-English poems differed from other practising dialecticians of late twentieth-century Cornwall in that they recalled genuine working-class experience. Elsewhere, in poems such as 'On a Bible Christian Chapel' Phillipps importantly expresses the view of the last of that generation to consider the experiences of Bible Christiandom which had so shaped identity since the late nineteenth century onwards, but which by the end of the late twentieth century had lost direction and drive even within the Cornish context. Phillipps therefore offers a lament for not only the Bible Christian movement, but for Methodism itself:

> If there is any God, these men will know,
> Who guide with courage, and who guard with fear,
> Their short, yet strong tradition of Heaven's glow;
> If there is any God, He will be here.[97]

The scope of Anglo-Cornish and Cornu-English poetry – particularly during the 1990s – has been wide and varied; yet the work produced has all assisted in the reclamation process. Other writers were constructing a similar agenda within the milieu of revived Cornish. As Deacon has detailed, the revival of Cornish has been in debate since the breakdown of the 'Nancean synthesis' in the mid-1980s.[98] The Cornish language debate of the 1990s has been dominated by competing 'experts', each with their own agendas of 'superiority' and 'authenticity',[99] each with their own band of loyal followers. Much of the discourse has unfortunately been couched in impenetrable linguistic jargon, often ignoring the wider aims of the Cornish language movement. However, the debate over orthographies would appear to be more ideologically driven than linguistic. We may see the entire debate as a kind of internal review – Deacon has argued that the debate is a response to post-modernist uncertainty.[100] The Revivalist project would appear to be still somehow seeking a modernist approach to Cornish, when it is clear that Cornish plurality is actually the reality. Thus, as Kenneth Mackinnon says, we should perhaps now be referring not to one 'Cornish' but to several different but related 'Cornishes', patterning the existence of various 'Englishes' across the world.[101]

This plurality can certainly be observed within the genre of contemporary Cornish poetry, where poets from various positions in the debate have continued to produce new work. Pol Hodge (b.1965) became a significant Cornish poet during the 1990s. Hodge found that his experience of exile from Cornwall, and unemployment in Cornwall, had prompted a series of poems which allowed constructive and important enquiry into his own identity and what it meant to be Cornish and a Cornish speaker in the 1990s. To do so, Hodge rejected many of the conventions set up by Revivalist poets, such as Edwin Chirgwin and Richard Jenkin, and was prepared to use unconventional verse forms, raps, dialect and forms of popular and mass culture in order to move forward Cornish verse and give it a recognizable contemporary poetic voice, committed to nationalism. Typical of Hodge's approach are his poems of Troon life intersecting with the processes of globalization; here seen in 'Eskisyow-Medhel Wella Moel/Willy Moyle's Slippers':

> An tanyow a Gendowrow, Goeld ha Grenville yw yeyn, mes y
> hwrav vy mos tre dhe doemmder hag eskisyow Wella Moel.
> > Piw?
> > *'Wella Moel ty a woer,*
> > *an den koth gans pymp hwoer,*
> > *mab kottha den koth Moel,*
> > *ev ne a dhemmedhis*
> > *benyn goth Tregaskis,*
> > *a-dhiworth Fordh Leti.'*

> [The fires of Condurrow, Gooldes and Grenville are cold, but I
> come home to warmth and Willy Moyle's slippers.
> > Who?
> > *'Willy Moyle, you knaw,*
> > *the ol' man wi' five sisters,*
> > *oldest son a ol' man Moyle,*
> > *'ee who married*
> > *ol' woman Tregaskis*
> > *from up Laity Road.']*[102]

Ironically, and perhaps even painfully, it is his Methodist heritage combined with pride in Cornish industrialism which forms the metaphorical basis of Hodge's work. His reaction against Methodism shows how a new generation, post-K.C. Phillipps, has dealt with the centrality of Methodism in the history of industrial and post-industrial Cornwall. Another target of Hodge's was an education system which on the surface – and according to the dicta of the National Curriculum – only served to force Cornish identity out of Cornish children.[103] Hodge's most recent work has seen him incorporate more Cornu-English into his expression in order to reinforce issues of identity and difference. This has recently culminated in poems such as 'The Queen's English':

> I'm not English,
> This idn England
> An' I dun want to speak
> the language of some ol' queen.[104]

Though continuing to assert a strongly nationalist poetic, Hodge's achievement has been in taking Cornish verse beyond the confines of the Language movement to wider readerships and audiences inside and outside of Cornwall.

Writing in almost a completely different form to Pol Hodge is Tim Saunders. Instead of choosing the verse forms and structures of popular culture, Saunders is more interested in writing Cornish poetry which was related to – and dependent upon – the traditions of Celtic poetry, and which was aware of its own internal themes, verse forms and part of a historical continuum. Thus, whilst Hodge uses free verse and English forms to construct his poetry, Saunders writes within what we may term a more 'classical' Celtic tradition. Early on in his writing career, Saunders recognized the limitations of the pseudo-medievalism of the Revival, and forged ahead, writing in isolation several hundred poems in Cornish, and poems about Cornwall in other languages.[105] Saunders also recognized the need to write in Cornish and to establish a modern literature of Cornwall.[106] Before the late twentieth-century revival in Anglo-Cornish and Cornish poetry, Saunders found his work marginalised, but as this contemporary movement developed, Saunders' crucial place within the continuum has been foregrounded. He is the most important poet writing in Cornish in the modern era. His recent *Collected Poems* guarantee his significance; this poem in praise of the Cornish inventor, Richard Trevithick:

> Ann hoarn ha'nn tan a'dhÿnyth toth
> yn kreuth vaen koth dre nerth ann daran,
> ha'nn kledhrow a'gan serc'h bellder del gôth.

> [It is the iron and fire that will beget speed
> in the womb of old stone through the strength of the thunder,
> and the rails that will sing fitting love of distance.][107]

Richard Gendall (b.1924), meanwhile, had continued to develop his poetry since his early involvement with the Revival. Gendall, one of the most significant scholars of Cornish of his generation, rarely published his work, though his songs are more widely known. Gendall came to the fore in the language movement in 1952 when he launched *An Lef/ The Voice*, and in 1956 a second magazine, *Hedhyu/Today*, which ran until 1961.[108] Paralleling his research into Modern Cornish, Gendall has resisted publication of his earlier work in Unified Cornish, yet has recently offered compelling poetry in Modern Cornish, which proves his status as a central Cornish poet, not only in the earlier phase, but also between the years 1980 and 2000.[109] Gendall's awareness of his Cornishness is typified in poems such as 'An Yrth/The Snow', where, as in the poetry of Richard Jenkin, the language itself is sufficient in expressing identity and difference, but here couched in the dilemma facing a Cornish miner:

An stennar, eve aweath,
palas dreath an doar,
kethew an kensa,
ne ell e boaz seere tha voaz dewetha
leba tene eve a whath.

[The tinner, he too,
digging through the ground,
though he is the first
cannot be sure to be the last
where he draws his breath.][110]

The work of Gendall, Saunders and Hodge has helped to define the direction of contemporary Cornish verse, though numerous other poets – among them Anthony Snell and Jowann Richards – have also written significant constructions of Cornwall.[111] Though important steps in moving forward Cornish poetry have been made, aside from these five, poets writing in Cornish have failed to have much impact on the literary mainstream, and remain circulated amongst the Cornish magazines only – and near-ghettoised. The first full-length novel in Cornish was *An Gurun Wosek A Geltya/The Bloody Crown of the Celtic Countries* (1984) by Melville Bennetto, which blends Arthurian mysticism with questions of nationalism.[112] A further novel *Jory* (1989) by Myghal Palmer has also appeared,[113] but it seems that the novel in Cornish, at least, is a limited proposition due to the limited readership. The Cornish novel is a direction which might one day be more viable – but more readers will be needed to make a sustainable literary enterprise. As Murdoch perceptively comments:

> In trying to evaluate the literature of revived Cornish, it is diffi-
> cult to separate the concepts of nationalism (which is itself fluid)
> and of elegy, the twin themes of the deserted engine house (or the
> lost language) and the bloody crown. . . The development of
> Cornish literature will depend upon new writers (and a new
> generation), the possibilities of enlarged readership and an agreed
> literary standard, as well as on the adoption of themes which are
> part of a broad cultural perspective, as was the case with the
> great works of the middle ages in Cornish.[114]

Alongside the resistance to attempts to diversify the themes of modern Cornish writing, part of the problem has been a desire – especially by the Cornish Language Board and Kowethas an Yeth Kernewek – to sacrifice quality texts for quantity, though this does appear to be slowly changing.[115] In addition, it is only recently that, despite the break-up of consensus within the 'Language Movement', language activity has become less reliant on Cornish activists operating on political fronts as well as cultural ones. This specialization should help promote an agreed literary standard. It has been difficult also for some of the magazines to drop the pseudo-medievalism which first prompted Saunders' earlier polemic.[116] However, a completed version of the Bible should emerge in 2004, the hundredth anniversary of Henry Jenner's *A Handbook of the Cornish Language*.[117] The Bible's completion will obviously be symbolic since it was its earlier incompletion which led to near linguistic extinction. All this does suggest that Cornish literature, if still having a long way to go in terms of its reception by the wider Cornish public, is in a healthy state and has produced some exciting poetry between 1980 and 2000. The past decade has seen extraordinary achievement, perhaps only dreamed about by the Cornish Revivalists of the early twentieth century.

However, the most exciting work within Cornish culture is presently being completed in film and screenplays. A breakthrough short film produced by Wild West Films titled *The Last Words of Dolly Pentreath* (1994) used the symbol of the 'last' Cornish speaker to wander as a ghost through late twentieth-century Cornwall, observing the changes which have occurred, finding much joy when she meets Cornish speakers.[118] A second pioneering film, *The Saffron Threads* (1995) demonstrates the journey of a group of Galician travellers through Cornwall, and their finding of saffron.[119] A biography of the Cornish poet, Pol Hodge, titled *A Smooth Guide to a Rough Cornishman*, also pioneers the use of the film poem, recording Hodge's reflections on his experiences.[120] The film *Splatt dhe Wertha/Plot for Sale*, (1997) written by Andrew Lanyon, is a short surrealistic comedy about three heroines from a nineteenth-century novel who escape from their author's imagination and, after visiting modern Cornwall, become inspired themselves to create.[121] These films are ground-breaking in the sense that they operate as a genuine Cornish cinema. Though technically there is a long way to go, Cornish 'film' is gaining ground and producing innovative work.

As well as new ways of writing Cornwall, such as film, the confidence in writing in Cornwall has opened up its thematic concerns. The iconography, image and culture of surfing is as much an important construction of contemporary Cornwall as poetry in Cornish. The lettering and logos of many surf boards, clothes and tattoos are pseudo-Celtic and tribal, suggesting a link between Cornwall's ancient past and the present. Surfing in many ways appears as a 'green' activity, in some measure connecting human beings and nature in a non-destructive and therefore Celtic way. Since 1980, there has been rapid growth in the sport. Initially, there was a considerable resistance from Cornish parish and local councils, but they now see the long-term benefit of the sport to the economy of Cornwall. In 1993, the Cornish Gorseth created the first Bard for services to Cornish surfing. With the economic and social background established, a surf literature was inevitable and an important new direction.

Both the film *Blue Juice* and Cathy Lester's *Surf Patrol Stories* were produced in 1995 as a response to Cornwall's surfing culture. *Blue Juice* is the story of a Cornish surfing hero – JC. He has to decide whether he can continue to opt into the 'forever young' culture of surfing or realize his responsibility to his girlfriend, Chloe.[122] The Cornish surfing community presented is fairly accurate. Aspects of rave culture, Cornish New Age-ism in the form of Heathcote Williams (playing a kind of Neo-Pagan Celtic-surfing shaman), and biker/outlaw culture are blended to offer insight into the immediacy of late twentieth-century youth culture in Cornwall. The film manages to write Cornwall by using its village location as the setting for a series of clashes between a number of sub-cultural groups. Against this, Cornwall is given a positive image – the raves take place in a post-industrial landscape of old copper mines and tin streaming works, and the Cornish youth are given positive identities – enjoying a vibrant life, while living on the periphery. The text is an accurate reflection of the conflicting communities within Cornwall in the mid-1990s. The voice heard is not 'nationalist', but it does give voice to Cornwall's youth culture, and in such a way also reclaims Cornwall for the young. Cathy Lester, meanwhile, moves forward an important new direction in the prose depiction of Cornwall in her volume of surf patrol stories.[123] The nine stories in the volume are based on the activities of the Perranporth Surf Life Saving Club, and the narratives presented reflect the typical events of a Cornish surfing community. However, what is perhaps needed to demonstrate the place of surfing culture is a text which manages to integrate it more thoroughly within other aspects of Cornish experience. That text has not yet been written, but it can only be a short while before it emerges, given the present fusion of place, sport and culture.

The fusion of popular and Revivalist culture is also seen in Cornish drama from 1980 to 2000. The drama (originating in the continuum from the work of Donald R. Rawe) is promoted by several peripatetic Cornwall-based groups including the more established companies, such as Kneehigh, Bedlam and Miracle Theatre, as well as emergent groups such as Grinning Gargoyle Theatre. Mainly devised by the players themselves, but from time to time scripted by professional and semi-professional playwrights, themes from Cornish folklore and history as well as modern social issues are being presented both in and outside of

Cornwall. As Craig identified, these types of theatre companies initially operated outside the usual conventions of British theatre by taking material to alternative venues and sites of performance.[124] Initially, though, this was more because Cornwall did not possess any permanent theatrical institutions for such companies to operate within. However, by the late 1980s it had become the established method of theatrical work in Cornwall; with only the late 1990s offering more permanent theatre space.[125] In such a way, Cornish theatre companies have pioneered much community theatre, though there may be a case for arguing that the companies were completing a re-working of Cornish medieval theatre, which was community-based. In Cornwall, companies like Kneehigh Theatre have presented material in such diverse theatre spaces as the Minack and the ruined industrial surrounds of Botallack Mine.[126] Among their more recent plays with Cornish themes have been *Tregeagle*, a retelling of the Faust folktale, *The Bogus*, a play detailing Cornish emigration, and *The King of Prussia*, a play considering the life and times of John Carter, the Cornish 'Freetrader', all contributing to the continuity of Cornish literature. Others texts were also up for reinterpretation. In *Figgie Hobbin*, Kneehigh Theatre presented dramatic versions of Charles Causley's Cornish poetry, whilst elsewhere they have brought about a dynamic dramatic synthesis of the industrial with the ancient – particularly seen in the work of one of their designers, David Kemp.[129]

Two important writers have emerged out of this scene, who are actively reclaiming the tongueless land. James Stock, operating outside of Cornwall, produced for the Royal Court Theatre, London, *Star-Gazy Pie and Sauerkraut* – a play which is set in Padstow, travelling back, via its characters' dreams and anxieties, to Nazi Germany and to a nineteenth-century asylum.[130] But perhaps the most significant name in contemporary Cornish theatre is Nick Darke. Written often for Kneehigh Theatre, Darke's subject-matter has always embraced resoundingly Cornish themes, and gives to his characters strong Cornish personalities. This is best seen in *Ting Tang Mine*, which began life as a community play, but was later redrafted, exploring events surrounding the mine.[131] In essence the theme of the play was barely different from some of the late nineteenth-century narratives of industrial Cornwall, and whilst producing some of the most exciting, and well-written drama between 1980 and 2000, Darke remains focused on pre-1900 Cornwall – perhaps because this is where he feels Cornish identity was at its strongest. Though Darke sometimes denies they are political texts, the plays do present Cornish characters – as in *The Bogus* and *The King of Prussia* – outwitting English characters, and being cunning – as in some of the nineteenth-century dialect narratives. His

1999 play, *The Riot*, has been toured both in and outside of Cornwall to much acclaim.[132]

As we approach the end of this study, and begin to understand the lively vista of reclamation, perhaps the most interesting text to re-emerge is the *Ordinalia* itself, taking us full circle. Symbolic of medieval, Celtic-Catholic Cornwall, the three plays of the cycle are certainly the most important texts within the canon of Cornish literature. In 1996, Alan M. Kent was commissioned by the Ordinalia Trust to complete a verse re-rendering of the *Ordinalia* into English, in order that the plays may be given a revived and relevant performance for the new millennium.[133] Apart from a solitary production in 1969 by students of Bristol University, the full cycle has not been staged in Cornwall for over 300 years. Kent's re-rendering of the text has maintained the rhyme scheme of the Cornish, and whilst the new version will mainly be in English, Cornish identity is once again foregrounded, as in the words of the Trader in *Passio Christi*:

> Yew! Caiaphas, haughty Bishop Sir!
> Help me! Jesus, all puffed up and full of stir,
> has been bedolin' and blustering in the stannon:
> and He has said to us straight
> that if the Temple was in a demolished state,
> in three days He'd up and raise 'un.[134]

Cornu-English itself appears be moving more centre-stage. Simon Parker has also chosen to re-assert the importance of Cornu-English in delineating difference. In the wake of more conflict over European fishing quotas, his timely monologue *A Star on the Mizzen* (1997) tells, through the imagined thoughts of one of the ringleaders, of a group of Newlyn fishermen who in 1896 refused to go to sea on Sundays (the theme also of Nick Darke's *The Riot*). Their livelihoods were threatened by Sabbath-breaking English crews from the East Coast. In May of that year, more than 300 fully armed troops of the Royal Berkshire Regiment were stationed on the streets of Newlyn, whilst three navy gunboats patrolled Mount's Bay, culminating in pitched battles being fought on the promenade. It is this moment which Parker chooses to tell; in so doing setting a new agenda and standard for Cornu-English dialect literature:

> 'We should ha' just stanked on over the top of 'en but instead we
> hesitated and squared up. Some of the boys started linging stones
> and ellins and when one well aimed bully caught Nicholas on the
> chacks and scat 'en over, that was it. . . We soon scattered and
> retreated to the Esplanade. There were whacks injured.'[135]

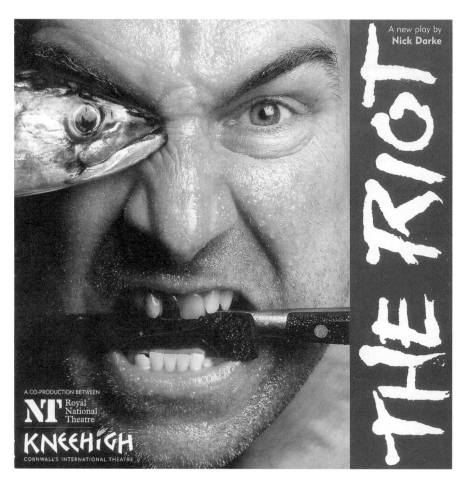

23. Programme cover for Kneehigh's production of Nick Darke's *The Riot*, first performed in 1999.

Parker's monologue re-establishes the centrality of Cornu-English in claiming the 'tongueless land'. Here, the voice is resoundingly Cornish, yet confident and realistic – expressing continuity, identity and difference. There is certainly more of the reclamation being achieved here to be completed, and yet Cornish and Cornu-English literature in 2000 is justified in looking at itself and realizing that there is much hope for the future. With Anglo-Cornish texts moving into more sophisticated explorations of Cornish experience, Cornish literature moving forward to demand more of its creators as well as taking it beyond the ghetto of Cornish speakers, and a confident and revived Cornu-English literature, it would seem that Cornwall's 'tongue' has reached, like the territory itself, new ways of defining its experience, its heritage and its development. Out of the eclecticism of *Kernopalooza!*, at the turn of the new millennium, the literary continuum of Cornwall can look back on its considerable achievement.

NOTES

1. Tim Saunders, *An Ros Du/The Black Heath* (Cardiff 1997). Privately published.
2. N.R. Phillips, *The Horn of Strangers* (Tiverton 1996), p. 5.
3. Helen Foster (dir.), *Kernopalooza!* (Plymouth 1998).
4. The Lollapalooza! travelling festival was organized by the musician Perry Farrell. It highlighted alternative music, left-of-centre politics such as Greenpeace and Amnesty International, and operated as an American mobile Glastonbury Festival.
5. Philip Payton, *Cornwall* (Fowey 1996a), p. 277. See also Allan M. Williams and Gareth Shaw, 'The Age of Mass Tourism' and Peter Mitchell, 'The Demographic Revolution' in Philip Payton (ed.), *Cornwall Since the War* (Redruth 1993a), pp 84–97 and pp 135–56. For a more critical view of late twentieth-century Cornwall, see Paul Theroux, *The Kingdom by the Sea* (Harmondsworth 1984), pp 113–31.
6. Jeremy Boissevain, 'Towards an Anthropology of European Communities?' in Victoria A. Goddard, Josep R. Liobera and Chris Shore (eds) *The Anthropology of Europe: Identities and Boundaries in Conflict* (Oxford 1994), pp 41–56. See also Sharon Macdonald *et al* in Sharon Macdonald (ed.), *Inside European Identities: Ethnography in Western Europe* (Oxford 1993).
7. See Douglas Williams, *Festivals of Cornwall* (St Teath 1987).
8. See *Lowender Peran: Festival of Celtic Culture Souvenir Programme* (Perranporth 1994); 'Golowan – John's Feast' in *Cornish World/Bys Kernowyon* 6 (1995), pp 20–1; 'Tom Bawcock's Eve: A Christmas Tide Story' (1994) in *Cornish World/Bys Kernowyon* 3 (1994), p. 11; 'Bodmin Riding and Heritage Week' in *Keskerdh Kernow/Cornwall Marches On: A Celebration of Cornwall Souvenir*

Programme (Truro 1997); 'St Austell and District White Gold Festival Week 11–18 July 1992' poster.

9. See *Daphne du Maurier Festival of Arts and Literature Souvenir Programme* (Fowey 1997); *18th International Celtic Film and Television Festival/18ves Goel Keswlasek Fylm ha Pellwolok Keltic Souvenir Programme* (St Ives/Porthia 1997).

10. For these festivals, see Fiona Earle, Alan Dearling, Helen Whittle, Roddy Glasse and Gubby (eds.), *A Time to Travel? An Introduction to Britain's Newer Travellers* (Lyme Regis 1994), p. 31.

11. See *The Cornish Guardian* July 31st 1997. See also Alan M. Kent, 'Celtic Ideology in Popular Music' in *An Baner Kernewek/The Cornish Banner* 75 (1994), p. 20.

12. Michael Tooby, *Tate St Ives* (London 1993); St Ives International, *A Quality of Light: Guide* (St Ives 1997). See also David Kemp, *Art of Darkness Museum Guide* (St Ives 1997).

13. Jerry Clarke and Terry Harry (eds.), *Tales of Twickenham* (Redruth 1991).

14. See *Keskerdh Kernow*, op.cit.

15. For North America, see Colin Robins, *Merlin's Diner* (Tiverton 1992); for Australia, see 'Celtic Stirrings Down Under!' in *Cornish World/Bys Kernowyon* 10 (1996), pp 28–9. For Cornish diaspora elsewhere, see Philip Payton, *The Cornish Overseas* (Fowey, 1999). See also Yvonne R. Lockwood and William G. Lockwood, 'Pasties in Michigan's Upper Peninsula: Foodways, Interethnic Relations, and Regionalism' in Stephen Stern and John Allan Cicala (eds.), *Creative Ethnicity: Symbols and Strategies of Contemporary Ethnic Life* (Logan, Utah 1991), pp 3–20.

16. See *Keskerdh Kernow*, p. 24; Bernard Deacon, Andrew George and Ronald Perry, *Cornwall at the Crossroads* (Redruth 1988); M.A. Havinden, J. Quéniart and J. Stanyer, *Centre and Periphery: Brittany and Devon and Cornwall Compared* (Exeter 1991); A.M.J. Galsworthy (ed.), *In Pursuit of Excellence: Cornwall* (Probus 1994).

17. For examples of Celtic spirituality literature in Cornwall, see Paul Broadhurst (1991) *Secret Shrines: In Search of the Holy Wells of Cornwall* (Launceston 1991); John Michell, *The New View Over Atlantis* (London 1985); Cheryl Straffon, *Pagan Cornwall: Land of the Goddess* (St Just 1993); Caeia March, *Reflections* (London 1995).

18. John Lowerson, 'Celtic Tourism' in Philip Payton (ed.), *Cornish Studies: Two* (Exeter 1994), p. 135.

19. See Amy Hale, *Gathering the Fragments* (California Ph.D 1998). For an opposite view to Hale, see 'The Galician crisis: definition of Celtic' in Peter Berresford Ellis, *The Celtic Dawn* (London 1993), pp 19–27.

20. For this debate, see Alan M. Kent, 'Smashing the Sandcastles' in Ian A. Bell (ed.), *Peripheral Visions* (Cardiff 1995), pp 173–80.

21. Ibid.; Donald R. Rawe criticizes writers of historical romance 'for the most part totally failing to grasp the Cornish character and way of thinking' after praising the 'socially committed poets of Cornish protest and patriotism'. See Donald R. Rawe, *A Prospect of Cornwall* (Chapel Amble 1996), p. 218. See also John Hurst 'Literature in Cornwall' in

272

Payton, op.cit. (1993a), p. 304.

22. See for example, Ella Westland, 'The Passionate Periphery' in Bell, op.cit., pp 153–72.

23. See the various explorations of this in Joan Tasker Grimbert (ed.), *Tristan and Isolde* (New York and London 1995).

24. Westland, op.cit., pp 154–9; Bernard Deacon, 'The hollow jarring of the distant steam engine' in Ella Westland (ed.), *Cornwall* (Penzance: 1997), pp 7–24.

25. Westland, op.cit. (1995), p. 153.

26. Ibid., p. 158.

27. Ibid.

28. Alan M. Kent, 'The Cornish Alps' in Westland, op.cit. (1997), p. 60.

29. See the historical romantic novels of Liverpool, such as Lyn Andrews, *Mersey Blues* (London 1995), and the 'North Country' in Josephine Cox, *More Than Riches* (London 1994).

30. Winston Graham, *The Twisted Sword 1815–16* (London 1990), *Ross Poldark 1783–87* (London 1945).

31. See *Poldark* on BBC video. First screened in 1975. See full bibliography for directorial details. *Poldark 3* was first screened in 1996. This version, despite its greater realism, was not well-received; in particular by the Poldark Appreciation Society.

32. Nickianne Moody, 'Poldark Country and National Culture' in Westland, op.cit. (1997), pp 129–36.

33. Symbolized in part by the re-publication of Winston Graham, *Poldark's Cornwall* (London 1994 [1983]). See also *Poldark Appreciation Society Newsletter* 25 (1994). See also David Clarke, *Poldark Country* (St Teath 1981); Robin Ellis, *The Making of Poldark* (London 1987).

34. David Cannadine, *The Pleasures of the Past* (Glasgow 1989), p. 266.

35. Graham, op.cit. (1945), p. 227.

36. Moody, op.cit., p. 133. See Winston Graham, *Demelza 1788–90* (London 1946), *Warleggan 1792–93* (London, 1953).

37. Winston Graham, *Jeremy Poldark 1790–91* (London 1950), *The Black Moon 1794–95* (London 1973) [This novel does not acknowledge the twenty-year break in the writing of the series], *The Four Swans 1795–97* (London 1976), *The Angry Tide 1798–99* (London 1977), *The Stranger from the Sea 1810–11* (London 1980), *The Miller's Dance 1812–13* (London 1982), *The Loving Cup 1813–14* (London 1984).

38. Graham, op.cit. (1945), p. 101.

39. Graham, op.cit. (1990), p. 25. Cornish language is also used in a scene in *Poldark 3*.

40. 'Cornwall of Mine' offered visitors tours of industrial heritage sites in Cornwall in the early 1990s. See *Cornwall of Mine* leaflet.

41. Victoria Holt, *Menfreya* (London 1966); Mary Williams, *The Granite King* (London 1982), *Heronsmere* (London 1983); David Hillier, *Trevanion* (London 1994), *Storm Within* (London 1995); Malcolm Ross, *Kernow and Daughter* (London 1994), *The Trevarton Inheritance* (London 1995).

42. Susan Howatch, *Penmarric* (London 1971).
43. Christine Bridgwood (1986) 'Family Romance: The Contemporary Popular Saga' in Jean Radford (ed.), *The Progress of Romance: The Politics of Popular Fiction* (London 1986); Westland, op.cit. (1995), p. 166. *Penmarric* was first televised in 1979. See full bibliography for further details.
44. Howatch, op.cit., p. 214.
45. See Judith Hubback in 'Women, Symbolism and the Coast of Cornwall' in Westland, op.cit. (1997), pp 99–106.
46. See 'Daphne du Maurier's Romance with the Past' in Alison Light, *Forever England* (London 1991), pp 156–207.
47. Cited on rear cover of Elizabeth Ann Hill, *The Driftwood Fire* (London 1996). See also Elizabeth Ann Hill, *Pebbles in the Tide* (London 1991).
48. Susan Hill, *Mrs de Winter* (London 1993).
49. Anita Burgh, *Daughters of a Granite Land: 1 The Azure Bowl* (London 1989), *Daughters of a Granite Land: 2 The Golden Butterfly* (London 1990), *Daughters of a Granite Land: 3 The Stone Mistress* (London 1991).
50. Cited on cover of Burgh, op.cit. (1989).
51. Gloria Cook, *Trevallion* (London 1994), *Kilgarthen* (London 1995).
52. Rosemary Aitken, *The Girl from Penvarris* (London 1995), *The Tinner's Daughter* (London 1996).
53. Daniel Mason, *Cousin Jack* (Fowey 1996).
54. Rosamunde Pilcher, *The Shell Seekers* (London 1988); Jean Stubbs, *Summer Secrets* (London 1990); Mary E. Pearce, *Polsinney Harbour* (London 1983); Katherine Sinclair, *Journeys of the Heart* (London 1989).
55. Cited on rear cover of Susan Sallis, *Summer Visitors* (London 1988).
56. See Rowena Summers, *Killigrew Clay* (London 1986), *Clay Country* (London 1987), *Family Ties* (London 1988); Mary Lide, *Tregaran* (London 1989); E.V. Thompson, *Ruddlemoor* (London 1995); Rumer Godden, *China Court* (London 1961).
57. Kent, op.cit. (1997).
58. Summers, op.cit. (1986), p. i.
59. Ibid., p. 281; Summers, op.cit. (1987), p. i.
60. Ibid., p. 310.
61. See Sam Llewellyn, *Hell Bay* (London 1980); Jim Crace, *Signals of Distress* (London 1994).
62. Sheila Reddicliffe, *The Cornish Serjeant* (London 1984), *The Cornish Mistress* (Callington 1992).
63. J.P. Mustill, *Summer Needs No Brightening* (Penzance 1997).
64. Joanna Hines, *The Cornish Girl* (London 1994).
65. E.V. Thompson, *Chase the Wind* (London 1977), *The Restless Sea* (London 1983), *Moontide* (London 1996), *Harvest of the Sun* (London 1978), *The Music Makers* (London 1979), *Singing Spears* (London 1982).
66. E.V. Thompson, *God's Highlander* (London 1989), *The Tolpuddle Woman* (London 1994).
67. E.V. Thompson, *Lottie Trago* (London 1990).

68. Thompson, op.cit. (1977), *Ben Retallick* (London 1980).
69. Thompson, op.cit. (1983), *The Stricken Land* (London 1986).
70. Westland, op.cit. (1995), p. 164.
71. Thompson, op.cit. (1977), op.cit. (1980).
72. N.R. Phillips, *The Saffron Eaters* (Exeter 1987), p. 162.
73. Ibid., pp 1–2.
74. Ibid., p. 20 and p. 83.
75. Ibid., p. 162.
76. See Westland, op.cit. (1995), p. 153.
77. Phillips, op.cit. (1996), p. 306.
78. See Deacon, George and Perry, op.cit.
79. Payton, op.cit. (1996a), p. 285.
80. Hurst, op.cit., p. 305.
81. Myrna Combellack, *The Playing Place – A Cornish Round* (Redruth 1989), p 3.
82. Hurst, op.cit.
83. Ibid., pp 305–6.
84. Alan M. Kent, *Clay* (Launceston 1991), p. 3.
85. Ibid., p. v.
86. Ibid., pp 1–2, p. 21 and pp 260–1.
87. Ibid., p. 2.
88. See A. Robert Lee (ed.), *Other Britain, Other British* (London 1995), pp 1–3; Mike Storry and Peter Childs (eds.), *British Cultural Identities* (London 1997), pp 18–25. See Hans-Werner Ludwig and Lothar Fietz (eds.), *Poetry in the British Isles* (Cardiff 1995). For a Cornish perspective, see Alan M. Kent 'A New Cultural Poetics' in *An Baner Kernewek/The Cornish Banner* 78 (1994), p. 20.
89. Bert Biscoe, *Accompanied by Larks* (Truro 1987).
90. 'The Mermaid's Song'. A regularly read poem.
91. Bert Biscoe, *Words of Granite* (Padstow 1998), pp 17–19 and p. 13.
92. Ibid., p. 44.
93. Alan M. Kent, *Grunge* (St Austell 1994), p. 14.
94. Alan M. Kent, *Out of the Ordinalia* (St Austell 1995), p. v.
95. Rawe, op.cit., p. 218.
96. Bill Headdon (ed.), *Cornish Links/Kevrennow Kernow* (Tunbridge Wells 1995), *A Homecoming of a Kind* (Winchester 1984); Harry Hickey, *Padstow Pride* (Chapel Amble 1996); Ann Trevenen Jenkin, *Gwel Kernow/A Cornish View* (Leedstown 1997).
97. K.C. Phillipps, 'On a Bible Christian Chapel' in *A Service for the Life of Kenneth Charles Phillipps*. Trezaise Methodist Chapel 26 June 1995, p. 2.
98. The term 'Nancean synthesis' was coined by Tim Saunders, 'Cornish – Symbol and Substance' (Dublin 1983), pp 253–58. See Bernard Deacon, 'Language Revival and Language Debate: Modernity and Postmodernity' in Philip Payton (ed.), *Cornish Studies: Four* (Exeter 1996), pp 88–106.

275

99. This debate is exemplified in the following key texts: Ken George, *The Pronunciation and Spelling of Revived Cornish* (Cornwall 1986), 'Which Base for Revived Cornish?' in Philip Payton (ed.), *Cornish Studies: Three* (Exeter 1995); Paul Dunbar and Ken George, *Kernewek Kemmyn: Cornish for the Twenty-First Century* (Cornwall 1997); P.A.S Pool, *The Second Death of Cornish* (Redruth 1995); N.J.A. Williams, *Cornish Today: An Examination of the Revived Language* (Sutton Coldfield 1995); Charles Penglase, 'Authenticity in the Revival of Cornish' in Philip Payton (ed.), *Cornish Studies: Two* (Exeter 1994), pp 96–107.

100. Deacon, op.cit. (1996b).

101. Citation of Kenneth Mackinnon in introduction to Payton (ed.) op.cit. (1996b).

102. Pol Hodge, *Mowth on Un like Dolcoath shaft* (Padstow 1997), pp 60–1.

103. Ibid. pp 58–9.

104. Ibid. p. 7.

105. Tim Saunders, *Teithiau* (Talybont 1977). For poems written in Welsh about Cornwall, see pp 36–9.

106. Tim Saunders 'Why I write in Cornish' in *Planet* 30 (1976), pp 29–33.

107. Tim Saunders, *The High Tide: Collected Poems in Cornish 1974–1999* (London 1999), pp 120–1.

108. See Richard Jenkin, 'Modern Cornish literature' in *The Celtic Pen* 1:3 (1994), pp 3–5.

109. See the poetry included in Craig Weatherhill, *Cornish Language and Place Names* (Wilmslow 1995), p. 22, p. 103 and p. 151.

110. Richard Gendall, 'An Yrth/The Snow'. Unpublished poem (n.d.).

111. For Anthony Snell, see 'Travyth yn Trogh/Nothing Broken' (1994) in *The Celtic Pen* 2:2 (1994), p. 20. For Jowann Richards, see 'Hwi a govha Hirawartha' in *An Gannas* 226 (1994), p. 8. Jowann Richards is also a frequent prose contributor to *An Gannas*.

112. Melville Bennetto, *An Gurun Wosek a Geltya/The Bloody Crown of the Celtic countries* (Redruth 1984).

113. Myghal Palmer, *Jory* (Taunton 1989).

114. Brian Murdoch, *Cornish Literature* (Cambridge 1993), p. 150.

115. Typical publications of both these organizations were characterized by card covers and staple-binding. Of late, this has altered. See Wella Brown, *Skeul an Yeth* (Cornwall, 1996). However, the Revivalist ideology remains with its colour cover of bards, a ruined mine, a quoit and craggy cliffs.

116. *An Gannas* 239 (1996) contains a play called 'Ia' by June Luxton which has a pseudo-medieval flavour. The logo of Kowethas an Yeth Kernewek remains remarkably medieval-looking, though modernisation is in process.

117. This proposal has frequently been detailed on BBC Radio Cornwall. The New Testament may be ready before 2004.

118. See Bill Scott (dir.), *The Last Words of Dolly Pentreath/An Dewetha Geryow a Dolly Pentreath* (Wild West Films 1994).

119. See Bill Scott (dir.), *The Saffron Threads* (Wild West Films 1995).
120. See Bill Scott (dir.) *A Smooth Guide to a Rough Cornishman/Ledyans Leven dhe Gernow Garow* (Wild West Films 1996).
121. See Bill Scott (dir.) *Splatt dhe Wertha/Plot for Sale* (Wild West Films 1997).
122. See Carl Prechezer (dir.) *Blue Juice* (Channel Four Films and Pandora Cinema 1995).
123. Cathy Lester, *Surf Patrol Stories* (Perranporth 1995).
124. See Sandy Craig (ed.), *Dreams and Reconstructions: Alternative Theatre in Britain* (Ambersgate 1980).
125. The Hall for Cornwall offers purpose-built theatre space for Cornish and touring theatre companies.
126. See 'Kneehigh Theatre' in *Cornish World/Bys Kernowyon* 11 (1996), pp 20–1.
129. Kemp, op.cit.
130. James Stock, 'Star-Gazy Pie and Sauerkraut' in *Star-Gazy Pie* (London 1995), pp 79–160.
131. Nick Darke *Ting Tang Mine and other Plays* (London 1987).
132. Nick Darke *The Riot* (London 1999). See also Nick Darke *Plays: One* (London 1999).
133. See The Ordinalia Trust , *The Cornish Mystery Plays* (Truro 1996).
134. Alan M. Kent, *Draft of Passio Christi* (2000) p. 9.
135. Simon Parker, *A Star on the Mizzen* (Liskeard 1997), pp 21–22.

Conclusion: *New Ordinalias and Beyond – Cornish Literary Pasts and Futures*

When the new Cornish *Ordinalia* is performed for the third millennium, continuity, identity and difference will come full circle – embodied in a single piece of Cornish literature. Despite the five hundred years between the performances, the literature will be as important as before in helping the community watching the play to define itself. Meanwhile, a thousand years of Cornish literature will come to an end. Here too, at the end of this study, we can come to some conclusions about this 'written' Cornwall. This book has sought to investigate how writers throughout history have constructed Cornwall, adopting a number of models which postulate that Cornwall's literary development has been dependent firstly on the changing nature of its peripheral status and its relationship to England; secondly, on the complex and altering identity of its people; and thirdly, on the perpetuation over a number of some-times interconnected, sometimes disparate literary developments, schools, and individual writers, of Cornish difference. This has been achieved by a marked sense of continuity, with breaks, halts, realign-ments and revivals which characterize most Western European cultures and literary development within them. Historical inquiry has noted distinct phases of this process, and explained them in the Cornish context, as well as relating them to other Celtic, British, European and world trends. This inquiry has led us to abandon both the myth of the non-existence of a literature of Cornwall, and the appropriation of Cornish, Cornu-English and Anglo-Cornish writing into the grand yet ultimately flawed model of English Literature. We have arrived at a radical understanding of Cornwall's literature which shows political, metaphorical and conceptual differences from literature from England, and indeed from other apparently similar Celtic cultures. Cornwall's literature needs to be recognized as part of a culture which must no longer be ignored by the conventional wisdom of British culture. The question of how Cornwall has been written about is thus answered by the following conclusions to be drawn from the story.

Despite a lack of surviving texts, it is clear that rather than being a literary backwater, and despite being on the geographical periphery,

278

Cornwall in the post-Roman and medieval period had a dynamic and extensive literary culture which was central in the development of European literature. The construction of Cornwall was at the heart of much European literature, since its status as a source of narrative and romance had been established early on. Cornish literature, meanwhile, was characterized by popular community theatre – based on biblical or hagiographical themes – though always given a resoundingly Cornish treatment, and fully expressing Cornish identity.

Cornish identity in the early modern period is characterized by a wider inclusion into the British scene, where the Cornish were given respect despite a broader process of incorporation. At the same time, though clearly in decline, Cornish texts continued to demonstrate a fusing of biblical narrative with Cornish experience; whilst Cornu-English and Anglo-Cornish texts demonstrated Cornish rebellion and refusal, at this early time, to be homogenized. The Renaissance period of Cornish literary history proved to be a particularly important shaping moment within the continuum of writing, for it witnessed the first meeting ground between English literary culture and Cornish hagiographical writing in the figures of Richard Carew and Nicholas Roscarrock. Both set up a watershed paradox of English allegiance and Celtic Revivalism which became fundamentally the markings of Cornish literary history. Cornish identity and difference may be expressed both in English and in Cornish, though given the historical accommodation of Cornwall, it was perhaps inevitable that Cornish literature would decline from here on.

The Civil War in Cornwall brought about what might be perceived as an end of confident Cornish identity which remained unasserted until the beginnings of the Industrial Revolution. Cornish literary culture was characterized by a decline in the production of texts in Cornish, though they did encompass more secular themes. The writings of Sidney Godolphin demonstrate an emergent Anglo-Cornish school of poetry, but one which could not be sustained, given the effects of the aftermath of the Civil War. A second revival of Cornish writing occurs at the end of the eighteenth century, producing a small set of highly interesting secular texts, but which was bound to recede given the increasing dominance of writing in English. This period was also characterized by travellers and visiting writers beginning to complete tours of Cornwall and creating a particular ideological view of Cornish experience. In effect these were the earliest tourist writings about Cornwall, a genre which was to last for the following centuries.

The Industrial Revolution brought about increased confidence in Cornish identity paralleled by a century of sustained and detailed writing of Cornish difference, based broadly upon industrial expertise and technical proficiency, together with a response to Methodism. The period was characterized in particular by confident poetry, and by historical novels, and was punctuated by other proto-Revivalist activity; this time completed in the fields of folktale and folklore. The twentieth-century collapse of industrialism within Cornwall was as devastating a blow as the loss of Cornish. A Revivalist ethic emerged which argued that to be more Celtic, Cornish people should revive the Cornish language. However, this was despite the fact that history and the Industrial Revolution had afforded to Cornwall a conceptualization of the Cornish as industrial Celt, with an identity based on the Cornish dialect of English. This is the major way in which Cornwall does not fit the model of traditional agrarian and non-technological Celtic identity.

The 'Revival' of the early twentieth century saw its best energies devoted to re-establishing Cornish language and writing, though a considerable Anglo-Cornish literature was also emergent, suffused with the conceptualization of visiting writers who were actively promoting Cornwall as a site of the Celtic Other, wherein it was still possible to find anti-materialism and spiritual fulfilment. Though there appeared a disparity between these groups, they actually had much in common in reinventing Cornish Celticity and a new kind of Cornish difference on the periphery. World War Two broke this emergent consensus, since Cornish identity needed to be merged again into a wider British identity. This incorporation took a long time to be questioned once again. The writers of the post-war period were characterized by allegiance to English culture, even though they were resolutely Cornish. However, towards the end of the twentieth century, paralleling growing pan-Celtic nationalist movements, more writers emerged with nationalist convictions.

Recently the Romantic construction of Cornwall has assumed a greater role within the wider writing of Cornwall, even though Romantic constructions of Cornwall had been present since the pre-industrial period. Paradoxically, this Romantic vision did much to present a vision of Cornwall as non-English and to express that difference; the texts part of a continuum of Cornish writing and interpretation of 'self' from the nineteenth century. A contemporary picture of Cornwall emerges which accepts the historical changes which have happened, and which asserts its place as a small nation within the new order of Europe, as well as a territory within an increasingly politically devolved Britain. Cornish, Anglo-Cornish and Cornu-English texts now co-exist with an increasing desire to move forward the old-style Revivalism and merge that with literary reclamation and development, blending the continuum from all the periods of Cornwall's literary history with new trends, texts and development. Crucially, Cornwall emerges as a territory which has then been misrepresented by those too keen either to fit it into a particular Celtic box, or to see it as a peripheral part of English literature.

As this story shows, Cornwall breaks the mould in several ways. It has also been characterized by a series of literary revivals which have sought throughout history to counteract the process of imperialism and accommodation into England. That a sense of separate Cornish identity still exists, and has existed throughout history, is testified to by the series of revivals attempted by Nicholas Roscarrock, the Penzance School, the nineteenth-century folklorists, the early twentieth-century Revivalists, and those at present still demanding readers to take notice of their Cornish voice. In addition, we may perceive Cornwall as the finest example of an Anglo-Celtic literary synthesis, where by nature of the territory and its specific history, both of the two literary continuums (Cornish and English) have had to acknowledge, then later combine and cooperate to articulate, the continuing sense of Cornish difference.

From these conclusions, Cornwall emerges as a territory which, though geographically small in area, has been written about extensively. In contrast to the observations of Hurst, who has argued that 'from the time of the *Ordinalia* to the coming of John Harris there was a literary silence over Cornwall', and 'there is not a great deal of work of high quality with a strongly Cornish face or character',[1] there is a strong case for asserting the existence and continuity of a Cornish, an Anglo-Cornish and a Cornu-English literature, with appropriate movements, changes and developments sometimes related, and sometimes not related, to English or other Celtic literatures. The historical picture up until the twentieth century was characterized by the decline of Cornish and the increase of Anglo-Cornish and Cornu-English literature, but substantial evidence now points to a continuing revival of writing in Cornish. This is the latest manifestation of the historical continuum of the literature of Cornwall. Considering the pressures of accommodation into the English state, the trend towards a 'South West' or 'West Country' regionalism, and the lack of indigenous Cornish media, the survival and growth of the Cornish Revival is one of the most remarkable cultural achievements of the modern era.

The perpetuation of difference in Cornwall has been constructed in all the literary texts considered here. Cornwall's difference is not only expressed through writing in the Cornish language. Paradoxically, literary romance in the form of historical novels has actually perpetuated a particular vision of Cornish difference drawn from one significant historical moment of Cornish culture – the Industrial Revolution – which has helped to build particularly strong images of Cornish identity and lifestyle for both Cornish and non-Cornish readerships. Similarly, Arthuriana, New Ageism, Paganism, Cornish art and texts with overtly traditional Celtic themes, have also contributed to popular constructions of why Cornwall is special or, in the words of Denys Val Baker, 'timeless'. Yet Cornwall does not fit the typical model of Celtic. Unlike other Celtic territories, Cornwall was the first to industrialize, and thus a growing sense of difference has been based on the Cornish conceptualization of itself as the aforementioned 'industrial Celt', vibrant as an emigrant to other parts of the world, and popularized latterly in the imagery of the candle and felt-hatted Cornish miner and the bal-maiden, symbolic of the rural and the industrial still in happy union. Cornwall breaks the rules of traditional conceptualizations of Celtic, and this is one reason it has not been afforded equivalent status to other Celtic literatures. This problem has been exacerbated by the lack of academic institutions operating in Cornwall ready to promote and defend a Cornish literature, its equal but different status in the Celtic canon, and its place as a historical and modern European literature of a small nation.

In terms of identity, despite moves towards homogeneity, both indigenous and visiting writers have continued to write of Cornwall's difference. Indeed the visiting writers have been highly influential in shaping in a positive way how that identity has been perceived. A survey of the historical process explains how the two groups actually met and co-operated more often than some observers might think. In the case of Daphne du Maurier, who is often held up as the very antithesis of what Cornish literature should be, a closer reading of her work reveals shifting allegiances and a deeper understanding of Cornish experience. Whilst critics have been quick to reduce the equal place of visiting writers in the overall construction of a 'written Cornwall', an argument of this study has been to assert those writers whose importance in the continuum of Cornish literature is too little known. Among such are Andrew Boorde, Celia Fiennes, Daniel Defoe, John Skinner, Edward Lhuyd, R.M. Ballantyne, Leo Walmsley and Arthur Caddick. The importance of several indigenous writers should also be more widely known: Humphry Davy, W. Herbert Thomas, J.T. Tregellas, James Dryden Hosken, Salome Hocking Fifield, and more recently, Edwin Chirgwin, Donald R. Rawe, Richard Jenkin and Tim Saunders. Fortunately this undervaluation is beginning to change. The next step will be to evaluate how Cornish men and women wrote about the territories to which they emigrated, and how their descendants now perceive their relationship to Cornwall.

Yet even though Cornish, Anglo-Cornish and Cornu-English literatures are now growing heathily, Cornwall still lacks sufficient
institutions for the texts generated to have the impact they deserve,
and for more cultural commentators to understand the development
of the literature and its history. Perhaps the saddest part of Cornwall's
literary history is the loss of so many texts in Cornish. Yet there is
good evidence that Cornish continues to grow in usage and importance within the culture in ways which were unheard of only a decade
ago. If we can criticize the Revivalists and others who have operated
in Cornish culture, then it must be for the neglected and subsidiary
place of Cornu-English within Cornwall. It is a great misfortune that
dialect was not recognized in the period 1890-1940 as a stronger
badge of identity; Phillipps' 'talisman',[2] that might have more readily
been the base of a modern Cornu-English literature, rather than the
sidelined position it has occupied for much of the twentieth century.

The literary future itself looks very healthy. Early in 2000, the main
campus site for a University of Cornwall was announced as being at
Tremough in Penryn, a stone's throw from the site of Glasney
College, perhaps fulfilling once again the ancient prophecy that 'In
Polsethow ywhylyr anethow' [In Polsethow shall be seen dwellings (or
marvels)].[3] Such a development is bound to help in both the writing of
new literature, as well as better informed scholarship upon the literature of Cornwall. More recently, a new level of publishing has begun
to professionalize the look and quality of the Cornish literary continuum, of which it is hoped this study is one part.[4] Such developments will not only facilitate better access for people wishing to read
the literature of Cornwall, but will also promote and develop new
writers. As for new writing, with the development of publishing on the
world-wide web and so-called 'hypertext', the future of writing about
Cornwall may well lie in this direction. On-line publishing may also
help in the development of better resources for the teaching of the
literature of Cornwall to students at primary, secondary and university
level.[5]

If there are observations to be made at the turn of the millennium, it
is that Cornish and Cornu-English literature needs to actually stop
being *so* Cornish – effectively to 'de-Revivalize'. It merely needs to
write about everyday occurrences, and give to those occurrences the
mark of Cornish difference. Allied to this is that Cornish, Anglo-
Cornish and Cornu-English literature must end its defensive stance
(effectively a 'cult of loss'), and stop 'gathering the fragments' of a past
which will not return. The dynamism of Cornish culture has proved
that whilst the lament for what is lost or will not return is appropriate,
Cornwall must also look forward to what it can become. It must

synthesize its ancient and modern, the Celtic and the industrial, Cornish and English, and develop the literature and culture so that each acknowledges its dependence on the other in defining and constructing Cornwall and Cornish identity in the new millennium. If the concept of Kernow/Cornwall has become difficult to define, that is because the black-and-white of St Piran's flag has metamorphosed into a brand new spectrum. The colours of the new *Ordinalia* blend into the rich pageant of Kneehigh Theatre's *The Riot*; the nationalist raps of contemporary Cornish poetry match Winston Graham's remarkable *Poldark* chronology. Over time, Cornish identity has altered and changed greatly, yet generations of writers have explored Cornish difference in remarkably new ways. To conclude, no one literature of Cornwall should dominate the others: each has its place in the continuum, each *onen hag oll* – one and all.

NOTES

1. See John Hurst 'Literature in Cornwall' in Philip Payton (ed.), *Cornwall Since the War* (Redruth 1993a), p. 307.
2. K.C. Phillipps, *A Glossary of Cornish Dialect* (Padstow 1993), p. 2.
3. Crystan Fudge, *The Life of Cornish* (Redruth 1982), p. 5.
4. Alan M. Kent (ed.) *Voices from West Barbary: An Anthology of Anglo-Cornish Poetry 1549–1928* (London 2000); Alan M. Kent and Tim Saunders (eds. and trs.) *Looking at the Mermaid: A Reader in Cornish Literature 900–1900* (London 2000); Amy Hale, Alan M. Kent and Tim Saunders (eds.) *Inside Merlin's Cave: A Cornish Arthurian Reader* (London 2000).
5. Numerous websites now promote Cornish language and Anglo-Cornish literature. For a brief selection, see the following:

> www.cornwall.net
> www.cornwall-calling.co.uk
> www.francisboutle.demon.co.uk
> www.kernewek.currantbun.com
> www.ozemail.com.au
> www.summerlands.com

BIBLIOGRAPHY

MANUSCRIPTS AND PAPERS

Beunans Meriasek. MS Peniarth 105, NLW, Aberwystwyth.
The Black Letter Pamphlet: News from Perin in Cornwall of a most Bloody and un-exampled Murder. Quarto, Bodley, 4 M G29(2), Oxford.
Gwreans an Bys. MS Bodley 219, Oxford.
Jenner Papers. Box Eight, Royal Institution of Cornwall, Truro.
John of Cornwall, *Prophetia Merlini.* Cod. Ottobonianus Lat. 1474, Vatican.
Nicholas Roscarrock, *Lives of the Saints.* MS Add. 3041, Cambridge.
Ordinalia. MS Bodl. 791, Oxford.
Tregear Homilies. BL MS Add, 46397, London.

NEWSPAPERS AND PERIODICALS

An Baner Kernewek / The Cornish Banner
An Houlsedhas
An Gannas
An Lef (pre-1953)
An Lef Kernewek (post-1953)
Annual Report of the Royal Cornwall Polytechnic Society
Artswest
Bolton Weekly Journal
Brice's Weekly Journal
Celtia
Celtic Pen
Cornish Guardian
Cornish Magazine
Cornish Review (Series 1)
Cornish Review (Series 2)
Cornish World / Bys Kernowyon
Delyow Derow
Devon and Cornwall Notes and Queries
Eythen
Folklore, and Folklore Society

285

Hansard
Hedhyu
Journal of the Royal Institution of Cornwall
Kernow (pre-war, *Tyr ha Tavas*)
Old Cornwall
Planet
Poldark Appreciation Society Newsletter
Publications of the Early English Text Series
Signal
Speculum
Studia Celtica Japonica
Transactions of the Philological Society
West Briton
Western Morning News

BOOKS, ARTICLES AND PAMPHLETS

Aitken, Rosemary, *The Girl from Penvarris*. London: Orion 1995
   The Tinner's Daughter. London: Orion 1996
Angarrack, John, *Breaking the Chains: Censorship, Deception and the Manipulation of Public Opinion in Cornwall*. Camborne: Stannary Publications 1999
Andrews, Lyn, *Mersey Blues*. London: Corgi 1995
Arnold, Matthew, *The Study of Celtic Literature*. London: Smith and Elder 1867
Arthur, Marshall, *The Autobiography of a China Clay Worker*. Cornwall: The Federation of Old Cornwall Societies 1995
Arthurson, Ian, *The Perkin Warbeck Conspiracy*. Stroud: Sutton 1997
Ashcroft, Bill, Griffiths, Gareth and Tiffin, Helen, *The Empire Writes Back: Theory and Practice in Post-Colonial Literatures*. London: Routledge 1989
Baker, James, *By the Western Sea: A Summer Idyll*. London: Longmans, Green and Co 1889
Bakere, Jane A., *The Cornish Ordinalia: A Critical Study*. Cardiff: University of Wales Press 1980
Balakrishnan, Gopal (ed.), *Mapping the Nation*. London: Verso 1996
Ballantyne, R.M., *Deep Down: A Tale of the Cornish Mines*. London: Blackie and Son 1868
Baring-Gould, Sabine, *The Gaverocks: A Tale of the Cornish Coast*. London: Smith, Elder and Co 1887
   In the Roar of the Sea. London: Methuen 1892

Beadle, Richard (ed.), *The Cambridge Companion to Medieval English Theatre.* Cambridge: Cambridge University Press 1994

Bédier, Joseph, *Le Roman de Tristan.* Paris: Privately published 1902–5

Bell, Ian A. (ed.), *Peripheral Visions: Images of Nationhood in Contemporary British Fiction.* Cardiff: University of Wales Press 1995

Bennett, David (ed.), *Multicultural States: Rethinking Difference and Identity.* London: Routledge, 1998

Bennetto, Melville, *An Gurun Wosek a Geltya/The Bloody Crown of the Celtic Countries.* Redruth: Dyllansow Truran 1984

Besant, Walter, *Armorel of Lyonesse: A Romance of Today.* Felinfach: Llanerch 1993 [1890]

Betjeman, John, *Summoned by Bells.* London: John Murray 1960
Collected Poems. London: John Murray 1988
Betjeman's Cornwall. London: John Murray 1994

Birks, Harold, 'Jamaica Inn: The Creation of Meanings on a Tourist Site'. In: Westland, Ella (ed.), 1997

Biscoe, Bert, *Accompanied by Larks.* Truro: Bert Biscoe 1991
Words of Granite. Chapel Amble: Lodenek Press 1998

Black, D.M., Redgrove, Peter, Thomas, D.M., *Penguin Modern Poets 11.* Harmondsworth: Penguin 1968

Blyton, Enid, *Five Go Down to the Sea.* London: Hodder and Stoughton 1990 [1953]

Boase, George Clement, *Collectanea Cornubiensis.* Truro: Netherton and Worth 1890

Bold, Alan, *Hugh MacDiarmid: The Terrible Crystal.* London: Routledge and Kegan Paul 1983

Borlase, William, *Antiquities Historical and Monumental of the County of Cornwall.* London: W. Bowyer and J. Nicholls 1754

Borlase, William Copeland, *Nænia Cornubiæ: The Cromlechs and Tumuli of Cornwall.* Felinfach: Llanerch 1994 [1872]
The Age of Saints: A Monograph of Early Christianity in Cornwall with the Legends of the Cornish Saints. Felinfach: Llanerch 1995 [1893]

Bosanketh, Edward, *Tin.* Marazion: Justin Brooke 1988 [1888]

Boissevain, Jeremy, 'Toward an Anthropology of European Communities'. In Goddard, Victoria, Llobera, Josep R. and Shore, Chris (eds.), 1994

Bottrell, William (ed.), *Traditions and Hearthside Stories of West Cornwall: First Series.* Penzance: W. Cornish 1870
(ed.), *Traditions and Hearthside Stories of West Cornwall: Second Series.* Penzance: Beare and Son 1873
(ed.), *Traditions and Hearthside Stories of West Cornwall: Third Series.* Penzance: F. Rodda 1880

Bowen, E.G., *Britain and the Western Seaways*. London: Thames and Hudson 1972

Brace, Catherine, 'Cornish Identity and Landscape in the Work of Arthur Caddick'. In: Payton, Philip (ed.), 1999

Bradshaw, Brendan and Morrill (eds.), *The British Problem, c.1534–1707: State Formation in the Atlantic Archipelago*. Basingstoke: Macmillan Press 1996

Brayshay, Mark (ed.), *Topographical Writers in South-West England*. Exeter: University of Exeter Press 1992

Brendon, Piers, *Hawker of Morwenstow*. London: Cape 1975a
(ed.) *Robert Stephen Hawker: Cornish Ballads and Other Poems*. St Germans: Elephant Press 1975b

Brice, Andrew, 'The Exmoor Scolding'. In: *Brice's Weekly Journal*. No.52 1727

Bridgwood, Christine, 'Family Romance: The Contemporary Popular Saga'. In: Jean Radford (ed.),1986

Brittain, F. (ed.), *Q Anthology: A Selection from the Prose and Verse of Sir Arthur Quiller Couch*. London: J.M. Dent 1948

Broadhurst, Paul, *Secret Shrines: In Search of the Holy Wells of Cornwall*. Launceston: Pendragon Press 1991
Tintagel and the Arthurian Mythos. Launceston: Pendragon Press 1992

Brown, Terence (ed.), *Celticism*. Atlanta: Rodopi 1996

Brown, Tony (ed.), *Welsh Writing in English: A Yearbook of Critical Essays*. Bangor: New Welsh Review 1995

Brown, Wella, *Skeul an Yeth*. Cornwall: The Cornish Language Board 1996

Buchanan, Robert, *The Master of the Mine*. London: N. Bentley 1885

Burgh, Anita, *Daughters of a Granite Land: 1 The Azure Bowl*. London: Chatto and Windus 1989
Daughters of a Granite Land: 2 The Golden Butterfly. London: Chatto and Windus 1990
Daughters of a Granite Land: 3 The Stone Mistress. London: Chatto and Windus 1991

Burke, Patricia, 'The Stained Glass Windows of the Church of St. Neot, Cornwall'. In: *Devon and Cornwall Notes and Queries*. No.33 1974–1978

Cable, James (ed. and tr.), *The Death of Arthur*. Harmondsworth: Penguin 1971

Caddick, Arthur, *A Croft in Cornwall*. Marazion: Wordons 1968
The Ballad of Michael Joseph: The Captain of Cornwall. Penzance: Headland, 1977
The Call of the West. Nancledra: Arthur Caddick Publications 1983

Cannadine, David, *The Pleasures of the Past*. Glasgow: William Collins 1989

Causley, Charles, *Runaway*. London: Curwen 1936

The Conquering Hero. London: Curwen 1937

Benedict. London: Muller 1938

Farewell, Aggie Weston! Aldington: Hand and Flower Press 1951

Hands to Dance and Skylark. London: Anthony Mott 1979 [1951]

Survivor's Leave. Aldington: Hand and Flower Press 1953

Union Street. London: Hart Davis 1957

Johnny Alleluia. Crediton: Richard Gilbertson 1961

Figgie Hobbin. Harmondsworth: Penguin. 1985 [1970]

Collected Poems 1951–1975. London: Macmillan. 1975

Secret Destinations. London: Macmillan 1984

A Field of Vision. London: Macmillan 1988

The Young Man of Cury and other poems. London: Macmillan 1991

The Spirit of Launceston: A Celebration of Charles Causley's Poetry. Launceston: Launceston Calligraphers 1994

Collected Poems for Children. London: Macmillan 1996

The Merrymaid of Zennor. London: Anderson 1999

Celtic Film and Television Association, *18th International Celtic Film and Television Festival / 18ves Goel Keswlasek Fylm ha Pellwolok Keltic Souvenir Programme*. St Ives/Porthia: 1997

Chambers, Harry (ed.), *Causley at 70*. Calstock: Peterloo Poets 1987

Chapman, Malcolm, *The Celts: The Construction of a Myth*. Basingstoke: Macmillan 1992

Chitty, Simon, *Charles Kingsley's Landscape*. Newton Abbot: David and Charles 1976

Clarke, David, *Poldark Country*. St Teath: Bossiney Books 1981

Clarke, Jerry and Harry, Terry (eds.), *Tales of Twickenham*. Redruth: Clarke and Harry 1991

Clemo, Eveline, *I Proved Thee at the Waters: The Testimony of a Blind Writer's Mother*. Ilkston: Moorley's Bible and Bookshop n.d.

Clemo, Jack, *Wilding Graft*. London: Anthony Mott 1983 [1948]

Confession of a Rebel. London: Chatto and Windus 1975 [1949]

The Clay Verge. London: Chatto and Windus 1951

'The Clay Dump'.1951. In: Val Baker, Denys (ed.), 1976

The Invading Gospel: A Return to Faith. Basingstoke: Marshall Pickering 1986 [1958]

The Map of Clay. London: Methuen 1961

Cactus on Carmel. London: Methuen 1967

The Echoing Tip. London: Methuen 1971

Broad Autumn. London: Methuen 1976

The Marriage of a Rebel: A Mystical-Erotic Quest. London: Victor Gollancz 1980

The Bouncing Hills. Redruth: Dyllansow Truran 1983

A Different Drummer. Padstow: Tabb House 1986

The Shadowed Bed. Tring: Lion 1986

Selected Poems. Newcastle upon Tyne: Bloodaxe Books 1988

Approach to Murano. Newcastle upon Tyne: Bloodaxe Books 1993

The Cured Arno. Newcastle upon Tyne: Bloodaxe Books 1996

Cobb, Francis F., *The Watchers on the Longships*. Redhill: Wells 1948 [1876]

Colley, Linda, *Britons: Forging the Nation 1707–1837*. New Haven and London: Yale University Press 1992

Collins, Wilkie, *Rambles Beyond Railways*. London: Westaway Books 1948 [1851]

Basil. Oxford: Oxford University Press 1990 [1852]

The Dead Secret. London: Chatto and Windus 1929 [1857]

Combellack, Myrna (ed. and tr.), *The Camborne Play: A Verse Translation of Beunans Meriasek*. Redruth: Dyllansow Truran 1988

The Playing Place – A Cornish Round. Redruth: Dyllansow Truran 1989

Combellack-Harris, Myrna (ed.), *Cornish Studies for Cornish Schools*. Redruth: Institute of Cornish Studies 1989

Cook, Gloria, *Trevallion*. London: Headline 1984

Kilgarthen. London: Headline 1995

Cook, Judith, *Daphne: A Portrait of Daphne du Maurier*. London: Corgi 1992

Cornish, John B. (ed.), *The Autobiography of a Cornish Smuggler (Captain Harry Carter, of Prussia Cove) 1749–1809*. Truro: D. Bradford Barton 1971 [1894]

Cornwall of Mine, *Cornwall of Mine*. Pamphlet explaining tourist project. Cornwall: n.d.

Courtney, Margaret, *Folklore and Legends of Cornwall [Cornish Feasts and Folklore]*. Exeter: Cornwall Books 1989 [1890]

Cox, Josephine, *More Than Riches*. London: Orion 1994

Crace, Jim, *Signals of Distress*. London: Michael Joseph 1994

Craig, Sandy (ed.), *Dreams and Reconstructions: Alternative Theatre in Britain*. Ambersgate: Amber Lane Press 1980

Craik, Dinah, *An Unsentimental Journey through Cornwall*. Penzance: The Jamieson Library 1988 [1884]

Cross, Tom, *The Shining Sands: Artists in Newlyn and St Ives 1880–1930*. Tiverton: Westcountry Books 1994

Geoffrey Cubitt (ed.), *Imagining Nations*. Manchester: Manchester University Press 1998

Curley, Michael J. (ed.), 'A New Edition of John of Cornwall's Prophetia Merlini'. In: *Speculum*. No.57 1982

Curnock, Nehemiah (ed.), *The Journal of the Rev. John Wesley*. Vols.1–8. London: The Epworth Press 1938

Daphne du Maurier Festival Committee, *The Daphne du Maurier Festival of Arts and Literature Programme*. St Austell: Restormel Borough Council 1997

Darke, Nick, *Ting Tang Mine and Other Plays*. London: Methuen 1987
Plays: One. London: Methuen 1999
The Riot. London: Methuen 1999

Davies, W. Ll., *Cornish Manuscripts in the National Library of Wales*. Aberystwyth: National Library of Wales 1939

Deacon, Bernard, 'Cornwall: Popular Culture and Guide Book Heritage'. In: Robins, Colin, 1992
'Language Revival and Language Debate: Modernity and Postmodernity'. In: Payton, Philip (ed.), 1996
'"The hollow jarring of the distant steam engine": Images of Cornwall between West Barbary and Delectable Duchy'. In: Westland, Ella (ed.), 1997

Deacon, Bernard, George, Andrew and Perry, Ronald, *Cornwall at the Crossroads: Living Communities or Leisure Zone?* Redruth: The Cornish Social and Economic Research Group 1988

Deacon, Bernard and Payton, Philip, 'Re-inventing Cornwall: Cultural Change on the European Periphery'. In: Payton, Philip (ed.), 1993b

Deane, Tony and Shaw, Tony, *The Folklore of Cornwall*. Totowa, New Jersey: Rowman and Littlefield 1975

Delany, Paul, *D. H. Lawrence's Nightmare: The Writer and His Circle in the Years of the Great War*. Hassocks: The Harvester Press 1979

De Sélincourt, Aubrey (tr.) and Burn A.R. (ed.), *Herodotus: the Histories*. Harmondsworth: Penguin 1954

Ditmus, E.M.R., *Tristan and Iseult in Cornwall*. Brockworth: Forrester Roberts 1970

Dixon, John, *A Schooling in 'English': Critical Episodes in the Struggle to Shape Literary and Cultural Studies*. Milton Keynes: Open University Press 1991

Doble, Gilbert H., *The Saints of Cornwall: Parts One to Six*. Felinfach: Llanerch 1997 [1923–1944]

Doel, Fran and Geoff, and Lloyd, Terry, *World of Arthur: King Arthur in History, Legend and Culture*. Stroud: Tempus 1998

Drayton, Michael, 'The Poly-Olbion'. In: Gilbert, Davies (ed.), 1838

Dudgeon, Piers, *Daphne du Maurier's Cornwall: Her Pictorial Memoir*. Chichester: The Chichester Partnership 1995

du Maurier, Daphne, *The Loving Spirit*. London: Arrow Books 1992
[1931]
I'll Never Be Young Again. London: Heinemann 1932
The Progress of Julius. London: Heinemann 1933
Jamaica Inn. London: Arrow Books 1992 [1936]
Rebecca. London: Arrow Books 1992 [1938]
Frenchman's Creek. London: Arrow Books 1992 [1941]
The King's General. London: Arrow Books 1992 [1946]
My Cousin Rachel. London: Arrow Books 1992 [1951]
Vanishing Cornwall. Harmondsworth: Penguin 1972 [1967]
The House on the Strand. London: Arrow Books 1992 [1969]
Rule Britannia. London: Arrow Books 1992 [1972]
Dumcombe-Jewell, L.C., 'Dr. Magnus Maclean and Cornish
Literature'. In: *Celtia*. November 1902
Dunbar, Paul and George, Ken, *Kernewek Kemmyn: Cornish for the
Twenty-First Century*. Cornwall: The Cornish Language Board 1997
Dunmore, Helen, *Zennor in Darkness*. Harmondsworth: Penguin 1994
Durkacz, Victor Edward, *The Decline of the Celtic Languages: A Study of the
Linguistic and Cultural Conflict in Scotland, Wales and Ireland from the
Reformation to the Twentieth Century*. Edinburgh: John Donald 1983
Earle, Fiona, Dearling, Alan, Whittle, Helen, Glasse, Roddy and
Gubby (eds.), *A Time to Travel? An Introduction to Britain's Newer
Travellers*. Lyme Regis: Enabler 1994
Ebbatson, Roger, *The Evolutionary Self: Hardy, Forster, Lawrence*. London:
Harvester Press 1982
Edwards, Ray (ed.), *The Charter Fragment*. Sutton Coldfield: Kernewek
Dre Lyther 1991
(ed.), *The Poem of Mount Calvary*. Sutton Coldfield: Kernewek Dre
Lyther 1993
(ed.), *The Tregear Homilies*. Sutton Coldfield: Kernewek Dre Lyther
1994
Elliot-Binns, L.E., *Medieval Cornwall*. London: Methuen 1955
Ellis, Peter Berresford, *The Cornish Language and its Literature*. London
and Boston: Routledge and Kegan Paul 1974
The Celtic Revolution: A Study in Anti-Imperialism. Talybont: Y Lolfra
1988 [1985]
Celt and Saxon: The Struggle for Britain AD410–937. London: Constable
1993
The Celtic Dawn: A History of Pan-Celticism. London: Constable 1993
The Chronicles of the Celts: New Tellings of their Myths and Legends.
London: Robinson 1999
Ellis, Robin, *The Making of Poldark*. London: Crossaction 1987

Ermarth, Elizabeth Deeds, *The English Novel in History: 1840–1895*. London: Routledge 1997

Evans, J. Gwenogvryn (ed.), *The Book of Taliesin*. Llanbedrog: Privately published 1910

Filbee, Marjorie, *Celtic Cornwall*. London: Constable 1996

Filleul, M., *Pendower: A Story of Cornwall at the Time of Henry the Eighth*. London: T. Nelson and Sons 1877

Ford, Patrick K. (ed. and tr.), *The Mabinogi and other Medieval Welsh Texts*. Berkeley: University of California Press 1977

Forfar, W.B., *The Exhibition and other Cornish Poems*. Truro: Netherton and Worth c.1891

Forster, Margaret, *Daphne du Maurier*. London: Chatto and Windus 1993

Fowler, Alistair (ed.), *The New Oxford Book of Seventeenth Century Verse*. Oxford: Oxford University Press 1992

Fowler, David, *John Trevisa*. Aldershot: Variorum 1993
  The Life and Times of John Trevisa, Medieval Scholar. Seattle: University of Washington Press 1995

Fox, Caroline, *Stanhope Forbes and the Newlyn School*. Newton Abbot: David and Charles 1993

Fredrick, Alan S. (ed. and tr.), *Béroul: The Romance of Tristan*. Harmondsworth: Penguin 1970

Fried, Harvey (ed.), *A Critical Edition of Brome's "The Northern Lasse"*. New York and London: Garland 1980

Fudge, Crystan, *The Life of Cornish*. Redruth: Dyllansow Truran 1982

Furnivall. F.J. (ed.), 'Andrew Boorde: The Fyrst Boke of the Introduction of Knowledge'. In: *Publications of the Early English Text Series*. Early English Text Society, Extra Series 10, 1870

Galsworthy, A.M.J. (ed.), *In Pursuit of Excellence*. Probus: Hawkins Publishing 1994

Gendall, Jan, 'John of Chyanhor & the Oral Tradition'. In: *The Celtic Pen*. Vol.1, No.4 1994

Gendall, Richard, *1000 Years of Cornish*. Menheniot: Teere Ha Tavaz 1994

George, Ken, *The Pronunciation and Spelling of Revived Cornish*. Cornwall: The Cornish Language Board 1986
  'Which Base for Revived Cornish?' In: Payton, Philip (ed.),1995

Gibson, James (ed.), *Chosen Poems of Thomas Hardy*. London: Macmillan 1975

Gilbert, Davies (ed.) *Mount Calvary*. London: Nichols and Son 1826
  (ed.), *The Parochial History of Cornwall*. Vols. 1–4. London: J. B. Nichols and Son 1838

Gillespie, Jack (ed.), *Our Cornwall: The Stories of Cornish Men and Women*. Padstow: Tabb House 1988

Goddard, Victoria, Llobera, Josep R. and Shore, Chris (eds.), *The Anthropology of Europe: Identities and Boundaries in Conflict*. Oxford: Berg 1994

Godden, Rumer, *China Court*. London: Macmillan 1961

Godfrey, Elizabeth, *Cornish Diamonds*. London: Richard Bentley 1895

Goodrich, Peter (ed.), *The Romance of Merlin: An Anthology*. New York and London: Garland 1990

Graham, Winston, *Ross Poldark 1783–87*. London: Werner Laurie 1945

    Demelza 1788–90. London: Werner Laurie 1946

    Jeremy Poldark 1790–91. London: Werner Laurie 1950

    Warleggan 1792–93. London: Werner Laurie 1953

    The Black Moon 1794–95. London: Collins 1973

    The Four Swans 1795–97. London: Collins 1976

    The Angry Tide 1798–99. London: Collins. 1977

    The Stranger from the Sea 1810–11. London: Collins 1980

    The Miller's Dance 1812–13. London: Collins 1982

    Poldark's Cornwall. London: Chapmans 1994 [1983]

    The Loving Cup 1813–14. London: Collins 1984

    The Twisted Sword 1815–16. London: Collins 1990

    The Poldark Omnibus. London: The Bodley Head 1991

Graham, W.S., *Collected Poems 1942–1977*. London: Faber and Faber 1979

Great Western/Arrow Books, *Daphne du Maurier: Du Maurier's Cornwall*. – Promotional tie-in with train tickets. London: Great Western 1996

Great Western Railway Company, *Legend Land*. 3 volumes. London: Great Western Railway Publications 1922–1923

Greenblatt, Stephen, *Renaissance Self-Fashioning: From More to Shakespeare*. Chicago and London: University of Chicago Press 1980

Green, Candida Lycett (ed.), *John Betjeman Letters, Volume One: 1926–1951*. London: Methuen 1994

    (ed.), *John Betjeman Letters, Volume Two: 1951–1984*. London: Methuen 1995

Grieve, Michael and Aitken, W.R. (eds.) *The Complete Poems of Hugh MacDiarmid*. Vols. 1 and 2. Harmondsworth: Penguin 1985 [1978]

Grimbert, Joan Tasker (ed.), *Tristan and Isolde: A Casebook*. New York and London: Garland 1995

Guest, John (ed.), *The Best of Betjeman*. Harmondsworth: Penguin 1978

Hale, Amy (1997) 'Rethinking Celtic Cornwall: An Ethnographic Approach' and 'Genesis of the Celto-Cornish Revival? L.C.

Duncombe-Jewell and the Cowethas Kelto-Kernuack'. In: Payton, Philip (ed.), 1997

Hale, Amy and Payton, Philip (eds.) *New Directions in Celtic Studies.* Exeter: University of Exeter Press 2000

Hale, Amy, Kent, Alan M., and Saunders, Tim (eds.) *Inside Merlin's Cave: A Cornish Arthurian Reader*, London: Francis Boutle 2000

Hall, Jim, 'Maximilla, the Cornish Montanist: The Final Scenes of Origo Mundi'. In: Payton, Philip (ed.), 1999

Halliday, F.E. (ed.), *Richard Carew: The Survey of Cornwall.* London: Melrose 1953

The Legend of the Rood. London: Gerald Duckworth 1955

A History of Cornwall. London: Gerald Duckworth 1959

Hals, William, *The Compleat History of Cornwall.* Truro: c.1736

Hardie, Melissa (ed.), *A Mere Interlude: Some Literary Visitors in Lyonnesse.* Penzance: The Patten Press 1992

Hardy, Evelyn, *The Countryman's Ear and Other Essays on Thomas Hardy.* Padstow: Tabb House 1982

Hardy, Thomas, *A Pair of Blue Eyes.* Harmondsworth: Penguin 1986 [1873]

A Pair of Blue Eyes. Oxford: Oxford University Press 1987 [1873]

The Distracted Preacher and Other Tales. Harmondsworth: Penguin 1979 [Various dates]

The Famous Tragedy of the Queen of Cornwall. London: Macmillan 1923

Harris, Markham (ed. and tr.), *The Cornish Ordinalia: A Medieval Dramatic Trilogy.* Washington: Catholic University of America Press 1969

Harris, John, *Lays from the Mine, the Moor and the Mountain.* London: Alexander Heylin 1853

The Land's End, Kynance Cove and Other Poems. London: Alexander Heylin 1858

The Mountain Prophet, the Mine and Other Poems. London: Alexander Heylin 1860

A Story of Carn Brea, Essays and Poems. London: Hamilton, Adams and Co 1863

Luda: A Lay of the Druids. London: Hamilton, Adams and Co 1868

Wayside Pictures, Hymns and Poems. London: Hamilton, Adams and Co 1874

Monro. London: Hamilton, Adams and Co 1879

Harvey, Graham and Hardman, Charlotte (eds.), *Paganism Today: Wiccans, Druids, the Goddess and Ancient Earth Traditions for the Twenty-First Century.* London: Thorsons 1996

Hatto, A.T. (ed. and tr.), *Gottfried von Strassburg: Tristan with the 'Tristan' of Thomas.* Harmondsworth: Penguin 1960

Havinden, M.A., Quéniart, J. and Stanyer. J., *Centre and Periphery:*

Brittany and Devon and Cornwall compared. Exeter: University of Exeter Press 1991

Hawkey, Muriel (ed.), *A Cornish Chorus: An Anthology of Prose and Verse.* London: Westaway Books 1944

Hays, Rosalind Conklin, and McGee, C.E. (Dorset) and Joyce, Sally L. and Newlyn, Evelyn S. (Cornwall) (eds), *Records of Early English Drama: Dorset/Cornwall.* Toronto: University of Toronto and Brepols 1999

Headdon, Bill, *A Homecoming of a Kind.* Winchester: Hesperus Press 1984

(ed.), *Cornish Links/Kevrennow Kernow.* Tunbridge Wells: Kernow Poets Press 1995

Heard, Doris, *The Spare Room and other Cornish Tales.* Redruth: Sidney James n.d.

Hecter, Michael, *Internal Colonialism: The Celtic Fringe in British National Development, 1536–1966.* London: Routlege and Kegan Paul 1975

Henwood, C.N., *Tales written in Cornish Dialect.* Newquay: Chugg n.d.

Hickey, Harry, *Padstow Pride.* Chapel Amble: Lodenek Press 1996

Higgins, Sydney, *Medieval Theatre in the Round: The Mutiple Staging of Religious Drama in England.* Camerino, Italy: Laboratorio degli studi Linguistici.

Hill, Elizabeth Ann, *Pebbles in the Tide.* London: Grafton 1991

The Driftwood Fire. London: Heinemann 1996

Hill, Susan, *Mrs de Winter.* London: Sinclair Stevenson 1993

Hillier, David, *Trevanion.* London: Warner 1994

Storm Within. London: Warner 1995

Hines, Joanna, *The Cornish Girl.* London: Hodder and Stoughton 1994

Hirth, Eric, *Never Sit Down in the Digey!: The Life and Times of Arthur Caddick, Cornwall's Premier Poet and Satirist.* Helston: Turnstone 1991

Hocking Fifield, Salome, *Norah Lang: The Mine Girl.* London: Andrew Crosbie 1886

Some Old Cornish Folk. London: Charles H. Kelly 1903

Hocking, Joseph, *Jabez Easterbrook.* London: Ward Lock and Co 1890

The Birthright. London: Ward Lock and Co 1897

Mistress Nancy Molesworth. London: Ward Lock and Co 1898

The Jesuit. London: Cassell and Co 1911

What Shall it Profit a Man? London: Hodder and Stoughton 1924

The Sign of the Triangle. London: Ward Lock and Co 1929

Not One in Ten. London: Frederick Warne and Co 1933

Hocking, Silas Kitto *Sea Waif: A Tale of the Cornish Cliffs.* London: Frederick Warne and Co 1882

Tales of a Tin Mine. London: Frederick Warne and Co 1898

A Desperate Hope. London: Frederick Warne and Co 1909

Nancy. London: Sampson Low, Marston and Co 1919

The Broken Fence. London: Sampson Low, Marston and Co 1928

Hodge, James, *Richard Trevithick 1771–1833*. Princes Riseborough: Shire 1995 [1973]

Hodge, Pol, *Mowth on Un like Dolcoath Shaft*. Chapel Amble: Lodenek Press 1998

Holmes, A.W., *Out of this Fury*. London: Hutchinson 1944

Holmes, Julyan (ed. and tr.), *An Dhargan a Verdhin gans Yowann Kernow*. Cornwall: Kesva an Taves Kernewek 1998

Holt, Victoria, *Menfreya*. London: Collins. 1966

Hooper, E.G. Retallack (ed. and tr.), *William Jordan: Gwryans an Bys/ The Creation of the World*. Redruth: Dyllansow Truran 1985

Hosken, James Dryden, *Poems and Songs of Cornwall*. Plymouth: Mitchell, Burt and Co 1906

Shores of Lyonesse: Poems Dramatic, Narrative and Lyrical. London: J.M. Dent c.1928

Howatch, Susan, *Penmarric*. London: Hamish Hamilton 1971

Hubback, Judith, 'Women, Symbolism and the Coast of Cornwall'. In: Westland, Ella (ed.), 1997

Hudson, W.H., *The Land's End*. London: Wildwood 1981 [1908]

Hughes, Helen '"A Silent, Desolate Country": Images of Cornwall in Daphne du Maurier's Jamaica Inn'. In: Westland, Ella (ed.), 1997

Hunt, Robert (ed.), *The Drolls, Traditions, and Superstitions of Old Cornwall: Popular Romances of the West of England (First and Second Series)*. London: John Camden Hotten 1865

Hurst, John, 'Literature in Cornwall'. In: Payton, Philip (ed.), 1993a

'Mine, Moor and Chapel: the poetry of John Harris'. In: Westland, Ella (ed.), 1997

'A Poetry of Dark Sounds: The Manuscripts of Charles Causley'. In: Payton, Philip (ed.), 1999

Ilinska, Zofia, *Horoscope of the Moon*. Padstow: Tabb House 1992

Address of Paradise. Padstow: Tabb House 1996

Isaac, Peter, *A History of Evangelical Christianity in Cornwall*. Cornwall: Peter Isaac 2000

Jackson, Kenneth Hurlstone (ed.), *A Celtic Miscellany*. Harmondsworth: Penguin 1971

Jago, Fred W.P., *The Ancient Language and Dialect of Cornwall*. Truro: Netherton and Worth 1882

An English-Cornish Dictionary. New York: AMS 1984 [1887]

James, Simon, *The Atlantic Celts: Ancient People of Modern Invention?* London: British Museum Press 1999

Jenkin, A.K. Hamilton, *The Cornish Miner*. Newton Abbot: David and Charles 1972 [1927]

The Story of Cornwall. London: Nelson 1934

Jenkin, Richard G., 'Modern Cornish Literature in the 20th Century'. In: *The Celtic Pen.* Vol.1, No.3 1994

'Cornish Literature in the Twentieth Century'. In: Price, Eurwen (ed.), 1997

Jenkins, Elizabeth, *The Mystery of King Arthur.* London: Michael Joseph 1975

Jenner, Henry, *A Handbook of the Cornish Language.* London: David Nutt 1904

'Some Possible Arthurian Place-Names in West Penwith'. In: *Journal of the Royal Institution of Cornwall.* No.12 1912

'The Tristan Romance and its Cornish Provenance' in *Journal of the Royal Institution of Cornwall.* No.14 1914

'The Fourteenth-Century Charter Endorsement'. In: *Journal of the Royal Institution of Cornwall.* No. 20 1915–1916

'The Men Scrifa'. In: *Journal of the Royal Institution of Cornwall.* No.69 1922

'The Bodmin Gospels'. In: *Journal of the Royal Institution of Cornwall.* No.70 1922

'A Cornish Oration in Spain in the Year 1600'. In: *Annual Report of the Royal Cornwall Polytechnic Society.* 1923

'The Bodmin Manumissions'. In: *Journal of the Royal Institution of Cornwall.* No.71 1924

Who are the Celts and what has Cornwall to do with them? Cornwall: The Federation of Old Cornwall Societies 1928

'Some miscellaneous Scraps of Cornish'. In: *Journal of the Royal Cornwall Polytechnic Society.* 1929

John, Catherine Rachel, *The Saints of Cornwall.* Padstow and Redruth: Lodenek Press and Dyllansow Truran 1981

Johns, C.A., *A Week at the Lizard.* Felinfach: Llanerch 1992 [1848]

Johnson, Trevor, 'Time was Away: *A Pair of Blue Eyes* and the Poems of 1912–13'. In: Hardie, Melissa (ed.), 1992

Johnston, Dafydd, *The Literature of Wales.* Cardiff: University of Wales Press 1994

Jones, Roger (ed.), *John Skinner: West Country Tour: being the Diary of a Tour through the Counties of Somerset, Devon and Cornwall in 1797.* Bradford upon Avon: Ex-Libris Press 1985

Kantaris, Sylvia, *Dirty Washing: New and Selected Poems.* Newcastle upon Tyne: Bloodaxe Books 1989

Kay-Robinson, Denys, *The First Mrs Thomas Hardy.* London: Macmillan 1979

Keating, Michael, *State and Regional Nationalism: Territorial Politics and the European State.* London: Harvester Wheatsheaf 1988

Kemp, David, *Art of Darkness Museum Guide*. St Ives: 1996
Kent, Alan M., *Clay*. Launceston: Amigo 1991
  'Cornish Politics, Society and Literature: A Plea for Correlation'. In:
  An Baner Kernewek / The Cornish Banner. No. 72 1993
  Grunge. St Austell: Lyonesse Press 1994
  'Celtic Ideology in Popular Music'. In: *An Baner Kernewek / The Cornish
  Banner*. No.75 1994
  'A New Cultural Poetics'. In: *An Baner Kernewek / The Cornish Banner*.
  No. 78 1994
  Out of the Ordinalia. St Austell: Lyonesse Press 1995
  'Smashing the Sandcastles: Realism in Contemporary Cornish
  Fiction' in Bell, Ian A. (ed.), 1995
  '"Art Thou of Cornish Crew?" Shakespeare, Henry V and Cornish
  Identity'. In: Payton, Philip (ed.), 1996
  'The Cornish Alps: Resisting Romance in the Clay Country'. In:
  Westland, Ella (ed.), 1997
  'One and All: Unity and Difference in Cornish Literature'. In:
  Price, Eurwen (ed.), 1997
  Dreaming in Cornish. Liskeard: Giss' On Books 1998
  *Wives, Mothers and Sisters: Feminism, Literature and Women Writers in
  Cornwall*. Penzance: The Jamieson Library and Patten Press 1998
  '"At the Far End of England. . .": Constructions of Cornwall in
  Children's Literature'. In: *An Baner Kernewek / The Cornish Banner*.
  No.98 1999
  (ed.) *Voices from West Barbary: An Anthology of Anglo-Cornish Poetry*.
  London: Francis Boutle 2000
Kent, Alan M. and Saunders, Tim (eds. and trs.) *Looking at the Mermaid:
  A Reader in Cornish Literature 900–1900*. London: Francis Boutle 2000
Keskerdh Kernow/Cornwall Marches On, *Keskerdh Kernow / Cornwall
  Marches On Souvenir Programme*. Truro: Keskerdh Kernow 1997
Kibler, William W. and Carroll, Carleton W. (ed. and tr.), *Chrétien de
  Troyes: Arthurian Romances*. Harmondsworth: Penguin 1991
King, Ronald, *Humphry Davy*, London: The Royal Institution of Great
  Britain 1978
Kingsley, Charles, *Two Years Ago*. London: Macmillan 1902 [1857]
  Westward Ho! London: J.M. Dent 1906 [1855]
Koch, John T. and Carey, John (eds), *The Celtic Heroic Age: Literary
  Sources for Ancient Celtic Europe and Early Ireland and Wales*. Malden,
  Massachusetts: Celtic Studies Publications 1994
Lach-Szyrma, W., 'Last Relics of the Cornish Tongue'. In *Folklore, and
  the Folklore Society*. c.1880
Langdon, Arthur G., *Old Cornish Crosses*. Exeter: Cornwall Books 1988
  [1896]

Lang, Flavia, *Daphne du Maurier: A Daughter's Memoir*. London: Mainstream Publishing 1994

Lawrence, D.H., *Kangaroo*. Harmondsworth: Penguin 1975 [1923]

Laws, Peter, 'The Cornish Riviera – Architects and Builders Provide the Necessary Ingredient'. In: Mattingly, Joanna and Palmer, June (eds.), 1992

Lean, H., *A Continuation of Short Dialect Stories; Books 1–5*. Camborne: H. Lean 1951–1956

Richard Harvey, The Smart Boy and other Stories. Falmouth: H.J. Jake n.d

Leavis, F.R., *The Great Tradition*. London: Chatto and Windus 1948

Lee, A. Robert (ed.) *Other Britain, Other British: Contemporary Multicultural Fiction*. London: Pluto Press 1995

Lee, Charles, *Paul Carah Cornishman*. London: James Bowden 1898
'The Widow Woman' 1899. In Quiller Couch, Arthur (ed.), 1941
Cynthia in the West. London: Grant Richards 1900

Leland, John, 'The Itinerary: So far as it relates to Cornwall'. In: Gilbert, Davies (ed.), 1838

Le Mat, Jean-Pierre, *The Sons of Ermine: A History of Brittany*. Belfast: An Clochán 1996

Lester, Cathy, *Surf Patrol Stories*. Perranporth: Windjammer 1995

Lhuyd, Edward, *Archaeologia Britannica*. Menston: Scolar Press 1969 [1707]

Lide, Mary, *Tregaran*. London: Grafton 1989

Light, Alison, *Forever England: Femininity, Literature and Conservatism between the Wars*. London: Routledge 1991

Llewellyn, Sam, *Hell Bay*. London: Michael Joseph 1980

Lockwood, Yvonne R. and Lockwood, William G., 'Pasties in Michigan's Upper Peninsula: Foodways, Inter-ethnic Relations, and Regionalism'. In: Stern, Stephen and Cicala, John Allen (ed.), 1991

Longsworth, Robert, *The Cornish Ordinalia: Religion and Dramaturgy*. Cambridge, Massachusetts: Harvard University Press.

Loth, Joseph, *De Nouvelles Théories sur l'origine du Roman Arthurian*. Paris: Privately published 1892

Lowender Peran, *Lowender Peran: Festival of Celtic Culture Souvenir Programme*. Perranporth: 1994

Lowerson, John 'Celtic Tourism: Some Recent Magnets'. In: Payton, Philip (ed.), 1994

Ludwig, Hans-Werner and Fietz, Lothar (eds), *Poetry in the British Isles: Non-Metropolitan Perspectives*. Cardiff: University of Wales Press 1995

Lupack, Alan (ed.), *Modern Arthurian Literature: An Anthology of English and American Arthuriana from the Renaissance to the Present*. New York and London: Garland 1992

Luzel, F.M., *Folktales from Armorica*. Felinfach: Llanerch 1992 [c.1870]

Lynch, Peter, *Minority Nationalism and European Integration*. Cardiff: University of Wales Press 1996

Macdonald, Sharon (ed.), *Inside European Identities: Ethnography in Western Europe*. Oxford: Berg 1993

Maclean, Magnus, *The Literature of the Celts*. London: Blackie & Son 1902

Maddox, Brenda, *The Married Man: A Life of D.H. Lawrence*. London: Minerva 1995

Magnusson, Sally, *Clemo: A Love Story*. Tring: Lion 1986

Mallet, Oriel (ed.), *Letters from Menabilly*. London: Weidenfield and Nicholson 1993

March, Caeia, *Reflections*. London: The Women's Press 1995

Marquis, John (ed.), *The Cornish Paradise of Daphne du Maurier*. Falmouth: Packet Newspapers 1997

Mason, Daniel, *Cousin Jack*. Fowey: Alexander Associates 1996

Matarasso, P.M. (ed. and tr.), *The Quest of the Holy Grail*. Harmondsworth: Penguin 1969

Matthews, John (ed.), *The Druid Source Book*. London: Blandford 1995

Mattingly, Joanna and Palmer, June (eds.), *From Pilgrimage to Package Tour*. Truro: Royal Institution of Cornwall 1992

Michell, John, *The New View over Atlantis*. London: Thames and Hudson 1995

Mildren, James (ed.), *The Cornish World of Daphne du Maurier*. St Teath: Bossiney Books 1995

Millgate, Michael, *Thomas Hardy: His Career as a Novelist*. London: Bodley Head 1971
Thomas Hardy: A Biography. Oxford: Oxford University Press 1985

Miners, Hugh, *Gorseth Kernow: The First 50 Years*. Penzance: Gorseth Kernow 1978

Mitchell, Emma, 'The Myth of Objectivity: The Cornish Language and the Eighteenth-Century Antiquarians'. In: Payton, Philip (ed.), 1998

Mitchell, Peter, 'The Demographic Revolution'. In: Payton, Philip (ed.), 1993a

Moody, Nickianne, 'Poldark Country and National Culture' in Westland, Ella (ed.). 1997

Moore, F. Frankfurt, *Tre, Pol and Pen*. London: Society for Promoting Christian Knowledge 1887

Morley, Geoffrey, *The Smuggling War: The Government's Fight against Smuggling in the 18th and 19th Centuries*. Dover: Alan Sutton 1994

Morris, Christopher (ed.), *Journeys of Celia Fiennes*. London: Cresset Press 1947

Moyer, Patricia and Hull, Brenda (eds.), *School House in the Wind: A Trilogy by Anne Treneer*. Exeter: University of Exeter Press 1998

Murdoch, Brian (ed.), *The Medieval Cornish Poem of the Passion: A Bibliography*. Redruth: Institute of Cornish Studies 1979
Cornish Literature. Cambridge: D.S. Brewer 1993
'The Cornish Medieval Drama'. In: Richard Beadle (ed.), 1994
(ed.), *The Dedalus Book of Medieval Literature: The Grin of the Gargoyle*. Sawtry: Dedalus 1995
'Is John of Chyanhor really a "Cornish Ruodlieb"?' In: Payton, Philip (ed.), 1996
'Legends of the Holy Rood in Cornish Drama'. In: *Studia Celtica Japonica*. Vol. IX 1997

Muret, Ernest (ed.) *Le Roman de Tristan par Béroul*. Paris: Firmin Didot et Compagnie 1903

Murray, Stuart (ed.), *Not on Any Map: Essays on Postcoloniality and Cultural Nationalism*. Exeter: University of Exeter Press 1997

Mustill, J.P., *Summer Needs No Brightening*. Penzance: Blue Elvan Press 1997

Nance, Robert Morton, 'Andrew Boorde on Cornwall, circa 1540'. In: *Journal of the Royal Institution of Cornwall*. No.75 1928
'Cornish Prophecies'. In: *Old Cornwall*. 1931
'The Charter Endorsement in Cornish'. In: *Old Cornwall*. 1947
The Cledry Plays: Drolls of Old Cornwall for Village Acting and Home Reading. Penzance: The Federation of Old Cornwall Societies 1956

Nance, Robert Morton, A.S.D. Smith and Graham Sandercock (eds. and trs.), *The Cornish Ordinalia, Second Play: Christ's Passion*. Cornwall: The Cornish Language Board 1982
(eds. and trs.), *The Cornish Ordinalia, Third Play: Resurrection*. Cornwall: The Cornish Language Board 1984

Neus, Paula (ed. and tr.), *The Creacion of the World: A Critical Edition and Translation*. New York and London: Garland 1983

Newlyn, Evelyn S. (ed.), *Cornish Drama of the Middle Ages: A Bibliography*. Redruth: Institute of Cornish Studies 1987

Newman, Paul, 'The Plays of Donald R. Rawe'. In: *Cornish Review*. No.24 1973
The Meads of Love: The Life and Poetry of John Harris (1820–84). Redruth: Dyllansow Truran 1994

Norden, John, *Speculum Magnae Britanniae pars Cornwall – A Topographical and Historical Description of Cornwall*. Newcastle upon Tyne: Frank Graham 1966 [1584]

Norris, Edwin, *The Ancient Cornish Drama*. London and New York: Blom 1968 [1859]

North, Christine, 'Travel in West Barbary'. In: Mattingly, Joanna and Palmer, June (eds.), 1992

Nutt, Alfred, *The Influence of Celtic upon Medieval Romance*. London: David Nutt 1904

Ó Luain, Cathal (ed.), *For a Celtic Future*. Dublin: Celtic League 1984

Ollard, Richard, *A Man of Contradictions: A Life of A.L. Rowse*. London: Allen Lane 1999

Ordinalia Trust, *The Cornish Mystery Plays*. Truro: Ordinalia Trust, 1996

Orme, Nicholas (ed.), *Unity and Variety: A History of the Church in Devon and Cornwall*. Exeter: University of Exeter Press 1991
(ed.), *Nicholas Roscarrock's Lives of the Saints of Cornwall and Devon*. Exeter: Devon and Cornwall Record Society 1992
The Saints of Cornwall. Oxford: Oxford University Press 2000

O'Sullivan, Sean (ed.), *Folktales of Ireland*. Chicago: University of Chicago Press 1966

Padel, Oliver, *The Cornish Writings of the Boson Family*. Redruth: Institute of Cornish Studies 1975
'Ancient Parishes with Possible Examples of the Plain-an-gwary'. In: Hays, McGee, Joyce and Newlyn (eds.), 1999

Page, John, *Jowan Chy an Horth Examined*. Redruth: Dyllansow Truran 1982

Palmer, Jas. L., *The Cornish Chough through the Ages*. Penzance: n.d.

Palmer, Myghal, *Jory*. Taunton: Gwask Bryn Frys 1989

Paris, John Aryton, *The Life of Sir Humphry Davy*. London: Henry Colburn and Richard Bentley 1831

Parker, Simon, *A Star on the Mizzen*. Liskeard: Giss' On Books 1997
(ed.), *Cornwall Marches On! Keskerdh Kernow*. Truro: Keskerdh Kernow 1998

Pascoe, R.A. (ed.) *Cornwall: One of the Four Nations of Britain*. Redruth: Cornish Stannary Publications 1996

Pawling, Christopher (ed.), *Popular Fiction and Social Change*. Basingstoke: Macmillan 1984

Payton, Philip, *The Making of Modern Cornwall: Historical Experience and the Persistence of 'Difference'*. Redruth: Dyllansow Truran 1992
(ed.), *Cornwall Since the War: The Contemporary History of a European Region*. Redruth: Institute of Cornish Studies and Dyllansow Truran 1993a
'"a. . . concealed envy against the English": A Note on the Aftermath of the 1497 Rebellions in Cornwall'. In: Payton, Philip (ed.), *Cornish Studies: One*. 1993b
(ed.), *Cornish Studies: One*. Exeter: University of Exeter Press 1993b
(ed.), *Cornish Studies: Two*. Exeter: University of Exeter Press 1994

(ed.), *Cornish Studies: Three*. Exeter: University of Exeter Press 1995
Cornwall. Fowey: Alexander Associates 1996
(ed.), *Cornish Studies: Four*. Exeter: University of Exeter Press 1996
(ed.), *Cornish Studies: Five*. Exeter: University of Exeter Press 1997
(ed.), *Cornish Studies: Six*. Exeter: University of Exeter Press 1998
The Cornish Overseas. Fowey: Alexander Associates 1999
(ed.), *Cornish Studies: Seven*. Exeter: University of Exeter Press 1999
Payton, Philip and Deacon, Bernard, 'The Ideology of Language Revival'. In: Payton, Philip (ed.), 1993a
Payton, Philip and Thornton, Paul, 'The Great Western Railway and the Cornish-Celtic Revival'. In: Payton, Philip (ed.), 1995
Pearce, Keith and Fry, Helen (eds.) *The Lost Jews of Cornwall*. Bristol: Redcliffe 2000
Pearse, Mary E., *Polsinney Harbour*. London: Little, Brown and Company 1983
Pearson, Alan, *Robert Hunt F.R.S. (1807–1887)*. Penzance: The Federation of Old Cornwall Societies 1976
(ed.), *Cornish Dialect: Prose and Verse*. Cornwall: The Federation of Old Cornwall Societies 1982
Penglase, Charles, 'Authenticity in the Revival of Cornish'. In: Payton, Philip (ed.), 1994
Penhaligon, Annette, *Penhaligon*. London: Bloomsbury 1989
Perry, Ronald, 'Economic Change and "Opposition" Economics'. In: Payton, Philip (ed.), 1993a
'Celtic Revival and Economic Development in Edwardian Cornwall'. In: Payton, Philip (ed.), 1997
Phelps, Kenneth, *The Wormwood Cup – Thomas Hardy in Cornwall: A Study in Temperament, Topography and Timing*. Padstow: Lodenek Press 1975
Philip, Neil, 'The Magic in the Poetry of Charles Causley'. In: *Signal*. 1982
(ed.), *The Penguin Book of English Folktales*. Harmondsworth: Penguin 1992
Phillipps, K.C., *A Glossary of Cornish Dialect*. Padstow: Tabb House 1993
The Cornish Journal of Charles Lee, 1892–1908. Padstow: Tabb House 1995
'On a Bible Christian Chapel'. In: *A Service for the Life of Kenneth Charles Phillipps*. Trezaise Methodist Chapel 26 June 1996
Phillips, N.R., *The Saffron Eaters*. Exeter: Devon Books 1987
The Horn of Strangers. Tiverton: Halsgrove 1996
Phillpotts, Eden, *Old Delabole*. London: William Heinemann 1915
Piggott, Stuart, *The Druids*. London: Thames and Hudson 1968

Ancient Britons and the Antiquarian Imagination: Ideas from the Renaissance to the Regency. London: Thames and Hudson 1989

Pilcher, Rosamunde, *The Shell Seekers.* London: New English Library 1988

Piltock, Murray G.H., *Celtic Identity and the British Image.* Manchester: Manchester University Press 1999

Pollard, Sidney, *Peaceful Conquest: The Industrialization of Europe 1760– 1970.* Oxford: Oxford University Press 1981

Polmear, K., 'Cornish Christmas Music'. In: Myrna Combellack-Harris (ed.), 1989

Pool, P.A.S., *The Life and Progress of Henry Quick of Zennor.* Redruth: Dyllansow Truran 1994 [1963]

The Death of Cornish. Redruth: Dyllansow Truran 1982

The Second Death of Cornish. Redruth: Dyllansow Truran 1995

William Borlase. Truro: Royal Institution of Cornwall 1996

Pounds, N.J.G. (ed.), 'William Carnsew of Bokelly and his diary, 1576–7'. In: *Journal of the Royal Institution of Cornwall.* No.114 1978

Poulson, Christine, *The Quest for the Grail: Arthurian Legend in British Art 1840–1920.* Manchester: Manchester University Press 1999

Price, Eurwen (ed.), *Celtic Literature and Culture in the Twentieth Century.* Bangor: The International Celtic Congress 1997

Pritchard, Alison (ed.), *The Poetry of Humphry Davy.* Penzance: Penwith District Council 1978

Pryce, William, *Archaeologia Cornu-Britannica.* Menston: Scolar Press 1972 [1790]

Quayle, Eric and Foreman, Michael, *The Magic Ointment and Other Cornish Legends.* London: Anderson Press 1986

Quiller Couch, Arthur, *The Astonishing History of Troy Town.* London: Anthony Mott 1983 [1888]

The Splendid Spur. London: Cassell 1889

The Ship of Stars. London: Nelson 1899

(ed.), *The Oxford Book of English Verse.* Oxford: Oxford University Press 1900

Hetty Wesley. London: Harper and Brothers 1903

Shining Ferry. London: Hodder and Stoughton 1905

Sir John Constantine. London: Smith and Elder 1906

The Mayor of Troy. London: Methuen 1906

From a Cornish Window. Cambridge: Cambridge University Press 1928 [1906]

The Delectable Duchy. London: J.M. Dent 1915

(ed.), *Cornish Tales by Charles Lee.* London: J.M. Dent 1941

Quiller Couch, Arthur and du Maurier, Daphne, *Castle Dor.* London: Arrow Books 1994 [1962]

Quiller Couch, M. and L., *Ancient and Holy Wells of Cornwall*. London: Chas J. Clark 1894

Radford, Jean (ed.), *The Progress of Romance: The Politics of Popular Fiction*. London: Routledge and Kegan Paul 1986

Rawe, Donald R., 'The Deep Sea Dream'. 1950. In: Val Baker, Denys (ed.), 1976

Petroc of Cornwall. Padstow: Lodenek Press 1970

The Trials of St Piran. Padstow: Lodenek Press 1971

Padstow's Obby Oss and May Day Festivities: A Study in Folklore and Tradition. Padstow: Lodenek Press 1990 [1971]

Geraint: Last of the Arthurians. Padstow: Lodenek Press 1972

'Night on Roughtor'. In: Val Baker, Denys (ed.), 1973

(ed.), *A Cornish Quintette: Five Original One Act Plays*. Padstow: Lodenek Press 1973

Haunted Landscapes: Cornish and West Country Tales of the Supernatural. Portloe: Lodenek Press 1994

A Prospect of Cornwall. Chapel Amble: Lodenek Press 1996

Reddicliffe, Sheila, *The Cornish Serjeant*. London: William Kimber 1984

The Cornish Mistress. Callington: Lightbody Publications 1992

Redgrove, Peter (ed.), *Cornwall in Verse*. Harmondsworth: Penguin 1983 [1982]

Rees, Alwyn and Brinsley (eds) *Celtic Heritage: Ancient Tradition in Ireland and Wales*. London: Thames and Hudson 1961

Restormel Arts Clay Stories Project, *Tales from the White Mountains*. St Austell: Restormel Arts and Verbal Arts Cornwall 1993

Roberts, Forrester, *The Legends of Tristan and Iseult: The Tale and the Trail in Ireland, Cornwall and Brittany*. Gloucester: Forrester Roberts 1998

Rogers, Pat (ed.), *Daniel Defoe: A Tour Through the Whole Island of Great Britain*. Harmondsworth: Penguin 1971 [1724–1726]

Robins, Colin, *Merlin's Diner*. Tiverton: Cornwall Books 1992

Rose-Troup, Francis, *The Western Rebellions of 1549*. London: Smith, Elder and Co 1913

Ross, Malcolm, *Kernow and Daughter*. London: Piatkus 1994

The Trevarton Inheritance. London: Piatkus 1995

Rowe, John, *Cornwall in the Age of the Industrial Revolution*. St Austell: Cornish Hillside Publications 1993 [1953]

Rowe, John and Andrews, C.T., 'Cholera in Cornwall'. In: *Journal of the Royal Institution of Cornwall*. No.111 1974

Rowse, A.L., *Tudor Cornwall*. Redruth: Dyllansow Truran 1990 [1941]

A Cornish Childhood. London: Anthony Mott 1982 [1942]

The West in English History. London: Methuen 1949

'The Stone that Liked Company'. In: Val Baker, Denys (ed.), 1951

Cornish Stories. London: Macmillan 1967

(ed.), *A Cornish Anthology*. London: Macmillan 1968

The Cornish in America. Redruth: Dyllansow Truran 1991 [1969]

'The Curse of the Clavertons'. In: Val Baker, Denys (ed.), 1976

Matthew Arnold: Poet and Prophet. London: Thames and Hudson 1976

A Life: Collected Poems. Edinburgh: William Blackwood 1981

The Little Land of Cornwall. Gloucester: Alan Sutton 1986

Quiller Couch: A Portrait of 'Q'. London: Methuen 1988

(1989) *The Controversial Colensos*. Redruth: Dyllansow Truran 1989

Ruhrmund, Frank, *Penwith Poems*. Padstow: Lodenek Press 1976

Brother John. Penzance: Rainyday Publications 1985

Russell, Paul, *An Introduction to Celtic Languages*. London: Longman 1995

St Ives International, *A Quality of Light Guide*. St Ives: 1997

Sallis, Susan, *Summer Visitors*. London: Corgi 1988

Saunders, Tim, 'Why I write in Cornish'. In: *Planet*. No.30 1976

Teithiau. Talybont: Y Lolfa 1977

'Cornwall – Symbol and Substance'. In: O Lain, Cathal (ed.), 1984

An Ros Du/The Black Heath. Cardiff: Privately published, 1997

The High Tide: Collected Poems in Cornish 1974–1999. London: Francis Boutle 1999

The Wheel: An Anthology of Modern Poetry in Cornish 1850–1980. London: Francis Boutle 1999

Scawen, William, 'Antiquities Cornuontanic: The Cause of Cornish Speech's Decay'. In: Gilbert, Davies (ed.), Vol. 4 1838

Schmidt, Michael, *50 Modern British Poets*. London: Pan 1979

Scott, Tim, *The Cornish World of Denys Val Baker*. Bradford on Avon: Ex Libris Press 1994

Shallcross, Martyn, *Daphne du Maurier Country*. St Teath: Bossiney Books 1987

The Private World of Daphne du Maurier. London: Robson Books 1993

Shaw, Thomas, *The Bible Christians*. London: Epworth Press 1965

A History of Cornish Methodism. Truro: D. Bradford Barton 1967

Simmonds, Posy, *Mrs Weber's Diary*. London: Jonathan Cape 1979

Sinclair, Katharine, *Journeys of the Heart*. London: Piatkus 1989

Sinfield, Alan (ed.), *Society and Literature 1945–1970*. London: Methuen 1983

Slack, Roger, 'D.H. Lawrence: Recollections and Poetry'. In: Hardie, Melissa (ed.), 1992

Smith, A.S.D., *The Story of the Cornish Language: Its Extinction and Revival*. Camborne: 1947

Smith, Baker Peter, *Trip to the Far West*. London: Sherwood 1839

Smith, M.G., *Fighting Joshua: A Study of the Career of Sir Jonathan Trelawny*. Redruth: Dyllansow Truran 1985

Squire, Charles, *The Mythology of the British Islands* London: Gresham 1905

Stanier, Peter, *Cornwall's Literary Heritage*. Truro: Twelveheads Press 1993

Stern, Stephen and Cicala, John Allan (eds.), *Creative Ethnicity: Symbols and Strategies on Contemporary Ethnic Life*. Logan, Utah: Utah State University Press 1991

Stevens, C.J., *Lawrence at Tregerthen: D.H. Lawrence in Cornwall*. New York: Whitson 1988

Stock, James, *Star-Gazy Pie*. London: Nick Hern Books 1995

Stokes, Whitley, 'The Passion: A Middle Cornish Poem'. In: *Transactions of the Philological Society*. 1860–1
(ed. and tr.), *The Life of Saint Meriasek, Bishop and Confessor: A Cornish Drama*. London: Trübner and Co 1872

Storry, Mike and Childs, Peter (eds), *British Cultural Identities*. London: Routledge 1997

Stoyle, Mark, *Loyalty and Locality: Popular Allegiance in Devon during the English Civil War*. Exeter: University of Exeter Press 1994
'"Sir Richard Grenville's Creatures": The New Cornish Tertia, 1644–46'. In: Payton, Philip (ed.), 1996

Straffon, Cheryl, *Pagan Cornwall: Land of the Goddess*. St Just: Meyn Mamvro Publications 1993

Stubbs, Jean, *Summer Secrets*. London: Macmillan 1990

Sturt, John, *Revolt in the West: The Western Rebellion of 1549*. Exeter: Devon Books 1987

Summerfield, Geoffrey (ed.), *Worlds: Seven Modern Poets*. Harmondsworth: Penguin 1979

Summers, Rowena, *Killigrew Clay*. London: Severn House 1986
Clay Country. London: Severn House 1987
Family Ties. London: Severn House 1988

Syed, Keith and Edwards, Ray (eds.), *Origo Mundi*. Cornwall: The Cornish Language Board 1998

Symons, Andrew, 'The Poetry of A.L. Rowse'. In: *An Baner Kernewek/ The Cornish Banner*. No.73 1993
'Clemo: The Authentic Voice'. In: *An Baner Kernewek/The Cornish Banner*. No. 78 1994
'John Harris – A Weaving of Traditions'. In: *An Baner Kernewek/The Cornish Banner*. No.82 1995

Tangye, Michael, 'The Wrasslin' Match'. In: *An Baner Kernewek/The Cornish Banner*. No.79 1995

Theroux, Paul, *The Kingdom by the Sea*. Harmondsworth: Penguin 1984

Thomas, Charles (ed.), *Cornish Studies/Studhyansow Kernewek 1–15*. Redruth: Institute of Cornish Studies 1973–1987

John Harris of Bolenowe: Poet and Preacher 1820–1884. Cornwall: Cornwall Methodist Historical Association 1884

Celtic Britain. London: Thames and Hudson 1986

'Hardy and Lyonnesse: Parallel Mythologies'. In: Hardie, Melissa (ed.), 1992

Tintagel: Arthur and Archeology. London: English Heritage and Batsford 1993

And Shall These Mute Stones Speak? Post-Roman Inscriptions in Western Britain. Cardiff: University of Wales Press 1994

Christian Celts: Messages and Images. Stroud: Tempus 1998

Thomas, Chris, 'See Your Own Country First: The Geography of a Railway Landscape'. In: Westland, Ella (ed.), 1997

Thomas, D.M. (ed.), *The Granite Kingdom: Poems of Cornwall*. Truro: D. Bradford Barton 1970

(ed.), *Songs from the Earth: Selected Poems of John Harris*. Padstow: Lodenek Press 1977

Birthstone. London: Victor Gollancz 1980

The White Hotel. London: Victor Gollancz 1981

Selected Poems. Harmondsworth: Penguin 1983

Memories and Hallucinations. London: Victor Gollancz 1988

Eating Pavlova. London: Bloomsbury 1994

Charlotte: The Final Journey of Jane Eyre. London: Duckworth 2000

Thomas, Ned, *The Welsh Extremist: Modern Welsh Politics, Literature and Society*. Talybont: Y Lolfa 1991 [1973]

Thomas, W. Herbert (ed.), *Poems of Cornwall by Thirty Cornish Authors*. Penzance: F. Rodda 1892

Thompson, E.V., *Chase the Wind*. London: Macmillan 1977

Ben Retallick. London: Macmillan 1977

Harvest of the Sun. London: Macmillan 1978

The Music Makers. London: Macmillan 1979

Singing Spears. London: Macmillan 1982

The Restless Sea. London: Macmillan 1983

The Stricken Land. London: Macmillan 1986

God's Highlander. London: Macmillan 1989

Lottie Trago. London: Macmillan 1990

The Tolpuddle Woman. London: Macmillan 1994

Ruddlemoor. London: Headline 1995

Moontide. London: Headline 1996

Thorn, Caroline and Frank (eds.), *Doomsday Book: Cornwall*. Chichester: Phillimore 1979

Thorpe, Lewis (ed. and tr.), *Geoffrey of Monmouth: The History of the Kings of Britain*. Harmondsworth: Penguin 1966 (ed. and tr.), *Gerald of Wales: The Journey through Wales and the Description of Wales.* Harmondsworth: Penguin 1978

Todd, A.C., *Beyond the Blaze: A Biography of Davies Gilbert.* Truro: D. Bradford Barton 1967

Tooby, Michael, *Tate St Ives: An Illustrated Companion.* London: Tate Gallery Publications 1993

Toorians, Lauran (ed.), *The Middle Cornish Charter Endorsement: The Making of a Marriage in Medieval Cornwall.* Innsbruck: Institut für Sprachwissenschaft der Universität Innsbruck 1991

Tor Mark Press (eds.), *A First Cornish Anthology.* Truro: Tor Mark Press n.d.

Trease, Geoffrey, *The Phoenix and the Flame.* London: Macmillan 1973

Tregellas, John Tabois, *Cornish Tales.* Truro: Netherton and Worth c.1863

Tregidga, Garry, 'The Politics of the Celto-Cornish Revival, 1886–1939'. In: Payton, Philip (ed.), 1997

Treneer, Anne, *The Mercurial Chemist: A Life of Sir Humphry Davy.* London: The Royal Institution 1963

Trenoodle, Uncle Jan, *Specimens of Cornish Provincial Dialect.* London: John Russell Smith 1846

Tresize, Simon, '"Off Wessex", or a Place in the Mind'. In: Hardie, Melissa (ed.), 1992

Trevenen Jenkin, Ann, *Gwel Kernow/A Cornish View.* Leedstown: Noonvares Press 1997

Trevose, Daniel, *Looking for Love in a Great City.* London: Cape 1956

Trewin, J.C. (ed.), *Robert Stephen Hawker: Footprints of Former Men in Far Cornwall.* London: Westaway Books 1948 [1857]

Tristram, Hildegard L.C. (ed.), *The Celtic Englishes.* Heidelberg: Universitätsverlag C. Winter 1997

Truran, Len, *For Cornwall – A Future!* Redruth: Mebyon Kernow 1976

Turner, Paul (ed. and tr.), *Thomas More: Utopia.* Harmondsworth: Penguin 1965

Val Baker, Denys (ed.), *One and All: A Selection of Stories from Cornwall.* London: Museum Press, 1951

Britain's Art Colony by the Sea. Bristol: Sansom & Company 2000 [1959]

The Sea's in the Kitchen. London: Phoenix 1962

The Timeless Land: The Creative Spirit in Cornwall. Bath: Adams and Dart 1973

(ed.), *Haunted Cornwall.* Tavistock: Heritage Publications 1980 [1973]

(ed.), *Cornish Short Stories.* Harmondsworth: Penguin 1976

The Spirit of Cornwall. London: W.H. Allen 1980

A View from Land's End: Writers Against a Cornish Background. London: William Kimber 1982

Vickers, Stanley and King, Diana (eds.), *The du Maurier Companion*. Fowey: Fowey Rare Books 1997

Wakelin, Martyn F., *Language and History in Cornwall*. Leicester: Leicester University Press 1974

Wallace, Gavin and Stevenson, Randall (eds.), *The Scottish Novel since the Seventies*. Edinburgh: Edinburgh University Press 1993

Walmsley, Leo, *Love in the Sun*. London: Anthony Mott 1983 [1939]

Weatherhill, Craig, *Cornovia: Ancient Sites of Cornwall and Scilly*. Penzance: Alison Hodge 1985
Cornish Place Names and Language. Wilmslow: Sigma 1995

Weatherhill, Craig and Devereux, Paul, *Myths and Legends of Cornwall*. Wilmslow: Sigma 1994

Welch, Robert, *Changing States: Transformations in Modern Irish Writing*. London: Routledge 1993

Westland, Ella, 'The Passionate Periphery: Cornwall and Romantic Fiction'. In: Bell, Ian A. (ed.), 1995
(ed.), *Cornwall: The Cultural Construction of Place*. Penzance: The Patten Press and the Institute of Cornish Studies 1997

Whetter, James, *Cornish Essays/Scryvow Kernewek 1971–76*. Gorran: CNP Publications 1977
The History of Glasney College. Padstow: Tabb House 1988
The Bodrugans: A Study of a Cornish Medieval Knightly Family. Gorran: Lyfrow Trelyspen 1995
Cornwall in the 13th Century: A Study in Social and Economic History. Gorran: Lyfrow Trelyspen 1998

Whitfeld, H.J., *Scilly and its Legends*. London: Simpkin, Marshall and Co 1852

Whitaker, John, *Supplement to the First and Second Books of the History of Cornwall by Richard Polwhele*. London: Cadell and Davies 1804

Whybrow, Marion, *St Ives 1883–1993: A Portrait of an Art Colony*. Woodbridge: Antique Collectors' Club 1994

Wilhelm, James J. (ed.), *The Romance of Arthur: An Anthology of Medieval Texts in Translation*. New York and London: Garland 1994

Williams, Alan M. and Shaw, Gareth, 'The Age of Mass Tourism'. In: Payton, Philip (ed.), 1993a

Williams, Derek R., *Prying into Every Hole and Corner: Edward Lhuyd in Cornwall*. Redruth: Dyllansow Truran 1993
'Robert Morton Nance'. In: *An Baner Kernewek/The Cornish Banner*. No.88 1997

Williams, Douglas, *Festivals of Cornwall*. St Teath: Bossiney Books 1987

Williams, Ifor (ed.), *Canu Taliesin*. Cardiff: University of Wales Press 1960

(ed.), *Canu Aneirin*. Cardiff: University of Wales Press 1970

Williams, J.E. Caerwyn (ed.), *Literature in Celtic Countries*. Cardiff: University of Wales Press 1971

Williams, Mary, *The Granite King*. London: William Kimber 1982

Heronsmere. London: William Kimber 1983

Williams, N.J.A., *Cornish Today: An Examination of the Revived Language*. Sutton Coldfield: Kernewek Dre Lyther 1995

Williams, Robert, *Lexicon Cornu-Britannicum*. Llandovery and London: 1865

Williamson, Duncan and Williamson, Linda (ed.), *A Thorn in the King's Foot: Stories of the Scottish Travelling People*. Harmondsworth: Penguin 1987

Wooding, Jonathan, *St Meriasek and King Tudor in Cornwall*. Sydney: 1992

Woolf, Virginia, *To the Lighthouse*. Oxford: Oxford University Press 1992 [1927]

Wormleighton, Austin, *A Painter Laureate: Lamorna Birch and his circle*. Bristol: Sansom & Company 1995

UNPUBLISHED SOURCES

Biscoe, Bert, 'The Mermaid's Song'. n.d.

Fulton, Helen, 'Individual and Society in Welsh and French Romances of Owein/Yvain'. Paper given at the Celtic Studies Association of North America, Annual Meeting 1999

Graves, Eugene van Tassel, *The Old Cornish Vocabulary*. Ph.D. Columbia: University of Columbia 1962

Gendall, Richard, 'An Yrth/The Snow'. n.d.

Hale, Amy, *Gathering the Fragments: Performing Celtic Identities in Cornwall*. Ph.D. California: University of California, Los Angeles 1998

Jenkin, Richard, *Selected Poems*. n.d

Letter to the author, April 13th 1996

Kent, Alan M., *Draft of Passio Christi: A Verse Adaptation*. 2000

Lowman, P.L., *Supernaturalistic Causality and Christian Theism in the Modern English Novel*. Ph.D. Cardiff: University of Wales 1983

Rawe, Donald R., *Hawker of Morwenstow*. 1975

Murder at Bohelland. 1991

The Last Voyage of Alfred Wallis. 1994

Selected Poems. n.d.

St Austell And District White Gold Committee, *St Austell and District White Gold Festival Week Poster*. St Austell: 1992

AUDIO-VISUAL SOURCES

Annett, Paul (dir.) *Poldark 1: Part Two*. BBC Video 1993 [1975]
  Poldark 1: Part Four. BBC Video 1993 [1975]
Berry, Christopher (dir.), *Poldark 1: Part One*. BBC Video 1993 [1975]
Dudley, Philip (dir.) *Poldark 2: Part One*. BBC Video 1994 [1977]
  Poldark 2: Part Two. BBC Video 1994 [1977]
Dudley, Philip and Jenkins, Roger (dirs.), *Poldark 2: Part Three*. BBC Video 1994 [1977]
  Poldark 2: Part Four. BBC Video 1994 [1977]
Foster, Helen (dir.), *Kernopalooza!* Carlton Westcountry 1998
Ives, Kenneth (dir.) *Poldark 1: Part Three*. BBC Video 1993 [1975]
Laxton, Richard (dir.) *Poldark 3*. HTV/First Independent Production 1996
Prechezer, Carl (dir.), *Blue Juice*. Channel Four Films and Pandora Cinema 1995
Scott, Bill (dir.), *The Last Words of Dolly Pentreath/An Dewetha Geryow a Dolly Pentreath*. Wild West Films 1994
  The Saffron Threads. Wild West Films 1995
  A Smooth Guide to a Rough Cornishman/Ledyans Dhe Gernow Garow. Wild West Films 1996
  Splatt Dhe Wertha/Plot for Sale. Wild West Films 1997
Wakerell, Tina (dir.), *Penmarric: Part One*. BBC Video 1994 [1979]
Wakerell, Tina and Martinus, Derek (dirs.), *Penmarric: Part Two, Part Three and Part Four*. BBC Video 1994 [1979]

WORLD-WIDE WEB SOURCES

www.cornwall.net
www.cornwall-calling.co.uk
www.francisboutle.demon.co.uk
www.kernewek.currantbun.com
www.ozemail.com.au
www.summerlands.com

LIST OF ILLUSTRATIONS

INDEX

Entries in bold relate to illustrations.

315

317

324

325